Understanding the Social Effects of Policy Reform

EDITORS

Lionel Demery
Marco Ferroni
Christiaan Grootaert

with

Jorge Wong-Valle

The World Bank
Washington, D.C.

Copyright © 1993
The International Bank for Reconstruction and Development/The World Bank
1818 H Street, N.W.
Washington, D.C. 20433, U.S.A.

The judgments in this study do not necessarily reflect the views of the Board of Executive Directors of The World Bank or the governments they represent. The material in this publication is copyrighted. Requests for permission to reproduce portions of it should be sent to Office of the Publisher, at the address shown in the copyright notice above. The World Bank encourages dissemination of its work and will normally give permission promptly and, when the reproduction is for noncommercial purposes, without asking a fee. Permission to photocopy portions for classroom use is granted through the Copyright Clearance Centre, 27 Congress Street, Salem, Massachusetts 01970, U.S.A.

The complete backlist of publications from the World Bank is shown in the annual *Index of Publications*, which contains an alphabetical title list and indexes of subjects, authors, and countries and regions. The latest edition is available free of charge from the Distribution Unit, Office of the Publisher, The World Bank, 1818 H Street, N.W. Washington, D.C. 20433, U.S.A., or from Publications, The World Bank, 66, avenue d'Iéna, 75116 Paris, France.

At the time of producing this study, Lionel Demery, Marco Ferroni, and Christiaan Grootaert were senior economists, and Jorge Wong-Valle was a consultant economist, all in The World Bank's Poverty and Social Policy Division, Africa Technical Department.

Library of Congress Cataloging-in-Publication Data

Understanding the social effects of policy reform / edited by Lionel
   Demery, Marco Ferroni, Christiaan Grootaert, with Jorge Wong-Valle.
      p.   cm.
     "A World Bank Study."
     Includes bibliographical references.
     ISBN 0–8213–2425–X
     1. Economic development—Social aspects.   2. Africa—Social
conditions—1960–   3. Africa—Economic conditions—1960–
I. Demery, Lionel.   II. Ferroni, Marco A., 1948–
III. Grootaert, Christiaan, 1950– .
HD75. U5   1993
306'.096—dc20   .   93–3805
                                                       CIP

Contents

Acknowledgments

Editing this volume has been enjoyable and rewarding. For this, we have to thank all the contributing authors, who have delivered state-of-the-art reviews of the impact of policy reform. We appreciated their patience and their willingness to make repeated revisions. We also owe a debt of thanks to those—too numerous to mention—who commented on earlier versions of the manuscript. Four anonymous referees made valuable suggestions to help bring the book to its present state. Finally, we thank Michel Noël and Ismaïl Serageldin, whose guidance and encouragement were instrumental in bringing this undertaking to a successful conclusion.

The editorial process benefited from the contributions of Meta de Coquereaumont, Leo Demesmaker, Claire Floyd, Jenepher Moseley, Alison Strong, and Katrina van Duyn. Joyce Petruzzelli designed the cover, which gives the book its own identity while integrating a visual link to the book's companion volume, *Making Adjustment Work for the Poor: A Framework for Policy Reform in Africa* (A World Bank Study, 1991). Last, we gratefully acknowledge the financial support of the Directorate of Development Cooperation of the Government of Switzerland, without which this book could not have been published.

Lionel Demery
Marco Ferroni
Christiaan Grootaert

March 1993

v

1

The social dimensions of policy reform: Concepts, data, analysis

Marco Ferroni and Christiaan Grootaert

For many developing countries, the 1980s have been the decade of adjustment: policy reform necessitated by worsening economic crisis. Collapsing world prices of many primary commodities reduced export earnings, expansionary fiscal policies proved unsustainable, and the debt burden rose. As a result, the economies of many countries were in a protracted slump throughout the decade, living standards fell, and poverty increased. Since the first half of the 1980s, a growing number of governments, especially in Africa and Latin America, responded by putting in place structural adjustment policies, often with the help of the World Bank and the International Monetary Fund, to regenerate sustainable growth.

Evidence to date indicates that these programs are beginning to pay off, and adjusting countries, particularly those that sustained the effort over a number of years, have begun to experience more growth than those that did not implement macroeconomic reforms (Corbo, Fischer, and Webb 1992). It has become clear, though, that structural adjustment is a slower process than had been assumed when the reforms were initially implemented. In the meantime, poverty and social conditions have continued to deteriorate in many countries (Cornia, van der Hoeven, and Mkandawire 1992). The situation is particularly precarious in Sub-Saharan Africa, where the number of poor has been growing rapidly. It is estimated that in Africa in 1985, 180 million people lived in poverty—47 percent of the population—two-thirds of them in extreme poverty. If current

trends continue, the number of poor in Africa could increase by nearly 100 million by the year 2000. In all other regions of the world, poverty is expected to improve (World Bank 1990b). Clearly in African countries, more attention must be given to the social dimensions of the economic crisis and of the reform programs, that is, to their impact on poverty, health, nutrition, education, and employment.

The importance of integrating these social dimensions into the design of adjustment programs is now well recognized (World Bank 1991b). However, the process by which this is best done is not fully understood, and the debate on this issue has been marked by uncertainty and confusion. In large measure, this can be attributed to the complexity of the linkages between macroeconomic and sectoral policy reform on the one hand, and the living conditions of households and individuals on the other. The analysis of these linkages has not always distinguished successfully between the effects of adjustment and the pre-adjustment crisis, between the contractionary and the expansionary effects of stabilization and adjustment, and between outcomes for the poor and the nonpoor. To a large extent, this stems from the difficulty of counterfactual analysis—the study of what would have happened without adjustment or with an alternative adjustment path. The shortage of reliable data (especially at the household level) has further hindered attempts to identify how the various groups in society have been affected by policy reforms.

The rising trend in poverty and the deteriorating social conditions have led many governments and the donor community to reassess their development and assistance strategies from the point of view of poverty alleviation. The World Bank has recently declared an intention to link its lending to government efforts at reducing poverty (World Bank 1991a). Application of this principle requires poverty monitoring; that is, analysis of the evolution of income, consumption, and basic needs fulfillment over time, and establishment of relationships between this evolution and the policy environment.

The successful undertaking of such policy-oriented analysis requires both a suitable framework of analysis and relevant data to support the analysis empirically. This book proposes a framework in which the transmission of structural adjustment policies to the living conditions of households is seen as a two-step process. Initially, the macroeconomic and social policies that make up an adjustment package affect market prices and the social and economic infrastructure, the backdrop for household economic and social decisionmaking. In a second step, when faced with changing prices of goods, services, and productive inputs, and changing availability of infrastructural services, households respond by modifying their behavior. Depending on the nature of the changes involved, household welfare will improve or deteriorate. In practice, the two steps in the process overlap and there is feedback upward resulting from the households' response, but, as this book hopes to show, the two steps provide a convenient stylistic distinction that facilitates analysis and clarifies the policy implications.

The objective of this book is to contribute toward a better understanding of how the process of policy reform in response to economic crisis affects the living conditions of households and individuals. The focus is on poverty and on the social aspects—broadly defined—of welfare: health, fertility, nutrition, food security, education, employment, and migration. Each of these aspects of living conditions is treated in a separate chapter, but the linkages between them are fully recognized. Policy change does not affect all groups in society in the same way, and three target groups receive explicit attention: the poor, women, and smallholders. The book has a strong orientation toward Africa—the continent where the need to focus on social aspects of adjustment is the highest. Most chapters were written, either explicitly

or implicitly, with the African reality in mind. Nevertheless, the general framework of the analysis and the analytical methods presented in the book have a general application to developing countries.

Before discussing our approach to the analysis of the social aspects of policy reform in more detail, we turn now to a brief presentation of the framework within which the analysis will be set and which outlines the transmission process from policy change to welfare.

Structural adjustment and the distribution of income

Structural adjustment aims at setting the economy of a country back on a path of sustainable growth when it is faced with a macroeconomic crisis characterized by unsustainable internal and external balances. These are often the result of terms-of-trade shocks, high external debt service obligations, and expansionary macroeconomic policies leading to an excess of aggregate demand over aggregate supply. In the case of a small open economy operating as a price-taker in world markets, an excess demand in the tradable sector leads to an external imbalance, that is, a deficit in the current account of the balance of payments. Excess demand for nontradable goods causes inflation and hence a rise in the price of nontradables relative to the price of tradables (that is, an appreciation of the real exchange rate). This encourages a shift of economic activity to the relatively more profitable nontradable sector. This shift may also be promoted by a restrictive trade regime—high export taxes and excessive government interference in production and trade. In such a policy context, production for export and efficient import substitution (that which is maintainable at low levels of protection) begin to falter. The economy's external constraint becomes ever more binding, and growth gives way to stagnation.

Structural adjustment can be defined as a process whereby the national economy is opened by means of the depreciation of the real exchange rate.[1] This is accomplished by a combination of demand- and supply-side policies, with or without a nominal devaluation. The measures available to depreciate the real exchange rate and to increase efficiency and competitiveness include, on the demand side, monetary, fiscal, and wage restraint, and, on the supply side, measures to restore the incentive structure in favor of exportables and efficient import substitutes. Currency devaluation and trade liberalization fall under this category. Supply-side measures also include the reduction of intra-sectoral price distortions, and other measures (for example, parastatal reform) to improve efficiency and create an institutional environment conducive to growth.[2]

Demand-side (or stabilization) policies are contractionary in effect, and they act rapidly. Supply-side measures are usually expansionary, but they require time to take effect. The social cost (and the political feasibility) of adjustment relates to the time it takes for the expansionary forces of the process to prevail over the recessionary ones. The lags involved are in part determined by private reactions to changes in incentives; these reactions are conditioned by the credibility of the economic reform program and by the ability of the infrastructure and institutions to allow the needed resource shifts between sectors and activities. The lags (and people's perceptions) are also influenced by the chosen combination of demand- and supply-side policies. The required relative weight of demand-side measures to restore macroeconomic balance can be reduced by simultaneous action to change relative prices and the composition of output between tradable and nontradable goods and services. (The main policy tool to achieve this is devaluation.) It can also be reduced by additional external finance and by an improvement in the country's external terms of trade.

Fiscal adjustment typically involves a decrease in public employment, a reduction in subsidies and transfers, tax reform, and the reform or privatization of parastatals and marketing boards. The first-order redistributive consequence of these actions will be a relative income loss on the part of public sector employees and all those who benefit from government subsidies and transfers. The precise pattern of redistribution will depend on the composition of public expenditure cutbacks and on the nature and speed of implementation of tax reform. In most circumstances though, few of those who are negatively affected by fiscal retrenchment are poor. For example, in the African context, results from household surveys show that those below the poverty line derive at best a marginal fraction of their income from public employment (see Kanbur 1990; Boateng and others 1990; République Rwandaise 1990; Grootaert 1993). The evidence also suggests that many poor tend not to be reached by government subsidies

and programs (Ferroni and Kanbur 1990).[3] But this will vary of course, country by country, depending on the chosen poverty line, the patterns of employment and consumption of the poor, and the pattern of public expenditure. Where the poor are not affected by fiscal retrenchment, the reduction of public employment and subsidies could imply a reduction in the average income gap between the poor and those who derive sizable shares of income from these sources.

Changes in public sector employment and wages are not the only impact of structural adjustment on the labor market. The general role of the labor market is to respond flexibly to the new pattern of demand for labor that follows the changes in the structure of incentives put in place by the policy reforms. This may well require a decline in real wages in certain sectors. In the short run, if the supply of tradables is to expand, the real-product wage[4] in this sector must decline relative to the real-product wage in the nontradable sector. This is necessary to induce employers to hire more workers in the tradable sector and, alternatively, to shed labor in the nontradable sector. The effect on the real-consumption wage (the relevant indicator of workers' welfare) is ambiguous, because it depends on the composition of workers' consumption baskets. If nontradable commodities loom large in the baskets, the real-consumption wage may rise even in the short run. Conversely, if food (the principal wage good in workers' budgets) is tradable, the real-consumption wage may fall.

In the long run, the redistribution of income induced by production switching depends on the relative factor intensity of tradable and nontradable activities. Production switching toward the tradable sector will redistribute income toward the more intensively used factors in this sector (World Bank 1991b). It is often the case that nontradable or highly protected industries are relatively more capital-intensive than tradable activities, such as, for example, agriculture. Where this characterization is correct, adjustment is expected to have a beneficial effect on labor incomes. If rural activities are more tradable and labor-intensive than urban industries, then adjustment will benefit the rural population more than city dwellers.

Naturally, many rural households produce both tradables and nontradables (even though agriculture as a whole has a larger tradable component than the rest of the economy in many countries). Under production switching, the long-run distributive effects in rural areas depend on the ratio of tradable to nontradable commodities in the pattern of household consumption, and on the relative weight of tradable and nontradable activities in the generation of income. For example, adjustment is expected to benefit small farmers who are both producing for export and growing a significant part of their own food. The cost of imported inputs, such as fertilizer, will rise, but will be offset by rising output prices.[5] In turn, adjustment is likely to hurt net buyers of food employed in the nontradable sector of the economy, which is the case of many urban dwellers. The net impact on this group will depend on their opportunities to migrate to jobs in the tradable sector, the composition of their consumption basket, and private transfers between rural- and urban-based family members.[6]

If these are the stylized distributional consequences of macroeconomic policy reform, what is the impact of adjustment on the poor? At the theoretical level, the net welfare outcome of policy reform cannot in general be predicted because households have considerable possibilities of substitution in both income and consumption and, more generally, because policy reform engenders change in many determinants of welfare, including those that relate to earned income and product market behavior, net private and public transfers, and the value and incidence of services provided by the public sector. Since some of these factors may work in opposite directions, net outcomes can only be established empirically. The development of a theoretical framework must thus be followed by a plan for empirical analysis (and, if needed, data collection). This necessary sequence is the main reason for this book.

The welfare reform: An empirical framework

Welfare in its different aspects—consumption, basic needs fulfillment, leisure—is ultimately experienced by households and individuals. Its analysis requires very much a micro-orientation. The analysis of the processes through which the effects of macroeconomic policy reform are transmitted to households is hampered because microeconomics and macroeconomics lack theoretical integration. Microeconomics deals with the decisionmaking behavior of individual units, whereas macroeconomics focuses on aggregate constructs without linking changes therein to the activities and welfare of households and individuals (Ruggles and Ruggles 1986, p. 245).

The gap between macroeconomics and microeconomics can be bridged by introducing the notion of a meso level—between the macro and micro levels. The meso level, for our purposes, consists of the markets in which households trade, and the economic and social infrastructure they use.[7] It is important to realize that households react to mesoeconomic changes engendered by macroeconomic change, rather than to macroeconomic change as such. Accordingly, the two-stage approach proposed in this volume for the study of macro-micro linkages consists, first, of an analysis of how changes in policy instruments affect relevant markets and infrastructure, and second, of an analysis of how household income-earning activities, consumption behavior, and satisfaction of basic needs respond to these mesoeconomic changes. The elements of the mesoeconomic level that command particular attention in the context of studies on the social and distributional consequences of structural adjustment are labor markets, credit and product markets, health and education services, and the state of economic infrastructure such as transportation and irrigation.

This approach to macro-micro analysis is illustrated in Figure 1.1. The main economy-wide and sectoral policy instruments used to bring about adjustment are listed at the top of the figure. These policies are shown to influence markets and infrastructure (the meso level). The analysis of these influences is termed macro-meso analysis and is reviewed in the next section.

Changes at the meso level will affect the income-earning and asset positions of households, as well as their expectations. Understanding these effects is the task of meso-micro analysis, whose data requirements and analytical procedures constitute the main body of this book and are summarized in this chapter. In the lower part of Figure 1.1, household welfare is depicted as depending on a range of outcomes: household consumption (from which measures of poverty may be derived), employment, migration, education, health, nutrition, and fertility. These outcomes are the result of the combined influence of supply and demand factors. For example, the educational status of household members (an outcome variable) is influenced by the availability of schooling (a supply factor) and the income of the household (a demand factor). Markets and infrastructure influence both the supply and the demand side of this equation. For example, changes in the labor market may affect teachers' salaries and the number

Figure 1.1: Macro-meso-micro analysis

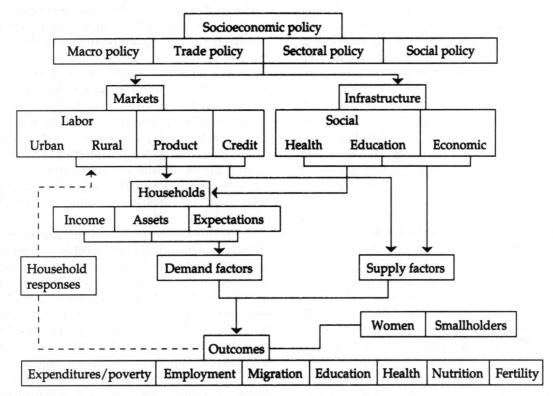

Source: World Bank 1991b.

Figure 1.2: A hierarchical information system for the social dimensions of adjustment

(1) Level	(2) Focus	(3) Analysis	(4) Constructs	(5) Data

Macro	*Policy*
	• Monetary, fiscal, and exchange rate policy
		• Macroeconomic models
		  -aggregate (RMSM)
		  -multisectoral (CGE)
			• National accounts
			• Social accounting matrix
			• Consumer price index
			• Balance of payments
			• Macro-indicators
				• Economic, trade, and financial statistics
				• Social and demographic statistics

Meso	*Effects* • Markets • Economic and social infra-structure	• Sectoral and institutional studies • CGE • Multimarket models	• Social accounting matrix • Food balance sheets • Sectoral quantity and price indices	• Community survey • Price statistics • Production statistics

Micro	*Impact*
	• Individual and household welfare
		• Household models and analysis	• Poverty profiles
			• Social indicators
				• Household surveys
				  -economic
				  -social
				  -anthropometric
				  -demographic

Source: World Bank 1991b, Table 6.1.

of teachers available, and thus the supply of education services. Changes in product markets (commodity price changes) will affect the incomes of households buying or selling those commodities and so influence the demand for schooling and other services. Household income may also be influenced by the availability of infrastructural services.

The existence of feedback loops from household welfare outcomes to markets is indicated by the broken lines in Figure 1.1. For example, an increase in the price of consumer goods will cause a reduction in consumption by households, as well as substitution effects, if price increases are uneven across commodities. This response of households will feed back as shifts in demand in the product market, which will lead to second-order effects on prices. In this way, the first-order effects of a price change (which ignore household responses) are likely to be different from the full effect (after allowing for higher-order changes).

To document change in the variables accounted for in Figure 1.1, information is required at each of the macro, meso, and micro levels. So it is useful to view information requirements in the context of a hierarchical information system where data and empirical analysis are explicitly considered at each of the three levels. Such a system relevant for social dimensions analysis is presented in Figure 1.2. (See World Bank 1991b for an explanation of the rationale underlying this system.) While some data on macro, meso, and micro variables are already collected in most countries (though they are of variable quality), household survey data are the most critically deficient information source currently hampering analysis of the social dimensions of policy reform, particularly in Sub-Saharan Africa—yet they offer the greatest potential payoff for understanding the impact of adjustment on households. This is a prime reason why this volume focuses on household-survey-based analysis.

With Figures 1.1 and 1.2 in mind, we turn now to a more detailed discussion of the data requirements to implement the two-stage analytical approach. We shall clarify the analytical procedures applicable to each of the two stages.

Macro-meso analysis: Data and analytical procedures

Macro-meso analysis can be defined as the study of aggregate economic and social sector achievements in the context of policy reform, and of changes in production and consumption incentives. Aggregate economic performance indicators are those that appear in the national income and product accounts and the balance of payments, augmented by data on the creation of money and the rate of inflation. Social sector performance indicators include such input and intermediate measurements as the number and distribution of primary schools and primary health care facilities, school enrollment, dropout and repetition rates, immunization coverage, and the share of population with access to safe water and sanitation. Output measurements in the social sectors include the literacy rate, infant and child mortality, and other measures of schooling and health achievement.

The quality and availability of public services is, in part, a consequence of the level and composition of government expenditure. (It is also a function of the efficiency of service delivery.) A useful set of indicators to study the evolution of social services provided by the government has been suggested in the United Nations Development Programme's *Human Development Report 1991* (UNDP 1991, pp. 5-6). The report argues that efforts to monitor the share of public spending devoted to human development should focus on the percentage of public expenditure earmarked for social services (the social allocation ratio) and the percentage of social expenditure devoted to human priority concerns such as primary education and primary health care (the social priority ratio), among other data.

Information on incentives (and incentive distortions) can be identified at both the macro and the meso level. Macro and trade policy indicators of incentives include the spread between the official and the parallel market price of foreign exchange, the real effective exchange rate, the rural-urban (or internal) terms of trade, the structure of protection, and the external terms of trade. For example, a rise in the spread between the official and the parallel market exchange rate may imply a rise in the rate of indirect taxation of smallholders, if they are selling their output to an official marketing board at the official exchange rate, and are buying their inputs on the parallel market at prices that reflect the dearer parallel exchange rate.

The three main prices that, at the meso level, transmit the impact of macroeconomic policy operating through markets to households and individuals are wage rates or the price of labor, the price of food and fuel, and, for farmers, agricultural output prices. In addition to the analysis of price movements, it is often necessary to study the institutional characteristics of the markets on which the poor depend. For example, labor markets may be characterized by institutional arrangements that inhibit wage flexibility and employment growth. Access to credit may be constrained because credit institutions are not sufficiently decentralized or are unable to respond to poor people's need for small amounts of credit. Relative price shifts and the reallocation of resources toward tradable activities in the context of structural adjustment may be inhibited by infrastructural shortcomings or a lack of supportive response from capital markets.

Two approaches to macro-meso analysis can be suggested: the analysis of time series of these variables to assess economic and social trends, and the development of economy-wide models to generate counterfactuals. Both approaches are the subject of Chapter 2. One difficulty of time-series analysis is the attribution of causality between observed trends and exogenous events such as policy reform. The problem can be solved at least in part by decomposing the series into historical sub-periods. Regression techniques can then be used to test whether the indicators deviate significantly from their secular trend during an episode of structural adjustment.

The use of numeric models is an important complement to the time-series-based, factual analysis of economy-wide changes in the context of policy reform. Such models are able to generate illuminating policy counterfactuals. For example, by changing relative prices, governments induce changes in the supply and demand behavior of firms and individuals. These direct changes induce indirect effects, leading to a new equilibrium in time. The outcomes, as reflected in the macroeconomic and distributional indicators associated with one set of policies, can be compared with alternatives. The main limitation of the economy-wide models available is their failure to trace the infrastructural effects of policy change.[8]

Meso-micro analysis: Data and analytical procedures

Meso-micro analysis is the study of income-generation processes, expenditure decisions, and basic needs achievements as functions of prices, household characteristics and endowments, and relevant infrastructure available to the household. This is the subject of Chapters 3 through 12. Household surveys constitute the basic data source needed for meso-micro analysis, augmented by community surveys on prices and infrastructure characteristics where possible.

In advising governments about efficient empirical options to monitor the social dimensions of adjustment, it is useful to distinguish between two generic kinds of household surveys: the light and rapid survey to collect data on key outcome or achievement variables; and the full-fledged, multi-topic household survey to permit multivariate analysis of household choices and welfare outcomes. Prototypes of surveys corresponding to each category have been developed under the joint UNDP, African Development Bank, and World Bank Social Dimensions of Adjustment (SDA) program, which is sponsoring the application of these surveys in many African countries. The surveys are briefly reviewed here.[9]

The light or Priority Survey (PS) is a data collection instrument aimed at identifying target groups and establishing for such groups key indicators on welfare and basic needs fulfillment. The PS has a restricted data content, but the data are collected over a large sample and permit fast tabulation and analysis. Ideally, the PS is conducted as the first component of a survey program, providing policymakers with an initial data base for targeting essential and urgent interventions. When repeated, the PS also becomes a monitoring tool for tracing changes in welfare and basic needs fulfillment across target groups. Repetitions of the PS are recommended, because the micro-level effects of macroeconomic policy reform are distributed over time and thus call for a combination of cross-sectional and over-time data. Analysis of initial PS data can thus provide both a benchmark for key welfare indicators and basic policy analysis (see Grootaert and Marchant 1991).

The more complex, multi-topic Integrated Survey (IS) is designed to collect, for a relatively restricted sample, comprehensive data on income and expenditures, assets, socioeconomic characteristics, and welfare indicators of households and their members. The survey's main goal is to permit in-depth analysis of household responses to changes in their living and working environment (see Delaine and others 1992). A key requirement of the analytical methods presented in Chapters 4 to 12 is that they be able to draw on integrated multi-subject household data sets.

Although a great deal of analytical work can be undertaken using single-subject surveys, the issue of measuring and understanding the standards of living of different household groups cannot be adequately dealt with unless there is the possibility of correlating economic and social data at the household level. While the IS is an ideal data source for the analysis plans on the social effects of policy reform in this volume, alternative data sources can be used. The living standards surveys sponsored by the World Bank's Living Standards Measurement Study are examples of an alternative integrated or multi-topic survey approach.

In general, IS-type surveys should be viewed as strategic investments to generate the data needed for longer-term policy planning and development strategy choice. They take time to implement (data collection usually requires a full year) and analyze. For this reason, short-term policy action, by definition, cannot be guided by IS-based conclusions and recommendations. Short-term action requires priority data collection and analysis that focuses on identification of policy target groups and on provision of the key items of information policymakers need to make rapid decisions in the area of social dimensions. Accordingly, the meso-micro analysis proposed in this book starts, in Chapter 3, with a plan for priority social dimensions analysis to be undertaken rapidly using simple analytical tools. While the PS is the preferred and simplest data source for this priority analysis, other surveys can also be used. Since the data requirements are less, the choice of alternative data sources is greater for priority analysis than for the analysis discussed in Chapters 4 through 12.

The next section gives an overview of the analytical approaches developed in the chapters on meso-micro analysis. However, the general procedure can be summarized as follows. Most chapters follow, explicitly or implicitly, a three-stage approach in the framework of standard utility maximization theory. First, the dependent variables are defined, depending on the particular aspect of household welfare of interest. Cross-tabulations of these variables against major classifying variables provide a first insight into the distribution of the characteristic in question. Second, in the context of the retained model of household behavior, independent or right-hand-side variables are selected to explain variations in the dependent variables. This relationship takes the following general form:

$$Z = a + b_1 X_1 + b_2 X_2 + b_3 X_3$$

where Z is the dependent variable of interest; X_1 a vector of predetermined household assets and characteristics; X_2 a vector of market variables (prices); and X_3 a vector of infrastructural variables (such as distance to health facilities and schools, indicators of quality of these services, and so on). The b's are the parameters to be estimated.

The third stage seeks to assess how changes in the X_2 and X_3 variables affect the dependent variable and thereby welfare outcomes. This is given by:

$$\Delta Z = b_2 (\Delta X_2) + b_3 (\Delta X_3)$$

where information on changes in the X_2 and X_3 variables comes from the macro-meso analysis described earlier. This type of analysis can be quite intricate in view of the interactions between different aspects of welfare and the feedback effects between the micro and meso levels. The meso-micro analysis chapters show what is practically feasible given existing analytic techniques.

An analysis guide for the social effects of policy reform

A successful analysis strategy for the social dimensions of policy reform in an adjusting country would have to consist of support to data collection efforts at the household level along the lines discussed in the two previous sections, and the application of macro-meso-micro analysis. The precise nature and sequencing of data collection and analysis efforts is country-specific and cannot be prejudged. This section presents a possible guide for the assessment of the social dimensions of adjustment, and summarizes important policy issues to be addressed. The issues, derived from the various chapters, combine to present a guide in planning a country program of analysis of the social effects of policy reform. Of course, departures from the proposals made here will frequently be dictated by country circumstances.

A country-specific analytic agenda might start with the implementation of *priority analysis* of social dimensions of policy reform, followed by more detailed analyses. In Chapter 3, Demery and Grootaert present a priority analysis, which focuses on symptoms and indicators of immediate need. It is strongly focused on poverty and basic needs because these are the key areas for immediate attention. Since the construction of income and expenditure measures cannot be undertaken in this context, the main challenge is the design of suitable proxy measures. Analytically, the task is to use these measures to identify target groups.

The policy focus of priority analysis is not to modify employment, education, or health policy, but to identify those groups in society that are particularly disadvantaged in any one of the dimensions that constitute the standard of living, and to document the extent of that disadvantage. The analysis will not necessarily provide indications about the type of interventions needed to solve the problem in the long term. This is the role of the in-depth analysis proposed in other chapters. In Chapter 3, the aim is to set short-run operational priorities based on observations of the extent of a problem in different socioeconomic groups.

Chapters 4 to 12 address our main concern—how to investigate the impact of policy reform on household welfare, given the availability of a multi-topic household data set. These chapters reflect the multi-dimensionality of poverty and the social effects of policy reform, as well as the fact that policy change affects various groups in society differently. Foremost comes the concern about the impact on the poor (Chapter 4). This is supplemented with an analysis of the ways in which households—poor and non-poor—generate income and how this can be enhanced in an adjustment context (Chapters 5 and 6). The social dimensions of policy reform have an important sectoral content relating to human resources, that is, education, health, food security, and nutrition. Health and nutrition are directly related to the survival of individuals, while education is the main element of capital acquisition that holds promise for future escape from poverty. Each of these sectors represents crucial welfare-related outcome variables at the household and individual levels, and is associated with important infrastructure determinants at the meso level (for example, schools and health facilities). Chapters 7 to 9 cover the sectoral aspects of social dimensions analysis.

Social dimensions analysis must be target-group-oriented. The identification of target groups of interest will be more country-specific than the identification of sectors. Nevertheless, at least three broadly defined target groups—the poor, women, and smallholders—must be considered in any analysis of the impact of policy reform. We have already mentioned the poverty profile (Chapter 4), which identifies the poor for policy purposes. Chapters 10 to 12 focus on women and small-holders. The selection of women as a target group follows because men and women do not face the same constraints in taking advantage of income and employment opportunities. The role of fertility needs to be emphasized in this context. The concern with smallholders follows from the fact that in most developing countries the majority of the population is rural, and agriculture—the dominant sector—takes place on small farms.

In the remainder of this section, the individual analysis plans are briefly presented, highlighting the policy issues they address.

In the *poverty profile* (Chapter 4), Demery reviews how the magnitude and depth of poverty—the key social problem in most countries—may be assessed. To analyze household welfare, a money-metric measure is proposed—namely, total household expenditure per capita (or per adult equivalent). To separate poor and non-poor households, a poverty line must be specified. The chapter suggests that where there is general agreement about the poverty line in the country, an absolute poverty concept is appropriate. Otherwise, analysts are advised to adopt a poverty line that represents some proportion of mean income.

The chapter presents a simple method for measuring the incidence, intensity, and severity of poverty—a poverty measure that is easy to compute and to interpret and that has the added advantage of decomposability. By decomposing the measure across socioeconomic groups, some understanding is gained of how poverty may be affected by policy reforms. Such decompositions will also indicate the extent to which leakages occur under different targeting options designed to reduce poverty. The poverty profile provides an overview of the poverty issues facing the country. This overview represents necessary background information for each remaining analysis plan. If a country has been collecting data over several years, the poverty profile in combination with the priority analysis of Chapter 3 can be applied to data from different years. This will provide the key elements necessary for poverty monitoring over time.

In the analysis plan on *employment and earnings* (Chapter 5), Addison addresses the radical changes in the incentives for different types of work brought about by adjustment. In general, adjustment shifts the incentives from sectors producing nontradable goods to those producing tradable goods. The impact of this shift on rural populations will depend very much upon whether food in the country in question is tradable or not. Also, adjustment frequently affects employment through restructuring the government and the para-public sector. This usually implies retrenchments as part of measures to enhance efficiency. The task is to find suitable employment opportunities for laid-off public sector employees.

In many countries (particularly in francophone Africa), the public sector wage has been persistently above market-clearing levels. In recent years, this margin has disappeared because of salary erosion. In many countries, the public sector acts as the leading sector for wage determination in the private sector. The latter frequently exhibits inflexible wages, so that the bulk of adjustment occurs through changes in the volume of employment rather than wages. All in all, adjustment can be expected to induce a greater mobility of labor and to reduce job security. This means that a greater number of people are holding secondary jobs or that labor turnover has increased or both. The extent of this phenomenon and the types of workers most affected (male or female, educated or non-educated) is a major area of analysis because it will help determine the shape of the employment-creation programs.

A group that deserves special attention is the unemployed—those who have not managed to take advantage of the new opportunities and incentives provided in the labor market. The question of youth unemployment is particularly critical. In many countries, the output of the educational system does not meet the demands of the labor market, and the educational system does not respond quickly enough to the changing incentives under adjustment. The extent of un-employment among recent graduates is a key indicator, and retraining programs may be needed.

Given the importance of the urban informal sector as a creator of jobs, the productivity and profitability of the enterprises in that sector deserve attention. The analysis has to relate profitability to the characteristics of the entrepreneur in terms of age, education, and migrant status. It will be important to monitor the sectoral composition of output to see to what extent informal enterprises respond to the shifts in incentives in favor of tradable goods. Significant bottlenecks can occur in terms of access to credit, access to capital goods (which in many countries are imported and typically become more expensive

under adjustment), and access to technical and commercial know-how. Special programs may need to be designed as part of an adjustment package to ensure that entrepreneurs have the ability to respond properly to the new incentives.

The reallocation of labor induced by the adjustment program across the different sectors of the economy may require considerable *migration*. A separate analysis plan (Chapter 6) is devoted to this issue for two principal reasons. First, adjustment is likely to change migration flows, possibly slowing down or reversing the long-standing (rural to urban) migration patterns observed in developing countries. Second, migration has important implications for human welfare. It offers opportunities for improvements in living standards, but it can also be socially disruptive—not only through the displacement of families, but because often families become separated when the adult males relocate to find work. The number of households headed by females can increase substantially, an issue addressed also in the chapter concerned with women's issues (Chapter 11). The subject of migration is politically sensitive in many countries, especially in Africa, in view of the high urban population growth rates—migration typically accounts for about half of urban population growth.

In Chapter 6, Montgomery proposes a migration analysis in three stages. First, out-migration profiles are constructed by age, sex, and initial location. Second, a multivariate model is developed to study out-migration as a function of personal characteristics and the characteristics of the place of origin. This model is rooted in the well-established human-capital perspective on migration, but fully recognizes the role of other variables, such as prices and infrastructure. Third, an analysis of origin/destination pairs is proposed, in a simplified way that keeps empirical estimation tractable. The analysis plan concludes by considering the crucial link between several dimensions of household responses to adjustment, in particular between migration, fertility, and the education and health of children.

The consideration of these links casts light on the next set of chapters (7 to 9), which provide the sector focus of the social dimensions of policy reform: education, health, nutrition, and food security.

Behrman argues that the analysis of *education* (Chapter 7) needs to distinguish between supply and demand factors as determinants of the output of the education system in a country. The supply side consists of schools and institutions as well as teachers and teaching materials. Structural adjustment often implies budget cuts, which may include expenditure cuts for public schooling, increases in user charges for education, reductions in the provision of education materials, and increased rationing of access to public schools. On the demand side, adjustment policies will affect household incomes as well as prices, which will have an impact on the amount of education services demanded.

Analytically, the income effect is to be distinguished from the price effect. The former operates through changes in income, which directly affect the demand for education. The price effect works through making schooling directly more expensive (user fees) or through changes in the opportunity cost of attending school or both. The analysis focuses on the determinants of the demand for schooling. There are three key policy issues here: How much will the ability of households to send their children to school be affected by a reduction in their income? In other words, what is the income elasticity of the demand for education? What is the impact from the price effect? Adjustment programs frequently increase user charges for education. What is the long-term impact of adjustment on the demand for education? If adjustment will truly generate growth, then there should be an increased demand for education because of an increase in the expected returns to education.

If a household is faced with a reduced demand for education, this reduction will not necessarily be uniform for different types of household members. The demand analysis must at a minimum be differentiated according to gender. In doing so, the analysis complements that addressed in Chapter 11 on women and structural adjustment.

Although Chapter 7 does not specifically address the internal efficiency of education delivery, this issue cannot be overlooked. Indeed, even though ministries of education may be faced with budget cuts, the same amount of money can be used to deliver very different packages of services. A package that is mainly oriented toward higher education will be biased against the poor. On the other hand, a package that strongly supports universal primary education and the provision of adequate teaching materials for primary education will have a strong egalitarian effect.

It is important to note that the effect of adjustment on education is not limited to the direct impact on the educational sector itself. There is an important indirect impact through the labor market, whose smooth functioning depends on a steady supply of suitably schooled workers. It will also affect the ability of smallholders and informal sector entrepreneurs to increase their productivity and take advantage of new opportunities expected to accompany the adjustment process. Last, education has an impact on health and nutrition status. The educational analysis therefore provides not just an input into the design of education policy, but also into the determination of policy with regard to nutrition, agriculture, and other sectors.

In Chapter 8 on *health*, Pitt suggests that structural adjustment may influence the health status of the population by affecting governmental expenditures on health-related services, by changing the cost of these services, and by altering real incomes. Health is multi-dimensional and difficult to measure. Drawing conclusions regarding health on the basis of nutrient intake is fraught with ambiguities. Nutrients are important inputs in the production of health, but unsatisfactory indicators of health status. Self-reported frequency of illness is another proxy for health that is frequently poorly reported. The chapter proposes anth-ropometric measures as the preferred indicators of health. It focuses on reduced-form demand equations for health, using prices of food, wages, measures of accessibility to public health programs, household assets, and household "public" goods (sources of drinking water, sanitary facilities) as independent variables. The policy discussion developed in the chapter is in terms of food prices and programs; that is, health facilities, fertility control programs, and household "public" goods.

The availability and quality of health facilities is in large measure a consequence of public expenditure choices, although private sector provision of health care (for example, through nongovernmental organizations) is important in many cases. Health sector governmental spending in Africa has tended to be concentrated on higher-order care (hospital-based and curative, as opposed to primary and preventive). These higher-order services tend to benefit the higher-income groups. There is, here, a policy issue in terms of the intra-sectoral allocation of resources. Also, the management of public spending in health and the prevailing program input combinations are often deficient, leading to low and, in many cases, still deteriorating health services. There is a need for more data on program placement and expenditures on recurrent inputs by district. Meso-level data on actual availability of health facilities and complementary inputs (drugs, disposable materials, health workers) may need to be combined with household data to obtain an accurate picture of the supply of health care.

An important doubt raised by the chapter is that simple associations between health programs and health outcomes may not measure accurately the effects of public spending on health care. The reasons for this include the possibility that the spatial distribution of government health programs may be influenced by environmental factors that are favorable to the occurrence of certain debilitating diseases. This may lead to positive observed correlations between health program spending and frequency of illness. The chapter recommends that estimates be made of how changes in local programs affect the health of the local population.

In Chapter 9, Eele, Hay, and Hoddinot discuss policy issues in the area of household *food security and nutrition*: (a) the analysis of adjustment-induced changes in wage and producer income, food prices, and consumption; (b) the identification of food-insecure groups from this, and an analysis of food budget shares, expenditure elasticities, and (where possible in view of data constraints) the comparison of food consumption with "requirements"; and (c) the various market and non-market forms of intervention available to governments to raise the food security and nutrition of specified groups. These interventions include targeted indirect income transfers in the form of commodity-specific subsidies; public employment schemes; and direct income transfers in the form of food aid, cash, food stamps, or ration cards entitling the holder to subsidized food. The practical difficulties of targeting are well-known. Self-targeting through inferior commodities (in a consumer preference, not a nutritional, sense) holds considerable potential to limit administrative cost and leakage of benefits to non-needy consumers. There are few successful experiences of self-targeted food subsidy schemes in Africa, and opportunities for self-targeting should be explored.

Following the analysis of the sectoral aspects of the social dimensions of policy reform in Chapters 7 to 9, the final set of chapters in this volume addresses group-specific investigations. Two analysis plans are devoted to women: Chapter 10

examines an important aspect of the role of women, namely fertility. Chapter 11 argues that adjustment affects men and women differently and explores the reasons why. The special situation of rural smallholders is addressed in Chapter 12.

Few factors have a greater effect on the ability of women to take advantage of social and economic opportunities than their reproductive role. Montgomery explores this issue in depth in the analysis plan on *fertility* (Chapter 10). Fertility, investments in children's health and education, and the supply of labor are the dimensions along which the household responds to changes in its economic environment. Analytically, these are the jointly determined endogenous variables in a conceptual framework where prices, infrastructure, and household assets are the exogenous factors. The key questions to be answered are: Do the economic contractions now felt in many developing countries encourage postponement of childbearing? Do they imply lower lifetime fertility? Could structural adjustment produce a pro-natalist response in rural areas and an anti-natalist response in urban areas? How might public investments in health care, education, and family planning influence fertility?

In deriving the answers for a given country, analysts should focus on the relationship between income and fertility, and allow for interactions between income and other covariates. Among these, the plan emphasizes the interaction between income and the cost of schooling. The key point is that proper service delivery in family planning and education has the potential to transform the relationship between income and fertility. Among the indirect effects, the influence of educational and health infrastructure on fertility must be singled out. These indirect effects underlie the tradeoff between child quantity and quality, which has proved to be an integral element of demographic transition outside Africa. Educational and health investments may complement, or substitute for, investments in family planning services. The estimation of the direct effect of the latter on fertility needs to be compared with the indirect influences of education and health investments on fertility.

In the analysis plan on *women* (Chapter 11), Collier observes that adjustment changes incentives and constraints for the generation of different types of income. It is conceivable that the constraints faced by men and women, and therefore their ability to respond to those incentives, are not the same. On the demand side, men and women are not likely to have the same propensities to consume goods and services such as education and health. So, the consumption of goods and services, and basic needs achievements, may be differentially affected for men and women faced with falling income or rising prices or both. Hence a gender distinction in analysis and policy design is warranted.

The supply response of individuals, both men and women, depends in essence on the resources they control. The two key resources are labor and credit. Because households do not necessarily function democratically, women may not have complete control over their time. The traditional division of labor may dictate that they spend significant time on specific functions such as fetching water and wood. Analysis must show (a) what the pattern of time-use by women is; (b) whether rural women have the necessary control to reallocate their time when, for example, the relative prices of different crops change; and (c) whether women can gain access to the necessary inputs such as land and credit.

A key question is the role of food in the adjustment process. If food is a tradable good, then major opportunities will open up for women since in many African societies food production is a traditional responsibility of women. However, this also means that resource mobility will have to be highest among women, and the question is whether the current functioning of the labor market will make that reallocation possible. Institutional, legal, or other constraints may impede this reallocation, resulting in allocative inefficiency, which may need to be addressed through special programs. In rural areas, an important element will be extension services. These are often biased in favor of men, and to the extent that promotion of new technologies and new crops occurs through these services, women may have less access to them. This may require redesign and retargeting of extension services.

There is complex interplay between the use of health and family planning services and access to employment and education. It will be critically important to examine rates of non-enrollment in primary schooling, where such rates are frequently twice as high for girls as for boys, creating a disadvantage for girls that they may never be able to overcome.

In the analysis of policy issues surrounding *smallholders* (Chapter 12), Mullen, Pearce, and Merid start with the assumption that under given agro-ecological conditions, the income possibilities of smallholders are largely determined by their labor use and their cropping choices, which are influenced by relative prices in relevant markets and the availability of labor. (Land scarcity is not a binding constraint to production and income opportunities in most African settings.) Smallholders typically pursue a combination of activities, including off-farm wage employment, and work on their plots, where they produce tradable or nontradable crops and rear animals. The relative importance of these activities as determinants of total income may be used to classify the smallholder population into predominantly export-crop producers, producers of tradable foods for import-substitution, rural laborers, and subsistence farmers—that is, rural families deriving a particularly small proportion of their income from exchange activities through labor or product markets.

The key policy issues related to smallholders under adjustment are the evolution of rural wages relative to product prices, the nature of changes in the use of labor and other farm inputs, and the farm output response. Rural wage labor (which is expected to benefit from adjustment in the longer run) might suffer a real-wage fall in the short run. This could occur if larger farmers producing for export or domestic market consumption were slow to expand their production. It is not certain whether smallholders would require a real-wage fall to induce an expansion of tradable production. The short-term effects of devaluation on real wages are therefore ambiguous, and food intervention or other compensatory assistance may be required for some groups.

Another policy issue arises when poorer groups fail to benefit from adjustment as producers because price signals are not transmitted to them, whether because of infrastructural and institutional shortcomings or because of an inadequate initial flow of consumer goods to the countryside. In many African countries, agricultural marketing processes work inefficiently. Thus if smallholders fail to shift to profitable (tradable) crops or to increase the relative importance of these commodities in their output mix, they cannot gain from adjustment as producers. Public investment in agriculture, and the development of institutions capable of serving the needs of smallholders, must accompany programs of macroeconomic reform.

A guide for analysis

The analysis plans in this volume discuss methods of both descriptive, tabular analysis, and multivariate investigation. Both types of analysis are likely to be required in country-based investigation. Tabular analysis possibilities are set out in detail, especially in Chapters 3 and 5. Space limitations precluded an exhaustive presentation of sample tables (called "frames" in this volume) in all the chapters. Readers are encouraged to develop their own sample cross-tabulations for their fields of particular interest.

Given the complexity of macro-micro linkages, in most situations some multivariate analysis is indispensable. The inevitable omission of important explanatory variables from cross-tables, and the fact that interactions can be studied only rudimentarily through tabular analysis, can lead to misleading policy conclusions in the absence of multivariate techniques. For this reason, the analysis plans include such techniques and discuss the proper specification of the most relevant estimation equations. However, the mathematical expositions are kept minimal and presented in special boxes to maintain text flow and to provide verbal explanations for all points of modeling expressed in equation form.

Most chapters propose a reduced-form approach to the estimation of outcomes as a function of household-choice variables, set in the standard household utility maximization framework. The derivation of such reduced-form equations is discussed in more detail in some chapters than in others. Therefore, although each chapter is designed to be self-contained, the reader might find it useful to consult other related chapters to maximize analytical guidance.

The selection of topics for the analysis of the social dimensions of policy reform is country-specific. The analysis plans presented in this volume should assist country-based analysts in their task of assessing the social and distributional consequences of structural adjustment and longer-term development policy. We hope that the choice of topics and analytic techniques will be found appropriate for that objective. Each chapter contains at least one empirical illustration of the analysis recommended, presented in a box. Most illustrations are set in the African context—Africa is the continent where poverty and social concerns are most pressing, and we have been particularly concerned that the conceptual and empirical framework underlying the analysis plans is relevant for African countries. However, as a guide for policy analysis, the approaches and techniques suggested in this book will be applicable in most developing countries undertaking policy reform.

Notes

1. Our assumption here is that real devaluation is both possible and expansionary. Positive evidence regarding the possibility of achieving real devaluation under African conditions is presented in World Bank and UNDP (1989).

2. Demand- and supply-side policies are interdependent and mutually reinforcing. For example, devaluation, normally viewed as a supply-side measure, also plays a role in fiscal adjustment. Where producer prices of export crops are fixed by the government, a devaluation means a reduction in fiscal outlays to support the producer price. Another example is parastatal reform. This is often necessary both to increase the efficiency of production and trade and to eliminate or reduce the fiscal burden of operating losses incurred by state-owned enterprises.

3. A recent study has found that the poorest groups in Africa are unaffected by policy reforms in general (Duncan and Howell 1992).

4. The real-product wage is the nominal wage relative to the output price. The real-consumption wage is the nominal wage deflated by the weighted price index of workers' consumption baskets.

5. For an analysis of changes in agricultural incentives in the context of structural adjustment in Africa, see Jaeger and Humphreys (1988) and Duncan and Howell (1992). For Latin America, see Ferroni and Valdés (1991).

6. Private transfers can significantly influence total real income consequences of a process of adjustment (see Mahieu 1990 for an analysis of individuals' rights and obligations in the community in a West African setting).

7. The macro-meso distinction, as an aspect of analyzing the impact of adjustment, was introduced by Cornia, Jolly, and Stewart (1987). However, our use of the term "meso" follows World Bank (1991b), where the term is used differently than in Cornia, Jolly, and Stewart.

8. A recent study by the Organisation for Economic Cooperation and Development (OECD) has highlighted the strengths and weaknesses of economy-wide models in analyzing the equity effects of adjustment policy (see Bourguignon, de Melo, and Morrisson 1991).

9. Other empirical approaches at the micro level (for example, the technique known as Rapid Rural Appraisal and participant-observer techniques) are not discussed in this volume.

2

Analyzing the mesoeconomic effects of structural adjustment

Lionel Demery

The previous chapter proposed a two-stage research design for analyzing the effects of structural adjustment on human welfare. The first stage traces the effects of adjustment on markets and infrastructure, and the second assesses how these changes in turn influence the various dimensions of household welfare. This chapter deals with the first stage, and is concerned with the real-economy effects of adjustment policy. The chapter will seek to explain how some economic variables taken as explanatory variables in other chapters are themselves influenced by policy interventions. The subset of explanatory variables with which we shall be concerned are at the *mesoeconomic* level. These variables come between the macro-policy interventions and the micro level, in this context the household-level variables.

The problems raised in the first part of this research design should not be underestimated. It is extremely difficult to predict the precise changes that policy interventions will induce in markets and infrastructure. There are a number of reasons for this. First, many transmission mechanisms link a policy instrument to markets and infrastructure. Some policy instruments lead to conflicting effects, and it is difficult to assess which will dominate. An exchange rate adjustment is a classic case of this—a devaluation generally leads to a mix of income and substitution effects, the relative strengths of which will determine the net outcome.

Second, an adjustment program is usually a package of several policy instruments; this com-

plicates even further the task of understanding what the net effects of the combined changes would be. A devaluation might be expected to raise the domestic currency price of importables, but if it is combined with trade liberalization, the net effect on such prices may be reversed. And if marketing institutions are also reformed at the same time, the net effect will be even more difficult to establish.

Third, it is by no means easy to disentangle the effects of policy reform from other changes occurring concurrently. Countries implementing an adjustment program might be faced with further external shocks (such as a continuing decline in their terms of trade). The observed historical changes in market prices will be due in part to the adjustment, but also to the recurring and destabilizing shocks. A fourth and related problem is that of the counterfactual. Ideally, what is required is a comparison of the effects of any given adjustment package with the outcomes of another package—which could either be an alternative adjustment program or no action on the part of the government. But without an economy-wide model through which such alternatives can be analyzed, this is a difficult undertaking.

Finally, the macro-meso analysis addressed in this chapter depends critically on data availability. Unlike the other chapters of this volume, the macro-meso analysis relies generally on data sources other than household surveys. It is therefore difficult to set out an analysis plan with the same precision as the other chapters, since what is done will depend on the available data. Consequently, the chapter suggests two broad approaches, each having different data implications. The first approach assumes only a fairly basic data set—essentially the national accounts, combined with some public sector accounts and price data. The methods used to trace the effects of macroeconomic policy change here are fairly crude, and little by way of generating counterfactual results will be attempted. This approach emphasizes the differences between trends in variables before and after the adjustment program. It has obvious limitations—particularly the problems of causation (observed changes may not be due only to adjustment policy) and the counterfactual.

The second approach, which assumes a more comprehensive data set, involves using modeling techniques. These provide a more robust analysis of the economic effects of adjustment, separating the effects of the adjustment from those of external shocks, and the like, and can be used to generate illuminating counterfactuals.

Before discussing these two approaches, it is useful to identify the relevant mesoeconomic variables. Each chapter of this volume seeks to understand one or more aspects of household welfare (income, expenditure, employment, health, education, nutrition, and so on). For this, a number of explanatory variables are specified, some of which relate to markets and infrastructure. The purpose of this chapter is to identify which of these mesoeconomic variables are important for household welfare, and to understand how they may be affected by policy change.

Table 2.1 attempts to bring this together in a simple analysis matrix, by identifying which meso-level variables are used in each analysis plan. A double star in the cell indicates that the variable is considered critical for meso-micro analysis. A single star indicates that the variable is used in the appropriate chapter, but is considered desirable rather than critical. The wide range of subjects examined by meso-micro analyses implies that a variety of meso-level variables is called for. However, the double star rating suggests that a more limited selection of key meso variables can be identified. These are product prices, wage rates, credit, agricultural services, education services, and health services—the main meso variables considered in this chapter.

Periods of destabilization and adjustment

In the absence of an economy-wide model, the macro-meso analysis suggested in this chapter emphasizes the changes in variable trends brought about by adjustment. If the analysis occurs after an adjustment program has been in place for some time, it will be possible to identify periods of destabilization and adjustment. During destabilization, major unsustainable macroeconomic

Table 2.1: Meso-level variables used in household data analysis

Meso variables	Poverty	Employment	Migration	Education	Health	Nutrition/ food security	Fertility	Women	Smallholders
Market variables									
Product market prices	**			*	*	**		*	**
Input prices	*			*		**			**
Market rationing						**			*
Market access	*	*	*			**	*	**	*
Market wages	*	**	**	**	**	*	**	**	
Wage inflexibilities		**	*						
Interest rates	*			*					*
Access to credit	*		*	*	*	*		**	**
Infrastructural variables									
Roads/communications			**	*					*
Irrigation services						**			**
Marketing institutions		*				*	*	*	*
Extension services	*			*		*	*	**	**
Health services	**		*	*	**		*	*	
Education services	**	*	*	**	*		**	*	
Other social services	*					*	**	*	

** Critical for meso-micro analysis.
* Desirable rather than critical for analysis.

imbalances emerge, creating the need for the adjustment program that follows.

During the adjustment phase, one would expect to find these imbalances being reduced. So, during periods of destabilization, inflation rates, external deficits, and government budget deficits are likely to increase. There might be other symptoms of imbalance, such as an acute scarcity of foreign exchange, the imposition of import restrictions, a shortage of imports (of consumer, intermediate, and capital goods), an appreciation of the real exchange rate, resource transfers into nontradables, and so on. These should all be examined to establish which period is best considered as one of destabilization. It would be helpful to have some account of the causes of these imbalances. In some instances, imbalances are caused by internal shocks, such as drought or political change. In others, external events (declining terms of trade, interest rates, recession in OECD countries) are the main underlying factors. The policy response to each shock is expected to be quite different.

Similarly, the analyst must identify the period(s) of adjustment, and the policy instruments used to achieve the adjustment. This will involve a brief historical account of the main policy reforms enacted, including major fiscal and monetary contractions, exchange rate adjustments, price and marketing reforms, and institutional changes (such as privatizations). It is important to establish both the timing of the application of the policy changes and their effects on the major macro balances—the trade and budget deficits (usually expressed as a percentage of GDP), the rate of inflation, and the rate of economic growth. Periods of destabilization and adjustment may not be as clear as this might suggest. There may be elements of policy reform during periods of destabilization, while some measures of macro performance (for example, the rate of inflation) may continue to worsen during periods of adjustment (when other indicators show an improvement). Although such analysis may call for best judgment, it is an essential exercise. Macromeso analysis as presented cannot properly be undertaken without some broad historical assessment of this sort.

The process of adjustment

An adjustment package is generally designed to achieve sustainable economic growth (which maintains the macroeconomic balances) and a more efficient allocation of resources. This frequently requires changes in relative prices to increase incentives to the tradables sector. Devaluation, trade liberalization, market reforms, and fiscal and monetary reforms are commonly used to achieve this. These policy instruments (even those purely macroeconomic instruments such as devaluation or monetary contraction) will lead to profound changes in the economy, influencing the structure of relative product and factor prices, and changing the availability of infrastructural services (such as roads, water supply, education, and health services).

The extent to which relative prices change as a result of adjustment depends on the degree to which *expenditure switching* characterizes the policy reforms implemented. If the adjustment program involves a significant exchange rate adjustment, and changes in price and trade policies, relative prices will change, and act as signals for resource reallocation (generally to exportables and unprotected importables, and away from nontradables). But, although infrastructural services may be influenced by the relative price shifts, they are likely to be particularly vulnerable to adjustment policies that emphasize *expenditure reductions*. A contractionary monetary and fiscal stance is likely to lead to cuts in government expenditure, which may reduce resources available for economic and social infrastructure.

As a first step toward understanding how relative prices and infrastructure might be influenced by the adjustment effort, one must assess whether adjustment was achieved mainly through expenditure switching or reduction. This can be achieved through a simple decomposition exercise.

An analysis of the effects of adjustment policy must respect basic macroeconomic identities. These are the National Income and Product Accounts (NIPA), which measure the flow of goods and services and incomes in the economy, the Balance of Payments (BP), which measures the flow of current transactions with the rest of the world, and the Monetary Survey (MS),[1] which measures the flow of money creation. The key point here is that these three sets of accounts are interdependent—any one can be derived from the other two. For simplicity, assume that all borrowing and lending abroad is undertaken by the government. The NIPA identity is given as:

$$C + I + (G_c + G_i) + (X - M) \equiv C + S + T \qquad (1)$$

where C is consumer expenditure, I is gross private domestic investment, G_j is government consumption ($j = c$) and investment ($j = i$) expenditure, X and M are respectively the exports and imports of goods and services, S is gross private saving, and T is total tax revenue. GDP measured as aggregate product is given on the left-hand side of (1), while it is measured as aggregate income on the right-hand side. Rearranging gives:

$$S - I \equiv (G_c + G_i - T) + (X - M) \qquad (2)$$

The left-hand side of (2) gives the net flow of savings from the private sector into the financial markets, and the right-hand side sums the government's demand for deficit finance and the foreign sector's demand for funds to finance its current account deficit.

The BP identity is given by:

$$X - M + \Delta L_{gf} \equiv \Delta R \qquad (3)$$

where L_{gf} denotes government liabilities abroad, R is the level of foreign exchange reserves, and Δ denotes changes in the variable indicated. Here the current account surplus plus government borrowing abroad sum to the change in foreign exchange reserves at the central bank.

Finally, the MS identity is written as:

$$\Delta B \equiv \Delta R + \Delta L_{gc} \qquad (4)$$

where B is the monetary base and L_{gc} the liabilities of the government to the central bank. Notice that the MS identity can be derived from the other two identities. Net saving by the private sector, the left-hand side of equation (2), can go to additional holdings of money balances (B) or to holdings of government debt (L_{gp}). Similarly, the government deficit $[(G_c + G_i) - T]$ can be financed by sales of debt to the private sector, to the central bank (L_{gc}), or abroad (L_{gf}). Thus, for each item in the NIPA identity we can derive a corresponding change in assets and liabilities held by the institutions involved. Thus, equation (1) can be rewritten:

$$(\Delta B + \Delta L_{gp}) \equiv (\Delta L_{gp} + \Delta L_{gc} + \Delta L_{gf}) \\ + (\Delta R - \Delta L_{gf}) \qquad (5)$$

Clearly then, (5) is equivalent in an accounting sense to the MS identity (4). These accounting relationships form an excellent basis for comparative work on adjustment policies across countries, ensuring internal consistency in the macro accounts.

Using this accounting framework, and given the availability of the national accounts data, it is possible to decompose changes in the balance of trade deficit into the various expenditure elements. From the national income and product accounts (equation 1),

$$\Delta(X - M) \equiv \Delta Y - \Delta E \\ \equiv \Delta Y - \Delta C - \Delta I - \Delta G_c - \Delta G_i \qquad (6)$$

where Y is GDP ($C+S+T$) and E is aggregate expenditure ($C + I + G_c + G_i$). Such calculations should be prepared in order to establish the extent to which the adjustment in the external accounts was brought about through increases in output (ΔY) or through decreases in expenditure. And if the latter, it should show which of the components of expenditure distinguished in the national accounts have borne the brunt of the adjustment.

These calculations are very straightforward, and they provide considerable insight into the processes of the adjustment program. First, the data should be compiled along the lines of Frame 2.1, which decomposes the change in the trade balance into the changes that occur in output (ΔY) and the various expenditure components as given in (6). The sum of the changes in output minus the changes in expenditure will just equal the change in the trade deficit. These changes in the values of each of these items should also be expressed in percentage terms—the changes in output and expenditures being expressed as a percentage of the total change in the trade balance. Notice also that the table suggests a memorandum item, in which the changes in the trade balance are aggregated over years to capture key periods. For example, the memorandum item in Frame 2.1 decomposes the change in the trade deficit over 1979-84 and 1985-90, assuming that the first period is one where the trade deficit worsened (hence the negative sign)—this being a period of destabilization—and that the deficit narrowed in the second (adjustment) period.

Unfortunately, the real world is often not as simple as Frame 2.1 suggests. It is possible, for example, that a country implementing successful policy reform may experience an increase in external resources and a related widening of its trade

Frame 2.1: Changes in the trade balance and its related identities

Year	$\Delta(X - M)$ Amount	(Percent)	ΔY Amount	(Percent)	ΔE Amount	(Percent)
1979		(100)				
1980		(100)				
1981		(100)				
...		...				
1989		(100)				
1990		(100)				
Memorandum items:						
1979-84	-	(100)				
1985-90	+	(100)				
1979-90	?	(100)				

gap. The period of "adjustment" would therefore not be reflected in the movement of the trade deficit, at least for a while. (Ultimately, adjustment must entail some closing of the gap, through a sustainable increase in export earnings.) Additional shocks might also adversely affect the trade gap, despite a successful program.

The purpose of Frame 2.1 is to show whether the changes in the trade deficit (and especially the improvement in the deficit during periods of adjustment) were associated with a change in output (which would be an expansion in output during the adjustment phase), or changes in aggregate expenditure (that is, declines of expenditures during the adjustment period). If the former, the adjustment is likely to have involved switching policies, which raised the production of tradable goods. But if the adjustment was brought about mainly by cuts in expenditure, either switching policies were not applied, or they were ineffective. This preliminary assessment should lead to a more in-depth analysis of the application and effects of switching policies and expenditure-reducing policies. The types of analysis that are required for each are addressed in the following sections.

Expenditure-switching effects

The analysis of the switching effects of adjustment must be divided into three broad sections. First, it must examine the effects of adjustment on relative product prices. Second, some assessment must be made of the real-wage effects of policy interventions. Finally, some analysis should

be conducted on changes in the credit market induced by adjustment policy.

A difficulty common to much of the analysis in this section arises from the presence in developing countries of parallel markets. These exist in product, credit, and even labor markets, and generally characterize the foreign exchange markets. Analysts should trace induced changes in both official and parallel prices, since these may well differ, depending on the nature of the policy reforms adopted. With some households trading mainly in official markets, and others in parallel markets, this distinction is important for meso-micro analysis.

Exportables, importables, and nontradables

The distinction among exportables, importables, and nontradables is central to the understanding of the real-economy effects of structural adjustment, since most adjustment policies can be expected to influence each product category differently (see Mundlak, Cavallo, and Domenech 1990). The classification of goods and services according to their degree of tradability is essentially country-specific.

Nontradables are goods and services whose prices are determined by domestic supply and demand. This is due to the nature of the good involved (such as public services, housing, and construction) or because transport costs prohibit either the import or the export of the good in question, and insulate it from world markets. Tradable goods are those that cross frontiers, and, in theory, their prices are determined directly by world market conditions, so that for a "small" economy, tradables prices can be taken to be exogenous.

One of the more important problems encountered in using this type of classification of product markets is that commodities can switch categories, frequently in response to the policy change under investigation. The most important reasons that goods are nontraded are commercial policy (for example, prohibition of imports) and transportation costs. Taking the transportation markup to be q, and the world price of a commodity to be P^*, the domestic price must be equal to or less than $P^*/(1+q)$ in order for it to be exportable (assuming no trade taxes/subsidies). Similarly, for the commodity to be importable, its domestic price must be equal to or greater than $P^*(1+q)$, as otherwise its importer would not be able to compete with domestic suppliers. Thus, we have a range of domestic prices for which the commodity is nontradable—neither an exportable nor an importable. This range is given by:

$$P_x \leq P^*/(1+q) < P_n < P^*(1+q) \leq P_m \qquad (7)$$

The difficulty is that a commodity can cross these boundaries and move from being nontradable to being either an exportable (if the domestic price falls sufficiently) or an importable (if the domestic price rises). Country-based empirical work will have to identify where such changes occur. A second difficulty is that commodity classifications may change geographically. A certain commodity may be importable at or near the port of entry, but as transportation costs increase its price in remoter areas, it may become entirely insulated from world markets. This may have become more common during periods of destabilization and adjustment, since transportation networks in Sub-Saharan Africa have deteriorated, and costs have risen accordingly.

There are sectors whose outputs clearly fall under the "tradable" label, such as production of cash crops for export. Similarly, many government services are unquestionably nontradable. In between these pure cases, there lies a grey area of conceptual ambiguity. Any sector protected by severe import quotas should be included under the nontradable category, since changes in the world price will leave domestic prices unaffected, and will influence only the margins obtained by importers. Chapter 11 suggests that a useful starting point for most African countries would be to consider manufactures as a protected importable (assuming that the good in question is not subject to highly restrictive import controls), and export agriculture as an unprotected exportable. With the nontraded sector comprising mainly construction, services, and the public sector, the main area of ambiguity lies in classifying food agriculture. How food production is classified will need careful assessment for each case.

Macro-meso analysis must establish this categorization of commodities for periods of destabilization and adjustment. This must involve identifying any changes over time in the classification. For example, in the early years, possibly during periods of destabilization, a good might be nontraded, simply because of the import protection its producers received. But as policy reforms are applied (possibly a reduction in import controls combined with a devaluation), the

commodity might become a tradable. One of the objectives of this analysis is to identify such switches over time.

The analysis must also identify any geographical switches in these categories. Given information on prices at or near the ports of entry, and estimates of transportation markups, it should be possible to predict what prices across the regions should be. Major departures from the predicted prices would suggest that the commodity in question is a nontradable.

Induced changes in relative product prices

One crucial way in which macroeconomic adjustment influences the structure of relative prices is through its effect on the *real exchange rate*—the price of tradables relative to the price of nontradables (P_t/P_n). Changes in this relative price are frequently the main driving force of the adjustment effort, and are brought about mainly through currency devaluations. The calculation of the real exchange rate is particularly meaningful when other trade policies (such as import controls, tariffs and export taxes) are not changed during the adjustment. This means that relative prices within the tradables category (for example, the exportable/importable relative price, P_x/P_m) remain unchanged, so that we may use the tradable composite.[2] Under such circumstances, the main relative price change induced by adjustment should be captured by changes in the real exchange rate. If other policy instruments change prices within tradables, then further relative price calculations will be called for.

There are broadly two methods for computing the real exchange rate: the first involves taking price indices of nontradables and tradables directly; the second, indirect method deflates the nominal effective exchange rate with appropriate price deflators.

Whether the *direct method* can be used to compute the real exchange rate clearly depends on the availability of the required price data. Prices of nontradables may be available in the published sources. If not, they may be proxied by taking either the services component of the consumer price index (or GDP deflator), or a specific index that is expected to move in sympathy with nontradables prices. The latter might include a price index of a single sector (like construction or housing) or, alternatively, a wage index (assuming that labor is a major component of nontradables production costs).

Choosing an appropriate index for exportables and importables also depends on data availability. If there are no quantitative restrictions to international trade, unit value indices may be used to indicate the movement of tradables prices. For example, the importables price index can be estimated using the unit value of imports (or a major component of imports such as manufactures). Similarly, the export price might be estimated using export unit values. There may be direct information on tradables prices from official sources (including the price data published by marketing boards). Such information is preferred when quantitative restrictions make unit value indices of little relevance in predicting the domestic price. But official data tend to give a misleading impression of market prices since they usually omit parallel market prices, which are always significantly higher than the official market price.

Frame 2.2 illustrates the type of table that might be prepared, reporting the direct calculations of the real exchange rate. The memorandum items, reporting the mean index during the sub-period, should prove useful in gauging the extent to which the relative price movement changed as a result of the adjustment program.

The *indirect method* of estimating changes in P_t/P_n over time involves deflating the nominal rate of exchange. In the simple three-sector dependent economy world, there are three related sets of relative prices:

$$P_m/P_n = eP_m^*(1+k)/P_n$$
$$P_x/P_n = eP_x^*(1+s)/P_n$$
$$P_x/P_m = [P_x^*(1+s)]/[P_m^*(1+k)] \qquad (8)$$

where e is the nominal exchange rate, k is the tariff rate imposed on imports, s is the subsidy/tax rate on exports, and the asterisk refers to world prices. Assuming (initially) that $s = k = 0$, and that P_x^*/P_m^* remains unchanged, then exportables and importables can be combined into a composite tradable commodity. It follows then that the real exchange rate, P_t/P_n, is given by,

$$\varepsilon = eP_t^*/P_n \qquad (9)$$

This index should reflect two important effects of adjustment. First, it should show the direction of induced resource allocations. A rise in ε, or a real exchange rate depreciation, should signal an increase in profitability in tradables, and therefore,

Frame 2.2: Relative price indices of tradables and nontradables
(1980 = 100)

Year	Services price [a] (1)	Import unit value (2)	Export unit value (3)	Relative price estimates (1)/(2)	Relative price estimates (1)/(3)
1979					
1980	100	100	100	100	100
1981					
...					
...					
1990					
Memorandum items:					
1979-84					
1985-90					
1979-90					

a. Alternatively, an index of construction/housing prices may be used.

a tendency for resources to flow into the sector, and out of nontradables. Second, it reflects the degree of the country's international competitiveness. A decline in ε reflects an increase in the real cost of producing tradables, and therefore a decline in competitiveness. Similarly, an increase in ε should signal an increase in a country's international competitiveness.

In calculating (9), the analyst will have to resolve three main difficulties: the selection of the best empirical counterparts to P_t^* and P_n with which to deflate the nominal exchange rate e; the possibility that e will vary across tradable commodities; and the effects that tariffs, import controls, and export taxes/subsidies will have on relative tradables prices.

The first issue concerns the choice of price indices to use in deflating the nominal effective exchange rate, the latter being defined as a trade-weighted index of the nominal exchange rates between the domestic currency and the currencies of each trading partner. Three deflators have been suggested and used in the empirical literature.[3] First, the consumer price index (CPI) of the country in relation to its competitors is used. Equation 8 then becomes:

$$\varepsilon = e(CPI^w)/CPI^d \qquad (10)$$

where the superscripts refer to world (w) and domestic (d) values. The world index can either be the CPI of a principal trading partner, in which case the calculation is on a *bilateral* basis, or it may be a weighted average of a number of trading partners' CPIs, in which case a *multilateral* real exchange rate is computed.

A second approach is to replace the CPI with wholesale price indices (WPI). This is not desirable, however, since WPIs comprise mainly tradable goods and the denominator in (9) should ideally reflect domestic prices of nontradables. Even as an indicator of international competitiveness, the use of WPI is inappropriate, since international variations in WPIs tend to be small. A third approach is to deflate using GDP deflators, that is, a weighted average of the GDP deflator of the country's trading partners divided by the country's own GDP deflator. One limitation of using the GDP deflator in computing the real exchange rate is that it contains both tradable and nontradable commodities, and therefore does not exactly correspond to equation (9). Moreover, it is made available only annually, usually after some time lag.

Analysts will probably calculate a number of estimates of ε, using various deflators, and using bilateral and multilateral real exchange rates. Following Edwards (1988 and 1989) and Harberger (1986), we suggest that ε is best estimated using the WPI of a country's competitor(s) in the numerator and the CPI of the country concerned as the denominator. The former gives greater weight to the price of tradables. Nontradables usually figure prominently in the CPI. In this way, the estimate of ε closely corresponds to equation (9). Alternatively, analysts may prefer to use only components of the price indices—taking the tradables components of the price indices of trading partners (be these CPI, WPI, or GDP deflators), and the nontradables component of the country's own price index (CPI, WPI, or GDP deflator). In this way, the world price of tradables is indexed in the numerator, and the domestic price of nontradables is indexed in the denominator.

This gives the "best" estimates of ε as:

$$\varepsilon_b = e\,(WPI^{\,US})/CPI^{\,d} \qquad (11)$$

and

$$\varepsilon_m = (\sum_{i=1}^{m} \alpha_i\, e_i\, WPI_i^{\,w})\,/CPI^{\,d} \qquad (12)$$

where the b and m subscripts refer to bilateral and multilateral versions of ε, e_i is an index of the nominal rate of exchange between the domestic currency and the currency of trading partner i, α_i is the trade weights used in computing the multilateral index, and $WPI_i^{\,w}$ is the wholesale price

indices of the trading partner i (there being m trading partners). Once calculated for periods of destabilization and adjustment, ε should be compared with the direct calculations of P_t/P_n. Generally, these should give similar patterns of relative price change, though the exact movement of the direct price series may lag behind the ε series.

These estimates of ε have been made assuming that the nominal exchange rate (e) is the same for all tradables, so that the index provides an accurate estimate of changes in the relative price of all tradables. This may not always be the case. Quite apart from the problem of multiple exchange rates (in which the official value of e will vary across sectors), some tradable sectors may purchase or sell foreign exchange in the parallel market, where the domestic currency price of foreign currency is generally higher.[4] Thus, the calculated value of ε will prove a misleading indicator of resource flows. If producers of exportables are more likely to sell foreign exchange in the official market, if importables consumers tend to purchase in the parallel market, and if an exchange rate depreciation narrows the gap between the official and parallel rates, P_x/P_m is likely to rise as a result of a devaluation. This means that resource flows into exportables will be greater (and into importables less) than that predicted by the calculated value of ε. If analysts think that such changes are significant, and likely to invalidate the use of ε, they may calculate sector-specific values of the real exchange rate, using the exchange rate that applies to the sector. This would also take into account sector-specific trade interventions, to which we now turn.

The third set of complications in calculating the relative-price effects of adjustment concerns the presence of, and changes in, other trade interventions, such as tariffs, import controls, and export taxes/subsidies. If these are important, and especially if they are changed under the adjustment program, it is essential that the macro-meso analysis proceeds beyond ε, since this index will give a misleading impression of relative price changes, and so of resource flows *within* tradables. For example, cuts in export taxes or in import tariffs will shift relative prices in favor of exportables. These relative price shifts should be measured as part of macro-meso analysis, since they will clearly affect the various household groups differently. Where domestic price data are good, the effects of such policies can be traced directly, with a table similar to Frame 2.2 being computed for the domestic importables and exportables relative price. It is particularly important to attempt direct calculations of changes in relative prices within tradables if quantitative restrictions are imposed (and adjusted) on imports, since the indirect methods using world prices are not generally valid. For such commodities, world prices are a poor guide to domestic price levels.

Where price data are poor, the analyst is obliged to use world prices and from them to compute the domestic price. This procedure is only valid for importables when quantitative restrictions are not applied. Assume that $s = 0$, but that $k > 0$, and that the government reduces k as part of its adjustment package. The effect on the domestic price of importables can be calculated from:

$$P_m = e[P_m^* (1 + k)] \qquad (13)$$

With changes in both k and e taking place under adjustment, it should be possible for the analyst to compute a time series for those importables whose prices have been changed as a result. Calculating the price changes in this way means that the analyst can derive the policy-induced changes directly. Estimates of ΔP_m (based on P_m^*, and Δe and Δk) can then be used in assessing the effects of policy changes. Similarly, computations can be carried out for P_x^* using Δe and Δs. An illustration of such computations is given in Box 2.1. (Box 12.2 in Chapter 12 also deals with methods for making these price computations.)

The analyst may wish to establish whether these relative price changes have indeed induced resource transfers. Estimates of changes in output (or value added) in the various sectors should provide evidence of whether adjustment is succeeding in shifting resources out of nontradables (and possibly previously protected importables), and into tradables, especially exportables. More direct evidence on labor transfers is discussed in the next section.

Labor-market effects

As with price data, the possibilities for analysis of the real-wage effects of adjustment are certain to be constrained by data availability. It is unlikely that reliable labor-force surveys will have been conducted at appropriate points for analytical purposes (that is, at the start of the periods of destabilization and adjustment, and some time after adjustment policies have taken effect). These data will usually refer only to formal sector wages, and movements in these are likely to be different

Box 2.1: An example of relative-price calculations

An illustration of the type of problems encountered in calculating a relative-price series is to be found in Collier's (1988a) assessment of adjustment in Malawi and Tanzania. For Malawi, he had access to reliable data on the domestic price of exportables, but not for importables. Since Malawi did not use either import quotas or price controls, he was able to infer from the world price and tariff rates the domestic price of importables. By contrast, Tanzania used both quantitative restrictions and price controls extensively, and this procedure could not be justified. For this country, Collier was able to use sector-specific GDP deflators. From these sets of calculations he was able to estimate a price series for both exports and importables for the two countries. He also computed nontradables prices from various sources.

Domestic prices of exports, importables, and nontradables, 1973-83

	Malawi			Tanzania		
Year	Exports	Import-ables	Non-tradables	Agricul-tural exports	Non-oil im-portables	Non-trad-ables
1973	100	100	100	100	100	100
1974	118	132	108	106	116	120
1975	127	158	117	125	139	134
1976	146	182	126	141	155	142
1977	163	206	131	209	172	161
1978	202	210	135	194	191	176
1979	213	243	143	186	215	199
1980	214	308	149	225	279	241
1981	212	377	171	246	390	284
1982	202		192	307	458	339
1983	209		209	342	522	397

Source: Collier 1988a, Table 9.

Methods of calculation:

Malawi: exports–direct data on domestic export prices; importables–cif import prices times one plus average tariff rate; nontradables–simple average of school fees, entertainment, personal services, travel, domestic help, and low-income housing.

Tanzania: agricultural exports–from 1985 Agricultural Price Review; importables–manufacturing value-added deflator; nontradables–weighted average of GDP deflators for construction, wholesale and retail trade, and transport.

The lesson from these calculations is that with limited data, some ingenuity must be used to compute meaningful price series. Note that for Malawi, the data clearly show that nontradables became markedly cheaper relative to importables, mainly as a result of expenditure-switching policies. In Tanzania, the evidence indicates that price movements encouraged resource transfers out of exportables into importables and nontradables.

(quantitatively, and possibly also qualitatively) from informal sector wages.

Generally, data on public sector wages are likely to be more readily available than for other wage series, and these can provide some clues of real-wage trends overall. Similarly, minimum wages can be used to estimate changes in wage trends during destabilization and adjustment. Of course, such wage trends should be expressed in real terms, with nominal wages deflated by the consumer price index.

Ideally, measures of wage differentials, especially between tradables and nontradables, and formal and informal sectors, should be computed, since these are likely to change during adjustment (at least in the short run). If private sector wage series are available, the analyst should compute changes in the public sector wage in relation to private sector (market) wages throughout the period under study. During destabilization, the public sector wage will have risen relatively, and fallen during adjustment. Similar patterns might be expected of the rural-urban wage differential. An analysis such as this can reveal how relative wage trends have been changed as a result of adjustment. The main data limitations are certain to be in the area of the informal sector (or market-determined) wage. It is very unlikely that such information will be available over time to permit meaningful macro-meso analysis.

Even without informal sector wage data, official wage trends can be compared with average levels of living for the population in general. An example of this is found in Collier (1988a). Using national accounts estimates and the CPI, he computed real private consumption per capita for Malawi and Tanzania. At the same time, he estimated a real-wage series for the formal sector from official sources, again deflating using the CPI. By expressing the real wage relative to average real consumption, he generated a time series that showed for both countries that the real-wage/ real-consumption index fell from 100 in 1973 to around 65/70 in 1984. He was able to show (albeit through an imperfect indicator) that formal sector wages had fallen in relation to peasant living standards quite dramatically.

In the absence of wage data, there is some scope for using the results of household surveys to assess the direction of likely wage changes. This derives from the fact that the real wage will rise (fall) as a result of an expenditure-switching policy if workers consume mainly nontradables (tradables). An examination of the expenditure patterns of wage-earning households should enable the analyst to infer something about the direction of the likely short-run real-wage change.

Changes in credit markets

In most African countries, fiscal contraction is closely associated with monetary contraction, so that adjustment is usually associated with significant changes in the credit markets. These invariably consist of a formal market, dominated by the organized, modern banking system, and an informal or "curb" market. The former is directly subject to the restraints imposed under monetary contraction, while the latter is affected only indirectly. Typically, a credit squeeze will reduce the supply of credit in the organized banking system, so that many borrowers have to shift to the informal market to obtain their credit requirements. Since interest charges are fixed (and generally low) in the organized market, such borrowers face increased interest charges on their new debt. Interest rates in the curb market, which are flexible, will therefore rise as the credit contraction in the formal market pushes more borrowers into the curb market. Monetary contraction restricts the availability of credit in the organized market, and increases interest rates in the curb market.

In some programs, the fixed-interest regime of the formal market (referred to as a "repression" of the money market in the literature) is dismantled, so that interest charges are allowed to settle at their market-clearing values. So, in addition to any decrease in credit availability in the formal market, borrowers may face increased interest charges in the market.

Once again, the extent to which these changes can be usefully analyzed depends critically on data availability. Information on credit and its terms is generally available from the official banking system, but this can prove totally misleading as a preparation for the meso-micro analyses if most households obtain their credit from the curb market. It may be, for example, that interest rates are not increased significantly among the larger banks, but because of credit restraint, curb-market rates increase. Using official rates would be inappropriate in analyzing households that borrow through the curb market. Data on the curb market are essential. Nominal and real rates of interest applying in the organized banking system and in curb markets should be computed for the period of destabilization and adjustment.

In this way, some historical estimate of the effect of adjustment on the credit market can be obtained.

Expenditure-reducing effects

The first stage in the analysis of the effects of expenditure-reducing policies is to identify which of the broad categories of expenditure were subject to cuts and to identify those items that expanded during the destabilizing phase. Expenditures should be disaggregated initially into the four categories of equation (6): private consumption and investment, and public consumption and investment.[5] By dividing equation (6) by Y (GDP), we can decompose changes in the trade deficit/GDP ratio as follows:

$$\Delta\left[\frac{(X-M)}{Y}\right] = 1 - \Delta\left(\frac{C}{Y}\right) - \Delta\left(\frac{I}{Y}\right) - \Delta\left(\frac{G_c}{Y}\right)$$
$$- \Delta\left(\frac{G_i}{Y}\right) \qquad (14)$$

A table such as Frame 2.3 should prove extremely useful in any preliminary assessment of the implications of destabilization and expenditure reduction. It may be, for example, that the expansion of the trade deficit/GDP ratio during the period of destabilization (assumed to be 1979-84 in our hypothetical case) was associated mainly with an increase in government investment, while the contraction of the deficit during adjustment was due to cuts in private consumption and investment. Such asymmetries in expenditure changes over the cycle of destabilization and adjustment are important to identify, since they have a direct bearing on the distribution consequences of adjustment. If the macro imbalance was caused by an over-expansionary fiscal policy, while its correction was borne mainly by private consumption, the social costs of the adjustment are likely to be high.

Given the central role of the government in providing infrastructural services (through both investment and recurrent expenditures), cuts in G_c and G_i will be of particular interest for macro-meso analysis. For our purposes, these expenditure items are not sufficiently disaggregated, since the meso-micro analysis plans require more refined estimates of changes in infrastructural services. Chapter 8, for example, explains the health status of individual household members in terms of changes in health services available to the household. Thus, macro-meso analysis must disaggregate further the changes in government

Frame 2.3: Decomposition of changes in the trade deficit/GDP ratio by expenditure item
(percent)

| Year | $\Delta(X-M)/GDP$ | Expenditure change | | | |
		$\Delta(C/GDP)$	$\Delta(I/GDP)$	$\Delta(G_c/GDP)$	$\Delta(G_i/GDP)$
1979	100				
1980	100				
1981	100				
...	...				
1989	100				
1990	100				
Memorandum items:					
1979-84	100				
1985-90	100				
1979-90	100				

expenditures during destabilization and adjustment, and must attempt to estimate how much the various items of expenditure have changed in real terms over the period, and especially during the adjustment period.

At the very least a time series should be computed for each country, showing the changes in public spending by major category. For this, a table along the lines of Frame 2.4 should be prepared. The expenditure categories depicted in the table ought to be considered as a minimum disaggregation. It would be helpful, for example, to distinguish among the three levels of education (primary, secondary, and tertiary), and between different categories of health expenditures (primary health care, hospitals, and so on). The whole table might be prepared for recurrent (distinguishing wage and non-wage costs) and development (or capital) expenditures.

The analyst should be careful to define an appropriate price index in generating a time series of expenditures in real terms. In most cases, the consumer price index (CPI) will be all that is readily available, but in others, alternatives may be tried (at least for the sake of comparison). These would include a money wage index (on the assumption that labor is the most important cost of many public services), the GDP deflator, or that part of the deflator that refers to the service/public sector. The proportion in total real government expenditure of each of the items depicted in Frame 2.4 should also be computed, and changes over time observed.

The data in this table merely show what has happened in real terms to expenditures on each of the items. Again we have the knotty

Frame 2.4: Real government expenditure by sector

Year	Social infrastructure				Economic infrastructure					
	Education	Health	Social security	Housing	Roads	Utilities	Transport/ communi- cation	Economic services [a]	Other items [b]	Total
1979										
1980										
1981										
1982										
...										
...										
1990										
Memorandum items:										
Percentage change										
1979-1984										
1985-1990										
1979-1990										

a. Including items such as irrigation and extension services. These may be listed separately if necessary.
b. Including general administration, defense, and so on.

research task of quantifying the change in infrastructural spending imposed as a result of structural adjustment. In making judgments on this, the analyst must bear in mind that:

• Taking deviations of expenditures from a time trend is an inappropriate method of assessing the impact of adjustment on that expenditure item. As we have been at pains to show, the period before the adjustment is unlikely to be typical of any long-term trend, being one in which expenditures are likely to have been unusually (and unsustainably) high.

• Changes in the real expenditures on each item may not necessarily reflect changes in the availability of services to households. This is because cuts in expenditures may be associated with more efficient use of resources, while the opposite may be true of periods of expansion.

• The effects of expenditure cuts will vary by region depending on how the cuts are applied within each sector. For example, expenditure cuts in higher education are unlikely to have any real effects on education services in rural areas. But if the cuts were applied mainly to primary schools, rural areas may suffer disproportionately. Similarly, cuts in teacher recruitment will inevitably harm rural areas more than urban, given the preference teachers attach to working in urban areas. The quantity adjustment of such a policy would be borne mainly by rural areas.

• Some changes in government expenditures may have taken place independent of adjustment and be associated with the adjustment program only chronologically. Obviously there is little that can be said by way of a generalization here—it is simply a matter for the analyst's judgment.

In most countries, data are available from line ministries and other sources. These can be used to trace how the overall budget cuts imposed on a sector (such as health and education) have been applied in practice. To obtain useful estimates of how these adjustments have affected the key mesoeconomic variables, two broad stages of analysis will be required. First, there must be a careful sifting of data to establish which services have gained and lost real resources as a result of the adjustment program. This should establish how these changes have been distributed across the regions of the country. This analysis is likely to be time-consuming, but it will yield high returns in gaining insight into how the expenditure changes have influenced household welfare.

The second stage of this analysis is the translation of real expenditure adjustments into changes in mesoeconomic variables. The latter, for example, might be expressed in terms of numbers of doctors, nearness to a health clinic, pupil-teacher ratios at the nearest school, and so on. How have these variables been influenced by the resource changes observed? There can be no universal formula for such analyses. Much will depend on the specifics of the case, and on the data available (for example, see Thorbecke 1992). Box 2.2 illustrates how the budgetary implications of

Box 2.2: Tracing infrastructural effects: The case of health in Nigeria

Analysts who wish to assess the likely effects of changes in the fiscal provision for any publicly provided service on the use of the service by households face a particularly difficult problem. If governments cut real expenditures on health, what are the effects on the use of health facilities by individuals in need of health care, and what is the ultimate effect on their health status? In a recent study of health services in Ogun, Nigeria (World Bank 1990a), the problem was posed in a slightly different way. This study sought to assess the budgetary implications of changes in the use of health facilities. The method used is therefore pertinent to the policy and analytical issues raised in this chapter.

The study involved three stages of analysis. First, an analysis was conducted of the determinants of health facility use by individuals. This was based on a household survey. A reduced-form equation was specified, which explained the use of public and private health facilities in terms of household and individual characteristics, and the prices and quality of the health facilities. A striking feature of the results was that the use of facilities increased significantly as the quality of the facilities improved. The second stage involved an analysis of the cost structure of the various health facilities covered (small hospitals, maternity clinics, and basic health clinics). These facilities were available in both the public and the private sector. Finally, by bringing together the demand and cost findings, the study was able to assess the revenue and cost effects of different ways of changing the use of facilities.

The objective of policy is to maximize the use of health facilities. However, the methods used to raise usage will have different implications for revenue and costs, and different implications for the fiscal budget. For example, increasing cost recovery might raise revenue and so effect budgetary savings, but it would reduce the use of facilities. Improving the quality of the facilities would improve usage, but it would be costly to implement, and would be a drain on the public purse (at least in the short run).

To resolve these conflicting effects, the study presented a number of cost recovery simulations. These changed the values of important independent policy variables to determine their effect on health facility usage. Using the estimated equations on facility usage, they could derive for any set of exogenous variables the probability of individuals using a public facility, using a private facility, or simply deciding on self-treatment. Changes in the use of public facilities can then be combined with the cost recovery assumption used in the simulation to estimate the revenue that would be obtained for that level of facility use. However, the manipulation of these explanatory variables has direct cost implications for the facility. These are also calculated in the simulations, based on the analysis of the facility's cost structure.

Simulation results: Simulation results are shown in the table below.

Case 1: No change: all variables set at mean values.

Case 2: Price increase: price of facility use increases from 1.2 naira per visit (which is the mean value) to 2.4 naira. Private facility costs unchanged.

Case 3: Quality improvement: expenditure per person served increases from 3.04 naira to 6.08 naira. Private sector reacts by raising its expenditure per person served from 1.36 naira to 2.72 naira.

Case 4: Price increase/quality improvements: price and quality adjustments as above; increased drug availability and improved condition of public facilities (along with various private sector reactions).

Simulations for public sector
(thousands of naira)

	Change in gross revenue	Change in gross costs	Surplus or loss	Frequency of use (public and private)
Case 1	0	0	0	0.48
Case 2	+3,400	-200	+3,600	0.47
Case 3	+200	+6,500	-6,300	0.50
Case 4	+6,000	+10,400	-4,400	0.53

Source: World Bank 1990a, Tables 5.16, 5.17, 5.18.

Interpretation: The objective of policy is generally to discourage the frequency of self-treatment and increase the use of facilities (private and public). If there were no budget constraint, Case 4 would be clearly preferred, since this maximizes facility use. This case increases cost recovery, but also makes significant quality improvements to the facilities. Despite raising revenue considerably, this strategy also increases costs, resulting in a net budgetary cost of 4,400,000 naira. Even the less ambitious Case 3, which simply raises one component of quality, only achieves increased health facility use at a budgetary cost. Of the cases considered in the study that resulted in budgetary saving, Case 2 produced the best outcome in terms of facility use, although this case suggests that facility use would decline marginally as a result of the budgetary savings. If these savings were devoted to raising standards of health care among poorer groups, however, there might be beneficial effects not covered by the simulation.

---

alternative approaches to encouraging health facility usage can be estimated based on household survey and health cost data. Here the link between the individual's use of health facilities and the fiscal budget is established.

Economy-wide modeling techniques

The analysis suggested so far relies on examination of the historical record. The key lies in identifying periods of destabilization and adjustment.

This permits the analyst to draw conclusions about how adjustment has affected markets and infrastructure. But this type of analysis is subject to a number of serious pitfalls. First, the historical record does not imply *causation*, since what is observed happening over time is influenced by a wide range of factors, and not simply the macro imbalances and the corrective adjustment policies. Movements in relative prices, for example, might reflect changes in supply conditions entirely unrelated to adjustment—including the favorable effects of technical progress and the adverse effects of drought. The methodology suggested cannot entirely separate out these factors.[6]

The second main problem with the suggested approach is that it does not distinguish between first-order and higher-order effects of a policy change. For example, a policy that raises the market price of a commodity will lead some households to purchase less of it, thereby reducing demand and causing the price to fall somewhat. This might be related to the time period that is allowed in tracing the effects. The firstorder effects are impact effects, with the full effects taking time to work their way through the economic system. The first-order impact on prices may well be greater than the full effect, since the initial change in prices is moderated by demand and supply responses.

The third weakness of the analysis suggested is that it ignores the interactions between markets and infrastructure. Yet we know that the economy functions as a system, with changes in any one market influencing what happens in others. For example, an increase in the price of food will increase production of food, which in turn will raise the demand for farm labor. This may raise rural wages. These effects need to be traced in a *systematic* manner.

Finally, the methodology does not produce any robust answers to the question, "What might have happened had a different set of adjustment policies been applied?" The *counterfactual* case is not readily derived from the historical approach suggested. Yet, in most cases, governments would like to have some idea of how alternative policies might have worked, and such impressions are difficult to form without more structured and rigorous methods.

The strengths and limitations of modeling

It follows that a more systematic approach to macro-meso analysis might be needed. The use of economy-wide models already has a tradition in development economics and policy design. In the remainder of this section, we shall review the potential of economy-wide modeling for macro-meso analysis. This is not meant, however, either as a review of such models, or as guidelines for the construction and use of models. Our purpose is to highlight the strengths and weaknesses of the approach, and to identify the main features an economy-wide model must possess to be of use in the analysis of the distributional consequences of adjustment.

At the outset, it is important to emphasize that a model of the economy is simply a tool. As such, it is intended to aid our thinking—not to substitute for it. Models should be combined with human judgment—not replace it. In this way, the user will not be tempted to react in an extreme way to the model—either to dismiss all its predictions as too mechanical and useless, or to accept without reservation anything produced by the model, simply because it appears to be "scientific." The proper use of the economy-wide model involves application of the analyst's own judgment and understanding of the country to which the model is applied and interpretation of the model's predictions accordingly.

The main strength of the model lies in its formalization of the thinking process—it makes explicit what is often assumed implicitly in less formalized logic. It also simplifies the real world, by ignoring minor detail and focusing on the more important interactions. Many models are important bridges between economic theory and the practice of economic policy (Dervis, de Melo, and Robinson 1982). While analytical models are an essential starting point in considering a real-world problem, they cannot take us very far. At best they can only provide qualitative predictions, while the policy practitioners must make quantitative decisions. Theory may suggest that a devaluation policy will work under certain circumstances, but the practitioner must know by how much to devalue. Theory is often ambiguous, even about the direction of change. This occurs especially in cases where there are two opposing effects of a change, the net result depending on which of the effects is the stronger. In this case, theory alone cannot provide an unambiguous answer. In such circumstances, the numerical model comes into its own, since it can simulate the two opposing effects and reveal which is the stronger. Many policy issues are of this type and require both quantification and simulation before an answer can be obtained.

The main weakness of modeling lies in its highly structured approach. First, it assumes that the economy can be described through a set of relationships that remain stable over time. Insofar as these might change, the predictions of the model will prove unreliable. Second, economy-wide models are generally not designed to take into account qualitative changes in the economy, which by their nature are not easily quantified. Finally, the degree of disaggregation feasible in an economy-wide model remains limited—not by the capacity of the computer, but by the understanding of the user. If the model is too detailed, it quickly becomes a black box to the user, resembling the vast complexity of the real world instead of providing a simplified version that would aid our thinking.

Required features of macro-meso models

These considerations apply to models in general, but there are specific requirements of our present concern—the macro-meso analysis in the context of a program to trace the income and consumption effects of macroeconomic policy changes. The main required features of an economy-wide model may be summarized as follows:

• The model is to be used for policy analysis. It should be designed to aid our understanding of the way the economic system operates rather than to forecast the future. It must treat policy instruments and targets explicitly. It should also be able to trace the causal mechanisms at work, linking the instruments to the targets.[7] Among the targets included should be the fiscal and external deficits.

• The model must involve a minimum degree of disaggregation, at the very least distinguishing among the main producing sectors of the economy: exportables, importables, protected importables, and nontradables. A macro model is inappropriate, since it is incapable of analyzing the critical structural shifts brought about by adjustment policies.

• The ideal model must be capable of representing macro-policy instruments. While many instruments are "real" economic variables (government demands for consumer and investment goods, many price policies), other policy instruments are monetary (monetary and interest rate policy). The macro-meso model must, to some extent, be able to track changes in both real and monetary policy instruments at the macroeconomic level.

• Since many adjustment policy instruments have their principal effects through changing the incentive structures of product and factor markets, the model should treat product and factor prices as endogenous. Product and factor supplies and demands must be modeled, and price changes must be related to excess demands. Price and wage endogeneity, however, may be constrained by rigidities that prevent markets from clearing instantaneously and that result in rationing in the markets and persistent excess demands. This would depend on the characteristics of the markets in the country concerned. These constraints can play a pivotal role in explaining how adjustment affects markets and thereby household incomes. Wage rigidity in particular can determine how the labor market transmits the effects of adjustment policy to households.

• Finally, the macro-meso model should include the household sector and trace how household incomes and expenditures are determined. We have already stated that the level of household disaggregation feasible in an economy-wide model may be too limited for many policy issues. And although the main purpose of the model is to trace mesoeconomic effects, the household sector remains an important ingredient in the model. This is for two principal reasons. First, the model can provide useful insights into household effects, even if this is not altogether sufficient for policymakers. Second, without the household sector, the model would be unable to trace the full mesoeconomic effects. Household responses play an important part in determining what happens in markets as a result of policy interventions. The determination of household incomes and expenditures should be considered as an essential element of the model.

Do applied general equilibrium models fill the bill?

Applied general equilibrium (AGE) models are frequently used in addressing policy issues in an economy-wide framework.[8] The main feature of AGE models is the general equilibrium nature of the model. Producing units are represented as purchasing factors from households, and so generating value added. In return for factor services, households receive income payments, which are allocated to savings and consumption. The sum of these production and consumption decisions yields supplies and demands in the various product and factor markets. These are reconciled through relative-price adjustments, which yield zero excess demands in the markets unless some rigidity is assumed to exist. Described in this way, the AGE model seeks to trace the operation of the real economy. It yields predictions of what is likely to happen to the structure of relative product and factor prices if the assumptions of the model, or if policy instruments such as trade taxes, change. It is more often than not an empirical application of orthodox real-economy theory (the exceptions being mainly "structuralist" AGE models, such as Taylor forthcoming).

AGE models show considerable promise for macro-meso modeling. They explain what determines relative product and factor price movements and show how resource allocation rules operate. Most AGE models use base-year social accounting matrices (SAMs), which represent how incomes generated by production activities are mapped across households and how expenditure decisions by households are allocated to sectors. AGE models have a built-in focus on incomes and their distribution. Finally, AGE models usually explicitly model the external sector, and can be used to analyze the effects of trade policy. Such qualifications make them eminently suitable for analysis of the redistributive effects of adjustment. (See Box 2.3 for an illustration of the AGE model approach.)

AGE models have two principal weaknesses from the macro-meso analysis perspective. First, they do not usually embrace the macroeconomy, especially its monetary components. Second, they only trace the effects of policy interventions on markets and do not treat infrastructural effects. We shall discuss both limitations.

AGE MODELS AND THE MACROECONOMY. AGE models are principally concerned with relative prices, resource allocation, and trade. They are not usually designed to analyze macroeconomic changes. Most AGE models follow fairly simple price normalization procedures, through which the aggregate price level is taken as exogenous, and all absolute prices are simply expressed in terms of some numeraire. Relative prices, of course, remain unaffected by such normalization. As a general rule, the choice of numeraire in such models is entirely arbitrary, since the model is not intended to explain the absolute price level. This means that such AGE models are incapable of

tracing the effects of macroeconomic policy, especially when such policy intervention is through the operation of monetary variables.

AGE models, however, can be modified to incorporate a macroeconomic superstructure. This can meaningfully interact with the multi-sector general equilibrium model, and enable the user to conduct macroeconomic experiments in an AGE setting. Bourguignon, Branson, and de Melo (forthcoming) have made an important recent contribution in this area. Their refinement of the AGE approach involves the addition of a macroeconomic model to the general equilibrium framework, in which the macroeconomic sub-model yields the level of aggregate demand in the economy (through a variant of an IS-LM system), while the general equilibrium sub-model computes the real-economy side, yielding aggregate supply. Their macro model contains general asset-market equilibrium conditions, which determine a vector of rates of return. These in turn influence the level of aggregate demand. In a simpler version of the same, Demery and Demery (1992) take two financial assets (money and bonds), and trace the link between the monetary and real economies through the interest rate in textbook fashion.

There are now AGE models in use that incorporate the macroeconomy into a multi-sector general equilibrium framework. It is perhaps too early to judge whether these models provide an empirically convincing description of how macroeconomic changes influence the real economies of developing countries.

AGE MODELS AND INFRASTRUCTURE. The second major limitation of AGE models when applied to the analysis of the effects of adjustment concerns their inability to capture the full effects of infrastructural changes, which are likely to be important for Africa. This applies as much to economic as to social infrastructure. If adjustment entails cuts in government expenditure on education, health, and physical infrastructure, there are two broad effects. First, there will be income losses for those employed in the sectors who previously benefited from these expenditures (teachers, doctors, those employed by road construction firms, and so on). These direct primary-income effects of expenditure cuts can be readily measured by AGE models, simply by tracing the full general equilibrium implications of the resulting contraction in sectoral demands.[9]

Box 2.3: Generating counterfactuals with applied general equilibrium models

Among the advantages of using the structured logic of an economy-wide applied general equilibrium (AGE) model, perhaps the most important for our purpose is its ability to produce counterfactual scenarios. These trace what might have occurred had events been different. The use of an AGE model to produce such counterfactuals is illustrated by Bourguignon, de Melo, and Suwa (1991). They use a model based on the macro-micro "maquette" developed by Bourguignon, Branson, and de Melo (forthcoming), in which a general equilibrium model is linked to the macro accounts via the standard IS-LM framework (see main text). They define an archetypical economy for Sub-Saharan Africa, in which both real and financial economies are represented. The main features of the model are described in the following assumptions:

Financial sector
- Money supply exogenous
- No bond market (government holds only foreign debt)
- Households hold cash and equities in firms
- Firms use working capital and hold liabilities from banking system

Foreign exchange market
- Limit on government borrowing; only government can borrow from abroad

Labor market
- Flexible agricultural wages; downward nominal wage rigidity in formal sector

Goods market
- Flexible prices throughout

The model is therefore a "stylized" model, designed to highlight (and perhaps exaggerate) specific features of African economies. It should be distinguished from an "applied" model, which is designed to be applied to a specific country case, and therefore should be more realistic than a stylized model (see Robinson 1988). Using this archetypical model, the authors derive counterfactual outcomes, based on assumptions about external shocks and adjustment policy responses. The main features of their results are summarized in the table in this box.

These simulations illustrate what might happen in the archetypical economy subject to an external shock (a deterioration in the terms of trade of 20 percent in period 2 and a permanent doubling of the interest rate on foreign debt from 4 percent to 8 percent). The initial simulations compare outcomes without the shock (the first column) with those with shock, a standard adjustment package containing a limit on public borrowing, and an exchange rate depreciation (the second column). The results of this exercise reveal that wage and price flexibility in the typical African case seem to minimize the adverse growth effect of the shock with adjustment, despite a rapid fall in investment. The fiscal deficit widens, mainly because of the increase in debt service brought about by the interest hike. Interestingly, these simulations show a decrease in poverty as a result of the shock/adjustment compared with the no-shock case. This is attributable to the effects of the devaluation, raising producer prices and favorably influencing the incomes of poor smallholders. It is likely that the no-shock poverty level would be lower than the shock-without-adjustment case. For an illustration of the effects of the shock, see World Bank (1990b, p. 105).

Simulations were also performed to illustrate outcomes of alternative adjustment packages. Among a number of simulations, the authors apply an adjustment-with-redistribution package. Under this simulation, an adjustment program is augmented by a food subsidy of 7 percent and a public works program. The overall macroeconomic indicators are not that different under adjustment with redistribution, although the fiscal deficit is noticeably greater compared with the standard package. The gains in terms of an improved poverty outcome are clear— the head-count index falling to 24.3 percent compared with 29.5 percent.

Another policy response traced in the simulations was adjustment through rationing—here the real exchange rate is held constant, and import rationing is introduced to correct the external deficit. In some senses, this can be described as postponed adjustment. The effects of this strategy are strikingly different from the standard adjustment: growth and investment are enhanced, and the inflation rate is lower. But the fiscal deficit is significantly higher (illustrating that the adjustment is only postponed), and poverty is very much worse. Rationing imports creates rents among better-off groups, redistributing income from the poorer to the richer socioeconomic groups.

This exercise illustrates the advantages of using AGE models to produce counterfactuals. Here we have only reported some of the main macroeconomic and poverty outcomes, but the AGE model can also report outcomes of the main mesoeconomic variables of interest—prices in product and factor markets.

Outcomes: Seven periods into the simulation exercise

	Without shock	With shock		
		Standard adjustment	Redistributing adjustment	Rationing adjustment
GDP (period 1 = 100)	120.0	117.0	117.0	121.0
Investment/GDP	20.5	15.5	13.1	25.5
Inflation	16.9	18.1	19.4	16.7
Devaluation rate	15.0	17.5	18.2	17.3
Interest rate	21.2	23.4	26.6	15.0
Overall deficit/GDP	6.2	9.0	11.1	12.6
Poverty rate[a]	31.1	29.5	24.3	39.2

a. Head-count ratio.

To do this, the cuts in government expenditure items need to be translated into sectoral demands, so that they can be readily input into the AGE model (or into a SAM).

The expenditure cuts will have indirect effects on the incomes of households that previously benefited from the infrastructural services that were produced. These effects are not traced in most AGE models. Cuts in expenditure on education will not only reduce the primary incomes of those engaged in the education sector, they will also adversely affect the education of those who previously benefited from the services, reducing current levels of household welfare and future levels of income. The same can be said of cuts in health expenditure. A reduction in other infrastructural services, such as road construction, will have similar effects. Households that cannot gain access to markets and inputs will experience declines in output and income. These indirect effects on incomes and welfare can be important in Africa, and further work should be undertaken to improve the capacity of AGE models to trace them.

Concluding observations

Macro-meso analysis in the research scheme is certain to be one of the most taxing of all those outlined in this volume. Yet this work is an essential prerequisite for what follows. Without an understanding of how adjustment policies influence the main explanatory variables considered by the meso-micro analysis plans in this volume, it will not be possible to link micro-level data with changes in economy-wide policy variables.

What can be done in analyzing the meso effects of adjustment policy depends on the available data. We have tried to keep the data requirements to a minimum. But in the last analysis, the data will constrain what can be achieved. At one extreme, we have presented some fairly basic analyses requiring only national accounts data. At the other, there is the application of AGE models, with their potentially voracious appetite for numbers. It is probable that most countries will lie somewhere in between these cases. As some of our illustrations have shown, analysts will need to use the utmost ingenuity to push the available data as far as they can convincingly go.

In cases where economy-wide modeling is not feasible, the approach recommended here concentrates on the historical record. The analysis program depends on the identification of periods of destabilization and adjustment, so that changes in the mesoeconomy between these periods can be attributed (for the most part) to the adjustment program. This is an imperfect solution, since we know that there may well be other factors that have a bearing on the historical record. The analyst has to use judgment in accounting for these extraneous influences.

Notes

1. Using IMF terminology.

2. This also assumes that the international terms of trade (P_x^*/P_m^*) remain unchanged.

3. We ignore here the use of money wage indices as deflators, although these have been used effectively, especially when indices of international competitiveness were required.

4. Edwards (1989, p. 105ff) computes real effective exchange rates using both official nominal exchange rates and rates that apply in parallel foreign exchange markets. He found that they bore very little relation to each other. Indeed, in 13 out of the 28 cases considered, the correlation coefficient between the two indices was negative. This suggests that where parallel markets are important, the use of the official rate can be seriously misleading.

5. This level of disaggregation is chosen because it is consistent with what is available from the national accounts. As we shall discover, a much more refined classification of expenditures will be required in assessing the infrastructural implications of adjustment.

6. Although the methodology attempts to separate out the effects of the "recession" from those of the adjustment by carefully subdividing the historical record, it does so rather crudely.

7. Forecasting models usually rely heavily on lagged endogenous variables and reduced-form specifications. Although they yield better forecasts, such models generally mask the causal mechanism involved.

8. For an excellent summary of the main features of such models, see Dervis, de Melo, and Robinson (1982, Ch. 5) and Robinson (1988).

9. By the same token, a SAM can perform similar assessments. Thorbecke (1992) traces the primary-income distribution effects of alternative fiscal policies in Indonesia using a fixed-price SAM multiplier model.

3

Priority analysis

Lionel Demery and Christiaan Grootaert

As was explained in the introductory chapter, this volume aims to provide the analysis plans needed to fully understand the social dimensions of the adjustment process. The implied analysis is in-depth and requires an important amount of time and data. These data requirements were elaborated in Chapter 1. The human and other resources available for analysis in most developing countries are such that the analysis proposed in this volume cannot be undertaken at once. In many cases, staff may need to receive preliminary training in data processing and analytic techniques.

An in-depth analysis covering the multiple social dimensions of adjustment may take two to three years or longer. In principle, this is quite acceptable—capacity building is a time-consuming process. The subject matter will retain its policy importance for many years to come, and thus such an investment in human capital is worthwhile. Also, analytic capacity is not subject-bound; once acquired, it can easily be applied to other matters of interest. Acquiring the ability to analyze the social effects of policy reform can be viewed as a suitable way to enhance a country's overall capacity to analyze and design social policy and to integrate it into economic policy at large. The analysis plans in this volume are tools in the process of building this capacity.

But it must be recognized—and emphasized—that many policy concerns cannot be left untouched until in-depth analysis has been completed. Action is needed now. This means that priorities have to be established in analytic tasks. This has to be done in two ways: across topics and within topics. The choice of topics is country-specific. In some African countries, food security and nutrition issues top the list of policymakers' concerns, while in other countries nutrition is satisfactory, and education and health concerns are in the forefront of the policy debate. The first task in applying the analysis plans is to rank topics to reflect policymakers' priorities. In practice, this task is not straightfoward, because social policies are generally closely interlinked, and priorities overlap. Even if nutrition is the overall top priority, and education ranks well below, *some* education issues may nevertheless be more important than *some* nutrition issues. Precedence *within* topics is also needed.

This chapter is concerned with this issue. It aims to highlight the key analytic concerns in the area of social dimensions, *within* each of the sectors and target groups to which individual chapters in this volume are devoted. In selecting these key issues, three considerations have played a role:

• On the policy side, issues were selected for their relevance and high priority in most countries.

• On the data side, issues were retained that had less demanding data requirements.

• On the analysis side, issues were retained that require the simplest analytical tools and thus can lead to rapid results.

Thus, this chapter aims to provide an outline for *priority analysis* (PA) in the social effects of adjustment. This analysis requires a minimal amount of data and uses simple analytical techniques. It can be undertaken in most developing countries, even those with limited data collection and analytic capacities. It was designed to yield policy-relevant findings in a timely fashion, to be an input for the most urgent concerns of policymakers. The three considerations in the previous paragraph do not always converge, and hence tradeoffs were made in the selection of topics. To the extent that such tradeoffs vary across countries, this PA plan may need to be adapted to specific country situations. In general, however, it is more immediately "ready for use" than the other analysis plans.

The data for the PA plan can be taken from many sources: single-topic surveys on employment, health, education, and so forth; integrated surveys; and household enterprise surveys. In the context of the hierarchical information system recommended to countries interested in the social dimensions of adjustment (see Chapter 1), it is clear that the Priority Survey is the ideal data source, in that it contains all the information needed for this analysis plan. However, this is not the only suitable data source, and alternative data can feed the analysis.

Analytic concepts

The basic goal of PA is to identify target household groups and establish key indicators through which the impact of adjustment on these groups can be monitored. No effective social policy is possible without knowledge about target groups and how their conditions evolve. The focus here is on those conditions that can evolve rapidly and that may require urgent policy interventions in the context of adjustment. The implementation of PA thus centers around two tasks: selecting indicators to capture the relevant social conditions; and defining target groups.

Selection of indicators

The indicators for priority analysis must be proxies for direct welfare measurement and be sensitive to changes in the economy. We need proxies because direct welfare measurement requires a great deal of information: total household expenditures, income, and assets. This information underlies most of the analysis in the sector- or target-group-specific analysis plans in this volume, but it does not meet the minimal data and rapid

analysis principles retained for the PA plan. The proxies chosen must be able to reflect the impact of adjustment or other macro policies. For example, the literacy rate in a country is a most important indicator of advances in human capital accumulation, and literacy is an important part of personal welfare. However, the literacy rate has a momentum of its own, and will not change much in the short run, say, as a result of a drop in educational expenditures. On the other hand, the student dropout rate will quickly respond to changes in the monetary and/or opportunity cost of schooling that can occur under adjustment. In this example, PA should focus not on the literacy rate, but on such variables as primary school enrollment and recent changes in it. Relevant indicators can then be constructed, such as the dropout rate among primary school children and the (mis)match between age and grade attended. Such indicators will readily reflect undesirable effects from adjustment on education. Similarly, as far as farm enterprises are concerned, PA cannot attempt to construct the income from such activities (this is an important focus of the analysis plan on smallholders in Chapter 12) but must focus on those aspects of operating a farm that can be influenced by adjustment, for example, price changes of crops, price increases and/or changes in availability of imported fertilizer.

A prime function of PA is to note undesirable changes in key indicators. This can be done by comparing results from successive surveys, or by relying on retrospective questions within a given survey (the approach used by the Priority Survey). In this PA plan, however, we will limit ourselves to discussing observations at one point in time and their interpretation. The two key tasks—the selection of indicators and the definition of target groups—have to be done first at one point in time. Once successfully completed, it is relatively straightforward to repeat the analysis for a second observation point. Then, of course, one will need to assess the statistical significance of observed changes. The techniques for doing so are fairly well-known and written up in textbooks. The specific procedures will depend upon the statistical features of the surveys being compared.

Our indicator-focused PA relies mainly on a tabular presentation. This reflects the need to keep the analysis simple and quick. But for selected topics, we shall also discuss multivariate regression analysis. This will be done where the importance of an indicator deserves a fuller analysis than tables can provide, and where it is possible to do so without having to invoke explanatory variables that fall outside the scope of PA (such as total income or expenditures, or price data).

Target groups and socioeconomic groups

The primary objective of PA is to identify target groups for social policy interventions in the context of adjustment. This means that such groups must be defined from a policy-relevant perspective. Hence, the first task of PA is to set up a classification of socioeconomic groups (SEGs). These are meant to be as homogeneous as possible from the point of view of the impact of adjustment on their welfare through the production and income-generation mechanisms of the economy. Such groups must be defined along dimensions that can become criteria for the implementation and targeting of government policy.

A priori, two major criteria can be put forward to define SEGs in that perspective:

• *Location*. The first distinction to make is the urban/rural distinction. Where possible, each can be broken down further; for example, rural areas can be split by agronomic or ecological zones, and the capital city can be distinguished within urban areas. It is generally not desirable to present results according to administrative entities (provinces, districts) because these rarely represent economic entities. Also, it is inadvisable to use "survey regions"(that is, the territories covered by survey teams), because this holds the danger that enumerator effects unduly affect comparisons across regions.

• *Assets/sources of income*. This is clearly the prime classifying variable if economic homogeneity is sought, since this is the main mechanism through which adjustment affects household welfare. In rural areas, the classification can be made according to whether the household owns a farm (and the size of it) and its major crop or type of crops (export versus subsistence crops). In some cases, the institutional arrangement under which the farm is operated can be part of the classification (for example, sharecropping). In urban areas, the work status of the household head and/ or the sector providing the household's main source of income can be used (for example, government, parastatal enterprises, formal private sector, informal private sector).

In some cases, the classification can be further refined by sociological criteria such as ethnicity, religion, and language, in countries where this is considered appropriate and policy-relevant. The SEG classification will be country-specific and should be built to reflect local conditions and policy issues. The following classification is offered as an illustration:

1. rural–export-oriented farmers (medium and large holdings)
2. rural–export-oriented smallholders
3. rural–food/subsistence farmers
4. rural–pastoralists
5. rural–landless agricultural workers
6. rural–non-agricultural workers
7. urban–skilled public sector employees
8. urban–unskilled public sector employees
9. urban–formal private sector workers
10. urban–informal private sector workers
11. urban–inactive or unemployed

An important variant would be to distinguish between the capital city and other urban areas. This is warranted if, as is the case in many African countries, the population of the capital city is several times that of the next largest city. The capital city then often has many unique economic characteristics and problems. For example, the concentration of economic activities (government, export businesses) may mean that the capital's economy will respond very differently to adjustment than other urban areas. However, splitting the urban SEGs in this way may lead to few sample observations per SEG, unless the sample size of the survey on which the PA is based is very large. In general, a tradeoff will be necessary by aggregating along another dimension. For example, instead of simply doubling the number of urban SEGs in the above sample classification (to five for the capital city and five for other cities), one can propose an increase to only six groups by using the following scheme:

7. urban–capital city–public sector employees
8. urban–capital city–formal private sector workers
9. urban–capital city–informal private sector workers
10. urban–other cities–formal sector workers (public and private)
11. urban–other cities–informal sector workers
12. urban–inactive or unemployed

Once the basic SEG classification has been established, it becomes a major dimension of PA.

Most tables will have SEG as a dimension, and the basic description of the population can usefully be done by SEG.

Before starting tabulations, one must clarify the relationship between target groups and SEGs. The way they are defined, SEGs form a mutually exclusive and exhaustive classification of households in society. They are fairly homogeneous internally with respect to major economic parameters. Target groups, on the other hand, are selected sub-groups of the population of concern to policymakers, and are defined along various economic and noneconomic criteria. Target groups can overlap so that one individual or household can belong to several target groups (or to none). For example, the poor, female-headed households, malnourished children, smallholders, coffee farmers, and so on can be target groups. Target groups need not necessarily be defined at the household level (for example, malnourished children) and can be quite heterogeneous (for example, the poor). In many instances, to target policies we need to rely on socioeconomic criteria that enable us to identify in practice the target group. To identify the poor, for example, one might examine location, lack of assets, selected activities, and so on. In other words, the poor are identified in relation to the socioeconomic group(s) to which they belong.

Three types of relations are possible between target groups and socioeconomic groups:

• A target group equals a SEG (for example, export-oriented smallholders).

• A target group is part of a SEG (for example, laid-off, unskilled public sector employees).

• A target group overlaps various SEGs (for example, female-headed households).

An important task of PA is to show the incidence of target groups within the different SEGs. This is essential to assess the efficiency and leakages of

programs that are targeted according to SEG criteria. This task (in addition to the display of the overall population distribution across SEGs) is the first step in PA.

Frame 3.1 shows the distribution of individuals by age and sex across SEGs, as well as the total population distribution. This basic demographic table can be checked with a recent census, if it is available, to assess the reliability of the survey(s) underlying the PA. The details of the age/sex distribution can reveal important differences in demographic patterns. For example, some SEGs may have less than the average share of adult males, perhaps as a result of migration.

Frame 3.2 tabulates, at the household level, the relative importance of the SEGs in the overall population. This is the key table to show the correspondence between target groups and SEGs. For example, if female-headed households are a target group, their distribution is shown in line 2 (which sums horizontally to 100 percent). Line 3 then shows the percentage of female-headed households within each SEG, that is, the incidence of the target group within the SEGs (together with male-headed households, this sums to 100 percent vertically). The table thus indicates the extent to which the target group is concentrated in a few SEGs, and to which SEGs any interventions need to be targeted to minimize program leakages to people outside the target group.

Basic needs

As we have already indicated, PA needs to emphasize basic needs indicators. The reasons for this are evident. First, these variables are important indicators of welfare, tracing both short- and long-run effects. Indications of morbidity and malnutrition, for example, are evidence of immediate stress among the population. But basic needs indicators also suggest long-run implications, because they are important inputs into human capital, and thus influence future income-earning

Frame 3.1: Distribution of the population by age, sex, and SEG

(percent)

Age	Sex	SEG 1 ....SEG 11	Total
0-5	M		
	F		
6-10	M		
	F		
....	....		
65+	M		
	F		
Total		100 100	100

Frame 3.2: Distribution of households across SEGs

(percent)

	SEG 1......................SEG 11	Total
All households		100
Female-headed households		100
Percentage of female-headed households		

capacity (and welfare). Second, they are relatively easy to measure (at least as compared with income- and expenditure-based indicators). Third, structural adjustment typically involves fiscal policy reforms, which seek to reduce the fiscal deficit through cuts in government expenditure. In many countries, expenditures in the health, education, and housing sectors are cut, while at the same time, subsidies of important food items are reduced, or removed entirely. These austerity measures can seriously limit the access of households to basic needs services, and adversely affect household members. At the same time, changes in household income-earning opportunities are likely to change the opportunity costs of health and education activities, and so affect the demand for these services.

PA focuses on four basic needs: education, health, nutrition, and housing. Each of these is now considered.

Education

As indicated earlier, education indicators such as literacy and numeracy rates have a momentum of their own. These are "outcome" variables—the outputs of the education system. The main concern of PA is with inputs, with tracing the numbers of the school-age population currently receiving education. The basic indicator underpinning most priority education analysis is the enrollment rate. This is defined as the number of children attending school divided by the total number of children of school age. Enrollment rates should be calculated for various levels of schooling, highlighting primary (age 5-11) and secondary (12-15) education. Unless special policy considerations suggest otherwise, the analysis should not deal with tertiary levels. Only a small proportion of the population will be attending at this level, and most of these will be from better-off households. Enrollment rates should be calculated for each socioeconomic group (and for each region if this is considered important for policy purposes). These calculations would yield tables following the structure of Frame 3.3.

Comparisons between the socioeconomic groups will be interesting in themselves, and will provide initial clues about the underlying factors that might be responsible for the variations in enrollment. For example, differences between rural and urban-based households might suggest variations in the availability of schooling. On the other hand, low levels of enrollment among

farming households may well indicate high returns to child labor in the agricultural enterprise. The differences in household income between SEGs will also explain some of the variation in enrollment. Such differences will not necessarily prove such causal links, but they may provide some initial guidance to policymakers. Tabulations should distinguish the sex of the children, so that the analyst can gain some understanding of any gender bias in school enrollment among the socioeconomic groups.

The enrollment rate may not be a sufficiently sensitive indicator to capture the effects of recent policy changes. It should be supplemented with some analysis of recent dropout rates from the education system—a more sensitive indicator than the enrollment rate. A tabulation along the lines of Frame 3.4 would be particularly useful for policymakers. The dropout rate is defined as the number of children who left school in the current school year divided by the total number of children enrolled in the current year (plus the dropouts). Again, the tabulations should be prepared separately for primary and secondary schooling and be disaggregated by sex. Of specific importance is what happens at the end of different educational levels (primary, lower secondary,

Frame 3.3: School enrollment rates, by level of schooling, sex, and SEG

	SEG 1.........................SEG 11	Total
Primary enrollment rates		
M		
F		
T		
Secondary enrollment rates		
M		
F		
T		

Frame 3.4: Educational dropout rates, by socioeconomic group

	SEG 1.........................SEG 11	Total
Primary-level dropout rates		
M		
F		
T		
Secondary-level dropout rates		
M		
F		
T		

upper secondary, and so on). In difficult economic conditions there may be a growing tendency to not continue to the next level of education and to enter the labor market sooner. This can be captured by the percentage of graduates who proceed to the next level. This indicator is likely to be sensitive to macroeconomic and policy change.

One final educational indicator to be computed is the relation between age and school grade. In each country, there is an accepted relation between the age of the child and his or her school grade. If children have dropped out of education for periods in the past, or if they have been obliged to repeat grades, they may find themselves in grades that are inappropriate for their age. This indicator is a further refinement of the enrollment and dropout indicators, since it reveals weaknesses in the education experience of those who are currently enrolled and attending school. For example, the enrollment and dropout rates

will not pick up changes in the incidence of repeats, which reflect some educational stress. So this age/grade assessment must be made for every child of school age who is currently attending school. There are two ways to tabulate data to reveal differences in age/grade experiences across socioeconomic groups. The first is to compute for each SEG the number of children whose age is above that for their current grade as a proportion of the total number of enrolled children. This is shown in Frame 3.5 and illustrated in Box 3.1.

Alternatively, a matrix can be prepared for each socioeconomic group, distributing the sample by age and grade, as illustrated in Frame 3.6. If there were no age-grade slippage in the socioeconomic group, all the sample would be across the diagonal. But with temporary absences and repeats, some children will be observed to the southwest of the diagonal. Only a few children in grades ahead of their age would appear to the northeast of the diagonal. Frame 3.6 reports only mis-

---

Box 3.1: Education and socioeconomic status in Côte d'Ivoire, 1985-88

In 1981, Côte d'Ivoire launched a structural adjustment program in an attempt to counteract economic decline induced by falling world prices of coffee and cocoa—the country's two main exports. The adjustment effort was sustained until 1986 and then abandoned. This was followed by a sharp recession in 1987-88—two years characterized by severe economic destabilization and a more than 20 percent decline in real household expenditure per capita. Poverty incidence increased substantially. An important question for policymakers is how access to basic needs evolved in such a changing macroeconomic environment. In education, the government succeeded in protecting the share of public expenditures devoted to education, but private spending fell sharply, especially among poor households. The net primary school enrollment rate for the country as a whole stayed at 54 percent, but the rate fell for very poor households. Falling income levels forced many parents to pull children out of school, either temporarily or permanently. One manifestation of this was a growing problem of age-grade mismatches, that is, children falling behind in educational progress. In 1985, 31 percent of children in primary school were at least one grade behind the one normally associated with their age. In 1988, this figure had risen to 42 percent. However, the situation became much worse for poor and very poor households. Age-grade mismatches for boys in very poor households increased from 38 percent to 64 percent between 1985 and 1988, and the increase for girls was from 28 percent to 53 percent.

Poverty is strongly related to socioeconomic status in Côte d'Ivoire. The poorest groups are farmers and urban informal sector workers. These groups also saw the highest

drop in educational progress as measured by age-grade mismatch (see table below).

In 1985, the most educational progress, that is, the lowest incidence of age-grade mismatch, was found among children of government and private formal sector employees. Those are also the socioeconomic groups for whom the incidence of mismatches increased least. In contrast, high rates of mismatch occurred among children of farmers, who fell further behind than any other group. In urban areas, the situation deteriorated most for girls in households of informal sector employees and the self-employed. These results provide powerful information for targeting educational interventions in Côte d'Ivoire.

Age-grade mismatches in primary school, Côte d'Ivoire, 1985-88
(percent)

Socioeconomic status of the head of household	Boys		Girls	
	1985	1988	1985	1988
Export crop farmer	29.0	50.3	30.1	61.3
Food crop farmer	31.5	54.8	33.6	45.7
Government employee	21.7	27.5	25.7	31.1
Private formal sector employee	25.6	36.0	33.3	31.5
Informal sector employee	35.6	28.3	12.7	58.5
Self-employed	35.6	43.4	27.7	48.9
Unemployed	39.9	29.4	83.3	46.4
Inactive	38.9	33.0	36.6	38.6
All households	29.5	43.0	31.9	41.6

Source: Grootaert 1993.

Frame 3.5: Age-grade mismatches as a proportion of total enrollments, by SEG, education levels, and sex

	SEG 1..........................SEG 11	Total
Primary level		
M		
F		
T		
Secondary level		
M		
F		
T		

Note: These mismatches are only for children above the age indicated for the grade.

Frame 3.6: Age-grade matrix for SEG 1

	Primary education grade						
Age	1	2	3	4	5	6	7
5							
6							
7							
8							
9							
10							
11							
12	Cells comprise numbers in sample						
13							
14							
15							

Frame 3.7: Mean household education expenditure per currently enrolled child, by SEG and region

	SEG 1...............................SEG 11	Total
Region		
1.		
2.	Cells contain mean expenditure values	
3.		
4.		
Total		

matches for primary education, since this is likely to be the most sensitive indicator of early educational problems for the households concerned.

Some surveys obtain information for the household as a whole on school fee expenditures. This can be used to identify differences across socioeconomic groups in expenditure on education. To account for variations in the numbers of children at school, household expenditures should be divided by the number of currently enrolled children in the household, and the mean values reported (along the lines of Frame 3.7). An alternative would be to present the share of education in total expenditures. The results should be disaggregated by region, since expenditures will likely be higher in urban areas (especially in the capital city), where private schooling is more readily available.

In many countries, policy reforms include elements of cost recovery in the public sector, which are often applied to the education sector. To what extent can households afford to pay for the education of their children? How willing are households to do so? These issues are vital, since they determine whether cost recovery in education will lead to lower enrollment rates and increased dropout rates among some socioeconomic groups. The information on education expenditures will give governments some preliminary indication of the types of households that commit resources to the education of their children and of the significance of such costs in their overall household budgets. The indications are preliminary since a more detailed investigation would be required for a thoroughgoing analysis.

Most survey data permit some multivariate analysis. Chapter 7 reviews the main considerations that are applied in specifying an estimation model for education analysis, and we shall not repeat this here. However, some priority multivariate analysis should be undertaken. Our main interest is in identifying the dependent and explanatory variables that can be used in ordinary least squares (OLS) estimation. Three dependent variables are available: the proportion of children of school age in each household currently enrolled; the proportion of dropouts in each household; and the share of household expenditure spent on education. The occupation, education, and income levels of the household head and spouse are generally important explanatory variables. Household assets (and income) can also be used as explanatory variables. Regional dummy variables may be used to capture the effects of variations in educational services.

Health

The PA focuses on the use of health services by the household, rather than on the health status of its members. Health status is a more responsive indicator than education performance variables. The health of a population can deteriorate quickly, as compared with literacy or numeracy rates, for example. The main problem with health indicators, however, is that it is difficult to obtain accurate information in a household survey—it is unlikely that the survey respondent will be familiar with the health condition of all household members. Moreover, since illness and injury have to be self-reported in such household surveys, indicators of health status tend to be relatively unreliable. For example, better-educated households tend to report more illness than poorer and less well-educated households. Similarly, infant mortality is an important and frequently used indicator of health conditions, but it needs to be calculated from specially suited demographic surveys with large samples and can rarely be calculated precisely at the sub-national level. For that reason it is not really part of priority analysis, where the focus is on socioeconomic and target group analysis, using easily available data sources. A focus on use of services is also justified on the grounds that health consultations may be influenced by policy reforms under a structural adjustment program (see Box 2.2 in Chapter 2). Whether these reforms involve significant cuts in programs, or the restructuring of health services, it is certain that they will change the access of the various socioeconomic groups to health care.

Two broad types of health data are required for PA. First, the incidence of health consultations —the numbers of persons who had a health consultation during a reference period divided by the total population in each group—must be computed and compared across the SEGs. Frame 3.8 disaggregates this by age and sex in order to isolate demographic effects. Three of these are noteworthy: infants and young children are more likely to receive medical attention than older children and adults; childbearing women are more likely to have medical consultations; and older age-groups will probably make greater calls on the medical services.

The second type of health PA concerns the type of consultation made. This is particularly relevant in situations of structural adjustment. This analysis should indicate the availability of modern health services to households. Differences in the type of consultation will reflect, among other things, the availability of medical services (Frame 3.9).

Finally, health analysis should use information on the household's health expenditures, if this is available. Some household surveys obtain expenditure data, so that a priority tabulation along the

Frame 3.8: Incidence of health consultations, by SEG, age, and sex
(percent)

Age		SEG 1.......................................SEG 11		Total
0-5	M			
	F			
6-15	M			
	F			
16-45	M			
	F			
46-60	M			
	F			
> 60	M			
	F			
Total				

Frame 3.9: Distribution of health consultations by type of consultation and SEG
(percent)

Type of consultation	SEG 1............................SEG 11		Total
Traditional healer			
Health assistant			
Midwife/nurse			
Doctor			
Other			
Total	100	100	100

lines of Frame 3.10 may be feasible. Others may record the cost of health consultations, permitting tabulations along the lines of Frame 3.11. This information will establish more directly what each type of health consultation costs the household.

Frame 3.11 provides some important information about the supply side of household health expenditures. The costs of health consultations vary across types of consultation, so variations down the columns of Frame 3.11 are to be expected. However, variations across socioeconomic groups for each type of consultation are more significant, since these will reflect how accessible the services are in economic terms. Because health facilities are available does not imply that they are accessible to all households. The table will show whether health costs are low enough to enable poorer groups to have effective access. Changes in these costs measured over time will help monitor changes in health costs, and show how these changes are affecting each of the socioeconomic groups.

Chapter 8 reviews the types of behavioral relations that might be estimated for health, and there is little point in repeating that here. Dependent

Frame 3.10: Mean per capita household expenditure on health, by SEG and region

	SEG 1............................SEG 11	Total
Region		
1.		
2.		
3.	Cells contain expenditure values	
4.		
Total		

Frame 3.11: Average health costs per consultation, by type of consultation and SEG

Type of consultation	SEG 1...............................SEG 11	Total
Traditional healer		
Health assistant	Cells contain average costs	
Midwife/nurse		
Doctor		
Other		
Total		

variables for multivariate PA of health may be defined at the individual and the household levels. The individual-level dependent variable reflects the demand for health inputs, in this case whether the individual has consulted a health practitioner during the reference week. This is a dichotomous variable, which takes the value of 0 for individuals who have not consulted a practitioner and 1 for those who have. Multivariate analysis therefore requires binary logit estimation methods. Per capita household health expenditure (or its share in total expenditure) is an alternative dependent variable, though this is defined at the household level. As this is a continuous variable, ordinary least squares procedures will generally apply.

The selection of regressors will depend on the level of analysis. With an individual-level dependent variable (consultation with practitioner), explanatory variables will be of three types:

• The characteristics of the individual concerned, such as age, sex, relationship to household head, and work status

• Household-level variables (including education/employment of household head and spouse, wages/incomes of household head/spouse and household, landholding, expenditures on food, water source used by household)

• A set of variables external to the household, ideally including prices of foods, costs of health consultations, and access to infrastructural services, such as health-care facilities.

With a household-level dependent variable (health expenditure), the individual-level regressors would be dropped. However, variables reflecting the age/sex structure of the household (such as the dependency ratio) might be included among the household-level regressors to take account of the demographic determinants of health expenditure. The household and external independent variables specified earlier should be retained for the household-level analysis.

Nutrition

Although household surveys cannot generally obtain reliable information on illness and injury for each household member, household surveys can effectively monitor one aspect of health: nutrition. This is one of the "outcome" indicators that can be readily measured in a one-visit household survey. Anthropometric information can be obtained on all children, usually age three months to five years. These data cover age, height, and weight and can be used to assess the extent of malnutrition, reflecting both stunting and wasting. The analytical underpinnings of data analysis on nutrition are discussed in Chapter 9. Two broad indicators should be computed from these data—height for age and weight for height. The former measures the degree of stunting, and the latter measures wasting. A child can be considered severely stunted if his or her height is less than 85 percent of the standard height for his or her age (the standard being drawn from a reference population—see Chapter 9). Similarly, a child can be considered severely wasted with weight less than 75 percent of the standard weight for height. Children in these categories are malnourished.

PA should identify malnutrition for each of the socioeconomic groups, preferably by region, using both height-for-age and weight-for-height indicators. This is one of the prime indicators requiring an immediate policy response if a problem is signaled by the indicator. The regional disaggregation will give policymakers more precise clues about the specific groups that are in need of food targeting. Frame 3.12 reports the sort of tabulation that is required for wasting. The same table should be computed for stunting.

As with education and health, some multivariate analysis should be possible for nutrition. The dependent variable in this case would be the weight-for-height and height-for-age indicators already discussed—these are defined at the individual level. In general, the set of explanatory variables defined for health analysis should be retained here—these being individual level, household level, and external categories of regressors.

Housing

Housing should be part of a PA program for two reasons. First, housing, and its related facilities, can be considered a basic need, reflecting the welfare levels of the population. Changes in these facilities (in part as a result of periods of austerity and adjustment) reflect changing welfare levels. Second, as stock variables, they are relatively easy to obtain in one-visit household surveys and censuses.

Many household surveys obtain information on the characteristics of the dwelling and the facilities that are available. Frames 3.13, 3.14, and 3.15 illustrate the types of tabulation that can be useful in priority policy analysis. They cover the tenurial arrangements of the dwelling (which can reveal economic stress if there is a decline in owner occupation) and the facilities available (drinking water, fuel, and so forth). The importance of housing indicators for the targeting of poverty alleviation programs is illustrated in Box 3.2.

Employment

One major way through which structural adjustment affects households is by altering their employment opportunities, which then induces changes in the time allocation of household members across different types of employment and different sectors of the economy. Such changes will not be the same across all households because different SEGs have different endowments, which will influence the ability of households to respond to a new incentive structure. The pattern of economic activity across SEGs, and how it changes, is one of the key tables in assessing the impact of adjustment and policy reform.

Frame 3.16 lays out for each SEG and for the country as a whole the distribution of individuals over broadly defined economic activities. Since the SEGs (the columns of the table) have been defined partly by the main economic activity of the head of household and since the rows are activity categories for all household members (age seven and older), the table directly shows the extent to which the household has differentiated

---

Box 3.2: Housing and poverty

The analysis of housing conditions is a high priority for poverty-oriented policies. Housing conditions for the poor are frequently abysmal and contribute to health risks. Housing conditions are an easily observed indicator, which because of the strong association with poverty, can also be used to target poverty alleviation interventions in areas where the poor are disadvantaged, such as access to education, health care, and employment.

Housing conditions in Côte d'Ivoire, 1988
(percent)

	Very poor households	Mid-poor households	Non-poor households
People with access to tap water	2.9	11.4	31.2
Households with flush toilet or pit latrine	25.9	42.9	62.9
Households with garbage removal by truck	5.5	17.0	38.1
People with access to electricity	10.9	29.2	53.3
Average floor area per person (square meters)	6.1	7.0	10.2

The gap in housing conditions between poor and nonpoor in Côte d'Ivoire is striking. But it is also striking that even among the poor, there is a group—the very poor—whose conditions are much worse than the other poor. Only 3 percent of very poor people in Côte d'Ivoire have access to safe tap water—one-fourth the rate of the midpoor and one-tenth the rate of the non-poor. Only 5.5 percent of very poor households benefit from garbage removal by truck—one-third the rate of the mid-poor and one-seventh the rate of the non-poor. These living conditions greatly contribute to poor health and hygiene. They provide important indicators to target policy interventions aimed at helping the poor.

Source: Grootaert 1993.

---

its activities relative to that of the head. For example, one may find that among the rural SEGs, most members of food/subsistence farm households work as farmers or unpaid family workers, while among export-oriented farmers a greater percentage of household members have other activities. Such a finding would imply that the latter group has a better chance of withstanding

Frame 3.12: Percentage of children (age 3 months to 5 years) indicating significantly low weight for height, by SEG and region

(percent)

	SEG 1............................SEG 11	Total
Region		
1.		
2.		
3.		
4.		
Total		

Note: The cutoff chosen for the table should be 75 percent of standard weight. Alternative cutoffs may be selected (for example, 85 percent to indicate moderate wasting).

Frame 3.13: Distribution of households by house tenure and SEG

(percent)

Dwelling arrangements	SEG 1....................SEG 11		Total
Owner-occupier			
Tenant			
Rent-free accommodation			
Squatting			
Total	100	100	100

Frame 3.14: Distribution of households by water source and SEG

(percent)

Water source	SEG 1............................SEG 11		Total
River/lake			
Well			
Public tap			
Own tap			
Other			
Total	100	100	100

Frame 3.15: Distribution of households by type of cooking fuel and SEG

(percent)

Cooking fuel	SEG 1............................SEG 11		Total
Wood/charcoal			
Kerosene			
Gas			
Electricity			
Other			
Total	100	100	100

an economic shock in the agricultural sector and/or has more successfully adapted to past shocks.

In urban areas, the table may reveal, for example, SEGs in which formal sector employment has diminished (a frequent result of adjustment) and in which a growing number of people have been able to switch to self-employment. To the extent that full-time enrollment is used as a row category, the table may give a first indication of low school attendance in certain groups.

A useful extension of Frame 3.16 is to split each row according to gender. There are strong arguments for expecting that structural adjustment affects men and women differently. (A detailed analysis of how and to what extent this occurs is presented in Chapter 11.) PA must provide a first insight on major differences in economic activity patterns between men and women, and on which SEGs these differences are most pronounced.

Since structural adjustment induces resource switching, it is important to identify types of individuals and households who have failed to make such a switch successfully, and as a result have become unemployed. Frame 3.17 shows a useful display of this information, allowing us to pinpoint the age/sex groups and the SEGs within which unemployment is a problem. The row totals give the demographic dispersion of unemployment, while the column totals give the incidence of unemployment in each SEG and for the country as a whole. When PA is repeated in subsequent years, this table will be able to show where unemployment is worsening or improving. A useful refinement of Frame 3.17 is to split each row further (especially the rows pertaining to young adults) according to the level of education achieved. This would then indicate whether the unemployment problem is more or less severe for well-educated people (especially recent graduates). This is important information for the design of employment and retraining programs. Such programs will be different indeed if, for example, the majority of unemployed are recent technical school graduates as opposed to people past age 40, with skills mainly acquired on the job, who have lost employment because of policy reform.

One way to avoid unemployment at the place of residence is to leave the household and to migrate to look for work elsewhere. Such a situation may be socially disruptive and have adverse side effects on the education and health of children.

Frame 3.16: Distribution of individuals (age 7 and older) by main economic activity and SEG
(percent)

Activity	SEG 1............................SEG 11		Total
Farmer			
Other self-employed			
Unpaid family worker			
Government employee			
Private sector employee			
Student			
Housekeeper			
No economic activity			
Total	100	100	100

Frame 3.17: Unemployment rate, by age, sex, and SEG
(percent)

Age		SEG 1............................SEG 11		Total
15-20	M			
	F			
21-25	M			
	F			
26-30	M			
	F			
31-40	M			
	F			
41-60	M			
	F			
Total	M			
	F			
Total				

If the data are available in the survey used for PA, analysts should investigate the incidence and distribution of this effect through tabular analysis. (Migration analysis is further discussed in Chapter 6.)

The classification of economic activities in Frame 3.16 was purposely kept broad to minimize data requirements. For many employment-related policy decisions, a finer occupational classification is needed. Ideally, the occupation list should reflect the tradables/nontradables distinction across which major resource shifts occur under adjustment. Such a list can often be derived from a labor force survey. In other types of surveys, more detailed employment information will only be available for the household head and, possibly, the spouse.

For tabulation of detailed occupation information, we recommend disaggregation to at most 50 to 75 occupations (this level of disaggregation corresponds roughly to the two-digit level within the International Standard Classification of Oc-

cupations—ISCO). Within agriculture, the occupations will be similar to the SEG classification; for example, farmer, pastoralist, and agricultural worker will be among the occupations, and these also form part of the SEG criteria. Similarly, within the category "farmer," the occupation list will differentiate according to major crop, which is also part of the SEG scheme. In other words, a table cross-classifying the occupation of the head of household with SEG will be largely tautological in rural areas. But in urban areas the occupation list will provide much refinement within the SEGs. Consequently, different occupational tables for rural and urban areas are called for. Frame 3.18 shows the distribution of the spouse's main occupation for rural SEGs (which were defined on the basis of the head's occupation), indicating the extent to which the spouse's work is different from the head's main activities. Differentiated work patterns within the household provide more protection against changes in the economic environment. An alternative to Frame 3.18 would be to cross-tabulate directly the occupation of the head of household with that of the spouse, although then the formal link with the SEG classification would be lost.

For urban areas, Frame 3.19 shows the main occupation of the head of household and spouse by SEG. Several alternative versions of this frame are possible, replacing (or combining) the occupation with work status or industry.

Many labor force surveys or employment modules in other surveys ask how long a person has been engaged in his or her current main occupation and what the previous occupation was. The two can be combined in a table to show shifts in occupational mix, using a relevant time cutoff of a given number of years ago. The cutoff point can be chosen to correspond to an event relating to structural adjustment or policy reform, such as the launching of an economic recovery program. If such a period is too distant in the past, the table could be constructed for a more recent period (say, the last one or two years) to show more recent job turnover. The information can be displayed in two ways.

In Frame 3.20, the current occupation is cross-tabulated against the previous one; to be of manageable size, this table has to be aggregated across occupations. The entries are, for each current main occupation, the distribution of people according to their previous occupation—allowing, of course, for the possibility that there was no previous

Frame 3.18: Main occupation of the spouse in rural SEGs
(percent)

	SEG 1 .... SEG 6		Total
Occupation 1			
Occupation 2			
....			
Total	100	100	100

Frame 3.19: Main occupation of the head of household and spouse in urban SEGs
(percent)

	SEG 7 .... SEG 11				Total	
	Head	Spouse	Head	Spouse	Head	Spouse
Occupation *j*						
Occupation *j*+1						
....						
Total	100	100	100	100	100	100

Frame 3.20: Patterns of occupational changes in the last *x* years, by occupation
(percent)

	Current main occupation				
	1	2	3	....	Total
Previous occupation					
1					
2					
3					
....					
No previous occupation					
Total		100			100

Frame 3.21: Incidence of occupational changes in the last *x* years, by current main occupation and SEG
(percent)

Current main occupation	SEG 1...................SEG 11		All
1			
2			
3			
......			
All			

occupation. Job mobility is indicated by non-zero off-diagonal cells (the main diagonal is empty by definition). The advantage of this presentation is that it shows the occupational flows. On the other hand, it lacks the link to SEGs. For that reason, an additional table is in order (Frame 3.21) to show, for each SEG, the percentage of people who have been in their current occupation for less than the chosen cutoff number of years. This shows which occupations have had recent accruals and in which SEGs they occurred. The "all" column shows total recent accruals for each occupation, and the "all" row shows average job mobility for each SEG, that is, the percentage of people who changed jobs in the last *x* number of years. A complement to this table would be to use previous occupations as rows and show which occupations have been abandoned.

It has been argued that structural adjustment programs not only increase job mobility but also job insecurity, thereby inducing people to hold more secondary jobs. Where data permit it, PA should include the construction of tables that display the extent to which this occurs, and in which occupations and SEGs this is concentrated. Frame 3.22 indicates the incidence of secondary job holdings by both SEG and current main occupation. This table can pertain to the household as a whole, but separate tables should be constructed for at least the head and the spouse because their incidence of second job holdings is likely to be quite different. The presentation in Frame 3.22 is SEG-specific, but it does not identify the prevalent primary-secondary job combinations. This is achieved by Frame 3.23, which cross-tabulates main with secondary occupation. (To keep the size of this table manageable, some aggregation, particularly of main occupations, will be necessary.) As with Frame 3.21, we recommend also constructing separate tables for head and spouse since prevailing job combinations will not necessarily be the same.

A final element of mobility that could be related to structural adjustment is geographical, that is, migration. If one or more household members have to leave the household to look for work, this can be seen as a distress variable in that, other things being equal, people would prefer to obtain jobs near their homes. The incidence of this variable across SEGs can indicate the extent to which local employment opportunities are missing for some SEGs.

The tables discussed so far are examples of how PA can be used to investigate ways in which structural adjustment and policy reform affect the patterns of employment. Box 3.3 provides a more complete set of tables concerned with this issue.

Frame 3.22: Incidence of secondary job holding, by SEG and current main occupation
(percent)

Current main occupation	SEG 1......................SEG 11	All
Occupation 1		
Occupation 2		
....		
All		

Frame 3.23: Pattern of secondary job holding, by current main occupation
(percent)

Secondary occupation	Current main occupation				All
	1	2	3	....	
1					
2					
3					
....					
Total	100				100

Note: This table is calculated only over those individuals with a secondary job.

Since employment is such an important area in assessing the impact of adjustment, we recommend selected multivariate analysis, in addition to the tabulations suggested. In particular, the following variables—important indicators of the employment situation—can be used as dependent variables in simple models of household behavior:

- Labor force participation
- Recent occupational change
- Secondary job holding
- Absence from the household for job search
- Wage earnings.

Depending upon the survey underlying the PA, these variables can be defined for all household members or for selected members, especially the head and spouse. Each variable can be the subject of a simple multivariate model, which may throw more light on the determinants of the phenomenon. Several of these models are discussed in a more complete way in the analysis plan on employment and earnings (Chapter 5). The discussion there on econometric issues of estimating models with binary dependent variables, and selectivity bias in the estimation of earnings functions, is also relevant here (for a more detailed discussion, see also Grootaert 1986). Here we limit ourselves to a brief description of the estimating equations.

Box 3.3: Tabulation plan—employment and migration

- Distribution of individuals by main economic activity and SEG
- Distribution of individuals by main economic activity and age/sex
- Distribution of individuals by main economic activity and education level
- Unemployment rate by age/sex and SEG
- Unemployment rate by education level and SEG
- Average wage income and direction of change by SEG
- Share of wages in total income by SEG
- Absence of head of household and spouse by reason and SEG
- Main occupation of head of household and spouse by SEG
- Work status of head of household and spouse by SEG
- Industry of head of household and spouse by SEG
- Average wages of head of household and spouse by occupation/SEG
- Recent occupational changes by current occupation
- Recent occupational changes by SEG
- Incidence of secondary job holding by SEG and current main occupation
- Patterns of secondary job holdings by current main occupation
- Duration of main occupation and previous occupation of head of household and spouse by SEG
- Main occupation of head of household and spouse by previous occupation
- Recent migration by place of origin and SEG
- Number of household members who left household for job search by SEG

Note: All tables pertaining to the head of household and spouse may also be tabulated separately for head and spouse, to highlight gender differences.

The labor force participation (LFP) model is usually estimated over all household members seven years of age or older (this age cutoff can be changed in the light of specific country situations) who are not full-time students. This exclusion is necessary because otherwise the model would confuse labor force participation with the schooling decision. The dependent variable is binary: it takes a value of zero if the main activity is "housekeeping" or "no occupation," and a value of one otherwise. In other words, labor force participation is defined to include work for wages, self-employment, and unpaid family work. The explanatory variables consist of the demographic and education characteristics of the individual, as well as selected household characteristics that may influence the decision to participate in the labor market, such as region (employment opportunities may vary significantly across different parts of the country) and the holding of farm or non-farm enterprises in the household itself (these provide ready access to unpaid family work). These household characteristics can be entered in the equation as regressors separately or combined through the SEG classification, which in fact summarizes them. We recommend that analysts test both specifications to see which gives the most meaningful results.

The estimating equation is:

LFP = f (age, gender, relation to head of household, education; region, household enterprises)

or

LFP = f (age, gender, relation to head of household, education; SEG)

Except for age, all the explanatory variables are discontinuous and thus enter the regression as sets of categorical (dummy) variables.

Two alternatives to this model are feasible (with the same set of explanatory variables). Instead of explaining the participation/non-participation decision, one may single out a particular mode of participation and examine its determinants, for example, comparing wage employment to other forms of participation (see Box 3.4). An alternative is to focus on unemployment and define the dependent variable as unemployed = 1, employed = 0. This model would provide a better explanation of unemployment than was possible in Frame 3.17, by controlling at the same time for various personal and household characteristics.

The dependent variable of the occupational change model is binary and equals one if an occupational change occurred in the last x years, with x being defined in the same way as for Frames 3.20 and 3.21. This ensures that the regression is consistent with the tables and provides a further explanation. In addition to the basic demographic variables, a major determinant of occupational change will be the situation before the change, in particular, the previous occupation. Another relevant factor is whether the household has migrated. The estimating equation is:

Occupational change = f (age, gender, relation, education, previous occupation; migration)

Whether a person holds a second job depends mainly upon his personal characteristics as well as upon the nature of the main job currently held (especially the earnings from that job). In addition, the socioeconomic status of the household can determine the access to a second job, for example, the place of residence and whether the household owns an enterprise. These features are captured by the SEG classification. The second-job model has a binary dependent variable, equalling one if a second job is held and zero otherwise. This model complements the tabulations in Frames 3.22 and 3.23. The estimating equation is:

Second job = f (age, gender, relation, education; current main occupation, duration, work status, industry, wage; SEG)

The next model explains whether a household member has been absent from the household for work reasons. The variables influencing this are the personal characteristics as well as the characteristics of the job currently held (or last held, if the person is now unemployed). The socioeconomic status of the household would also be relevant in determining an absence. The estimating equation is as follows:

Absence = f (age, gender, relation, education; occupation, work status, industry; occupational change, migration, change in assets; SEG)

A model similar to this could be constructed for the household as a whole, indicating the number of household members who have been away for work reasons. The differences are that here the dependent variable is continuous and the explanatory variables are limited to the household level. The assets situation of the household, especially with respect to productive assets, could be of specific relevance. As an option, the personal and occupational characteristics of the head of household could be included. The basic estimating equation would be:

Number of absent household members = f (agricultural enterprise, number of non-agricultural enterprises, assets, change in assets, migration; SEG)

Income and assets

Income is an important variable in the analysis of social welfare, particularly during structural adjustment. Not only is there every prospect of

Box 3.4: What determines access to employment?

Priority analysis in the area of employment aims to identify the most important determinants of jobs—especially the role of education and whether personal and socioeconomic characteristics play a role. In the case of gender, ethnic group, and so on, this analysis may provide warning signals of labor market segmentation or discrimination.

A model along the lines of the labor force participation model discussed in the text was estimated for Côte d'Ivoire to find the key factors that determine access to public sector and formal private sector employment—the two highest-paying sectors with the greatest job security. Selected probit coefficients are shown in the table below.

The education variables were included in a very detailed way to provide guidance for education planning. The results show that education beyond the secondary level is necessary in Côte d'Ivoire to gain access to the modern sector—public or private. Education in the form of apprenticeships is a deterrent to formal sector access and prepares people for work in the informal sector, either as an employee or in self-employment. Obtaining diplomas is essential for access to government jobs, highlighting the "credentialism" displayed by the public sector. In contrast, diplomas are not critical factors for access to formal private sector jobs. Results not reported here indicate that work experience is valued more in the private sector than in the public sector.

Demographic factors are also important determinants of access to the public sector: women are more likely to be employed in the public sector than in the private sector, particularly if they have no small children in their household. In contrast, people of non-Ivorian origin have a much better chance of working in the modern private sector, regardless of their education and work experience.

Determinants of access to public and private formal sector employment

	Public sector	Private formal sector
Education variables		
Years of primary schooling	-0.059	-0.039
Years of secondary schooling	-0.066	0.088
Years of higher schooling	0.206*	
Years of secondary VTE	-0.049	0.042
Years of post-secondary VTE	0.648*	
Years of teacher training	1.53*	
Years of apprenticeship	-0.121*	-0.085*
Primary education diploma	0.865*	0.269
Lower secondary education diploma	1.44*	0.384
Other diploma	1.01	
Secondary VTE diploma	1.56*	0.990*
Post-secondary VTE diploma	-0.176	
Teacher diploma	0.210	
Demographic variables		
Female, with child under age 5	0.461*	0.253
Female, without child under age 5	0.578*	-0.380
Non-Ivorian	-2.37*	-0.015
Sample	All employees	All private sector employees

* Significant at the 95 percent level.
Source: Grootaert 1990.

---

significant change in real incomes, but the sources of income are also likely to shift as policy reforms change the structure of incentives in the economy. Households previously relying on nontradable sectors for a livelihood will be obliged to switch to tradable sectors as adjustment policies take effect. Yet income is known to be a difficult variable to obtain through household surveys. It is typically under-reported in most surveys for a number of reasons. Respondents may not fully know the incomes of all household members, they may deliberately understate income for fear of taxation, or they may find it difficult to recall income over the specified reference period. Income is also subject to seasonal and other variations, so that its measurement becomes particularly difficult in household surveys that involve only one visit to the household.

Income analysis should begin with a general assessment of the main sources of income of the household, establishing the major changes observed. This should then be complemented with more detailed analysis of three principal components of this income—wage income of the household head and spouse, revenue from agricultural enterprises, and revenue from non-agricultural enterprises. Finally, the asset holdings of the household, and their recent changes, should be analyzed.

Sources of income

The PA is unlikely to be based on income measures of household welfare, in part because of the time required to compute meaningful estimates of income, including imputed income (for example, from home ownership). In some surveys, cruder estimates of income are obtained from respondents by simple direct questions, but these data are generally not a sufficiently reliable basis for quantitative analysis. This is why the PA presented in this chapter is concerned mainly with more easily measured proxies for household welfare. However, it may be possible under PA to examine the *sources* of income. While measurement errors preclude the use of the absolute level of income in priority analysis, these errors are unlikely to change the rank-ordering of income sources.[1] As an option for the priority analysis, it may be possible to present the data along the lines of Frame 3.24.

This addresses three major issues. First, to what extent do households diversify their income sources? This is critical for the analysis of the social dimensions of adjustment. Periods of policy reform and austerity frequently lead to household members working in multiple jobs, and cropping patterns might also become increasingly diversified. It is important to establish whether the diversification of income sources is greater for some groups than others. Is there evidence, for example, that urban-based households previously relying on wage employment diversify toward agricultural activities—such as food production for own consumption?

Second, to what extent is the occupational status of the household head (or possibly spouse as well) a useful indicator of the family's income source? In most cases, the socioeconomic classifications will use the characteristics of the household head, but this may not be a complete representation if the household earns a significant proportion of its income in activities outside those typically associated with the socioeconomic group. For example, farming households as a group may earn a significant proportion of their total income outside farming—either from non-farm enterprises or from wage labor. Frame 3.24 will provide a basis for making some assessment of this. Finally, Frame 3.24 will provide clues about how the poorer socioeconomic groups are likely to be affected by policy reforms. If such groups rely entirely on income from food crops, and if the latter are nontraded, it is likely that such groups will suffer during adjustment.

With income from some sources expected to fall and others to rise during the structural changes brought about by policy reform, we would expect to find patterns emerging from the data analysis. These changes should be related to the economy-wide changes that have occurred in the recent past. Some impression may be gained about which of the socioeconomic groups appear to be losing out and which (if any) seem to be gaining as a result of adjustment.

Wage income

Information on wage earnings can be tabulated along the lines of Frame 3.25. This frame can pertain to all household members or, in line with earlier tabulations on employment, single out the head of household and the spouse. The table splits wage earnings according to the source: public and private sector, the latter by industry. In computing the wage, the time period should be constant across all observations. Recomputations are usually required to recast the wage data into a common time unit. The data of Frame 3.25 can be used to assess whether labor market signals are in line with the main objectives of the structural adjustment program. In the very short run, wage differences can be expected, encouraging labor to move into tradable-oriented employment. Thus, private sector wages should (other things being equal) be higher than state sector wages, and within the private sector, wages in exportables and importables should be expected to gain relative to those in nontradables. The table also identifies wage variations across the socioeconomic groups. These differences will depend on the characteristics of the workers concerned—particularly their human capital. For example, wages may be higher in one SEG than another because wage earners are better educated. Tabulations of this sort can only be indicative of such effects. The application of multivariate techniques, however, may resolve some of the mystery.

The estimation of a simple wage-earnings model, based on the human capital theory, is

Frame 3.24: Mean shares of income source by SEG
(percent)

	SEG 1................SEG 11	Total
Agriculture		
Export crops		
Food crops		
Livestock		
Other products		
Non-farm enterprises		
Wage employment		
Public sector		
Formal private sector		
Informal sector		
Rents		
State and private transfers		
Total	100	100	100

useful to assess whether the relative returns to education and work experience have changed during an adjustment period. Many labor markets in developing countries are segmented: workers cannot easily move between different sections of the market (for example, between the informal and formal sectors, or between regions), and/or different types of workers are not considered substitutes for one another by employers (for example, male and female workers). The human capital model allows the inclusion of such variables to test for the presence of such segmentation. Variables related to occupation should not be included for this purpose as they represent factors subject to choice by household members. For actual estimation, the dependent variable (wages) needs to be converted to a common time unit and is best expressed in natural logarithmic form:

$$Ln(wages) = f \text{ (education, experience, experience squared; gender, region)}$$

Agricultural activities

Most households in developing countries rely on agriculture as a major source of income. Data on agricultural activities can be obtained from a variety of sources, including agricultural censuses and household surveys.

For PA, it is not recommended that detailed estimates of agricultural output and the income generated thereby be made. These are difficult to obtain and are not suited to PA. However, some indications of the changes in production are needed. These will reveal which crops are being favored by the changes in relative prices brought about through structural adjustment and which are not. A tabulation along the lines of Frame 3.26 (if feasible with available data sources) will provide the information needed.

If the survey also obtains information on the reasons for the output changes, this could enrich the PA further, enabling a table similar to Frame 3.27 to be prepared. Of the households reporting changes in each crop area planted, the proportions giving each of the stipulated reasons are computed. In this way, the table provides some indication of the predominant factors leading to changes in crop area (and by implication, production). The reasons given will to some extent be country-specific, but some will relate to price changes, and others to the liberalization of markets and the improved access to productive factors. These factors are particularly subject to change as a result of structural adjustment. For example, an adjustment program that liberalizes imports may improve the availability of fertilizers, and consequently increase the rate of return to fertilizer-responsive crops. Alternatively, it may reduce subsidies on agricultural inputs, which reduces rates of return. The area planted may increase or decrease during adjustment, depending on the induced changes in output prices and on the availability (and prices) of inputs.

Some household surveys allow a more detailed analysis of the changes experienced by farmers in the use of inputs—such as fertilizer, credit, extension services, and labor. Frame 3.28 tabulates the use of these inputs by main crop produced. We have already reviewed how adjustment can improve farmers' access to fertilizers (and also change their price). But it can also change

Frame 3.25: Mean wage income of household head and spouse, by SEG and sector

	SEG 1.........................SEG 11	Total
Household head		
Private sector		
1		
2		
......		
State		
Total		
Spouse	Cells contain values	
Private sector		
1		
2		
......		
State		
Total		

Frame 3.26: Proportion of farmers experiencing changes in production and area planted, by crop (and by livestock, for production)
(percent)

	Production		Area planted	
	Increase	Decrease	Increase	Decrease
Maize				
Yam				
Plantain				
Cocoa				
Coffee				
Livestock [a]			not applicable	

a. Changes in the number of livestock.

Frame 3.27: Reasons for change in area planted, by direction of change and crop
(percent)

	Maize		Coffee	
Reason	Increase	Decrease	Increase	Decrease
Price change				
Fertilizer availability				
Labor availability				
Marketing opportunities				
Credit availability				
Other				
Total increases/ decreases	100	100	100	100

Frame 3.28: Proportion of farming households using inputs, by type of input and main crop produced
(percent)

Main crop	Fertilizer	Credit	Extension services	Labor
Maize				
Yam				
...				
Coffee				

Note: Examples of variables:
Fertilizer: farmers having obtained and used fertilizer last season.
Credit: farmers having obtained credit for farming during last season.
Extension: farmers visited by extension worker during last season.
Labor: farmers hiring more workers in last season than season before.

the availability of credit and extension services, with the direction of change depending on the details of the adjustment package. It can also tighten (or slacken) the labor market, thus changing the availability (and profitability) of labor services. Farmers employing more labor than previously are likely to be benefiting from recent policy changes and expanding their operations. These inputs are all brought together in Frame 3.28, the precise content of which will depend on the data available.

Non-farm enterprises

As with agricultural activities, non-farm enterprises are certain to face changing constraints and opportunities as a result of adjustment. Market opportunities will open up for tradables and decline for nontradables. Infrastructural changes may improve access to product, factor, and credit markets. These will combine to change the profitability of non-farm activities, so that some will expand and others decline. A critical first stage of PA is the classification of these activities into exportables, importables, and nontradables, since this forms a vital link back to policy reforms. The next task is purely descriptive—to identify which groups operate enterprises in each of the sectors. Frame 3.29 shows the type of tabulation that is useful depending on data availability. Its purpose is to identify which SEGs are most involved in household-based non-farm enterprise, and the sectors in which they are active. Some judgment can be made from the table about which groups are likely to gain from adjustment—those that are particularly active in sectors likely to gain as a result of policy reforms.

Whether an activity benefits from adjustment can be assessed. As with agricultural enterprises, the objective of the PA of non-farm enterprise is not to estimate income generated by non-farm enterprises, but to assess which activities are increasing and which are declining. A tabulation similar to Frame 3.30 would provide this information. The interpretation of the tabulation is self-evident—sectors in which output or employment is expanding are likely to be benefiting from policy reforms. The combined evidence of Frames 3.29 and 3.30 will enable policymakers to make some judgment about how policy reforms have affected the different socioeconomic groups, at least as far as their non-farm enterprises are concerned.

Assets

Assets occupy a special place in PA because they are a key measure of economic welfare and of changes in it. Very few surveys will contain an exhaustive list of household assets. However, many surveys do contain some information on selected productive assets (such as land, farm, and equipment) and consumer durables (cars, bicycles, and so on). Such information is extremely useful in assessing a household's welfare (even if the value of the assets is not known). Even more important are changes in assets. Losses of assets, particularly, can be an alarm signal that the household is forced to dispose of its assets to meet current consumption needs—a situation that is dangerous for the household's future income-earning abilities.

Any one asset is not likely to be a sufficiently reliable proxy for welfare or change of welfare, but if a buy or sell trend is observed over several assets, the interpretation is strengthened. For that reason we do not propose tabulating results by asset, but rather calculating a simple score consisting of the number of categories of assets owned by the household (proxy for welfare level) and a net change score, that is, the number of categories with an increase minus the number of categories with a decrease (proxy for welfare changes). The asset score will range from zero to the number of assets in the survey. For example, if the survey contains information on 10 assets, the ownership score will range from zero (no assets owned) to 10 (all assets owned). The net change score in principle can then range from −10 (a decrease in all assets) to +10 (an increase in all assets), but in practice it will vary in a narrower range around zero. Two exceptions to this treatment could be made for land and cattle, which in rural settings are of greater importance than other assets, and which merit being shown separately, as is done in Frame 3.31. Information on changes in assets may need to come from the results of successive surveys, although the Priority Survey (see Chapter 1) obtains information on changes in asset holdings by households through simple retrospective questions.

Conclusion

The PA recommended in this chapter is based on three broad considerations: the issues selected are considered to be of high policy priority, requiring urgent attention from the analyst; the data requirements for the analysis should be less demanding; and the analytical methods used should be relatively simple and well understood among most analysts . This has led to the identification of three key areas of PA: basic needs (education, health, nutrition, and housing); employment and occupational structure; and income and asset holdings. For each area this chapter has highlighted the types of indicator that can be readily computed and analyzed through simple tabulations.

The challenge facing PA is twofold. First, indicators selected must reflect changes in the welfare of different groups in the population. Second, such indicators should be sensitive to the changes brought about by structural adjustment policies. In most cases, the indicators recom-

mended meet both criteria—they reflect the well-being of the groups concerned, and they can be expected to respond fairly rapidly to policy reform.

In practice, the type of PA conducted will be constrained by the available data. If a multisubject household survey has been conducted recently in the country, it may be possible to base most of the analysis on that one source. In cases where single-subject surveys are undertaken, PA has to be based on a number of surveys. In some coun-

Frame 3.29: Number of non-farm enterprises, by sector and SEG

Sector	SEG 1............................SEG 11	Total
1		
2	Cells contain total	
3	number of enterprises identified	
.....		
Total		

Frame 3.30: Proportion of enterprises experiencing output and employment changes, by sector

(percent)

	Output			Employment		
Sector	Increase	Decrease	No change	Increase	Decrease	No change
1						
2						
3						
......						

Frame 3.31: Asset ownership

	SEG 1.......................SEG 11
Ownership	
Score of assets owned	
Percentage of households that own land	
Percentage of households that own cattle	
Change in ownership	
Net change score of assets owned	
Percentage of households that lost land	
Percentage of households that gained land	
Percentage of households that lost cattle	
Percentage of households that gained cattle	

Note: See text for definition of score.

tries, however, a shortage of household data will severely constrain what can be achieved by way of PA. This provides an argument for undertaking the Priority Survey (further detailed in Grootaert and Marchant 1991). Such a survey would be able to support all the analysis proposed here.

Note

1. In the SDA Priority Survey (see Grootaert and Marchant 1991), information is collected on the main sources of income, without collecting detailed information on the full income accounts of the household.

4

The poverty profile

Lionel Demery

This chapter is concerned with poverty, and how it might be affected by policy reforms. It sets out an analysis plan to guide policymakers and analysts in using household data in developing countries. The methods proposed are relatively simple, and most results can be presented in tabular form. The principal objective has been to keep the analysis as simple as possible.[1] The chapter emphasizes the purely economic aspects of poverty—households are considered poor because they have low levels of income and consumption.

Chapter 1 has suggested a number of ways in which the poor are affected by government policies. The poverty profile is a first step in gaining some understanding of these effects. There are a number of reasons for making this assessment. First, if the poor are adversely affected, they may bear a disproportionate burden of the costs of adjustment. The challenge facing policymakers under such circumstances is to resolve this conflict between economic adjustment and growth on the one hand, and equity on the other. Second, an increasing incidence of poverty can undermine the economic sustainability of policy reforms. Poverty implies low levels of human capital, both today and in the future, which in turn harms prospects for economic growth. Finally, in extreme cases, an increase in poverty threatens the political sustainability of a reform program. For these reasons, governments must be able to make ex ante assessments of the potential poverty problems arising from policy interventions.

Such assessments are frequently constrained by the sparsity of data, especially at the household

level. To reflect this in a practical way, this chapter is based on the assumption that household data are only available for one point in time. This limits the analysis in a number of ways. An analysis based on policy-on/policy-off comparisons is excluded. In general, the analysis must be more cautious in attributing causation. It only draws inferences from the data about the likely effects of policy change. The analysis presented here is meant to be a first cut at identifying poor groups, establishing their main socioeconomic characteristics, and assessing how they are likely to fare during a period of policy reform.

The next section is concerned with measures of welfare that can be readily derived from a typical household survey. Then follows a discussion of what is meant by poverty, and how it can be measured in a single index. The discussion then outlines a four-step methodology for tracing the first-order effects of a policy change. Higher-order effects are considered only briefly. After a review of the basic needs aspects, the chapter concludes with a short discussion of the dynamics of poverty.

Measuring welfare

Poverty exists in a society when some of its members fail to attain a level of well-being considered by that society to be a reasonable minimum standard. For policy purposes, it is important to measure the extent of poverty in society, to establish which groups are more prone to it, and to gain some understanding of its causes. The poverty profile seeks to do this. In setting about this task, three key questions must be resolved. First, what *measure of welfare* is to be adopted as a basis for poverty analysis? Second, how can we determine whether or not an individual is poor? Third, how do we aggregate the information on all individuals to obtain a measure of poverty that is in some sense representative of the distribution we are dealing with? Discussion of the latter two questions is taken up in the next section.

The main problem faced in analyzing individual (or household) welfare is that utility is never observed directly. Some counterpart to welfare is required that can be readily observed. A strong theoretical case can be made for using expenditure as our proxy for welfare.[2] Assume that individuals consume two broad classes of commodities—those that they purchase in product markets, and those that they produce themselves. For such individuals, the problem is to:

$$\text{Maximize } U(x_1, x_2)$$

$$\text{Subject to } p_1 x_1 \leq p_2(q_2 - x_2) + A - C \qquad (1)$$

where x_i represents vectors of market-purchased goods ($i = 1$) and the consumption of home-produced goods ($i = 2$), p_i is the corresponding prices, q_2 is a domestic output vector, A is other (exogenous) income, and C is total production input costs. The values of q_2 and C are pre-determined through the household's production (net-revenue-maximizing) decisions.[3]

The dual expression of (1) represents the individual's objective as minimizing expenditure subject to some utility constraint:

$$\text{Minimize } p_1 x_1 + p_2 x_2$$

$$\text{Subject to } U(x_1, x_2) \geq U^* \qquad (2)$$

where U^* is some minimum acceptable level of utility. Solving (2) gives the *expenditure function*:

$$E = E[(p_1 \, p_2), U^*] \qquad (3)$$

Expenditure is a monotonically increasing function of U^*, so that if all individuals share the same preferences (or utility function), and if they face the same prices (both explicit market prices and implicit own-production prices), the ranking of expenditures will be the same as the ranking of utilities. This is a sound theoretical justification for the use of expenditure as a proxy for utility in

poverty analysis. It is based on the assumption that individuals are utility maximizers, and that the main arguments of their welfare function are the commodities they consume.

The use of expenditure as an indicator of welfare also assumes that individuals face the same set of prices. In the real world, however, they may face different prices—of both purchased and own-produced commodities. In such cases, it is not valid to use nominal expenditure as a welfare indicator, because some variation in expenditures will be due to price differences. Thus, if we are comparing expenditures across regions, we must be careful to account for regional price variations in computing an expenditure variable to reflect relative welfare levels. To do this, we need to choose a reference region, and make cost of living comparisons with other regions. For deflating regional expenditures into the prices of the reference region, the Paasche cost of living index is suitable. The Paasche price index (I_p) for region 1 is given by,

$$I_{p1} = \frac{\sum_{i=1}^{n} (q_{1i} \, p_{1i})}{\sum_{i=1}^{n} (q_{1i} \, p_{0i})} \qquad (4)$$

where p_{0i} and p_{1i} are the prices of commodity i ($i = 1,...,n$) in the reference (0) and non-reference (1) regions respectively, and q_{1i} is the expenditures on commodity i in region 1. The index uses the non-reference region expenditures as weights to compute the regional price index. Alternatively, (4) may be written,

$$I_{p1} = \frac{\sum_{i=1}^{n} V_{1i}}{\sum_{i=1}^{n} V_{1i} \left(\dfrac{p_{0i}}{p_{1i}}\right)} \qquad (4a)$$

where V_{1i} is the value of expenditure in region 1 on commodity i. Using this index to deflate expenditures across regions will yield a Laspeyres real expenditure index, in which expenditures in each region are valued at the prices of the reference region. These computations will require a reliable data set on prices across regions in the country. Price data may be derived from a community survey or from other sources, and expenditures (used as quantity weights in the Paasche index) can be derived from the household survey itself.

If comparisons of expenditure are made over time, changes in the overall price level must be accounted for. Ideally, regional consumer price indices (CPIs) should be used for changes in prices over time, but these are rarely available. In practice, only a national CPI will be available. The use of this index is valid if there are no significant variations in the rate of inflation among the regions of the country.

Within this framework, a number of income- and expenditure-based indicators present themselves. Each will need to be computed from the raw data collected in the survey, since they are not obtained from the respondent in a directly usable form.[4] The following lists possible measures of welfare:

- Total household income
- Total household expenditure
- Per capita household income
- Per capita household expenditure
- Total household income per adult equivalent
- Total household expenditure per adult equivalent
- Per capita food consumption
- Proportion of household budget spent on food.

These measures do not always produce the same results, and so it is important for the analyst to be sure that the indicator selected is appropriate for the purpose at hand.[5] The debate over whether welfare is better measured by income or expenditure (discussed in Grootaert 1983) derives in part from the empirical problems encountered in measuring income through household surveys. In general, household surveys give expenditures in excess of income for many household groups, which raises questions about the reliability of the income estimates. Our suggestion is to adopt an *expenditure-based* welfare measure.[6] "Total expenditures" should be the sum of all monetary expenditures made by the household, consumption of own production, and the imputed value of services derived from the ownership of consumer durables and housing. Expenditure data must be corrected for regional price variations, using the Paasche or other suitable regional price indices.

Our main interest lies in individual welfare. But since most household surveys are designed to collect expenditures at the household level only, household-level indicators must be adjusted to reflect more accurately the well-being of the individuals within it. To account for differences in household size, total household expenditure should at least be measured on a *per capita* basis.

Alternatively (and preferably), *adult equivalence scales* should be used to take into account differences in the age and gender structure of households, though this will make analysis more complex (see Deaton and Muellbauer 1980, Chapter 8).

Adult equivalence scales are preferred because children are generally less demanding, in the sense that an additional child requires fewer additional expenditures to maintain household welfare than would an additional adult. Simply dividing total household expenditure by household size (the per capita measure) will give a misleading impression of welfare differences. For example, compare two households with the same level of total expenditure and of the same size, but with one comprising all adults and the other consisting of an equal number of adults and children. The household with the children will enjoy a higher level of welfare, simply because its child members do not require the consumption levels of adults.

Dividing total household expenditure by household size implicitly ascribes a weight of unity to all household members, irrespective of their age. In applying an adult equivalence scale, some members will be assigned a weight between zero and unity, depending on their age. Thus, a child between 13 and 17 might be given a weight of 0.5, implying that consumption requirements are approximately one-half those of an adult. Similarly, children under seven years of age might be assigned a weight of 0.2 on the adult equivalence scale. Thus, instead of dividing total expenditure simply by the number in the household, each household member is assigned a weight depending on age, and the sum of the weights is used to divide total expenditure. Since the procedure to construct adult equivalence scales is beyond the scope of this chapter, interested readers are directed to Deaton and Muellbauer (1986) and Ravallion (1992) for further details. The issue that analysts must face here is whether to use weights derived from external sources or to attempt their estimation using household data. In his analysis of welfare in Côte d'Ivoire, Glewwe (1987) uses weights derived from Sri Lanka and Indonesia. These are given as:

Age of child	Adult equivalence scale
< 7 years	0.2
7–12 years	0.3
13–17 years	0.5
≥ 18 years	1.0

Even if analysts have no opportunity to compute their own country-specific weights in the poverty profile, they may wish to use weights such as these, and compare the results with those using simple per capita expenditure.

These money-metric measures of welfare should be supplemented by other indicators, as we shall see. Our rationale for using an expenditure-based welfare indicator assumes that only commodities enter the welfare function. There is nothing in principle against including other elements in the welfare function, such as various basic needs that are not obtained through market purchases (such as health and education). The main problem arises in selecting shadow prices at which to value these services. Our preference is to treat education and health separately (Chapters 7 and 8, respectively). By the same token, some may argue that the welfare function of the poor does not consist of the commodities they consume, but of more fundamental quality-of-life determinants. For example, for many poor households, welfare may depend on whether there is sufficient food available, or whether children are sufficiently nourished. A case can be made for considering other indicators of poverty that may reflect this—such as food consumption or measures of nutrition. Lipton (1983) argues that the poverty line should be placed at the income level at which the income elasticity of demand for staple food is unity, on the premise that "ultra-poor" households will not experience declines in the share of their incomes spent on food. There are other arguments for focusing on food expenditures as the welfare indicator. Such expenditures are less susceptible to economies of scale (thus not requiring the use of adult equivalence), and are easier to measure accurately, since respondents tend to recall more clearly the frequently purchased items. Using food expenditures does not require any complex imputation of expenditures. Analysts may wish to adopt a food expenditure measure of welfare in addition to total expenditure, and compare the results.[7] These considerations are taken up in other chapters of this volume—especially Chapter 9 on food security and nutrition. Here we shall concentrate on total-expenditure-based welfare measures.

The nature and measurement of poverty

If the indicator of welfare is to be per capita or per adult equivalent household expenditure in most cases, this leaves a second key question: how can one determine the extent of poverty within the community? Data analysis must adopt measures of poverty that will be helpful in guiding policymakers and in making links between poverty and the main structural characteristics of the economy, which are themselves likely to be influenced by policy reforms. In any measure of poverty, two broad issues present themselves: the identification of the *poverty line* below which we consider an individual to be poor; and the choice of a *single aggregate index* to measure poverty in a given distribution.

The poverty line

Much of the literature on poverty has been concerned with the respective merits of absolute and relative concepts of poverty.[8] Recent work has questioned the usefulness of absolute poverty, since what constitutes poverty in one society (at one point of time) may not be the same for another society (or the same society at a different time). While Sen (1983) restates the "absolute" case, he retains much relativity. He distinguishes between the "capabilities" that incomes confer on individuals, and the goods and services needed to produce those capabilities. According to this view, poverty is the absolute absence of certain critical capabilities—such as self-respect, avoiding shame, and community participation. But the bundle of goods required to provide these capabilities varies from place to place and from time to time, and it is in this respect that poverty is relative. If the absolute aspect of poverty is ignored, as Sen (1983, p. 156) puts it, "poverty cannot—simply cannot—be eliminated and an anti-poverty programme can never really be quite successful."

This distinction between capabilities and the commodities needed to achieve them suggests that a poverty line (based on capabilities but measured in commodities) for an urban area might be quite different from a rural poverty line, since the commodities needed to achieve a given set of capabilities would be different in each case. For example, if the capability underlying the poverty concept is to engage in social interaction without shame, it is likely that a much larger bundle of nonfood commodities (in the form of clothing, housing, and transportation) would be required of urban populations than of rural populations. Thus, to achieve the same capability, the poverty line would be higher for urban than for rural areas. However, the use of separate poverty lines for different groups or regions in the country is not recommended given that the domain of study is the country as a whole. Such differences in poverty lines can lead to misleading results, especially if there are movements of individuals across groups. For example, if the rural poverty line is lower than the urban, the migration of a rural nonpoor individual to a higher paid job in the urban area might raise aggregate poverty in the country if the individual's new income level is below the urban poverty line. Thus, measured poverty will increase, even if the individual concerned is unambiguously better off. In generating a poverty profile, the analyst should use the poverty line *consistently* throughout the domain of analysis. In most cases, the domain is to be the country as a whole.

The debate on whether absolute or relative concepts are appropriate is really about the choice of *poverty line*, and this is certain to need further clarification at each country level. The analyst must decide at the outset whether the poverty line is determined in some absolute sense (either by policymakers themselves or based on other criteria, such as minimum nutrition levels), or in relation to the income distribution in general.

Calculating an *absolute* poverty line is usually fraught with both conceptual and empirical ambiguities. What is the minimum caloric intake and level of food consumption required to avoid malnutrition? What combinations of food items meet this caloric requirement? What is the corresponding income required to buy this food? What nonfood commodities should be considered as essential for the commodity basket that defines absolute poverty? These calculations will inevitably involve the personal judgment of the analyst, and a measure of arbitrariness. If an absolute poverty line is to be calculated and used, the assumptions on which it is calculated (the basket of goods on which it is based and the vector of prices that is used to translate this real bundle into income terms) must be made explicit. Should the poverty line be based entirely on nutritional requirements, there are obvious implications for the welfare indicator used. To be consistent with a nutritionally based poverty line, welfare must be measured only in terms of food consumption.

Ravallion (1992) has suggested a simple method of estimating an absolute poverty line in which both food and nonfood expenditures are incorporated.[9] Given a generally accepted *food energy requirement*, k^* (say, 2,100 calories per person per day), and the implied food expenditure needed to achieve this intake, there remains the problem of identifying the level of basic nonfood expenditure that should be included in the poverty line.

Ravallion sets out three stages for calculating an absolute poverty line that includes both food and nonfood items. In the first stage, a reference household is defined, this being a typical or average poor household. Since at this stage (that is, prior to the computation of the poverty line) we will not have precisely identified the poor, he suggests selecting the poorest 15-30 percent of households as a first approximation. The consumption patterns of this representative household will then be used to determine the poverty line.

In the second stage, the food expenditure component of the poverty line is calculated. An estimate is made of the food energy intake that is yielded by the food bundle consumed by members of the reference household. Given an actual food consumption vector of x^r and a vector of corresponding caloric values (k), actual food-energy consumption is given by $k^r = k.x^{r'}$. Comparing k^* with k^r gives the food-energy shortfall of individuals in this representative household. How much additional food expenditure is required to fill this gap? There are an infinite number of combinations of additional food items that could raise the food-nutrition intake to the required level. Ravallion recommends using the shares of individual food items in total food expenditure of the representative household. The additional food expenditure needed to cover the food-energy shortfall would comprise a bundle of food goods identical in composition to the observed food consumption bundle of this representative group. More formally, the food expenditure component of the poverty line, x^*, is derived by multiplying every element of x^r by the constant k^*/k^r.

It remains now to estimate the nonfood component of the absolute poverty line in the third stage. Given the conceptual difficulties of defining a basic bundle of nonfood goods, whatever method is selected is certain to be somewhat arbitrary. Ravallion suggests that an appropriate criterion for defining basic nonfood goods is the willingness of an individual or household to forgo food in order to obtain nonfood goods. He therefore defines the nonfood component of the poverty line as the value of nonfood spending by a typical poor household that is just capable of meeting food requirements.[10] Adding the food and nonfood requirements will yield an absolute poverty line. The information needed to compute such a line is generally available in household income and expenditure surveys.

Using an absolute poverty line (with its attendant value judgments) is best justified where there is already general agreement among planners and policymakers about it. Of course, the analyst should be encouraged to use alternative poverty lines, and make comparisons with results derived from the official line. In such cases, analysis should use the results of the household survey to cross-check the realism of the official poverty line. For example, if planners are using a poverty line that was originally computed some years previously, but that has been updated using, say, the consumer price index, it would be important to check whether the inflated poverty line is consistent in real terms with the poverty line as originally defined. The consumer price index may not be a reliable indicator of changes in the prices of the basket of commodities that originally determined the poverty line.

The ambiguities of an absolute poverty line, and its subjectivity and arbitrariness, have led many analysts to adopt an explicitly arbitrary *relative* poverty line. In some cases, poverty is defined as that income below which a certain percentile of the population is to be found. Thus, the poor may be defined as the poorest, say, 40 percent of the population.[11] The poverty line is that income below which 40 percent of the population are distributed at the time of the survey. Kanbur (1990) selects a poverty line that defines 30 percent of the population as being poor, and an alternative "hard-core" poverty line that places 10 percent of the population below it. This makes the selection of the poverty line arbitrary, but there is always an element of arbitrariness and subjectivity in deriving a poverty line, and such a procedure makes this explicit.

However, there are at least two drawbacks to this approach. First, the interpretation of the poverty line becomes extremely difficult—exactly what level of deprivation does a poverty line so generated imply? Are people suffering malnutrition below this line? Just what level of suffering is suggested? There is nothing in the procedure used to derive the line to provide answers to these questions. Some additional assessment may be needed to give the analyst and policymaker some impression of the extent of deprivation implied by the poverty line derived in this manner. A second drawback to this method is that it implies that poverty will always be with us—if the poorest 30 percent of the population are poor by definition, poverty will never be eradicated. And this was one of Sen's basic objections to an unqualified relativist approach to poverty. Kanbur (1990) avoids this by identifying the poverty line as that which gives 30 percent of the population as poor in the base year, and then retains this poverty line in an absolute sense for the analysis of later years.

Fortunately, there is an alternative relativist approach to the selection of the poverty line which does not suffer from these drawbacks (nor from the drawbacks of the absolutist procedure). This defines the poverty line in relation to *mean income* (or possibly median income). For example, the poverty line might be defined as a half of mean income—those individuals earning less than half the average income are considered poor. The extent of deprivation implied by such a benchmark is more readily appreciated than with the percentile approach, since the analyst and policymaker will have some grasp of the standard of living to be obtained from the mean income, and therefore from some specified proportion of it. Defining poverty in this way does not imply that poverty is never eradicated. It is possible for incomes to be distributed entirely above one-half of mean income.

To summarize, in calculating the poverty line one of three broad approaches should be considered, with the analyst possibly using (and comparing) more than one approach:

• *A relativist approach.* Where there is no universally accepted notion of the poverty line, the analysis should take the poverty line to bear some relation to mean income (say two-thirds or one-half of mean income). Given its relativist assumption, this poverty line may vary over time, depending on whether mean incomes rise or fall. This procedure yields measures of poverty that have no "absolutist" significance. Here the significance lies not so much in the absolute numbers in poverty, but in the *patterns* of poverty across the various groups in society.

• *An absolutist approach.* Analysts may wish to compute an absolute poverty line incorporating food and nonfood components, and based on the method discussed above. Alternatively, in countries where a particular poverty line is well understood and generally accepted as dividing the population into the poor and the non-poor, analysts should be encouraged to adopt it. This is particularly important if the threshold is accepted and used by planners and policymakers, since the findings of the analysis would gain in policy significance. The principle should be established that where a poverty line is currently in use among planners, it should be used in the poverty profile. The key point to note here is that in such cases, the absolute level of poverty will have some meaning—policymakers and planners will be interested in just how many households are below this level (see the annex to this chapter on the accuracy of poverty estimates). The advantage of the absolute approach is that the poverty indicator will be sensitive to the effects of increased growth in GDP, which policy reforms seek to achieve. Purely relativist approaches may not be as sensitive to these effects.

• *A pragmatic approach*. Here, the poverty line is selected in an arbitrary manner for any one year (using a percentile cutoff, or taking some ratio of mean income), and this line is retained in real terms throughout the analysis, including the analysis of later years. As with the first approach, the absolute level of poverty will not have significance—but the patterns of poverty across groups and changes over time will.

The poverty index

Having established which individuals are to be considered as poor, it now remains to aggregate this information into a single index of poverty. Apart from the selection of the poverty line itself, the degree of poverty will depend on three basic factors:

• The *incidence* of poverty, as measured by the numbers in the total population living below the poverty line

• The *intensity* of poverty, reflected in the extent to which the incomes of the poor lie below the poverty line

• The *severity* of poverty, which reflects the degree of inequality among the poor, in that transferring income to the poorest from the better-off poor should lower the poverty index.

Any measure of poverty should ideally reflect all three dimensions. For our purposes, we need an index that can be used to assess the effects of adjustment. Since adjustment frequently entails changing the sectoral composition of output—from nontraded to traded goods, from import-competing to exporting sectors, and favoring agriculture—our poverty index must be decomposable across sectors (Kanbur 1987).

A useful index that meets these requirements is suggested by Foster, Greer, and Thorbecke (1984). Their class of poverty index takes the following form,

$$P_\alpha = \frac{1}{n} \sum_{i=1}^{q} \left(\frac{Y_p - Y_i}{Y_p} \right)^\alpha \tag{5}$$

where Y_p denotes the poverty line, Y_i the income/expenditure of the ith poor person, n the total population, and q the number of income earners below the poverty line. Essentially, the index takes the poverty gap of each poor person as a fraction of the poverty line $(Y_p - Y_i)/Y_p$, raises it to a power, α, and sums over poor units. Not only does this index take into account the incidence and the intensity of poverty, for values of $\alpha > 1$ it is also sensitive to the degree of inequality among the poor.

This class of poverty measures is flexible in two important respects. First, α is a policy parameter that can be varied to reflect correctly poverty "aversion." If $\alpha = 0$, it can be readily shown that (5) simply becomes,

$$P_{\alpha=0} = \frac{q}{n} = H \tag{5a}$$

where H is the head-count ratio, that is, the proportion of total income-receiving units below the poverty line. Note that if $\alpha = 0$, it means that the measure is entirely indifferent to how poor each poor unit is—it does not matter how far below the poverty line each poor person is. Therefore, with $\alpha = 0$, the index is simply the *head-count ratio*.

Alternatively, with $\alpha = 1$, the poverty index becomes

$$P_{\alpha=1} = \frac{1}{n} \sum_{i=1}^{q} \left(\frac{Y_p - Y_i}{Y_p} \right) = H I \tag{5b}$$

where the "income gap ratio" (I) is given by

$$I = \frac{1}{q} \sum_{i=1}^{q} \left(\frac{Y_p - Y_i}{Y_p} \right)$$

I is simply the average of the poverty gaps expressed as a fraction of the poverty line. $P_{\alpha=1}$ or HI takes into account how poor on average the poor are, and reflects both the incidence of poverty (as reflected in H) and its intensity (as given by I). It can also be used to calculate the amount of income, under perfect targeting, that needs to be transferred to the poor in order to exactly eradicate poverty. However, the $P_{\alpha=1}$ measure is insensitive to income distribution among the poor. Transferring income from the poorest unit to a richer (but still poor) unit will leave $P_{\alpha=1}$ unchanged (as both H and I will be unaffected). For this to be reflected in the index, greater weight has to be given to the poorest income-earning units. This can be achieved in this class of poverty indices by assuming values of α in excess of unity. With $\alpha > 1$, a transfer of one dollar to the poorest units from other (better-off) poor units will decrease the poverty index. In short, the P_α indices suggested by Foster, Greer, and Thorbecke permit the user to specify α, and thereby select an index that reflects his or her aversion to poverty.

The P_α class of poverty indices is flexible also in that it is sub-group decomposable (Kanbur 1987). The "overall" index of poverty can be shown to comprise the summation of poverty indices among all the sub-groups in the population. If the study population consists of m groups or sectors, then

$$P_\alpha = \sum_{j=1}^{m} z_j \, P_{j,\alpha} \qquad (6)$$

where $P_{j,\alpha}$ is the poverty index of group j, and z_j the population weight of group j ($j = 1, \ldots, m$), $\Sigma z_j = 1$. As we shall discover, this decomposition property will prove useful in analyzing poverty changes, since it is possible to generate both overall indices in each country and indices for each of the regional and socioeconomic groupings under consideration.

Poverty and adjustment

We now come to an important part of the poverty profile: analysis of the interactions between the adjustment program and poverty. In most instances, data will not be available on changes in poverty—all the analyst may have initially are data across households at one point in time as given by a household survey. From these data, and from the analysis of the macro-meso interactions outlined in Chapter 2, links have to be established between adjustment (as it has taken place over the years preceding the survey) and poverty, as evidenced at the time of the survey. But before coming to the analysis proper, some thought needs to be given to the peculiar problems raised in having a data set (initially at least) for only one point in time.

The poor and the vulnerable

In deciding upon the broad domains of policy concern, two criteria are used: *poverty* and *vulnerability* (World Bank 1991b). A household is poor if its income (or total expenditure) falls short of the standard that society sets—the poverty line. A household is vulnerable if it is particularly open to adverse external events or shocks, and cannot make the necessary adjustments to protect its standard of living. While it is true that ultra-poor households are certain to be vulnerable because of their poverty, these are two quite distinct dimensions of need. Some households may be poor and not vulnerable, because they are not affected by external events (for example, subsistence farmers), or because they can readily cope with the changes (for example, production and consumption switching in the light of relative price movements). Others can be vulnerable but not poor, a case illustrated by retrenched public sector workers.

There are three broad groups of concern to policymakers in the period of adjustment.

• *The chronic poor*, whose situation is caused by multiple deprivations, such as low productivity due to poor health and nutrition, or poor access to productive assets. This poverty is deep-rooted, existing before the recent deterioration in economic circumstances and the implementation of adjustment programs. It includes the extremely poor or destitute. Some are vulnerable to recession and adjustment-related shocks, which may have increased their poverty further. Others in this group, however, may be relatively unaffected, while yet others may in fact benefit from adjustment.

• *The new poor*, who were above the poverty line before the shock and adjustment measures, but who have fallen into poverty as a result.

• *Other vulnerable groups* that remain above the poverty line but are severely affected by adjustment and so merit policy consideration.

The poverty profile is aimed particularly at the chronic and new poor groups. It does not attempt to cover non-poor groups that happen to be particularly vulnerable to external shocks and adjustment. With survey results available for only one year, it is difficult to distinguish between the chronic poor and the new poor, and to ensure that all the poverty effects of policy reform are covered in the analysis. For example, suppose that a household survey is conducted shortly after an adjustment program. To what extent can the poverty profile give an assessment of the poverty effects of adjustment? Three "poor" groups are of interest: the chronic poor who remain poor after the adjustment (some may have benefited from the policy reforms, but not enough to take them out of poverty); the poor who benefit from adjustment, but benefit sufficiently from the reforms to move out of poverty; and the new poor, who become poor as a result of the adjustment. The survey will fail to cover the second of these groups, and so will present a pessimistic picture of adjustment—it will be subject to a selectivity bias, giving greater weight to those who lose, and less weight to those who gain, from the adjustment.

Much will depend on the timing of the survey. If the survey is conducted before the adjustment program, its main purpose will be to forecast the likely effects of adjustment—both harmful and beneficial—rather than make an ex post assessment. In this way, it may give a more balanced assessment of the gainers and losers from the reforms.

The one-off nature of a household survey limits what can be gained from the analysis. It must be recognized that a poverty profile based on a survey following an adjustment program will be subject to selectivity bias, and might present a more pessimistic view of the poverty effects than is the case. Even if we are prepared to forgo coverage of the groups that have ceased to be poor because of the adjustment, we are still left with the difficulty of distinguishing between the chronic and the new poor. There may be cases that can be defined with some confidence, for example, poor smallholders/rural-landless are likely to be chronic poor, whereas poor civil servants—or former civil servants—are likely to be new poor. But other poor groups identified by the survey may or may not have been poor before adjustment.

An overall assessment

If the macro-meso links are reasonably well understood, and the real-economy effects of policy can be approximated in terms of changes in the growth of real output per capita, relative price changes, infrastructural changes, and differences in sectoral growth rates, the challenge of the data analysis now becomes one of linking what is observed at the household level with these sectoral changes. This will involve four basic stages in the analysis. First, socioeconomic groups will need to be identified into which all households are categorized. This may require regional categorization. Second, poverty indices should be computed for these regional and socioeconomic groupings. Third, analysis should establish the main primary income sources (by sector) of each of the groupings. Finally, each of the categories affected by adjustment policy should be assessed.

STEP 1: DEFINING SOCIOECONOMIC GROUPS. The classification of households by socioeconomic group constitutes an essential element in all chapters in this book but especially in the priority analysis (see Chapter 3) and in this poverty profile. The issues raised in selecting socioeconomic classifications are considered in World Bank (1991b). Some of these considerations are repeated here in brief. Any number of criteria might be used to establish the classification of socioeconomic groups, but the basic requirements of a useful criterion are that it should be unambiguous and have a clear policy focus. Apart from the obvious importance of policy targeting, classifications should be selected so that households within them are reasonably homogeneous in the ways they are affected by (and respond to) adjustment policy. Since households are most often multi-individual units, a classification should be chosen that is applicable to all individuals in a given household or, alternatively, to the household as a whole; otherwise, the fundamental notion of the household being a "unit" is lost.

A broad set of criteria have been used for classifying households, including wealth, income, or expenditure (economic criteria); sociology; location; and characteristics of household head:[12]

• *Wealth, income, or expenditure.* Wealth is a fundamental factor affecting household behavior. In rural areas, access to land is critical. Landless or near-landless households can be affected differently from the smallholder by adjustment policy. Among the relatively poor, those with some assets might be distinguished from those who have none. Wealth, as with income or expenditure, has the advantage of being a household-level criterion. However, the use of income, expenditure, and, to some extent, wealth as classifiers suffers from a major drawback in that, according to any of these criteria, a household's relative position, and hence its classification, might change over time or as a result of policy intervention. For instance, the mobility of households between income deciles makes total income a poor classifier for targeting policy on particular households. The wealth criterion is more effective because households are relatively less mobile between wealth groups in the short or medium run.

• *Sociology.* These criteria include a range of factors such as race, religion, or language, and assume significance in African societies where market fragmentation or even ethnic discrimination might be a common characteristic of the majority of the poor.

• *Location.* Location is usually justified on the grounds that policy often has a locational element. Rural households need to be distinguished from urban households but, even beyond this, there is a strong spatial dimension in the way policy effects are transmitted through markets and infrastructure. Thus, it might be important to use an even finer locational division for the purpose of classifying household groups and to capture the regional effects directly. However, administrative boundaries rarely make analytical sense.

• *Characteristics of the household head.* The socioeconomic characteristics of the household head (such as occupation or employment status) are often used as criteria for classifying households. In doing so, one implicitly assumes that the behavior and level of well-being of all individuals in the household can be determined or adequately represented by the status of the head. However, the economic status of the household might be determined by the characteristics of the main earner, who need not be the household head. So this criterion has to be used with much care in its practical application (see Rosenhouse 1989).

In Sub-Saharan Africa, an indication of some broad categories of socioeconomic groups that might figure in a number of taxonomies is as follows:

Rural sector
• Export-oriented medium-size and large farmers
• Export-oriented smallholders
• Food/subsistence farmers
• Pastoralists
• Landless (or near-landless) agricultural workers
• Non-agricultural workers.

Urban sector
• Government employees (skilled)
• Government employees (unskilled)
• Private/formal sector employees
• Private/formal sector employers
• Informal sector self-employed
• Inactive or unemployed.

This classification may be refined by distinguishing between the capital city and other urban areas. The primacy of the capital city, which often makes it significantly different from other urban centers, suggests that this distinction is important in data analysis. If possible, the selection of socioeconomic groups should bear some relation to the structural changes brought about by adjustment. For example, as macro-meso analysis distinguishes between a number of sectors, it would be useful for the selection of socioeconomic categories to use this sectoral disaggregation. However, this

may lead to a serious problem of empty cells. Too detailed a disaggregation of socioeconomic groups might lead to small numbers appearing in the cells, given the relatively small sample usually contemplated for household surveys.

The selection of socioeconomic categories must be country-specific. It must reflect the specific characteristics of the country, and the policy priorities of the government. Policymakers must be fully consulted before the socioeconomic classification of households is finalized. The purpose of the classification is twofold: it makes the data analysis more manageable, and it enhances the ability of governments to design policies that can assist the groups in a targeted way. Because the poorest x percentile in most developing countries of Africa is heterogeneous, income distribution data in themselves are generally unhelpful for practical policy design. Casting the analysis in terms of readily identifiable socioeconomic groups makes it more policy-relevant. Box 4.1 outlines how a simple analysis of variance can provide some insight into the usefulness of the socioeconomic grouping selected.

STEP 2: P_α COMPUTATIONS. Once the regional and socioeconomic classifications of households are decided on, the analysis proper may begin. We suggest at the minimum that computations be made of the P_α indices (based on total household expenditure per capita or per adult equivalent) for $\alpha = 0, 1, 2$ (or 1.5). These should be computed for the country as a whole, for the regions of the country, and separately for each socioeconomic category. Any estimate based on cells in which the number of observations is less than 30 should be explicitly identified. Estimates should be reported for a number of poverty lines (for example, two lines representing one-half and two-thirds of mean per capita income, or giving 30 percent and 10 percent of the population as poor). Frame 4.1 provides an example of the basic type of tabulation that should be prepared under the poverty profile, taking a percentile approach to defining the poverty line.[13]

Before we discuss the inferences that can be drawn from such findings, it may be helpful to establish exactly what the figures reported in Frame 4.1 mean. Because all the P_α measures take the poverty gap as a proportion of the poverty line, they are all in the range of 0 and 1. As α increases, P_α becomes smaller, so that $P_{\alpha-1} > P_\alpha$. Beginning with the simplest case where $\alpha = 0$, the poverty index is simply the head-count ratio (H). In 1985,

$P_{\alpha=0}$ was equal to 0.30 for Côte d'Ivoire as a whole, which means that 30 percent of the total population of the country was poor. Similarly (reading down the first column under $P_{\alpha=0}$), nearly 50 percent of food crop farmers and only 3 percent of government employees were poor. Analysts should note that the n and q (and of course Y_i) values are different for each group. So in the calculation of group poverty indexes, q is the number of poor in the group, and n is the population of the group.

To decompose the total poverty index across the sectors, each sectoral poverty index is multiplied by its population weight (z_i), and this value is expressed as a proportion of the poverty index for the population as a whole. For example, for export farmers, the computations are:

$$(P_{\alpha=0,\,export})(z_i) / P_{\alpha=0,\,overall} = \text{contribution}$$

$$(0.365)(0.186)/0.30 = 0.223 \text{ (or 22.3\%)}$$

The population of export farmers comprises 18.6 percent of the total population of Côte d'Ivoire, so that with $P_{\alpha=0}$ for export farmers being 36.5 percent and for the country as a whole, 30 percent, the contribution of export farmers' poverty to aggregate poverty (with $P_{\alpha=0}$) is 22.3 percent. For $\alpha = 0$,

the interpretation of this is very straightforward. It means that 22.3 percent of the poor are found among export farmers. Decomposing poverty across the various groups (given in the second column under $P_{\alpha=0}$) tells us, for example, that only 1.9 percent of the total poor in the country were formal sector employees, while 59 percent were food producers.

The interpretation of $P_{\alpha=1}$ is a little more complicated, but nevertheless an intuitive explanation is possible. With $\alpha = 1$, P_{α} equals HI, where I is the income gap ratio. Recalling equation (5b), it is clear that I is also somewhere between 0 and 1. It is the poverty gap as a proportion of the poverty line, averaged across all poor units. Since both H and I are in the range 0 to 1, $P_{\alpha=1}$ (which equals HI) is also in this range. It also follows that $H > HI$, or $P_{\alpha=0} > P_{\alpha=1}$. For example, reading Frame 4.1, we can derive the income gap ratio (I) simply by dividing $P_{\alpha=1}$ by $P_{\alpha=0}$ (or H). For the country as a whole, since $P_{\alpha=1} = 0.10$, it follows that I is given by

$$I = HI/H = P_{\alpha=1}/P_{\alpha=0} = 0.10/0.30 = 0.33$$

It remains now to explain intuitively what I and HI really mean. With $I = 0.33$, the gap between the poverty line and the average income of the poor is 33 percent (or one-third) of the poverty line. Since

---

Box 4.1: Assessing the groupings

The key to selecting socioeconomic groups lies in some measure of homogeneity within the group. In this way, households within a group can be assumed to be affected by adjustment (and to respond to it) in a similar way. To check whether the selected grouping is meaningful, the analyst may assess the extent to which it explains how incomes are distributed across households. Income variance, of course, does not prove homogeneity within the groupings, but it can be interpreted as a useful indicator of it. A simple method for this test would be to decompose the total variance in income (or expenditure) into two broad components—the variance in incomes *between* and *within* groups. The greater the proportion of overall income variance explained by between-group variance, the more successful is the grouping in capturing income variations. The overall variance (σ^2) in income can be decomposed as follows:

$$\sigma^2 = \sum_{j=1}^{m} z_j \sigma_j^2 + \sum_{j=1}^{m} z_j (\mu_j - \mu)^2 \qquad (7)$$

within-	between-
group	group
variance	variance

where σ_j^2 is the variance in income within group j, μ is the overall mean income, μ_j is the mean income of group j, and z_j is the population weight of each group (recalling that $\Sigma z_j = 1$).

The objective of the grouping exercise would be to maximize the second term on the right-hand side of (7), so that as much of the overall variance in incomes/expenditures is explained by the grouping selected. If the between-group variance explains only a small proportion of overall variance (say, on the order of only 20 percent), the analyst must inspect the within-group variance for each group, to identify groups in which income variance is high (and which contribute significantly to overall variance). If the income/expenditure variance within a group is found to explain a significant proportion of the overall variance (as compared with the contributions of other sectors), this suggests that the group is not sufficiently homogeneous for analytical purposes.

The analyst may consider subdividing the group further to enhance homogeneity. The more groups that are distinguished, the greater the explanatory power of the grouping. The decision of when to stop further disaggregation and use the proportion of variance explained by the grouping has to be a judgment for the analyst.

Frame 4.1: Decomposition of P_α poverty measures by socioeconomic group, Côte d'Ivoire, 1985 (30 percent cutoff

Socioeconomic group	$P_{\alpha=0}$ Value	$P_{\alpha=0}$ Contribution (percent)	$P_{\alpha=1}$ Value	$P_{\alpha=1}$ Contribution (percent)	$P_{\alpha=2}$ Value	$P_{\alpha=2}$ Contribution (percent)
Export farmers	0.365	22.3	0.114	20.4	0.050	18.8
Food producers	0.495	59.0	0.184	64.1	0.090	65.9
Formal employees, government	0.031	1.3	0.002	0.2	0.0002	0.1
Formal employees, private	0.061	1.9	0.009	0.8	0.003	0.6
Informal sector	0.193	15.5	0.062	14.5	0.030	14.6
All	0.301	100.0	0.103	100.0	0.049	100.0

Note: Based on a poverty line giving 30 percent of the population as poor.
Source: Kanbur 1990.

$$(Y_i/Y_p) = 1 - (Y_i - Y_p)/Y_p$$

it follows that the average income of the poor is two-thirds (given by $1 - 0.33 = 0.67$) of the poverty line. Values of I for each of the groups may also be computed and interpreted in this way. For example, the income gap ratio for food producers was 0.372 ($= 0.065/0.495$), and for government employees it was 0.065 ($= 0.002/0.031$). This means that, on average, the incomes of poor food producers are 62.8 percent ($= 1 - 0.372$) of the poverty line, while those of poor government employees are 93.3 percent ($= 1 - 0.065$) of the poverty line. This highlights the extra information that is provided with $\alpha = 1$. We not only know that the incidence of poverty is greater among food producers than, say, government employees (through the headcount ratio), but also that the intensity of their poverty is greater.

Recalling equation (5b), it is clear that $P_{\alpha=1}$ or HI sums the gaps between each poor person's income and the poverty line, and divides by the total population. It is sometimes referred to as the "per capita aggregate poverty gap." This can be used to calculate the amount of income in per capita terms that is necessary (under perfect targeting) to exactly eradicate poverty. It shows that if every member of the population contributed 10.3 percent of the poverty line, there would be just enough to bring all poor people to the poverty line. Similarly, if all food producers contributed 18.4 percent of the poverty line, there would be enough to bring all food producers up to the poverty line. Government employees would only need to contribute, on average, 0.2 percent to exactly eradicate poverty among their colleagues. As with $P_{\alpha=0}$, the $P_{\alpha=1}$ index can be decomposed across sectors. This shows how the aggregate per capita poverty

gap is distributed across the groups. Of the resources needed to eradicate poverty (this being 10.3 percent of the poverty line in per capita terms), 64.1 percent would go to food producers, only 0.2 percent to government employees, and so on.

With $\alpha > 1$, no such straightforward intuitive interpretation is available, since the index now gives greater weight to the poorest groups. However, the principles are the same. The first column under $P_{\alpha=2}$ gives the index computed for each sector separately, and the second column reports the decomposition of the aggregate index across the groups. As with the other indexes, the group indexes are computed for group-specific values of n, q, and Y_i, and the decomposition applies population weights to the group values to generate contributions to overall poverty.

We turn now to review some of the implications of these findings. Frame 4.1 shows the usefulness of the decomposition property of P_α in understanding how poverty is affected by adjustment. Assuming that it is known how the various groups are affected by adjustment (a subject to which we return shortly), a great deal of information can be derived from a simple table such as this. Taking the incidence of poverty first ($\alpha = 0$ in Frame 4.1), clearly the poor are to be found mainly among food producers (a sector containing 59 percent of the total poor in Côte d'Ivoire). Of the poor, 22.3 percent are export farmers and 15.5 percent work in the urban informal sector (or are unemployed). Poverty is hardly present among formal sector employees. Notice that the contribution to poverty of food producers rises (from 59 percent to 65.9 percent) as higher values of α are taken. Higher values of α mean that greater weight is being given to the poorest groups. This suggests that a relatively large proportion of food producers are among the poorest of the poor. If greater weight is to be given to those in the extremes of poverty (that is, taking $\alpha = 2$), almost two-thirds of measured poverty in Côte d'Ivoire in 1985 is endured by food producers.

Frame 4.1 can be readily extended to include regions of the country. Tabulations that report poverty by both socioeconomic group and region will be particularly useful to policymakers. In the case of Côte d'Ivoire, it is essential to establish where the poor export crop producers are to be found. A tabulation such as Frame 4.2 can readily provide this information. Most of the poor export crop producers are located in the Savannah region, and these are mainly cotton producers. The table shows that the most poor food crop producers and informal sector workers are to be found in the Savannah region. Such two-way tabulations can be extremely helpful to policymakers, and can be computed for other values of α (Frame 4.2 is computed for $\alpha = 0$).

The rank ordering of socioeconomic groups according to their poverty status is the key to most policy analysis. As we have already emphasized, where the poverty line is explicitly arbitrary, it is the pattern of poverty across groups in society that is important. Two issues arise in interpreting the differences and orderings of poverty between groups. First, are these differences statistically significant? One region may have higher measured poverty than another, but this may simply be due to chance, so that repeated surveys might not give the same result. Differences between head-count indices of poverty can be tested in the same way as for any other sample *proportion*. For other poverty indices, the standard error is more complex. However, Kakwani (1990b) has derived a formula for the standard error of P_α as $\sqrt{\{(P_{2\alpha} -$

$P_\alpha^2)/n\}}$. By applying these standard errors to obtain confidence intervals for poverty indices for each group, the analyst can determine whether differences in poverty between the groups are statistically significant.

The second issue concerns the robustness of the poverty orderings. In the example from Côte d'Ivoire, these remain the same, regardless of the value of α chosen.[14] But this need not always be the case. It is possible that changing the poverty index, or changing the poverty line, will yield different rank orderings. To what extent can we be confident that the poverty orderings obtained with the P_α class of indices would also apply if another poverty line were chosen, or if another index of poverty were adopted? An assessment may be made of this through the use of *dominance conditions*.[15] This test involves comparing the cumulative distributions of income/expenditure up to some maximum poverty line of all pairs of socioeconomic categories that are distinguished. Thus, if the cumulative income distribution of one socioeconomic group (say, group A) lies nowhere below that of another (group B), then poverty can be said to be unambiguously greater in group A than group B. This is called first-order dominance.[16] It means that for all admissible poverty lines (that is, for all lines below the stipulated maximum poverty line), poverty in group A will be greater than in group B regardless of the choice of poverty measure.[17] This dominance test could be applied to all pairs of socioeconomic groups. In most cases, the test should prove conclusive, and the ordering obtained with the P_α index can be considered robust. But where the test is not conclusive, the P_α orderings should be suitably qualified.

STEP 3: IDENTIFYING PRIMARY INCOME SOURCES. The analysis thus far is based on fairly aggregative classifications of households. Insofar as it is based on income sources, it relies only on the main occupation of the household head or on the principal crop grown. There are two main problems with this type of analysis if some judgments are to be made about how adjustment is likely to affect the poor. First, a greater degree of disaggregation is usually required for policy analysis. For example, "export crop producers" should be further disaggregated into cocoa, coffee, and cotton producers, since adjustment policy is likely to affect each differently. But such disaggregations often lead to small-cell problems, given the relatively small sample size of most surveys. The socioeco-

Frame 4.2: Incidence of poverty by region and socioeconomic group, Côte d'Ivoire, 1985 (30 percent cutoff)

(percent)

Socioeconomic group	Abidjan	Other urban	West forest	East forest	Savannah	All
Export crop farmers	-	-	15.4	39.3	79.7	36.5
Food crop farmers	-	-	24.1	53.3	60.6	49.5
Formal, government	1.2	3.0	0.0	8.3	19.4	3.1
Formal, private	2.6	6.7	43.8	79.2	0.0	6.1
Informal	9.5	19.1	26.1	58.2	71.7	19.3
All	5.2	13.1	21.1	45.9	61.3	30.1

Source: Kanbur 1990.

nomic classification can be based only on the main occupation of the household head or the main crops grown. It acts only as a rough guide to the income source of the household concerned. During times of adjustment, it may be a very weak guide indeed, for two reasons: the household head may increasingly engage in multiple occupations (or diversify output) to cope with deteriorating economic circumstances—the main occupation may be one of a number; and other household members are usually engaged in different occupations (or grow other crops), and may in fact contribute more to total household income than does the household head. For these reasons, it is necessary to trace the income sources of poor households in more detail.

Information on sources of income, including farm and non-farm enterprise income, wage income, and other income sources (such as rental income and income transfers) is probably useful. From these computations, tabulations can readily be prepared to trace the main sources of income of poor households. Frame 4.3 reports the type of tabulation required for this, while Box 4.2 provides an illustration based on Côte d'Ivoire data. From such a table, one can check whether the income source of the household head (or the main crop produced) is a useful indicator of the main source of income of the household. For example, we can assess whether a household in which the head is employed, say, in the public sector also receives most of its income from that sector—or whether the household (both the head, through other occupations, and other household members) earns significant income from other activities. This is critical from a policy perspective. It would be misleading to draw the conclusion that a poor household whose head works for the government will lose out from public sector wage freezes if that household is also engaged in activities likely to become more profitable (say, wage income from employment in export manufacturing). Similarly, it would be essential to establish how much other income sources are tapped by agricultural producers. Frame 4.3 should be computed for poor and non-poor households separately, since income sources among the poor may differ from those of the non-poor within each socioeconomic group.

These data are helpful in identifying the diversity of income sources of the household. However, we need to establish how different socioeconomic groups are affected by adjustment. So it would be

Box 4.2: Income sources: An illustration

As an illustration of the type of tabulation suggested by Frames 4.3 and 4.4, the following is based on the results of the LSMS survey in Côte d'Ivoire, 1985.

Sources of income for various groups, Côte d'Ivoire, 1985
(percent)

		Farm households		
Income source	All households	All	Large	Small
Cocoa	7.0	14.7	22.0	3.5
Coffee	3.6	7.6	10.6	2.9
Other crop	5.2	11.0	11.0	10.9
Home-produced food	13.6	28.4	30.2	25.7
Livestock	1.0	2.1	2.3	1.7
Other farm income	0.4	0.8	1.3	0.0
(Total agricultural income)	(30.8)	(64.6)	(77.4)	(44.8)
Wage income	34.5	11.6	5.9	20.3
Rents, dividends, interest	13.8	9.0	6.9	12.6
Net transfer income	-0.4	-0.8	-1.1	-0.5
Net business income	19.8	14.0	9.3	21.0
Consumer durable services	2.5	1.7	1.6	1.7
(Non-agricultural income)	(69.2)	(35.4)	(22.6)	(55.2)
Total	100	100	100	100
Mean monthly income (CFA Fr. '000)	1,580.4	1,145.9	1,440.8	870.0

Note: The bottom row gives the mean values of income, which is important in judging how the various groups compare. Large farmers in Côte d'Ivoire earn only 72 percent of average income. Small farmers earn less (55 percent). Reading down the columns shows the diversity of income sources among groups; note how smaller farmers are more diversified —earning more than half their income from non-agricultural sources. Notice the importance of home-produced food in most household incomes.
Source: Derived from Deaton and Benjamin 1988, p. 34.

helpful to trace the sector of origin of income earned by the various groups. For this, we need only be concerned with primary income—income earned from productive work. Frame 4.4 presents the type of tabulation required for this. The disaggregation of the productive sectors is designed to separate tradable from nontradable, exportable from importable, protected importable from other importable, and government from private nontradable.

STEP 4: AN ASSESSMENT OF THE EFFECTS OF POLICY REFORM. Having prepared these basic tables, the analyst must now attempt to interpret them, and to make some judgment about how the poverty groups so identified have been affected by policy reforms. This analysis should proceed in two

Frame 4.3: Sources of income by socioeconomic group

Socioeconomic group		Percentage of total income by income source					
	Wage	Agricultural enterprise	Non-farm enterprise	Rent	Transfers	All
Export crop farmers							100
Food crop farmers							100
Formal, government							100
Formal, private							100
Informal							100
All							100

stages. The first is conducted at the group level, and seeks to identify how each socioeconomic group has been affected by adjustment. The second delves into the issue of within-group differences, concentrating on groups in which most of the poor are found (as evidenced by Frame 4.1).

Group-level analysis. There are two main questions:

• Are the poor engaged in economic activities that are favored by the policy changes?

• Are the poor able to respond to the incentives offered?

The first deals with the current activities of poor households. To answer this question, the analyst has to relate the findings of Frames 4.3 and 4.4 to the results of the macro-meso analysis discussed in Chapter 2. At the time of the survey, were the poor engaged in activities that are likely to expand as a result of policy reforms? Were poor households deriving their incomes mainly from tradables rather than nontradables, exportables rather than importables, and non-protected importables rather than protected importables? If the poor are to be found mainly among food producers, for example,

reading across the appropriate rows in Frames 4.3 and 4.4 will reveal whether this group is engaged in activities in which returns are likely to increase as a result of policy reforms. It may be that a non-trivial proportion of the incomes of food producers is gained from wage income (as evidenced in Frame 4.3), which means that such groups might be influenced in two broad ways by the adjustment. They are affected as food producers by the effects of policy reform on food markets (which may or may not be favorable, depending on whether food is a tradable commodity). They are also affected as suppliers of labor. The likely effect on the latter will depend on the direction of change in the real wage and on employment opportunities (see Chapter 5).

This analysis provides only a static picture of the implications of adjustment for poverty in the country. The analyst must make some judgment about how poor households are likely to respond to the costs and opportunities associated with policy reforms. Some households may be producing types of commodities favored by adjustment, but may not be able to raise production, or may not have access to market opportunities. Simi-

Frame 4.4: Share of poor household primary income by socioeconomic group and sector of origin
(percent)

Socioeconomic group	Sector								
	Tradables					Nontradables			
	Agriculture		Manufacturing						
	Export crop	Food crop	Exportable	Protected importable	Other	Construction	Government	Other	Total
Export crop farmers									100
Food crop farmers									100
Formal, government									100
Formal, private									100
Informal									100

larly, households may be producing products that are not favored, so for them the critical question is whether they can make the necessary adjustments to move into favored product lines.

To get some idea of this at the group level, the analysis should assess the access of these groups to *productive assets*, on the assumption that this will reflect the ability of households to realize the potential gains offered by adjustment. If households hold key productive assets (such as productive land, livestock, farm equipment, tools, labor) and if they have ready access to important inputs (such as fertilizer, extension services, irrigation/water, and credit), it is more likely that they can respond positively to adjustment. Frame 4.5 illustrates two types of data that are obtained through household surveys. The first concerns the amount of credit actually obtained by the household; the second concerns difficulties in obtaining credit. Whichever approach is adopted, the tabulation should uncover any significant problem encountered by socioeconomic groups in obtaining credit, and should establish whether poorer households experience greater difficulties (in this case, in obtaining credit) than other households in the same socioeconomic group. If this is the case, the analysis would suggest that the adjustment program incentives may not be sufficient to raise incomes among the poor (even though non-poor households in the same socioeconomic group seem likely to benefit). This would indicate that adjustment policies need to be complemented with credit-market interventions to assist poorer households in gaining credit.

Within-group analysis. Tabulations of the sort described have two limitations. The first is that they aggregate across households within groups. In most cases they describe group means, and do not give any impression of significant variations

Frame 4.5: Access to credit by socioeconomic group

(percentage of households obtaining credit over past year or percentage of households unable to obtain credit over past year)

Socioeconomic group	Poor households	Non-poor households	All
Export crop farmers			
Food crop farmers			
Formal, government			
Formal, private			
Informal			
All			

within the group. In effect, the analysis has assumed that within-group variations in incomes do not change in response to policy change. This permitted us to use group means as the basis of our analysis. The groupings were selected to reveal the major effects of adjustment through their influence on between-group differences. As tabulations, they can only take into account a limited number of influences.

The analysis should accordingly be taken one stage further, through within-group multivariate analysis. In this way we can investigate whether adjustment is likely to influence the within-group variations in expenditure, which were deliberately suppressed in the between-group analysis. For example, assume that adjustment favorably influences export farmers as a group so that, other things being equal, the mean income of this group will rise. Does this necessarily mean that poverty will be reduced? This depends on whether within-group variations in income change at the same time. If income variance remains unchanged (or is reduced), poverty will fall. But if within-group variance actually rises as a result of adjustment (for example, through a reduced access of poorer export farmers to credit), there can be no presumption that poverty will be reduced. This is why some analysis of the within-group variation in income/expenditure is a necessary component of the poverty profile.

The dependent variable for the multivariate analysis should be the same as that selected in computing the poverty index—taken in our case to be per capita total household expenditure. We specify the following general estimation equation for within-group analysis:

$$Y = Y [X, A, R, F, E] \qquad (8)$$

Per capita total household expenditure (Y) is assumed to depend upon five broad groups of regressors: household characteristics (X), asset holdings (A), a vector of relevant price variables (R), a vector of factor price variables (F) covering labor and credit prices, and a vector of appropriate infrastructural or environmental variables (E), such as access to roads, education/health services, credit, and so on. Equation (8) is a reduced form of an implicit structural model in which income/expenditure of the household is viewed as the outcome of a decisionmaking process. The household is assumed to maximize utility and net income, subject to its resource constraints. This process depends on its characteristics and asset holdings, and on the market opportunities it faces. As a result of these decisions, there will be significant differences between households in the ways in which they generate incomes. Some households possessing productive assets will rely on family enterprises. Others, having only their labor, will depend mainly on wage income. These differences formed the basis of the socioeconomic grouping.

The reduced form will obviously depend on the income-earning opportunities facing households. As a producing unit (operating either an agricultural or a non-farm enterprise), a household's income will depend on its productivity, which depends on its holdings of non-labor assets. It will also be determined by the costs of purchased inputs (such as labor and fertilizer). But households relying on wage labor will find that real-wage rates and their human capital assets have a critical influence on income. Therefore, the specification of (8) will differ according to the source of income of the household. So the reduced form should be estimated separately for each socioeconomic group, since we expect to obtain different coefficient estimates in each case. It may not be necessary to investigate expenditure variations within groups where few poor households are to be found. From Frame 4.1, for example, there would seem to be little point in investigating within-group variations among government employees, since only 3 percent of such households were poor, and poverty among them represented only 0.2 percent of total poverty (with $\alpha = 1$). Within-group analysis, however, would be fruitful for export crop farmers, food producers, and informal sector workers.

This exercise establishes which of the right-hand-side variables significantly influence per capita total household expenditure. In this way, it will establish which factors determine variations in income/expenditure within the group. For example, are export crop households poor because of their location, small landholdings, crop mixes, low levels of education, high dependency rates, use of and access to inputs or credit, access to markets, and so on? Having established the most important determinants of income/expenditure variation, we can understand why some households in the group are poorer than others, and whether such factors are likely to be affected by policy reform. Some of the right-hand-side variables (such as land size or dependency rates) are unlikely to be influenced by adjustment policy; others (such as market access, or credit) may be

significantly influenced by policy reforms. In this way, a more complete picture of the implications of adjustment for poverty can be gained. Box 4.3 illustrates some of the issues that arise in estimating the reduced-form (8).

Selective price interventions

The analysis thus far will have established the poverty effects of the adjustment through its general repercussions on the structure of the economy. The level of disaggregation feasible for this part of the data analysis will be circumscribed by the detail available on the mesoeconomic effects of the adjustment. In many cases, however, adjustment will also entail the deliberate manipulation of key prices, through changes in tax and subsidy policy. This may be to achieve an improvement in resource allocation, by taking a domestic price nearer to the border price, or to reduce the fiscal deficit. For whatever reason, the analysis of the poverty effects of an adjustment program is likely to be called upon to assess the effects of specific price changes.

The commodities selected for this more detailed analysis are inevitably country-specific, and will depend on which prices are likely to be manipulated by the government and for which reason. The first (and obvious) point is that data analysis must take into account the effects on the poor as both consumers and producers of the commodity in question. Household data can establish, in the first place, which groups of households produce and consume the commodity. Without this critical information it would be impossible to make any poverty assessment. We shall present two frames to illustrate the types of tabulation useful for these policy issues, dealing with the effects on the poor as consumers and producers.

Frame 4.6 reports expenditure patterns by a fairly broad category of expenditure. It distinguishes between food and nonfood consumption, each reported separately for market purchases and home-produced consumption. Other items are remittances paid out and expenditure relating to employment income in kind. Each cell in the table contains two entries. The top right-hand entry reports a column percentage, while the bottom left-hand entry is a row percentage. Thus, poor households spend 36.1 percent of their total expenditures on market purchases of food, but their purchases amount to only 14.1 percent of total market purchases of food.

A key point emphasized by Besley and Kanbur (1988) is that when governments seek to raise taxes or lower subsidies to reduce the fiscal deficit, it is more policy-relevant to consider the effects on poverty *per unit of deficit reduction*. This has implications for how a table such as Frame 4.6 is used. For this, the relevant share is not the proportion of the income of the poor spent on the commodity in question, but the fraction of total consumption in the economy accounted for by the poor. If the government were considering subsidizing the price of food to raise the real incomes of the poor, the relevant ratio is not that the poor spend 36.1 percent of their total expenditure on market purchases of food, but that their purchases represent only 14.1 percent of total market purchases. So, of one dollar spent in subsidizing food, only 14 cents would benefit the poor. Clearly, Frame 4.6 should be computed at a higher level of disaggregation and should identify most food commodities, and any commodities subject to tax/subsidy policy review under structural adjustment.

Similarly, price policy can have a profound effect on households as producers of the commodity in question. The poverty profile ought to present basic tabulations that can give initial guidance to the policymaker on this issue. Frame 4.7 gives an idea of the sort of tabulation needed. The interpretation of this table is similar to Frame 4.6. Ghana's most important export crop is cocoa. Of the total revenue

---

Box 4.3: Explaining household welfare: The two-stage least squares approach

Some of the issues raised in estimating equation (8) are illustrated in an analysis of household welfare in Côte d'Ivoire by Paul Glewwe (1991). Glewwe does not estimate the expenditure reduced form separately for each socioeconomic group as suggested in the text. However, he does estimate reduced forms similar to equation (8) for urban and rural areas separately (his methodology requires that relative prices do not differ widely across households).

The data: The 1985 Côte d'Ivoire Living Standards Survey.

The dependent variable: Household expenditure is defined to include explicit expenditures on food and non-food items, the value of food produced and consumed by the household, and the imputed use value of housing and consumer durables owned by the household. Glewwe uses the Tornqvist price index to correct for differences in price levels across regions, this being defined as:

$$I_j = \exp\left[\sum_{i=1}^{n} W_i \log\left(\frac{P_i^j}{P_i}\right)\right]$$

where W_i is the national expenditure share for good i, P_i is its average price, and P_i^j is the average price of good i in region j.

The independent variables: For the rural analysis that we report here, these were divided into four groups: human capital (age and education of most educated person in household); household assets (home ownership, land used, agricultural and non-farm business assets, livestock, savings); household characteristics (ethnicity of household head, region of residence, age and sex composition of the household); and community characteristics (rural wage, and nearness to roads, markets, extension centers, medical facilities, and Abidjan).

The estimation method: For the rural analysis, the inclusion of community-level variables raised difficulties in using ordinary least squares for estimating the reduced form. This is because some of the community variables are not strictly exogenous. Most community variables are determined prior to the present levels of household welfare. However, some variables (for example, the distance to the nearest market and medical center, and the wage rate for male agricultural laborers) may themselves be determined by levels of household welfare. Increased household income may lead to reduced labor supply and a rise in the rural wage; it may also lead to the development of a new market in response to increased output produced by the household, or to the establishment of medical facilities nearby, with health practitioners locating themselves in wealthier areas. Because of the endogeneity of these explanatory variables, a two-stage least squares estimation procedure is appropriate. The first stage of estimation treats these variables as endogenous, regressing them on a range of instrument variables. The estimated values of the variables are then used in the second stage to estimate the household welfare equation.

The results: Glewwe reports that over 50 percent of the total variance in household expenditure is explained by the reduced-form equation; this is more than satisfactory for cross-sectional analysis. Two features of his results are of particular interest in the context of this chapter. He finds that formal schooling does not explain variations in household welfare in rural Côte d'Ivoire. This is surprising, and Glewwe suggests that for agricultural practices in Africa, education may not be as important as it is in Asia and Latin America. It may also be due to the small number of observations of workers in rural areas with more than a primary education. The community variables are highly significant: long distances to paved roads and markets have a negative effect on welfare. The distance to Abidjan is particularly significant—"households in a village 250 miles outside Abidjan have a 40 percent lower level of welfare relative to those adjacent to Abidjan, ceteris paribus" (Glewwe 1991, p. 329). The study also finds evidence that nearness to medical facilities has a favorable effect on welfare—which suggests that health-care services may reduce the number of working days lost because of poor health.

raised from the sale of cocoa, about one-quarter (24.1 percent) goes to the poor. Thus, at the margin, every cedi used in raising the producer price of cocoa will be divided in the ratio 1 to 3 between the poor and non-poor households. From Frame 4.7, it is clear that pineapples should not be supported if the objective is to raise incomes of the poor. Groundnuts and oil palm should receive higher priority.

Feedback effects

This analysis is only a first approximation of the full effects of price changes. It ignores the feedback responses that occur both in the product markets themselves and in other markets. For example, households facing a changing set of relative prices will be induced to change their patterns of consumption in line with their preferences. These changes are not accounted for in the analysis. And yet there is good reason not to ignore them. The above analytical approach asserts that households are poor if their income/ total expenditure level is lower than some prescribed level, this level being chosen to reflect a fixed bundle of goods required to avoid poverty. But even the poor might be able to exercise some choice in their consumption behavior, and to im-

pose the requirement that a certain fixed bundle of commodities is needed to avoid poverty might be an unnecessary value judgment for the analyst. This is less clear for the destitute poor, for whom there are few choices. Hungry people need to be fed, and a case can be made for applying a restricted commodity bundle in defining their poverty. But for other poor groups, some consumption flexibility may exist and should be accepted.

To correct this, Ravallion and van de Walle (1988) propose measuring poverty by using a suitable *utility index*. Their method, which is based on "equivalent income," takes into account household preferences in deriving the poverty measure. Their method ranks households by a money-metric measure of utility, with the poverty line defined in the same space. Households exercise choice in selecting the bundle of commodities required to achieve whatever level of utility is permitted, so that they are not obliged to consume any specified bundle of goods.[18] They are considered poor only if measured utility falls short of the poverty line. We shall not go into further detail here, but it may be that some analysts would wish to adopt this approach as a means of taking into account the consumption responses of households.

The responses to policy-induced price changes will not be only the consumption response of the poor households concerned. There will be demand responses by non-poor households as well as supply responses. These all combine to produce product market outcomes that differ from the price outcomes assumed under the first-approximation approach. Similarly, there may be repercussions in other markets that significantly affect poor households. Take food-deficit poor households facing a policy-induced rise in the price of food. The analysis suggests that the households would be made worse off, and that measured poverty would rise. But the rise in food prices might induce increased food production among (non-poor) food-surplus households, and a general increase in the demand for labor and wage levels. If food-deficit households benefit from these improved conditions in the labor market, the full effect on their incomes will not be as adverse as that indicated in taking the first-order approximation. This feedback response through the labor market may counteract the direct consumption effects. It is possible to take some account of these feedbacks using basically the same "partial-equilibrium" approach proposed earlier, by making assumptions about what the likely wage response might be to any given price rise.

Frame 4.6: Expenditure patterns by poverty group, Ghana, 1987/88
(percent)

		All		*Non-poor*		*Poor*
Market expenditure		42.6		43.9		36.1
on food	100		85.9		14.1	
Consumption of		24.0		22.2		33.0
home-produced food	100		77.0		23.0	
Consumption of		1.9		1.9		1.7
home-produced	100		84.5		15.5	
nonfood items						
Other consumption		27.9		28.1		27.0
expenditure	100		83.9		16.1	
Remittances paid		2.1		2.3		1.4
out	100		89.3		10.7	
Expenditure relating		1.5		1.6		0.8
to employment	100		90.8		9.2	
income in kind						
Total expenditure		100		100		100
	100		83.3		16.7	

Source: Boateng and others 1990.

An example of this can be found in Ravallion (1990).[19]

Basic needs and the poor

Poverty is a multifaceted condition, and many of its dimensions will not be captured properly through the analysis of household expenditures. To complete the poverty profile, analysts must direct their attention to other aspects of poverty, focusing on the basic needs of poor groups. The social infrastructure is an important element of the mesoeconomic system—linking poor households to macroeconomic policy. We consider this to be a critical element of adjustment/poverty interactions. Not only can access to human capital-enhancing services increase welfare in the short run (improved health, for example, being desirable in and of itself), but it can have far-reaching economic effects into the long run—enhancing also the productive capacity of poor households (thus placing them on upward "income escalators"). It may be possible to estimate these longer-run effects on productivity of a change in human capital among poor households (for example, through enhancing their education and health status), but this should not be a preoccupation of the poverty profile. For present purposes it will be sufficient to trace whether their access to services has been affected by adjustment, and whether this is having noticeable short-run effects on poor households. The longer-run effects will just have to wait until later.

As with other elements of household data analysis, a two-stage approach is called for. The first stage should analyze how adjustment policies (notably fiscal adjustment) have affected the *availability* and *quality* of services across the country. The second stage should assess whether these changes in the supply of services have interacted with demand factors to change *outcomes* at the household level.

The first stage (the macro-meso stage discussed in Chapter 2) will involve tracing how adjustment has affected the resources available for health, education, and other programs of social support (such as nutrition programs). If it has involved fiscal cuts, the analyst must identify how the cuts have been distributed across the various functional components of the exchequer accounts. By applying appropriate price indices,[20] these nominal changes should be translated into real-resource adjustments facing each of the sectors. These calculations are needed to place the analysis of house-hold data into the context of the adjustment program. They should then be combined with the community-level data. These data should include information on the availability of education and health services, and on the quality of the services (covering, for example, the availability of drugs, textbooks). In this way, the analysis should identify how the real-expenditure changes imposed under the discipline of adjustment have affected the supply of social sector services in the communities covered by the survey. Various indicators can be computed (teacher-pupil ratios, number of doctors/hospital beds per capita, non-salary recurrent expenditures) that will indicate how the observed changes in resource availability have affected services across the country. Initially a community data set will be for just one point in time, but as such a survey is repeated, it will be possible to have more accurate estimates of how services have changed at the community level. It might also be possible to distinguish those regions/communities where the poor are mainly to be found. In this way, one can assess whether the burden of fiscal adjustments has been borne disproportionately by poorer communities.[21]

Frame 4.7: Revenue from the sale of crops, Ghana, 1987-88

(percent)

		All		Non-poor		Poor
Cocoa		22.9		23.5		21.0
	100		75.9		24.1	
Oil palm		3.4		2.9		4.9
	100		62.3		37.7	
Plantain		9.6		10.1		7.9
	100		78.2		21.8	
Bananas, oranges, other tree fruits		2.4		2.5		2.3
	100		75.1		24.9	
Groundnuts		4.3		3.9		5.7
	100		65.4		34.6	
Pineapple		0.2		0.2		0.04
	100		94.3		5.7	
Cassava		10.5		11.1		8.8
	100		78.1		21.9	
Yam, cocoyam		7.8		6.8		10.7
	100		64.0		36.0	
Maize		16.7		16.6		16.8
	100		73.6		26.4	
Rice		3.3		3.2		3.7
	100		70.8		29.2	
Vegetables		16.2		16.9		14.3
	100		76.9		23.1	
Others		7.7		7.3		9.0
	100		69.5		30.5	

Source: Boateng and others 1990.

73

The second stage examines the meso-micro relationships using a household data set. The poverty profile should assess the health and education status of the poor, by tabulating a number of key indicators. These are the outcomes of the combined influences of supply- and demand-side factors. In other components of analysis (notably the analyses of education and health in Chapters 7 and 8, respectively), more detailed analysis of these relationships is presented. The poverty profile should identify the level of the indicators for poor and non-poor groups, and seek to understand them in the light of the changes induced by the adjustment program.

Health

Tabulations on health should achieve two broad objectives. They should identify whether the incidence of illness (or injury) is greater among poverty groups than elsewhere in the community. A table showing the percentage of individuals reporting illness during the reference period, by poor/non-poor, region, and socioeconomic group would be a useful starting point. Unfortunately, illnesses and injuries are self-reported in most household surveys, and experience to date (with the LSMS surveys in Ghana and Côte d'Ivoire) has suggested that better-off households are more likely to report illness. However, this does not mean that the incidence of illness is greater among such households. A second broad objective is to establish the main repercussions of illness, measured in number of days lost through illness, and consultations with medical personnel. Tabulations on number of days lost and type of consultation by socioeconomic group and by poverty group would be conditional on the respondent reporting an illness.

Tables should be prepared on the incidence of illness, number of days lost, and type of consultation by poverty group and by socioeconomic group. Frames 4.8 and 4.9 are drawn from Ghanaian data. The mean number of days inactive because of illness (conditional, of course, on being ill) is less for the poor than the non-poor in Ghana. This is to be expected—the poor cannot afford to lose working days through illness. Nevertheless, the fact that five days on average were lost over the reference period (of 28 days) among very poor ill persons is a serious problem for them. Frame 4.9 presents some sobering statistics. It shows that more than two-thirds of the very poor who are ill do not consult any medical personnel (comparing unfavorably for the ill population as a whole,

among whom only one-half consult no one). These results should be compared with (and possibly explained through) the macro-meso analysis.

Education

Some simple tabulations should be prepared to highlight the education of individuals in poor and non-poor households. Two simple groups of indicators present themselves. These are "outcome" indicators, which reveal the effects of past education experience and past human capital investments. In some respects, these indicators can be considered as part of the *cause* of poverty, especially as they apply to adult members of the household. These are mainly literacy and numeracy rates. Tabulations on the current education "status" of household members should be presented. These tell us something of the *effects* of poverty on the human capital of succeeding generations. Frames 4.10 and 4.11 give examples of the types of tabulations of outcome and status variables that prove useful.

Literacy and numeracy rates are significantly worse among the poor, and rural areas are consistently outperformed by urban areas. Both literacy and numeracy are highest among the better off in Accra. Status variables suggest that educational disadvantage is likely to affect the next generation of individuals living in poor households. Among

Frame 4.8: Mean number of days inactive due to illness, by region and poverty group, Ghana, 1987/88

Region	Very poor	Poor	All
Rural	5.0	5.0	5.3
Accra	-	2.4	4.5
Other urban	3.0	4.5	4.5

Source: Boateng and others 1990.

Frame 4.9: Percentage distribution of ill people by type of consultation and poverty group, Ghana, 1987/88
(percent)

Type of consultation	Very poor	Poor	All
Doctor	13.1	16.9	25.6
Nurse	3.2	3.7	4.7
Medical assistant	10.0	11.9	11.0
Other	5.2	6.1	6.2
None	68.5	61.4	52.5
All	100.0	100.0	100.0

Source: Boateng and others 1990.

the very poor rural households, only 40 percent of children of secondary school age attend school. This compares with 58.5 percent for the poor and non-poor combined in Accra. Obviously, such tables should be prepared for other levels of schooling, including primary schooling if universal primary education is not yet attained. Notice in Frame 4.11 that the number of observations for some of the cells is very low. Such instances should be identified explicitly. Again, the analyst must attempt to relate the findings of the micro outcomes observed for education to the macro-meso analysis described earlier.

The dynamics of poverty

Thus far, our concern has been with the poverty analysis of a data set at a given point in time. However, household surveys are often repeated after a passage of time (say, three or four years). If we have observations for two or more points in time, the opportunities for analysis are widened considerably, to include an analysis of changes in poverty over time. These dynamic issues are considered in this section.

The timing of the surveys in relation to structural adjustment is critical in interpreting the data, especially where data for two or more points in time are available. We need to understand what changes have occurred in the economy in the interval between the surveys, and the extent to which these changes have been brought about by adjustment policy. Much of the over-time poverty analysis will involve repeating the tabulations described here, and comparing the two sets of results. The aim of such comparisons is mainly to establish whether the cross-section inferences drawn through the point-in-time analysis of the base-year data are confirmed in the time series. For example, the analysis of the base-year data may suggest that adjustment will benefit the poor, since most are engaged in export crop production.

Observing what happens to poverty over time in the export-producing sector should confirm (or correct) this expectation.

The P_α measures for each region and socioeconomic group should be computed for each year, and compared. Two observations are in order:

• A choice must be made about whether or not to be rigorously relativist in the treatment of the poverty line. Poverty line(s) may be selected for the base year, and kept constant in real terms for subsequent years. Alternatively, a poverty line defined in relation to mean income might be applied, in which case there is no certainty that it will remain constant over time. The interpretation of the results for such a case will be quite different.

• Dominance results can also be applied to comparisons of poverty over time. In this case, the cumulative distribution function in the terminal year is compared with that of the base year. If it is everywhere below the base year, poverty has unambiguously fallen, regardless of the poverty line and index selected. These calculations can be applied to overall poverty indices or to poverty in each of the groupings selected.

Having data for two or more points in time clearly extends the potential scope of the poverty profile in a number of ways. We shall highlight one important extension: decomposing poverty changes in *growth and inequality effects*.

There are two proximate causes to any change in the poverty index over time: a change in the mean income/expenditure; and a change in the distribution of income/expenditure around the mean. The first is the effect of a general growth in incomes; the second is the result of changing inequality. It is a simple matter to decompose any change in poverty over time into that which is due to a change in mean incomes (keeping inequality at its base year) and that arising from a change in inequality (keeping mean income constant).[22] Let $P_{\alpha,b}$ be the overall poverty index in the base year and $P_{\alpha,t}$ be the index for the terminal

Frame 4.10: Literacy and numeracy rates by region and poverty group, Ghana, 1987-88

Region	Very poor		Poor		All	
	Literacy	Numeracy	Literacy	Numeracy	Literacy	Numeracy
Rural	10.1	18.7	17.3	29.1	23.0	35.0
Accra	-	-	51.4	62.9	62.6	71.7
Other urban	20.0	27.1	24.0	35.7	35.4	49.0

Source: Boateng and others 1990.

Frame 4.11: Percentage of children (age 12-18) currently attending school, by region and poverty group, Ghana, 1987-88

Region	Very poor	Poor	All
Rural	40.7	50.2	50.5
Accra	-	57.1 [a]	58.5
Other urban	-	55.7 [a]	61.4

a. Observations = 7.
Source: Boateng and others 1990.

year. Now denote $P^*_{\alpha,t}$ as the poverty level that would have occurred in the terminal year if the change in the mean income over the period had not been accompanied by any change in inequality. This is obtained by applying the terminal-year mean to the base-year Lorenz curve. Similarly, let $P'_{\alpha,t}$ be the poverty level in the terminal year that would arise if mean incomes had stayed constant over the period, but only changes in inequality occurred. For this, the base-year mean is applied to the terminal-year Lorenz curve. The change in observed poverty between the two years can then be decomposed as:

$$P_{\alpha,t} - P_{\alpha,b} = (P^*_{\alpha,t} - P_{\alpha,b}) + (P'_{\alpha,t} - P_{\alpha,b}) + residual \quad (9)$$

The first term on the right-hand side of (9) is that component of the change in poverty due to the change in the mean income, holding the base-year Lorenz curve constant. The second term indicates that part which arises from the change in the Lorenz curve, holding the base-year mean constant. This analysis can throw light on the proximate causes of inequality change. Has poverty decreased mainly because of economic growth, or has there been a marked reduction of inequality?

Concluding observations

This chapter has described how household data can be analyzed to present a poverty profile. The profile is designed to provide insights into how poverty is likely to be affected by adjustment, although, as we have cautioned, the profile cannot provide rigorous grounds for attributing causation. The analysis has been kept relatively simple. The computations involved are straightforward, and most of the results are presented in tabular form. Such tabulations can be easily understood by policymakers. Further analysis should be applied to the data, some of which is described in other chapters. These studies will provide a more in-depth understanding of the reasons why some households are poor and others are not.

The main objective of the analysis is to provide policymakers with an improved empirical basis for protecting poorer groups in times of policy reform. It should signal clearly where poor groups are particularly vulnerable to policy change, and where they need immediate assistance. More important, it should suggest ways in which policy interventions might be adjusted to dampen adverse effects, and enhance the beneficial effects of policy.

Annex: Errors and bias in poverty measurement

If there are measurement errors in the data that underlie poverty analysis, the estimates of poverty will themselves be subject to error. The effects of these errors on poverty measures will depend on the nature of the errors involved. For example, suppose the welfare measure (per capita expenditure) is subject to additive error with zero mean. Estimates of mean expenditure will be unaffected, but each observation might be subject to error. The effect that this error has on poverty estimates will depend on the position of the poverty line in the distribution, and the poverty index selected. Ravallion (1988) states the necessary and sufficient conditions for greater variability in the welfare indicator to increase the expected value of the poverty measure.

It is important to highlight one source of error in welfare indicators derived from household data that may affect the reliability of the poverty estimates generated. A feature of household-level data is the relatively short reference period often used in obtaining estimates of some components of income and expenditure, in some cases only two weeks. Although the income/expenditure experience of a household will rarely be exactly typical of annual income/expenditure for that household, by summing across households, unbiased estimates can be obtained for the population as a whole (or for sub-groups of the population) of mean incomes and expenditures. However, as estimates of annual income at the individual household level will not be accurately measured using the short (two-week) reference period, estimates of the dispersion in incomes (and other statistics that depend on the dispersion—for example, the Gini ratio, variance, standard deviation) will be biased.

Scott (1989) has shown that this upward bias in the measure of annual income/expenditure dispersion or variance is both inevitable and large (possibly of an order of over 30 percent). The extent of this bias will obviously depend on the importance of those components of income/expenditure (for which short reference periods apply) in total income/expenditure. For example, most food expenditures are obtained over a short reference period; other, less frequently purchased items are measured over a longer reference period. Similarly, some income data (for example, wage income) are obtained over a shorter reference period than others.

Any upward bias in the measure of income variance has serious implications for poverty analysis, since the measures of poverty are also certain to be biased. The direction of the bias for P_α measures can only be determined empirically, since this effect on P_α is indeterminate (depending, among other things, on the position of the poverty line in relation to the mean). However, the analyst faced with this problem has two sources of consolation. First, insofar as the analysis is based on arbitrary poverty lines, the absolute extent of poverty is not so important. It is the pattern of poverty across the various groups that is of policy concern. It is unlikely that the poverty ranking of the various groups will be seriously affected by this bias (unless the source of the bias—the non-representativeness of reference-period incomes/expenditures—happens to be significantly worse for some groups).

It is possible that while the measurement of income dispersion using short reference periods is subject to this bias, the measurement of expenditure dispersion will be less so (assuming that both measures take the same reference period). This is because households faced with income variations will tend to smooth out expenditures over the year, because of their expectations of the "permanent" income for the year. The evidence Scott compiles to show that the bias is potentially serious is derived from measures of income. Some of the expenditure items derived may be obtained over a one-year reference period, which will reduce the resulting bias. Whether the measurement of income is more prone to this problem than measured expenditure depends on how they are derived. If income is reported over the year, then this bias would not be present at all for income measures.

Errors that affect the mean of the welfare indicator have different implications. An underestimate of mean expenditures will imply an overestimate of poverty. For the head-count index, and based on experience, Ravallion (1992) estimates that in general, a 5 percent underestimate of mean expenditures would lead to a 10 percent overestimate of poverty (that is, an elasticity of the head-count index with respect to the mean welfare indicator of about 2). This assumes that the error in the mean is not associated with errors in the Lorenz curve. If this is not the case, the effects on poverty measures will clearly depend on the nature of the errors involved.

Notes

1. The methods of poverty analysis presented here are consistent with those of a user-friendly computer package recently developed by the World Bank. The program (POVCAL) is for use on any IBM-compatible PC (for the documentation on this program, see Chen, Datt, and Ravallion 1991).

2. In making expenditures a proxy for welfare, we commit ourselves to measuring the poverty line and an individual's distance from it in "commodity" space. An alternative, taking this welfarist approach to its logical conclusion, is suggested by Ravallion and van de Walle (1988). This involves specifying the poverty line in "utility" space, and using an empirically estimated expenditure system to derive household utility levels. This is discussed below.

3. We assume that production decisions can be solved separately from consumption decisions. See World Bank (1991b) for a discussion of such recursive household models.

4. For a discussion of the methods used in deriving these aggregates, see Johnson, McKay, and Round (1990).

5. For a discussion of the differences in results obtained using alternative measures of welfare in the case of Côte d'Ivoire, see Glewwe and van der Gaag (1987).

6. Our theoretical justification of the expenditure-based measure assumed that only commodities enter the welfare function. The main limitation of this measure is that it ignores utility derived from leisure. To capture this, a full-income approach would be needed, which assigns a monetary value to leisure using the opportunity wage concept.

7. For a review of the relative merits and demerits of food expenditure as a welfare measure, see Ravallion (1992).

8. For useful reviews of recent developments in the measurement of poverty, see Atkinson (1987), Foster (1984), Sen (1983 and 1987), and (especially) Ravallion (1992).

9. Ravallion's approach emerged in part from his work in Indonesia, where there has been a longstanding consensus among policymakers about the nutritionally determined poverty line. There is a stronger case for the use of the absolute poverty concept under such circumstances.

10. In fact, Ravallion suggests two methods of calculating basic nonfood needs, one based on the nonfood expenditure of poor households that have the *potential* to just purchase the basic food requirement. In choosing not to, they devote some expenditure to nonfood items. If nonfood is a normal good, this gives a lower bound to nonfood requirements. The second is to select nonfood expenditures of households that *actually* just consume the basic food requirement, giving an upper bound.

11. During the 1970s, poverty was popularly defined as the poorest 40 percent, mainly as a result of the analysis presented in Chenery and others (1974).

12. Pyatt and Thorbecke (1976) discuss the merits of wealth, sociological criteria, and location as means of classifying households.

13. The selection of socioeconomic groups used in the tables is different from that proposed. No significance should be read into this—the categories in the tables are those used in studies on Côte d'Ivoire and Ghana.

14. This is also regardless of the poverty line selected. The same orderings were obtained using the 30th percentile cutoff as the 10th percentile.

15. See Atkinson (1987) and Foster and Shorrocks (1988).

16. The weaker second-order dominance test can only be specified for the index in use. For the $P_{\alpha=1}$ index, it is that the *area* under the cumulative distribution function for group A is greater than that for group B.

17. This is so long as the poverty measure satisfies certain mild conditions, notably that it is continuous, separable, symmetric, and weakly monotonic.

18. To generate these indicators, the analyst must have at his disposal an empirical expenditure system from which to assess the households' responses to the price changes under consideration.

19. An alternative would involve using a general equilibrium framework, though there is some evidence that little would be gained. In the case of Côte d'Ivoire, Kanbur (1990, p. 48) argues that "taking account of the feedback effects via a complex general equilibrium model does not seem to invalidate the policy guidelines that emerge from the poverty profile analysis."

20. Weights used in such price indices should ideally reflect the input combinations used in the sector concerned. It may not be possible to compute separate price indices for each social sector, in which case proxy deflators might be used (for example, the consumer price index, or, since labor comprises the main input, a money wage index).

21. As with our observations on the economic infrastructure, whether this is possible will depend on the sample drawn. If the poor are dispersed across all the communities, it will be difficult to identify how these infrastructural changes have affected them (as distinct from other household groups). However, unlike the economic infrastructure, social infrastructural changes will have noticeable effects at the household level, and these may reveal differential impacts of adjustment on the poor and the non-poor.

22. See Ravallion (1992). For an application of this decomposition, see Kakwani (1990a) and Grootaert (1993) for Côte d'Ivoire, and Ravallion and Huppi (1989) for Indonesia.

5

Employment and earnings

Tony Addison

Structural adjustment affects employment and earnings through its impact on the level and structure of economic activity. But there are diverse views of this impact. Some observers argue that adjustment depresses livelihoods over the short run without much (if any) long-run improvement. Others argue that adjustment improves livelihoods over the long run compared to non-adjustment. All commentators recognize that adjustment has particularly strong effects on certain occupations, but pessimists argue that adjustment fails to generate alternative employment sources, while optimists take the view that adjustment encourages new employment opportunities. Pessimists would replace current adjustment programs with greater market intervention and more import substitution, which they believe has stronger employment effects than export promotion.

Among those favoring market-oriented adjustment, there are differences over how much the poor share in adjustment-led growth. If the poor as a group benefit from adjustment, then special assistance is not required; it will suffice to make sure that the correct policies are in place. But if the poor do not gain significantly or lose out in the process, then assistance is called for. This involves reducing social, institutional, and economic impediments to their economic participation, improving their human capital, providing direct assistance through employment projects, and improving their geographical and occupational mobility.

This chapter provides guidelines for analyzing the employment and earnings effects of structural adjustment. We focus on wage earners and non-farm household enterprises. Agricultural self-employment is the subject of Chapter 12. Here we concentrate on the allocation of time to directly remunerative employment, referring to time use for the purposes of education, health care, and housework only in as much as they affect employment and earnings. The chapter is organized as follows. First, product-, labor-, and capital-market effects of structural adjustment are reviewed. Second, detailed descriptive analyses of employment and earnings effects are proposed, and appropriate cross-tabulations are suggested. Third, approaches to multivariate analyses of the determinants of labor supply, earnings, and household enterprise profit are set out.

The impact of adjustment on employment and earnings

Structural adjustment affects employment and earnings through product markets, labor markets, and capital markets. These are considered in turn.

Product markets

Product market effects work through:
• *Contractionary fiscal and monetary policies.* These policies reduce aggregate demand (the precise effects depend on the mix of government

expenditure cuts and revenue increases used to reduce the budget deficit). The prices of nontradable goods and services fall relative to the prices of tradables, because domestic supply and demand determine the former prices whereas tradable prices (for small open economies) are given by world price levels. This encourages tradables production to expand, and nontradables production to contract; the speed and extent of these changes depend on supply responsiveness.

• *Devaluation and import liberalization.* The former increases the domestic prices of tradables relative to nontradables, which further encourages tradables expansion. Not all tradables expand, however, because cuts in tariffs and quotas reduce the prices of importables relative to exportables. Sectors producing previously protected importables (usually manufactures) therefore contract relative to exportables. In the case of African countries, exportables are mostly unprotected (or suffer from negative protection).

• *Sectoral price adjustments.* The lessening of price controls, the adjustment of controlled prices to market levels, and the reform of marketing institutions to increase their efficiency together alter the structure of producer prices.

• *Changes in the provision and rehabilitation of economic infrastructure.* Public investment budgets are recast in the light of new priorities. This alters the returns that producers derive across product markets; new transport and processing facilities improve profitability in key sectors (such as agriculture), while investment cutbacks in disfavored sectors reduce their profitability.

These product market adjustments alter the derived demand for labor, thereby completing the transmission of policy effects through to household livelihoods. If tradables are more labor-intensive than nontradables, then in the long run employment and returns to labor (in both self-employment and wage-employment) will increase, provided that no labor market rigidities exist. The opposite result occurs when tradables are less labor-intensive than nontradables. The short-run outcome depends on labor mobility; if substantial retraining is involved, or if geographical mobility is difficult, then workers in expanding sectors will earn a premium on their labor returns, while those in contracting sectors will face a larger wage fall or greater unemployment than if they were mobile. But how the gains and losses are shared also depends on government policies in the labor market itself.

Product market adjustments also affect labor supply. Price increases for essential commodities may raise labor force participation and hours worked. Reduced incomes among the main earners of households will increase participation among other members (more school-age children may work, for example) and induce multiple job holdings. The changes in product markets that occur under adjustment and the induced changes in demand for labor inevitably imply reduced job stability, since many workers may need to change jobs or occupations. This factor, too, may contribute to increased multiple job holdings, whereby workers try to reduce the risk of unemployment or wage loss in a given sector.

Labor markets

Adjustment directly affects labor markets through:

• *Changing the process of private sector wage determination.* Government minimum-wage setting sometimes encourages a dual employment structure; wages cannot be adjusted downward to clear formal labor markets and the unemployed must resort to the informal sector. Minimum wages may be relaxed under market liberalization, with significant implications for formal and informal livelihoods.

• *Changing the process of public sector wage determination.* In some countries, public sector wages are still set above market levels. But in others, wages for professionals have fallen below those in the private sector. Most adjustment programs try to rectify these anomalies through reforms of the public sector.

• *Retrenchments in public sector employment.* Where public employment is overextended, thereby contributing to budget deficits, retrenchments of unskilled staff release resources to pay more to scarce professionals. Given the concentration of public employment in specific locations, large changes in local labor markets are implied.

Whether labor markets operate efficiently, via rapid adjustments in wages to shifts in labor demand and supply, is crucial to adjustment's impact on labor welfare (Johnson 1986). Labor-market segmentation induced by inappropriate policies can impede this efficiency, but segmentation can also occur irrespective of policy. Causes include unionization and monopsony, monopoly employers, imperfect information, barriers to mobility, discrimination, and distortions in capital markets (Mezzera 1981). Whatever its cause, segmentation greatly affects the impact of output fluctuations on employment and earnings.

Consider, for instance, a fall in the demand for nontradables. With inflexible formal sector wages, the formal labor market in the nontradables sector takes the brunt of the employment contraction, since some workers cannot retain employment by taking a lower wage. The informal labor market in the nontradable sector will take the brunt of the wage fall, both because informal labor demand falls, and redundant formal workers move into it (this may result in more informal workers dropping below the poverty line). The formal-informal wage differential therefore rises (McDonald and Solow 1985).

Capital markets

Adjustment affects capital markets through:

• *Alterations in the price of capital to producers.* This occurs through decontrol of the prices of capital equipment and changes in the prices of imported capital equipment consequent upon devaluation and import liberalization.

• *Changes in the structure of fiscal incentives offered to users of capital.* Programs often include the reduction of tax allowances on capital purchases, and the elimination of capital subsidies.

• *Elimination of financial repression.* In many countries, loan interest rates are kept below market levels, thus cheapening the cost of financing capital purchases by borrowing. The upward adjustment of interest rates to market-clearing levels is an important policy reform.

Each of these alters the relative factor-price ratios facing both households and enterprises, leading to changes in the factor combinations used. On balance, in most countries, such changes will tend to make capital more expensive relative to labor, thus favoring employment and wage growth. The strength of the latter will, however, depend on how quickly adjustments in capital stocks can be made, and on the elasticity of substitution between capital and labor.

A descriptive analysis of employment and earnings under adjustment

The analysis of employment and earnings can proceed in two stages. First, tabular data presentation can be used to inform policy analyses. For this purpose, it is important to present the information in a manner readily understood by decisionmakers. To achieve this, analysts and policymakers should agree on a *standard data-presentation framework* that will complement existing information on employment and earnings, and alert policymakers to problems requiring public interventions. The second stage of analysis, discussed later in this chapter, involves the construction of multivariate models that can account for more influences on a given variable than is possible in tables.

Although the features of a data-presentation framework can only be established at the country level, in general, it will have to cover the following topics:

1. The structure of employment
    1.1 characteristics of the labor force
    1.2 distribution of the labor force between tradable and nontradable sectors
    1.3 urban employment
    1.4 public employment
    1.5 non-farm self-employment

2. Changes in the structure of employment: mobility and migration
    2.1 mobility between occupations and sectors
    2.2 migration

3. The structure of earnings
    3.1 the composition of household income
    3.2 wage earnings
    3.3 earnings from non-farm self-employment

The following discussion aims to provide a basic insight into the employment and earnings effects of structural adjustment. The priority analysis of adjustment effects (Chapter 3) emphasized the importance of socioeconomic groups as a dimension of the analysis. This is retained here. For some aspects, such as the structure of the labor force, the socioeconomic classification is an important overall dimension, while other aspects of the employment issue pertain to one or more specific socioeconomic groups, such as in the case of public or urban employment.

The structure of employment

Adjustment will influence not only the level of employment (and unemployment) but also the structure of employment. There are many facets to this: employment in tradables versus non-tradables, public versus private sector employment, rural versus urban employment, and so on.

Characteristics of the labor force

THE DISTRIBUTION OF THE ACTIVE POPULATION BY MAIN EMPLOYMENT. Frame 5.1 shows the "economically active population"[1] distributed across their main employment, with disaggregation by gender, age, socioeconomic group, and whether the individual's household is above or below the poverty line.[2] A relatively fine disaggregation by age is recommended given life-cycle variations in employment prospects. Since most occupational mobility occurs among the young, the period from 7 to 25 years should contain the largest number of age-groups.[3]

Frame 5.1 offers a useful *static* picture of the labor force, clarifying (for instance) the structure of youth employment, and the role of public employment. Reporting Frame 5.1 at regular intervals, from successive surveys, provides a *dynamic* picture of how employment changes under adjustment.

For instance, in the short run, both private and public employment may fall heavily as a result of demand contraction affecting both private and public expenditures. In turn, this employment loss may be disproportionately spread; young workers often have less job security than older workers, and more women may be made redundant than men. Employment alternatives also vary significantly; young men may have fewer opportunities for self-employment than older men (because the latter may have greater access to productive assets), so open unemployment may be higher among younger males.

Obviously care must be taken in drawing such inferences, and the use of such tables should be part of wider analyses. But the presentation of the data in this way does provide a first indication of situations for further investigation. In this regard, with successive surveys, the magni-tude of changes in cell values should be reported.

LABOR FORCE PARTICIPATION AND UNEMPLOYMENT. Frame 5.2 presents labor force participation rates and unemployment rates by location, gender, age-group, and household headship. Some cells may contain only a small number of observations. For example, unemployment among the 7-14 age-group in rural areas may be very small, and this

should be indicated to the user, or excluded. However, child unemployment may be very significant in urban areas. In some countries, orphans and abandoned children have migrated to towns in search of work. Increasing unemployment and participation rates among this age-group would indicate a serious child-welfare problem, including schooling deficiencies, since children in this situation are unlikely to be enrolled and attending school.

Disaggregation by location shows the situation in local labor markets following sectoral policy changes, and how these have an impact on target groups. For instance, the employment effects of industrial rationalization are often concentrated on particular localities. This may have severe effects on a particular group because of the characteristics of the industry's employees (for example, if the factory employs large numbers of female operatives). Frame 5.2, reporting the results of successive surveys, will give an overview of local labor market adjustment to such policy reforms. In the first survey, a high rate of female unemployment in (say) the "other urban" category might be observed; the next survey would indicate whether that unemployment had persisted. A further refinement of the analysis is possible by replacing the "location" column headings in the frame by socioeconomic group (which typically includes location as one dimension, but adds other dimensions). Whether this is feasible in practice depends mainly on the sample size of the survey that underlies the analysis. Care has to be taken that the number of observations in each cell

Frame 5.1: Distribution of the active population by main employment status, gender and age-group, and socioeconomic group, and by poor and non-poor households
(percent)

	Unemployed	Employed private	Employed public	Self-employed
Female				
Age-groups				
All				
Male				
As above				
All				
As above, plus:				
Socioeconomic groups				
Poor				
Non-poor				

of the frame does not become too small for meaningful analysis.

Female labor force participation is, on average, lower than that of males because women have lower opportunity costs of non-participation when their wages are low. Unemployment rates are often higher among women because their opportunity costs of job search are lower, and discrimination in hiring leads to a lower job-opening rate for them. Information is therefore reported by gender. It is also reported by household headship, since household heads (of either gender) usually have a higher participation rate and a lower unemployment rate than other household members (who are partly supported by the household head). This is particularly the case for females: females who are heads of households often have a much higher participation rate and a much lower unemployment rate than females in general.

Finally, Frame 5.2 could also include marital status, since divorced\separated\widowed women generally have the lowest unemployment rates, and the highest participation rates, of all women. In losing the financial support of their spouses, these women face very high opportunity costs if they do not participate in the work force.

Disaggregations such as these highlight the situation of different groups and, over successive surveys, show whether particular groups are faring better or worse than the average. The multivariate analysis presented later in this chapter pursues these issues further.

EMPLOYMENT STATUS AND PARTICIPATION BY EDUCATIONAL ATTAINMENT. Frames 5.1 and 5.2 can be supplemented by tables showing employment status, labor force participation, and unemployment by educational attainment (with further breakdowns by gender). Such tables have identical columns to those of Frames 5.1 and 5.2, but the rows are no education, years of primary, secondary, and tertiary education, and so forth. This will show whether men and women with the same educational attainment have significantly different employment patterns and, over successive surveys, whether these patterns change (because, for example, men are more easily absorbed into certain types of employment than women). An illustration of such a table for Ghana is given in Box 5.1.

Distribution of the labor force between tradable and nontradable sectors

Since adjustment alters the output shares of tradables and nontradables, Frame 5.3 suggests the decomposition of employment status by the tradability of sectors. If the available household survey provides data on the industrial affiliation of respondents' activities, this allows us to classify the activity into various tradable and nontradable categories, as shown in Frame 5.3. Where a correspondence with conventional classifications is desired, Frame 5.3 could be disaggregated according to manufacturing, trade, services, and so on.

Labor moves between nontradables and tradables, but labor reallocations also occur within the tradable and nontradable categories. Two types of tradables are defined: protected tradables (import substituting industries under import quota protection) and unprotected tradables

Frame 5.2: Labor force participation ratio (L) and unemployment rate (U), by region, gender, age-group, and household headship
(percent)

	Capital		Other urban		Rural		National	
	L	U	L	U	L	U	L	U
Female								
Age-groups								
Household heads								
Other household members								
All								
Male								
As above								
All								
Age-groups								

Frame 5.3: Distribution of the employed labor force between tradables and nontradables
(percent)

	Self-employed	Wage earners	Total
Tradables			
Protected			
Unprotected			
Nontradables			
Consumer goods			
Capital goods			
Public services			

Box 5.1: Employment status and education in Ghana

The table below shows how the labor force with different levels of education is distributed by employment status. It highlights some important labor force characteristics—for example, those with only primary education or no education are found predominantly among the self-employed. The unemployment rate is highest among secondary-school-leavers, identifying a problem in their labor market that requires further investigation. Changes in the cell values over time will indicate how adjustment affects the educated labor force: in Ghana, for instance, private employment will take an increasing share of secondary-school-leavers and those with university education as public sector employment is reduced and as employment in tradable (predominantly private sector) activities grows.

Distribution of active population by employment status and educational level
(percent)

| Education level | Unemployed | Employed | | Self-employed |
		Private	Public	
None	0.7	4.4	2.5	92.5
Primary	0.7	10.1	2.2	86.9
Secondary	3.0	11.2	20.3	65.5
University	0.0	6.7	73.3	20.0
All	1.5	7.3	9.0	82.2

Source: Republic of Ghana 1988.

(mainly agricultural products).[4] Nontradables are disaggregated into consumer and capital goods, and into public services. These tabulations show the structure of employment at any one time, and successive surveys allow employment shifts to be tracked.

Two additional tables should be presented. First, the distribution of employed persons resident in poor households across tradable and nontradable sectors, disaggregated by wage-employment and self-employment, should be reported. Second, the distribution of the labor force by occupation across tradable and nontradable sectors should be given. This can be done in a format similar to Frame 5.3, with the tradable and nontradable sectors defining the rows, and occupations defining the columns.

Urban employment

Large changes can be expected in urban livelihoods under adjustment since nontradable services, and protected tradables, are urban-based, and these take the brunt of demand deflation. Formal job losses add to the informal sector, which may already be absorbing large amounts of labor if formal economic activity is stagnant before adjustment.

Frame 5.4 therefore decomposes urban employment (both wage- and self-employment) into its formal and informal parts, using criteria such as whether workers have an employment contract, whether minimum wage legislation applies, and/or whether workers enjoy social security benefits. The table indicates how important formal and informal employment is to different age-groups and to males and females. Shares for the poor and non-poor can also be reported. Finally, the wage- and self-employment components of the formal and informal employment categories can be reported (although there may be insufficient observations to report this information by age-group). Changes in the structure of urban employment can then be monitored as policy reforms are implemented.

Public employment

In the past, government employees have enjoyed above-market salaries together with benefits such as subsidized housing and security of tenure. But these benefits have been eroded considerably in many countries, and the structure of public employment is now changing fundamentally. Since public employment is usually distributed unevenly, job retrenchments can affect local employment severely. Therefore, Frame 5.5 shows the distribution of public employment across regions. Employment in government and state enterprises is shown, since job retrenchments can fall unevenly across the public sector.

Established and non-established public sector employment is also distinguished. The latter has become more prominent as established posts have

Frame 5.4: Distribution of urban employed labor force between formal and informal sectors, by age, gender, and household headship
(percent)

	Capital		Other urban	
	F	I	F	I
Female				
Age-groups				
Household heads				
Other household members				
All				
Male				
As above				
All				
Age-groups				

I indicates informal.
F indicates formal.
Note: Either wage earner or self-employed.

Frame 5.5: Shares of government and state enterprise employment in regional labor forces, and shares of established and unestablished public sector workers in the national labor force
(percent)

	Each region		National			
	G	S	G	S	E	U
All						
Composition of public employment						
Female						
Male						
Persons from poor households						

G indicates government.
E indicates established.
S indicates state enterprise.
U indicates unestablished.
Note: An additional column for each region may be added giving the aggregate of *G* and *S*.

been frozen, but "temporary" hiring of staff has been permitted. Unestablished jobs carry few fringe benefits and are vulnerable to retrenchment since the unskilled are concentrated in these jobs, and the costs of their dismissal are low.

The table also disaggregates the information by gender and for the poor. Thus, in a given region, 10 percent (say) of the regional labor force may be government employees and 5 percent in state enterprises. Of the region's government employees, 80 percent might be males and 20 percent females, while 10 percent might come from poor households.

Women and men are usually spread disproportionately across the column categories because of variations in local hiring practices and participation rates, and differences in the educational attainments needed by public employees. Public sector retrenchments are therefore likely to have disproportionate effects on male and female employment. Females may also be concentrated in unestablished occupations, which further heightens their vulnerability to redundancy.

Verifying whether the poor share in public employment is important information for countries beginning retrenchment, since substantial assistance to redundant public employees is not warranted if few of them are poor (Demery and Addison 1987b). However, the poor may be concentrated in the unestablished category, in which case assistance should be targeted to this group. Successive surveys, as well as information on the job listing of respondents available in some surveys, will also show whether the poor have been disproportionately affected by retrenchment. To date, only circumstantial evidence has been available on this issue (see Addison 1987 on the Gambia, for example).

Non-farm self-employment

Frame 5.6 shows the share by region of the labor force in non-farm self-employment. Since this employment usually becomes more important as people grow older, decomposition by age-group is shown (see Vijverberg 1988a on Abidjan, for instance). Gender differences are usually evident, as are differences across urban centers.

Frame 5.7 seeks to capture the importance of different non-farm enterprises across regions; for instance, services are generally more important in urban than in rural areas. The table also shows the relative roles of different non-farm enterprises in the employment of poor households. They may predominate in services and food commerce, where capital requirements are small, rather than in manufacturing, which needs more capital. We can track how this changes as projects are implemented to improve their businesses.

Adjustment will cause changes in the shares of these activities over time. For instance, services and non-food commerce usually become less important since these are predominantly non-tradable activities, while informal manufacturing,

Frame 5.6: Share of the employed labor force that reports non-farm self-employment, by region, gender, and age
(percent)

	Capital	Other urban	Rural	National
Female				
Age-groups				
Household heads				
Other household members				
All				
Male				
As above				
All				
Age-groups				

Frame 5.7: Distribution of household non-farm enterprises across activities by region, and for poor and non-poor households
(percentage of column total)

	Each region			National		
	AH	NP	P	AH	NP	P
Manufacturing						
Services						
Food commerce						
Nonfood commerce						

AH indicates all households.
NP indicates non-poor households.
P indicates poor households.

being predominantly tradable, will most likely increase. A reduction in rent-seeking upon the removal of market distortions will also reduce the role of nonfood commerce in the short term. The table should capture these effects.

Changes in the structure of employment: Mobility and migration

As with other aspects of economic life, the structure of employment is likely to change quite rapidly during adjustment. We deal with two aspects of such change: the occupational and sectoral mobility of labor; and its geographical mobility (or migration).

Mobility between occupations and sectors

Frame 5.8 clarifies the occupational changes that occur under adjustment, using information on employment histories. The current main occupation or other time use (housekeeping, education) is cross-tabulated with the previous main occupation or time use. The table then shows, for each current main occupation, the percentages of those who were previously in full-time education, unemployed, in the same occupation, or in other occupations.

The table indicates the flow of persons between occupations as adjustment takes effect. For example, we can see how government workers are reemploying themselves by checking the percentages of urban businessmen and farmers who were formerly in government. The table could also be repeated for each gender, to capture differences

in the occupational mobility of men and women (barriers to entry may affect women more than men, for instance). Finally, the information should be reported for those in poor and non-poor households to highlight the difficulties faced by the poor in achieving occupational mobility.

A table similar to Frame 5.8 can be presented with occupations aggregated into groups of formal wage-employment (with sub-categories of public and private), informal wage-employment, non-farm household enterprise, and farm enterprise. Each of these can be disaggregated for various categories of tradables and nontradables: for instance, using a threefold classification of tradability, formal wage-employment in the private sector can be split into unprotected tradables, protected tradables, and nontradables.

Such a table would, for example, show the percentage of those wage earners currently in unprotected tradables who had previously been wage earners in protected tradables or nontradables. This provides important information (especially when successive surveys are available) on the short- and long-term mobility of labor between nontradable and tradable sectors, which is a major determinant of the labor welfare consequences of structural adjustment.

Migration

Because adjustment causes substantial changes in the economy, a reversal of past geographical migration of labor may occur. Specifically, labor may return to agriculture, if (as is likely) adjustment shifts the urban-rural income differential in favor of rural employment.

Frame 5.9 captures important dimensions of migration under adjustment. For each region, the

Frame 5.8: Current occupation/time use in relation to previous occupation/time use
(percent)

		Current			
		E	H	S	01, 02 ... etc
Previous	E				
	H				
	S				
	01				
	02				
	...				
	etc.				

E indicates full-time education.
H indicates housekeeping.
S indicates searching for work.
01, 02, etc. indicates main occupations.
Note: All columns add to 100 percent.

Frame 5.9: Regional migration and characteristics of migrants
(percent)

	Each region		
Age	M	MU	MY
7-24			
Over 24			

M indicates recent migrants as a percentage of region's labor force.
MU indicates percentage of M who are currently unemployed.
MY indicates household income of recent migrants as a percentage of average household income in the region.

share of recent migrants (moved during the last year) in the region's work force is given. To establish how well they have adjusted to the local labor market, the percentage currently unemployed is shown. Finally, the income of households in which recent migrants now reside is reported as a percentage of the region's household income. This indicates how they have adjusted to the local labor market. If successive surveys are available, then their progress can be tracked; over time their unemployment rate may fall, and their household's income may rise relative to the average.

A small sample of migrants will limit decomposition by personal characteristics. Frame 5.9 therefore gives two age-groups only; the cutoff age is the mid-twenties, since younger people are more likely and able to migrate. If sample size permits, then decomposition by gender and poverty criteria should be used.

The structure of earnings

Associated with changes in the level and structure of employment, a new structure of earnings in the labor market is likely to emerge. This will particularly affect the distribution of earnings between wage-employment and self-employment.

Sources of household incomes, occupational earnings across tradable and nontradable sectors, and tabulations and indices of real earnings are the subjects of this section.

THE COMPOSITION OF HOUSEHOLD INCOME. Frame 5.10 decomposes household income by source

for poor and non-poor households.[5] It might be observed, for instance, that unearned income accounts for more than wage-employment among poor rural female-headed households (reflecting their dependence on remittances) or that non-farm enterprises make only a small contribution to the incomes of some poverty groups. Successive surveys, together with other information sources, can map changes in sources of income as adjustment proceeds. For example, self-employment income could fall among urban poverty groups if policy reforms depress the informal sector. Suitable project interventions can then be implemented to deal with this problem (and tabulations from successive surveys will highlight how income sources change as the projects are implemented). Frame 5.10 disaggregates the information by region since in most countries economic opportunities differ significantly across regions. As in other frames, a useful distinction could also be made between the capital city, other urban areas, and rural areas. If the sample size permits, Frame 5.10 should also be presented for each socioeconomic group.

Employed persons can be classified according to their occupational and industrial status, and each industry can be further classified according to its degree of tradability. For each occupation-industry cluster, mean and median values for earnings can be calculated and reported in a table such as Frame 5.11. Given the likely skewness of the data, it is important to report the median value in addition to the mean. If repeated surveys were available, it would be possible to see how the structure of occupational earnings changes as measures such as devaluation improve earnings in tradables relative to nontradables, as trade liberalization alters the structure of earnings within tradables, and as

Frame 5.10: The structure of household income in rural and urban areas, by poor and non-poor households, and gender of household head
(percent)

	Each region			
	Poor households		Non-poor households	
	Female-headed	Male-headed	Female-headed	Male-headed
Wage-employment				
Formal				
Informal				
Self-employment				
Agriculture				
Non-farm				
Enterprises				
Transfers				
Private				
Other				

Note: All columns add to 100 percent.

Frame 5.11: Earnings in tradable and non-tradable activities, by occupation
(in local currency over a one-month period)

	Each occupation		Overall	
	Mean	Median	Mean	Median
Tradables				
Protected				
Unprotected				
Nontradables				
Consumer goods				
Capital goods				
Public services				
Average by occupation				

earnings in nontradables are affected by measures such as civil service reforms. For example, adjustment might raise the earnings of manual workers in tradable sectors, but depress their earnings in nontradables. But as time passes, and workers are able to move out of nontradables, the differential in favor of manual workers in tradables will fall.

Regional price indices should be used to calculate the real earnings provided by different employment sources. For example, the mean and median values of real earnings derived from wage-employment (both formal and informal), self-employment (both agricultural and non-farm), and transfers can be reported for each region, with breakdowns for poor and non-poor households. Over successive surveys these will reveal changes in the structure of earnings as policy reforms take effect.

Last, given the effect of adjustment in changing the formal-informal wage differentials, it is important to provide real wage indices for both formal and informal workers. Wage dispersion can narrow or widen during adjustment depending on the nature of the policy package.

Wage earnings

In the analysis of earnings, an important task is to establish the determinants of observed differences in wages between individuals. What are the re-

spective roles of supply-side variables (for example, educational attainment, post-school experience) and demand-side variables (hiring practices, discrimination) in determining observed wage differentials? Finding an answer to this question requires multivariate analysis. But suitable cross-tabulation of the data can provide some guidance.

The wage differentials of particular policy interest are those between genders, between regions, and between the private and public sectors. All these are likely to change under adjustment. Frame 5.12 reports on these differentials expressed as ratios between, for instance, mean female and male wage rates. In some occupations, workers receive fringe benefits in the form of health, housing, and transport subsidies. Earnings differentials including both wage and non-wage payments should therefore be reported.

The rows of Frame 5.12 are distinguished by educational level, with further subdivisions in terms of age to proxy for post-school experience. If wages are mainly determined by human capital and work experience, then the ratios will be close to one. How far actual values diverge from unity provides an indication of demand-side influences. For instance, government wage setting may generate a significant public-private wage differential. It may be found that the public sector pays above the market rate for young persons with primary education, but substantially less for those with tertiary education.

Regional wage differentials may exist because of geographical immobilities, so that interregional labor flows do not equalize regional wage rates.[6] The differential between the "capital" and "other urban" categories may be closer to unity for those

Frame 5.12: The structure of wage differentials by education level and age
(as ratios of mean wage rates)

	Wage differentials			
Education level	Female/ male	Capital/ other urban	Urban/ rural	Public/ private
No schooling				
Age-groups				
Primary education				
Age-groups				
Secondary education				
Age-groups				
Tertiary education				
Age-groups				

Frame 5.13: Earnings of household non-farm enterprises for poor and non-poor households
(local currency per month)

	Each region							
	Gross revenue				Net revenue			
	Poor		Non-poor		Poor		Non-poor	
	ME	MD	ME	MD	ME	MD	ME	MD
Manufacturing								
Services								
Food commerce								
Nonfood commerce								

ME indicates mean.
MD indicates median.

with tertiary education, but greater than one for those with no education. Analyzed further in the light of what is known about the operation of urban labor markets, it may be found that the uneducated face a particular barrier to entry into the capital city's labor market.

Gender discrimination in hiring practices will create a significant male-female wage differential, by definition. The male-female differential may be close to unity for persons with secondary education, but much below unity for those with no schooling, indicating—perhaps—discrimination against uneducated women that needs further investigation. Comparisons of the differentials over successive years can reveal that a particular facet of adjustment is strengthening or weakening discrimination.

Depending on the sample size, further disaggregations of the columns of Frame 5.12 may be possible. For instance, disaggregating the public sector into government and state enterprises may reveal that a substantial public-private wage differential is due to wage setting in only part of the public sector. Or disaggregating the female-male differential between public and private sectors may show that the differential is concentrated in only one of these sectors.

Tables summarizing the characteristics of households deriving a wage income from sectors covered by minimum wage legislation should be presented. From this it can be ascertained whether minimum wages do benefit the lowest-income households.

Earnings from non-farm self-employment

The profitability of household enterprises is measured by net revenues. Under adjustment, these are affected by product- and input-price movements due to demand effects, exchange rate adjustments, changes in trade interventions, and the relaxation of price controls. Net revenues are calculated from information on the values of outputs and inputs. Frame 5.13 reports these for various enterprise categories, and for poor and non-poor households. Successive surveys will show how profit incomes among the poor fare as adjustment proceeds and as project-based interventions to assist target groups take effect. Median values should be reported since evidence to date shows a skewed distribution of earnings among most categories of enterprise. Gross revenues are reported as well, since changes in these are indicative of demand conditions facing households. Frame 5.13 proposes a way to decompose activity earnings by region, thus capturing changes in enterprise profits depending on their location. For example, the demand for, and profitability of, urban services may fall if adjustment substantially reduces urban formal incomes. But as policy reforms encourage the growth of agricultural incomes, the demand for rural services, and their profitability, may rise.

A multivariate analysis of employment and earnings under adjustment

Cross-tabulations of employment and earnings are limited in what they can show. With only three- or four-way classifications, they frequently omit important explanatory variables, and can therefore lead to misleading policy conclusions. Multivariate estimation techniques can resolve these difficulties. We shall examine the determinants of labor supply, wage earnings, and earnings differentials.

The determinants of labor supply

PARTICIPATION AND HOURS OF WORK. With multivariate analysis it is possible to go much further than the cross-tabulations proposed in understanding the impact of structural adjustment on labor supply. The determinants of both the decision to participate in wage-employment (or not) and, for participants, the number of hours supplied must be established. A dichotomous dependent variable *LP*, whose value is 1 if workers participate, and 0 if they do not, and a dependent variable *HW* (hours of work per week or per month) must be defined. The equations to be estimated are:

$$LP = f(w, Y, T, P, Z, X) \qquad (1)$$

and

$$HW = f(w, Y, T, P, Z, X) \qquad (2)$$

where w = the market wage, Y = profit incomes, T = transfer or unearned income, P = an index of consumer prices,[7] Z = a vector of the characteristics of the household and individual, and X = the characteristics of the community. Similar explanatory variables are used in the first estimation of each equation (although the final estimations will differ when some variables are insignificant for one equation but not the other). Separate equations can also be estimated for males and females; individuals from poor and non-poor households; and rural and urban workers. In this case, the dummy variables for these characteristics are omitted.

Box 5.2 presents in more detail the types of variables that can be included. Since age and marital status significantly affect labor supply, these are included. Education is likewise a standard variable in such equations. Time allocated to both housekeeping and the care of young children limits both participation and hours worked (Grootaert 1986, p. 164). Since the burden of these responsibilities usually falls on women, we can expect these variables to be particularly important in explaining their labor supply. Community variables are also included, since poor access to health and education facilities may limit participation by raising the time spent ill, and

---

Box 5.2: Wage-employment: Independent variables determining (i) the decision to participate and (ii) the number of hours supplied by participants

Key variables	Details of variables included
Wages	Wage rate per period
Profit incomes	Profit of farm enterprises Profit of non-farm enterprises
Transfers	Household unearned income
Consumer prices	Consumer price index
Age	
Gender	
Marital status	Unmarried Divorced/separated Widowed Spouse of household head
Education	Years of primary schooling Years of secondary schooling Years of vocational training Years of higher education Diplomas obtained
Effect of children	Child 0-4 years Child 5-9 years
Housework variables	Time spent collecting firewood Time spent collecting water Time devoted to other housework
Nationality group	
Location	Capital city Other urban Rural
Socioeconomic group	
Community variables	Childcare facility Health-care facility Index of area development

---

because of the need to spend time taking children to remote health facilities, and the like. Likewise, an index of area development using community data is included. The estimated equations can be used to assess policy-induced changes in these variables. For instance, the impact on urban female labor supply of providing more education for females, providing childcare facilities, and improving community social services can be predicted.

Decisions concerning the supply of wage labor are interdependent with decisions to apply labor to household enterprises, and to consume goods and services. These three sets of decisions are best viewed as the outcome of the same household maximization process. This is why profit income from household enterprises (both farm and non-farm) and the prices of consumer goods are included in both (1) and (2).

Adjustment will simultaneously affect wage rates, profit incomes, and commodity prices, and the household will reallocate the labor of its members accordingly. Changes in wage rates caused by policy reforms will not only have the usual income and substitution effects on labor supply, but will also affect the latter through changing household profits where the household uses hired labor. The profit effect on labor supply might be large in the urban informal sector, but small in rural areas where households use less hired labor (this is one reason for estimating separate urban and rural versions of equations 1 and 2).

Profit income is affected by changes in producer prices, input prices, and economic infrastructure under adjustment. We would expect profit income to be negatively related to both LP and HW, because a rise in profits will cause households to reallocate their labor supplies from wage-employment to self-employment. The estimated equations can be used to simulate the effects of (say) producer price increases on household profits, and eventually on labor supplies.[8]

Unearned income (T) is included to capture the effects of changes in both private and public transfers to households, both of which are affected by adjustment. For example, a fall in urban-to-rural remittances (due to adjustment's impact on urban nontradables) might lead rural households to compensate by increasing their labor supply. A fall in public transfers (for example, food assistance) as part of budget cuts could have a similar effect or, through diminishing nutrition, actually reduce the hours supplied by poorer households. The latter is a particularly important effect to capture for policy purposes.

ESTIMATION ISSUES. Both (1) and (2) can be estimated by ordinary least squares (OLS) regression. However, a number of important econometric problems can arise.[9] The first of these concerns the choice of whether to participate. The estimated version of equation (1) can be interpreted as the probability that an individual will participate in the labor market, given information about the person's characteristics. However, although the underlying probability model might be correct, a given sample of observations on the independent variables may correspond with LP values outside the [0,1] interval. This means that if we used the estimated version of equation (1) to predict the values of LP, some of those predicted values would fall outside the [0,1] range.

A standard solution to this problem is to apply the probit technique. This essentially transforms the original model in such a way that the predictions will lie in the [0,1] interval for all values of the explanatory variables.[10] The technique is computationally more involved than OLS (probit uses non-linear maximum likelihood estimation), but unbiased estimates are essential if policy conclusions are to be drawn.

The second econometric problem is the problem of selectivity bias arising in the estimation of the hours of work equation (2). Essentially, the sample on which equation (2) is estimated is self-selected, given the prior choice whether to work or not, and is therefore non-random. This could lead to biased parameter estimates when OLS is used. The correction of this bias involves the estimation of the "Mills ratio" from the probit estimation of the participation equation (1). The inverse of the Mills ratio is then inserted into equation (2) and OLS is applied.[11]

A third econometric problem is simultaneity arising from the fact that the profit income in (1) and (2) is not a truly exogenous variable, since it is determined by labor allocation decisions of the household. If uncorrected, this could also lead to biased estimates. The solution is to use the predicted values from the estimated profit function (10) and to insert these in place of y in equations (1) and (2).

Analysts are advised to experiment with a variety of functional forms and estimation procedures to determine the most effective methods for obtaining parameter values of policy interest.

The determinants of wage earnings

THE EARNINGS FUNCTION. The key tool to analyze wage differentials is the earnings function, which in general can be expressed as:

$$w = f(S, E, Z) \qquad (3)$$

Box 5.3: Interpreting earnings profiles: The role of education and experience

The issue: The influence of education and experience on earnings is a complex one, and cannot always be understood using the estimating equation (3). This is because there is a tendency for experience to have a greater impact on earnings for workers with higher levels of education. It is possible that a large proportion of the measured gross returns to education (using [3]) are due to this difference between the returns to experience. What appears to be a return to education may be due to work experience.

The method: Using data from specially commissioned surveys, Knight and Sabot (1990) estimate an equation similar to (3) for Kenya and Tanzania. This indicates measures of returns (in increased wage earnings) to education and work experience. To assess whether the earnings-experience profile is steeper for the more educated, they then estimated (3) separately for two levels of education attainment, primary completers and secondary completers.

The results: The three equations estimated are reported in the table below. From these results, Knight and Sabot conclude that in Kenya, the increment to earnings per year of employment experience is 51 percent higher for secondary completers than for primary completers. In Tanzania, it is 29 percent higher. It follows that this interaction between educational attainment and work experience explains a substantial proportion of the return to secondary education, as conventionally measured. Knight and Sabot extend this analysis in seeking an explanation for this interaction. It might be due to the fact that better-educated workers are more able (for example, in terms of cognitive skills), and therefore more likely to benefit from further (vocational) training. Alternatively, it may be due to the fact that better-educated workers had to take white-collar jobs, which give greater rewards to seniority—the "credentialist" explanation. They found that the data were not consistent with the latter hypothesis, but favored the conventional human capital explanation. More-educated workers appear to have higher returns to work experience because the skills acquired in school are also required in post-school training and skill acquisition.

Human capital earnings functions

Country and variable	Whole sub-sample	Primary completers	Secondary completers
Kenya			
S	0.476	—	—
	(6.70)		
L	0.042	0.035	0.053
	(8.40)	(4.64)	(7.79)
Constant	6.30	6.39	6.70
$\bar{R}^2$	0.29	0.23	0.31
N	205	71	134
Tanzania			
S	0.280	—	—
	(4.30)		
L	0.055	0.049	0.063
	(9.70)	(7.09)	(6.62)
Constant	6.07	6.11	6.28
$\bar{R}^2$	0.38	0.32	0.39
N	179	107	72

— Not applicable; t-statistics in parentheses.
Note: S, secondary education; L, employment experience.
Source: Knight and Sabot 1990, p. 81

where w is the wage rate over a chosen period, S is educational attainment, E is work experience, and Z is characteristics of the individual and household (see Box 5.3).

The inclusion of education and work experience variables is standard to earnings functions derived within a human capital framework.[12] Table 5.1 shows the variables that a typical earnings function might include under each of the above headings (Chiswick 1976; Grootaert 1986, p.

203). The dummy variables for gender, location, nationality, and socioeconomic group are included to capture the effects of wage differences due to market segmentation (which is more fully analyzed later). In addition, if the data permit, separate earnings functions should be estimated for each socioeconomic group, or at the very least for urban and rural workers.

Some community variables can also be included in the wage equation (for example, a measure of area development). The presence of good social infrastructure can positively affect wages (see Bardhan 1984). Where workers have good access to health facilities, productivity, and thus wage earnings, will increase. The estimated equations may then be used to predict the earnings effects of projects at the household and community levels designed to improve economic and social infrastructure. They also reveal the loss of wage earnings (especially among poor groups) that occurs if such infrastructure is cut back during adjustment.

CORRECTING FOR SELECTIVITY BIAS. Earnings studies generally exclude the self-employed from the sample, since their earnings represent returns to both capital and labor. The resulting OLS estimates may suffer from the selectivity bias noted under labor supply, since individuals can choose between wage-employment and self-employment. Hence, the sample of wage earners is again non-random or "self-selected" (Chiswick 1983). Various solutions have been offered, including using a dummy variable for activity status (Blaug 1974), or the share of self-employment income in total income (Chiswick 1976), but these are unsatisfactory since the variables are not truly exogenous. The best procedure is to include in the estimated version of (3) the inverse of the Mills ratio calculated from the probit estimate of the participation equation (1) and then estimate (3) by OLS (Grootaert 1986).

Explaining public-private wage differentials

If labor markets are perfectly competitive, workers with the same characteristics will earn the same wage regardless of their sector of employment. However, if some employers set wages above market-clearing levels (and restrict access to jobs in their sector by rationing), then different wages may be observed for workers with the same characteristics. The earnings function (3) can be a first step toward the analysis of wage differentials by incorporating such variables as location and socioeconomic group. Similarly, gender and nationality variables can be included to capture possible discrimination by employers against women or minority nationality groups.

However, one can go further by estimating separate earnings functions for wage-earner groups of policy interest. At the end of the procedure we can thus report the percentage shares of observed

Table 5.1: Independent variables for an earnings function
(dependent variable: wages per hour)

Key variables	Details of variables included
Education	Years of primary schooling
	Years of secondary schooling
	Years of vocational education
	Years of tertiary education
	Diplomas obtained
Work experience	Years in current main occupation
	Years in labor market
Characteristics	Gender
	Location
	Nationality group
	Socioeconomic group

wage differentials between sectors or types of workers due to differences in worker characteristics and differences in wage structures. In the following example, earnings functions would be estimated for government, state enterprise, and private sector workers, where the subscripts denote the type of employer (g = government, s = state enterprise, and p = private sector). To facilitate the exposition, let X stand for all the explanatory variables used. Three earnings functions would therefore be estimated of the general form:

$$W_g = f_g(X_g) \tag{4}$$

$$W_s = f_s(X_s) \tag{5}$$

and

$$W_p = f_p(X_p) \tag{6}$$

Earnings equation (3) implicitly assumed that the three sectors have the same wage structure, and that wages for workers with identical characteristics will differ across the sectors only by a markup, captured by the equation's intercept. This is obviously a restrictive assumption that will not hold in many labor markets. The assumption can be formally tested by comparing the coefficients of equations (4), (5), and (6). This is usually done by means of a Chow test.[13]

Having estimated (4)-(6), we can construct "representative" workers for each sector. This is done by calculating the mean value of each independent variable for all the workers in each sector. Each of these mean values is multiplied by the respective estimated coefficient of (4)-(6), and the sum of the products gives the predicted wage for the representative worker in that ownership category, that is:

$$\overline{W}_g, \overline{W}_s, \overline{W}_p \qquad (7)$$

The next step is to calculate what the predicted wage would be for a representative worker from (say) the private sector if paid according to the government wage structure (f_g), that is:

$$\hat{W}_p = f_g(\overline{X}_p) \qquad (8)$$

In other words, $\hat{W}_p$ is the predicted wage for someone having the average characteristics of private sector workers, but subject to a government wage structure. Alternatively, we could predict the wage for someone having the average characteristics of government workers but subject to a private sector wage structure. Thus the difference (D) in wages paid (for example) to representative workers in the government and private sectors is decomposed as:

$$D = \overline{W}_g - \overline{W}_p = \{\overline{W}_g - f_g(\overline{X}_p)\} + \{f_g(\overline{X}_p) - \overline{W}_p\} \quad (9)$$
$$= \qquad E \quad + \quad U$$

The first term (E) of (9) is the part of the differential explained by private and government workers having different characteristics, while the second term (U) is the unexplained difference between government and private sectors in their wage functions. The term (U) is an indication of the extent to which sectoral wage differences are due to different wage structures between the sectors, which can reflect discriminatory or other wage-setting practices. Box 5.4 shows an application of this decomposition method for Tanzania.

Wage differentials: Gender, formal/informal, and traded/nontraded

The procedure can be applied to decompose the observed male-female wage differential into that caused by employer discrimination against females, and that caused, for example, by females having less education. If discrimination is the main cause, suitable employment legislation is needed. If it is due to different characteristics, then female education and other characteristics need improvement. Policy interventions in these areas may be of great importance during adjustment, if women are to be enabled to benefit from new labor market opportunities.

The private sector in most developing countries can be split into formal and informal sectors. A wage differential usually exists between the two sectors, and this can also be decomposed into a component due to the differences in workers and an "unexplained" component. The latter may be due to formal sector employers setting above-market wages if this results in profit improvements through higher worker productivity (the "efficiency wage" argument). Alternatively, workers and employers may have an "implicit contract" to keep wages stable when demand fluctuates. Both efficiency wages and implicit contracts may occur in the formal sector, because formal enterprises have lower turnover rates and use more skilled workers than informal enterprises (since in the formal sector, capital intensities are higher). These practices are unlikely to occur in the informal labor market, where labor is often hired by the day, and where wages are expected to adjust rapidly to changes in market conditions without the lags that occur under longer labor contracts.

Identifying differences in formal/informal wage-setting procedures within the private sector is important, since they may intensify the dual labor market structure (unemployed workers cannot bid down formal wages and must therefore resort to informal employment), and exacerbate the costs of adjustment to informal workers. Decomposing the informal-formal wage differential on the basis of data from successive surveys will reveal whether adjustment has caused formal employers to become more flexible in their wage-setting practices (in which case the formal-informal differential may fall), or whether rigidities have persisted (in which case, as the beginning of this chapter stated, informal wages will fall disproportionately under adjustment, and the formal-informal differential may rise).

One reason why formal enterprises can sometimes pay above-market wages is that they are monopolies in domestic markets, thereby permitting managers to share excess profits with workers (whose bargaining position is strengthened by the lack of competitive pressures). For nontradables, limited market size may cause "natural" monopolies, while the lack of foreign competition to businesses in "protected tradables" encourages similar monopoly positions in small domestic markets for importables. The latter cause has become more pronounced in recent years as governments have extended import restrictions as a means of cutting trade deficits. These causes

Box 5.4: Public-private wage differentials in Tanzania

The issue: In Tanzania, government employees earn, on average, 51 percent more than employees of private firms, while employees of state enterprises earn 56 percent more (male employees only). But nearly 30 percent of government employees, and 20 percent of state enterprise employees, have a post-primary education, compared with only 6 percent of private sector workers. And, on average, workers in government and state enterprises are older, and have more work experience. So, is the difference in the characteristics of public and private employees sufficient to explain the average wage differential between them? Is at least some of this differential caused by the public sector paying workers of given education and experience more than they would earn in the private sector?

The method: Lindauer and Sabot apply the decomposition procedure discussed in the text. They construct representative workers for each sector and predict the wage rates of government and state enterprise employees if they were paid according to the private sector salary structure. The two wage differentials of interest are $(\overline{W}_g - \overline{W}_p)$ and $(\overline{W}_s - \overline{W}_p)$, and their decomposition is shown in the table in this box.

The results: The decomposition shows that nearly three-quarters of the large differential between government and private employees is explained by differences in the characteristics of employees (E). The remaining quarter of the differential is unexplained by characteristics and represents the difference in wage structures between government and private employers. Government employees receive a significant premium (as given by U) over private sector work-

ers with the same characteristics. Employees in state enterprises receive an even greater premium, since only half of the state enterprise–private sector wage differential is explained by the difference in employee characteristics between the two sectors (see table).

Since state enterprises pay their employees a wage above the comparable market rate, they can reduce their operating costs by bringing their wage structure into line with that of the private sector. This will reduce the deficit typically run by such enterprises, thereby reducing the size of the subsidies paid by the central government (the latter being a major source of fiscal imbalance in Tanzania).

Sources of public-private wage differentials
(as percentage of differential)

	Government-private wage differential $(\overline{W}_g - \overline{W}_p)$	State enterprise–private wage differential $(\overline{W}_s - \overline{W}_p)$
Contribution of employee characteristics		
Total (E)	74.4	49.4
of which:		
Education	58.4	23.6
Experience	9.8	8.4
Age	8.7	10.1
Location	-2.5	7.3
Unexplained difference (U)	25.6	50.6

Source: Lindauer and Sabot 1983.

---

are, however, likely to become less important during adjustment, as trade regimes are liberalized.

To capture these effects on wage determination, analysts may categorize the private formal sector according to private tradables, private protected tradables, and private nontradables. It is suggested that earnings functions be estimated for each category, and that the predictive test outlined here be applied (for instance, predicting the wage of a representative worker from the unprotected tradables sector if the worker were employed in the protected tradables sector or in nontradables). The proportion of wage differential not explained by worker characteristics gives an estimate of the effect of different product market structures on wage setting. This indicates the effects that import liberalization would have on wage earnings in protected tradables. Once employers face international competition, their monopoly profits would fall, thereby reducing their ability to pay workers more than in unprotected sectors.

Much of the informal-formal wage differential may be due to wage determination in only one part of the private sector (for example, nontradable monopolies). The differential between each part of the formal private sector and the informal sector should be estimated, and again the differential decomposed into worker characteristics and wage-setting practices.

The determinants of the earnings of non-farm enterprises

PROFIT FUNCTIONS. Profit functions are used to analyze the determinants of the profits of household enterprises. Let Y stand for the net revenues of the household enterprise (which is gross revenue minus all variable costs). Then:

$$Y = f(L, K, X) \qquad (10)$$

where L is household labor, K is capital stock, and X represents selected household characteristics

Box 5.5: The determinants of the profits of household non-farm enterprises

Key variables	Details of variables included
Household labor	Total working hours of household workers in the enterprise (for a given period)
Non-household labor	Total working hours of hired labor, or Number of hired laborers and apprentices in the enterprise
Own capital	Total value of owned capital stock used by enterprise (in local currency)
Rented capital	Total value of capital rented for use by enterprise (in local currency)
Government registration	1 if the enterprise is registered with a government agency, 0 if not
Employment contracts	1 if hired labor has formal contract, 0 if not
Foreign or domestic purchaser	1 if foreign, 0 if domestic
Formal or informal purchaser	1 if formal, 0 if informal
Credit	1 if enterprise uses credit, 0 if not
Location	1 if urban, 0 if not
Urban location	1 if capital city, 0 if not
Business age	1 if "old" business, 0 if "new" (criterion: number of years operating)
Gender of head	1 if female, 0 if not
Education variables	Number of years of primary, secondary, tertiary, and vocational education for household head, and averages for other household workers
Experience in this occupation	Number of years of experience of household head and averages (years) for other household members
Age	Age of household head, and average age of others
Nationality	1 if national, 0 if not

(Vijverberg 1988b, p. 5; Chiswick 1983).[14] The coefficient for the capital variable is the return on capital, while the coefficient on L is the return on labor.

Household labor is a variable constructed by aggregating working hours across household members. The period of aggregation (week, month, year) should be the same as that used for the dependent variable, that is, net revenues. Similarly, the total hours of work of hired labor should also enter the regression. However, as this is much less likely to be known from survey data, it can be proxied by the number of hired laborers and apprentices working in the enterprise. Alternatively, the monthly wage bill for hired labor can be entered. However, since apprentices are paid only intermittently, the wage bill can be an imperfect proxy for hired labor input. Both owned capital and rented capital are entered. These are the aggregate values of buildings, equipment, machinery, and so on used by each enterprise.

The type of variables capturing enterprise and household characteristics that can be included depends very much on the content of the survey on which the analysis is based. Box 5.5 presents a set of relevant candidate variables. Dummy variables for government registration and contracts for hired workers are used to capture the effects of enterprise formality/informality. A dummy variable for foreign and domestic buyers can proxy the effect of whether the enterprise produces tradable goods. Buyers can be grouped into either formal (public enterprise, large private enterprise, and so on) or informal (other households, local trader, and so on), and dummy variables entered for these characteristics (this captures the benefits of supplying the formal sector market, which may be less competitive than the informal market). Credit is of key relevance, because access to credit can determine how much an enterprise can take advantage of emerging opportunities, for example, by borrowing to purchase new equipment. Since access to credit is difficult to quantify, actual use of credit may have to be used as proxy. The location variables capture the effects of differences in local markets on enterprise profits. For instance, household enterprises may face more competition in the capital city than in rural areas.

Household characteristics include the gender of the household head, the average education levels of household members engaged in the enterprise, experience, and nationality (the latter can reflect, for example, the dominance of for-

Box 5.6: Profits from household enterprises in Côte d'Ivoire

Non-farm enterprises provide an important income source for households during periods of adjustment. Vijverberg (1988b) has estimated a profit function of the type described in the text for these types of enterprises in Côte d'Ivoire. The explanatory variables include those in Box 5.5. Of particular interest are the coefficients on the hours-of-work variable used in profit functions estimated for different types of household enterprises. These coefficients give the returns to labor.

The table in this box shows that the return (measured in CFA francs) from an extra hour of labor varies significantly across household enterprises. With the exception of services, the return from selling that hour in the labor market is substantially greater. Although households will also earn a return on the capital employed in their enterprise, most poor households have very little capital. Therefore, the magni-

tude of the difference in returns to labor (particularly between wage-employment and manufacturing or food commerce) suggests that many households engaged in these enterprises do so because wage-employment is rationed (which may be the result of formal sector wages being set above market-clearing levels).

Comparisons of returns on an hour of labor
(CFA francs)

	Non-farm enterprises	Wage-employment
Manufacturing	23	122
Food commerce	65	124
Nonfood commerce	100	133
Services	150	154

Source: Vijverberg 1988b.

---

eigners in some informal activities in West Africa).

Profit functions should be estimated for the main types of household enterprise: food commerce, nonfood commerce, services, and manufacturing. Estimated coefficients can then be compared to highlight differences in the structure of each activity (Box 5.6). Since food commerce, nonfood commerce, and services are primarily nontradables, while manufacturing includes tradables, a comparison of profit functions estimated from several surveys can indicate the effects of adjustment on the non-farm sector.

Separate profit functions for each activity should be estimated for enterprises in (i) male- and female-headed households, (ii) rural, capital city, and other urban households, and (iii) poor and non-poor households. Regarding (i), estimating profit functions for male- and female-headed households gives a clearer indication of the different constraints facing each across the activity range. Thus, the procedure adopted above for estimating the effects of discrimination on female wage earnings can be adapted to self-employment earnings. This involves estimating a profit function for enterprises in male-headed households, and then inserting mean values for the independent variables of female-headed households to predict the profits of the latter if they faced the same circumstances as male-headed households. This may reveal significant differences across the activity types: for example, there may be little difference in enterprise earnings of male- and female-headed households in services,

once characteristics are controlled for. But there may be substantial differences in manufacturing if (say) male-headed households have favorable access to capital and inputs (due, for instance, to discrimination against women entrepreneurs in informal and formal credit markets). Adjustment will aggravate or improve these constraints depending on the policy package.

Profit functions can be used to predict the effects of projects targeted to improving the assets of household enterprises, as part of strategies to raise their benefits from the adjustment process. In many countries, the returns on owned and rented capital are high, reflecting a lack of access to capital assets among households. The earnings of many households would increase significantly if their capital were improved. Similarly, the estimated returns on the different levels of education together with vocational training indicate how useful the country's education structure is to earning a livelihood in household enterprises. Separate profit functions for the groups outlined provide estimates of the likely returns on targeted projects; for example, credit schemes for self-employed women, infrastructure projects of special importance to rural non-farm enterprises, and targeted vocational assistance to poor households.

Comparing the returns to labor in non-farm self-employment and wage-employment

An important issue is the degree to which participation in non-farm self-employment, especially in the urban informal sector, is "voluntary" (chosen in preference to wage-employment), or involuntary because insufficient wage opportunities are available. The latter can occur when labor markets are segmented into a formal sector, paying above-market wages, and an informal sector, to which those unable to obtain jobs must resort for employment. This dualism in the employment structure can be exacerbated when adjustment causes a formal labor shake-out, leading to the swelling of the informal sector, and a further depression of earnings there.

At the margin, the returns to an individual's labor in self-employment and wage-employment should be equal. Some guidance about whether self-employment is voluntary can be obtained by calculating the return to labor in self-employment using the estimated coefficient on the labor variable in the profit function in Box 5.6 (Vijverberg 1988b). Given the estimated wage function (3), the predicted wage for someone with the mean characteristics of the self-employed is calculated. If this wage is substantially higher than the return on labor in self-employment, this indicates that self-employment may not be a voluntary choice.

Producer-household models

The decisions involved in the operation of household enterprises can be examined explicitly through the use of producer-household models. To date, these have been applied in the analysis of farm-household enterprises (see Singh, Squire, and Strauss 1986a and 1986b). However, they can be applied to households in the non-farm sector, without major changes, provided that one can assume that households face exogenous prices determined by complete product and labor markets (this assumption is easier to make for non-farm enterprises—at least in urban areas—than farm enterprises). In addition to showing how the demand for own-labor adjusts when relative prices change, household models also derive the effect on hired labor demand. When used alongside an estimate of labor supply to the sector, the induced change in wage levels can be calculated in addition to the change in household profits.

Such modeling requires a comprehensive data set since the household's decisions concerning time allocations, commodity demands, product choices, and investments are all jointly determined. A multi-topic survey is needed for the deployment of a wide variety of model structures.

Concluding observations

Because adjustment causes profound shifts in labor markets, the formulation of employment policies becomes more difficult at such times (van der Hoeven 1987). Employment targets in national plans may have to be changed substantially as the whole economic base of the country alters under adjustment (Richards 1986). The related fields of government activity (for example, education) are affected.

Consequently, the kind of information that policymakers need changes considerably under adjustment. The policy questions that arise vary. For example: Does adjustment influence female urban labor supply? Will financial reform affect the earnings of rural non-farm enterprises? Are the employment prospects of school-leavers improved by policy reforms? What are the effects of devaluation on urban versus rural incomes? The examination of these and other policy issues requires a range of analytical techniques. Analysis must be accurate if it is to serve policymaking. But it must also be timely given the pace at which policy formulation proceeds. Inevitably there may be tradeoffs between analytical rigor and meeting deadlines, and analysts will have to present their conclusions with a wider confidence interval than desired. The balance to be struck is a difficult one. The simplest techniques may be recommended on the grounds that they are the quickest to apply. However, simple tabulations may lead to erroneous conclusions and can seriously misinform policymaking. Multivariate techniques provide a more reliable research method for policy prescription.

Notes

1. The "active population" covers people in work, looking for work, or currently ill. Persons enrolled in school or who have been enrolled during the previous 12 months are usually excluded. Standard international definitions should be used (see Turvey 1990).

2. Chapter 4 discusses the construction of poverty lines. The main policy interest in Frame 5.1 is how the employment status of the poor differs from that of the non-poor.

3. For example, the Ghana Living Standards Survey Abstract reports employment data using age-groups of 7-14, 15-19, 20-24, 25-44, 45-54, and over 55 (Republic of Ghana 1988, p. 61).

4. The classifications here follow those of Chapter 11.

5. The data could be presented by household income quintiles, but the difference in income sources for poor and

non-poor households is the principal issue of policy interest.

6. Alternatively, a significant money-wage differential between regions may exist to compensate for differences in costs of living. In such cases the real-wage differential should be computed using the regional cost of living series if they are available.

7. The inclusion of P in these regressions assumes that a price index is available for different regions or other groupings. If only a national index exists, then it cannot be included in the regression, since it would show no variation across observations.

8. If the data set permits it, labor supply and commodity demand should be jointly estimated, since each arises out of a joint utility maximization. This results in more efficient parameter estimates (Blundell and Walker 1982).

9. These are treated in detail in Killingsworth (1983). See Killingsworth and Heckman (1986) for female labor supply, and Pudney (1989) for an advanced treatment.

10. The values of the explanatory variables can be any number, depending on the given sample. The process underlying the probit technique translates these values into probabilities (which range from 0 to 1), while maintaining the property that increases in these transformed values are associated with increases (or decreases) in the dependent variable (in this case LP). The cumulative probability function provides a suitable transformation, since its range is the [0,1] interval.

11. See Killingsworth and Heckman (1986, p. 182) for the derivation of the Mills ratio and Grootaert (1986) for an application of the method.

12. A measure of school quality could also be included among the education variables (Behrman and Birdsall 1983).

13. See Chow (1960) for a description of this test and Grootaert (1986) for an application.

14. We use profit functions instead of production functions because our concern is with earnings rather than output, although of course the two functions are related by assuming household profit maximization (see Lau 1978).

6

Migration responses to adjustment

Mark Montgomery

Until recently, African governments have been far readier to express concern over the spatial distribution of their populations than their population growth rates (Abumere 1981). A number of African countries could still be described as laissez-faire in respect to population growth, and some could even be regarded as pro-natalist. But few if any countries maintain a laissez-faire attitude toward population distribution. Much policy attention has been directed to the issue of rural-to-urban migration, where the urgency in policy has to do with the perceived consequences of over-rapid city growth.

The percentages of African populations living in urban areas are not high by developing-country standards; nor are these percentages increasing at an unusually rapid rate. What is unusual are the rates of growth in urban populations; these rates are extraordinary by both developing-country and historical standards. Perhaps a half of city growth can be attributed to natural population increase —to the excess of urban births over deaths. African urban fertility levels are not much lower than rural fertility levels. There is considerable scope for family planning and other policy measures aimed at reducing urban fertility, even if policy-makers remain narrowly concerned with population distribution and the consequences of rapid urban growth.

This chapter examines the implications of structural adjustment for the spatial deployment of labor. It examines how the prices and policies that emerge in adjustment affect decisions about migration at the individual level, and how these effects may be analyzed. It is clear that the structural changes brought about by adjustment policy will require resource shifts, including labor mobility. Migration can be considered in many cases as a requirement for a successful adjustment program. Without some migration response, resource misallocations may persist, despite changes in the system of incentives. Indeed, if adjustment redirects migrant flows, perhaps by encouraging urban-to-rural movement or by channeling migrants away from capital to secondary cities, there are implications for public sector planning and investment in infrastructure.

At the same time, migration is an important determinant of human welfare. Households generally make migration decisions to maximize lifetime income flows, or to acquire human capital for members. In extreme cases, migration can be a response to severe hardship, acting as a safety valve during periods of deprivation and economic stress. For these reasons, it is crucial to understand migration responses as part of an assessment of the social dimensions of adjustment.

Markets, infrastructure, and migration

A United Nations–sponsored inquiry in 1977 showed the level of concern among African governments about population distribution. Of 48 African governments responding to the inquiry, 45 characterized the spatial distribution of population as "extremely" or "substantially" unacceptable; 37 expressed a desire to decelerate or reverse rural-to-urban movement (Kosinski and Clarke

1982). While comparatively few countries have well-articulated and explicit population distribution policies, a number have sought to address distribution issues as a component of overall development planning, usually as a part of regional or rural development objectives.

Adepoju (1982) points to three areas of difficulty in the formulation of population distribution policy:

• Poor or non-existent data bases for studying interrelations between socioeconomic conditions and internal migration

• Predominance of so-called "spontaneous" moves, motivated by economic factors, among all migratory movements

• High per capita costs associated with explicit population resettlement and land colonization schemes.

The disappointing record of *explicit* redistribution policies in Africa and elsewhere implies that government policy regarding migration must focus for the most part on *implicit* policies, whereby migration is affected primarily through the economic determinants of spontaneous movements (United Nations 1981).

The discussion that follows gives priority to the economic determinants of internal migration. We recognize the importance of international migration on the African scene (Zachariah and Condé 1981), and also recognize the role of non-economic factors that influence population movements (such as political and ethnic disturbances, and famines). Consideration of these important issues, however, lies outside the scope of this chapter.

Background

There is a remarkable degree of intra-country diversity in levels of population density (Hill 1990). Kenya, for example, has three areas of high population density clustered around Lake Victoria. Cameroon displays a core of high-density settlement in the western highlands bordering Nigeria and around Yaoundé. In Benin, Ghana, and Côte d'Ivoire, population densities reach 200 persons per kilometer in the coastal regions—yet fall below 20 per kilometer in the north; a similar pattern prevails in Nigeria.

These variations in population density reflect ecological factors (climate, soil types, the incidence of disease) and longstanding historical influences as well as current responses to economic conditions. According to Abumere (1981), in a number of countries there is an imbalance between the distribution of population and the distribution of potential agricultural resources. Abumere argues that food-crop-producing areas, such as the middle belt of Nigeria, were neglected in the colonial era relative to areas producing for export, and to some degree those areas continue to be underdeveloped today.

Urbanization rates and levels are of particular concern to African policymakers. Four features of urbanization in Sub-Saharan Africa are distinctive.[1] First, urban proportions remain low in comparison with those in much of the developing world (Montgomery and Brown 1990). Second, there is marked country-specific variation about the average. In East Africa, for example, Somalia and the Sudan display urban proportions considerably higher than the average for the sub-region. At the other extreme are two neighboring countries, Burundi and Rwanda, with very low levels of urbanization (4.5 percent in the late 1970s). Estimates for Uganda are also low (9 percent in 1980), while the Kenyan 1979 level, at 13 percent, is close to the norm for East Africa. Similar country variation is evident in West Africa, where the coastal countries display higher levels of urbanization than do those of the Sahel.

A third salient feature of urbanization in Sub-Saharan Africa is perhaps at the root of policy concern: extremely high rates of city growth. Although these rates have historical precedent—the cities of tropical Latin America and South Asia experienced a similar pace of growth in the 1950s —growth in total African urban populations is occurring at rates that considerably exceed those experienced by industrial countries at a comparable period in their histories. For almost all Sub-Saharan countries, recent annual growth rates in total urban population are higher than 5 percent, and a significant number of countries exhibit rates of 10 percent or above. Tanzania's annual urban growth rate was nearly 12 percent over the 1967-78 period; Kenya's rate of growth was 6.4 percent over the period. In general, urban growth rates are higher in East Africa (6.9 percent over the 1975-80 period) than in West Africa (5.3 percent) or Southern Africa (3.6 percent).

It is important to recognize that high natural rates of population growth are a major contributor to the high rates of African urban growth. The natural rate of population growth (crude birth rates less crude death rates) itself accounts for some 40-60 percent of urban growth, with the remainder due to rural-to-urban migration and conversion of rural areas.

The fourth important feature of African urbanization is the concentration of urban population in a few large cities or towns. In most countries, more than half the urban population live in cities of at least 50,000 inhabitants; the majority of countries have no more than six cities of this size. Malawi in 1977 had 68 percent of its total urban population in two towns with more than 50,000 inhabitants, and over 50 percent of its urban population lived in the largest city. Senegal in 1976 had three-quarters of its total urban population in the six cities with more than 50,000 inhabitants. Thus, the typical African urban dweller lives in a medium-size city that is growing very quickly.

This pace and concentration of urban growth raises many development concerns. African urbanization does not seem to have been accompanied by a conventional structural economic transformation. In particular, growth in manufacturing output and employment has been disappointing in many Sub-Saharan countries (Becker and Morrison 1988; Montgomery and Brown 1990). Policy-related distortions (such as pricing schemes that penalize agriculture and benefit urban consumers) may have encouraged over-rapid rates of cityward migration. Rural out-migration removes from rural areas the needed human capital and skills embodied in young migrants.

In an adverse macroeconomic climate, rapid urban growth places severe stress on public sector capabilities. Urban administration, the development of revenue instruments, and the planning and management of infrastructural investments and interventions in the labor market are all made more difficult by the rapid pace at which African cities are growing (Linn 1982). The difficulties in providing infrastructure are particularly apparent in Africa's secondary cities, many of which do not possess the infrastructure necessary to attract firms and employment (Montgomery and Brown 1990).

Policy issues

Specific development concerns about population distribution, rural out-migration, and urban growth vary from country to country in Sub-Saharan Africa, but at least three issues are of common concern in the region and can be addressed in the context of structural adjustment:

• What is the impact of earnings levels and agricultural prices on rural-to-urban migration? To what extent do investments in rural agricultural infrastructure reduce out-migration? To what

extent is rural-to-urban migration encouraged by the greater availability and accessibility of public services (for example, education) in urban areas?

• What economic factors have the greatest impact on migration to African secondary cities? What factors encourage relocation from capital to secondary cities, and from rural areas to secondary cities?

• How important are agricultural development measures, as expressed in levels of rural infrastructural investments, and agricultural prices and earnings, in redirecting rural-to-rural migration?

With these priority issues in mind, we now turn to a more detailed examination of the role of economic factors in African migration.

Macro-meso linkages

A number of African countries have exhibited a degree of "urban bias" in their pricing and service delivery policies, and among urban areas, have tended to promote policies that directly or indirectly favor the largest cities. Structural adjustment programs have aimed to rationalize pricing and service delivery. For African economies, this has meant devaluation of the exchange rate, removal of bureaucratic controls and licenses on trade, and increases in the real prices of agricultural goods. As these price and policy distortions are removed, the longer-run labor supply response will be determined in large part by the reallocation of labor across economic sectors and locations.

What is known about the impacts of macro-level policy variables on the spatial allocation of labor? Kelley and Williamson (1984) considered the issues in the context of a detailed general equilibrium model of rural-urban migration. Their principal finding is that changes in the external terms of trade between manufactured and agricultural goods exert a powerful influence on the rate of rural-urban migration. As they put it, " the terms of trade between urban-based manufactures and rural-based primary products appears to be a far more critical determinant of future Third World urban performance than the relative price of imported fuels and natural resources." Among all factors influencing urbanization rates (changes in the percentage of the population that is urban), terms-of-trade effects are rivalled in magnitude only by sectoral rates of technological progress. The Kelley-Williamson model suggests that the external terms of trade are considerably more important than foreign aid flows, agricultural land scarcities, or population pressures (although see Preston and Greene 1985 for a critique).

In the scenario studied by Kelley and Williamson, an externally produced increase in the ratio of manufactured to agricultural prices P_M/P_A engenders an initial rightward shift in the demand for labor in urban manufactures. This initial shift in labor demand sets off cityward migration and induces a host of changes in urban markets for nontradable goods and services. Equilibrium is restored by a combination of two forces. First, the returns to labor in agriculture begin to respond positively to the withdrawal of labor from that sector. In addition, elements of the urban cost-of-living index—particularly housing rents, congestion costs, and prices of urban services—increase in tandem with urban labor force growth. Taken together, these factors diminish the real-earnings benefit that can be derived from rural-urban migration. As the full set of wages and prices is reconfigured, the rural-urban division of labor settles into its new equilibrium.

To the extent that structural adjustment in Africa succeeds in altering the terms of trade between exportable and nontradable goods in favor of the former, one might expect to see the neoclassical outcome envisioned by Kelley and Williamson working in the reverse. There would occur a rightward shift in the demands for agricultural and other exportable goods, which might (depending on the spatial location of their production) reduce incentives for rural-to-urban migration, relieve pressures on urban rents and public services, and increase agricultural outputs and incomes.

When one leaves the Kelley-Williamson neoclassical model, however, the spatial implications of terms-of-trade adjustments lose this crisp definition. We must recognize that exportables are produced in both urban and rural African sectors; hence, returns to exportables production need not imply diminution of rural-urban migration. For many African economies the magnitudes of agricultural price elasticities of supply are in doubt. Agricultural land suffers from environmental degradation aggravated in some regions by population pressures and climatic change. Owing to the difficulties of technological advance and the limited penetration of marketing infrastructure, agricultural supply elasticities may remain low even in the face of substantial adjustments in the external terms of trade. It is conceivable that the terms of trade between manufacturing and

agriculture could exert only a modest influence on sectoral and spatial demands for labor.

In summary, the issues raised in Kelley and Williamson's elegant formulation require more careful scrutiny on a country-by-country basis before they can be accepted as valid for Sub-Saharan Africa. Becker and Morrison (1988) have attempted to refashion certain aspects of the Kelley-Williamson model for African economies. Unfortunately, the limited data available to Becker and Morrison do not permit key parameters of the model to be estimated.

Markets and the migrant

At the heart of the debate about long- and short-run supply responses is the question of household labor allocation. How powerful are the effects of relative prices and infrastructure on migration decisions? There is now little debate over the proposition that economic factors, broadly construed, play the dominant role in migration decisions (see Yap 1977). Migration can be viewed as a form of human capital investment (see Sjastaad 1962, and Schwartz 1976 for early formulations) in which individuals move to take advantage of location-specific lifetime streams of real earnings. Differentials in migration propensities by economic sector, urban or rural location, age, sex, and education reflect differentials in the streams of earnings with respect to these characteristics.[2]

The human capital perspective on migration has been furthered by Todaro (1969) and Harris and Todaro (1970), who developed the notion that *expected* real earnings motivate migration. Expected earnings are the product of the real earnings level, for those who acquire employment, and the probability that the employment search is successful. A one-period version of the Todaro model is illuminating. Let w_R represent the real rural wage or earnings level, and let w_U represent its urban counterpart. Imagine that unemployment exists only in urban areas and let the one-period probability of unsuccessful job search be u, where u is the unemployment rate for the urban economy. If we can ignore relocation costs, then it is evidently rational to migrate from a rural area to an urban area if the expected urban real wage exceeds the rural real wage, that is, if

$$w_U(1-u) > w_R \qquad (1)$$

This formulation shows how high rates of urban unemployment u can be expected to discourage rural-urban migration and, conversely, how high rates of migration can remain rational even in the face of urban unemployment, provided that urban real wages are pegged sufficiently high relative to rural wages.

The model also points up another micro-meso connection, in the implications of continued migration for urban labor markets. If urban real wages are rigid[3] and unresponsive to market forces, cityward migration will persist until the point at which the urban expected wage $w_u(1-u)$ is driven down to equality with the rural wage. In equilibrium, the urban unemployment rate will be:[4]

$$u^e = 1 - \frac{w_R}{w_u} \qquad (2)$$

Thus, at a point in time, market wages and unemployment levels drive migration; but over time, migration shapes the urban labor market and the level of the expected wage. Harris and Todaro (1970) explore these issues.

It is now recognized that the Harris-Todaro formulation gives perhaps too much prominence to urban unemployment rates. In Sub-Saharan Africa, open unemployment is an option only for a select category of urban job seekers, namely those who have the means to sustain themselves by savings or family connections while searching for work. Only for a select category of potential migrants would unemployment rates be likely to exert an important influence on locational decisions. This point is confirmed in the migration analysis by Schultz (1982), which shows unemployment rates to matter only for better-educated potential migrants.

We should broaden the Harris-Todaro perspective and inquire into the role played by other factors in the adjustment to locational equilibrium. As Kelley and Williamson remind us, increases in transport costs, land rents, and the prices of urban services are all likely to accompany a demand-induced increase in the urban labor force. How might these elements of the urban cost of living feed back into household migration decisions? The literature contains surprisingly little analysis of this central issue, owing to the scarcity of detailed price data for developing countries. In consequence, very little is known about the influence of urban rents, transport costs, or public service pricing on migration decisions in Africa. Neither has the role of infrastructure availability and quality received systematic attention with regard to migration.

Table 6.1 provides a summary list of prices and other indicators relevant to migration that can be constructed from the data supplied in household and/or community surveys. We will treat the variables in Table 6.1 as representing the fundamental exogenous economic variables that guide migration. Note that income, as such, does not appear in the table; the key prices and wages that determine income appear instead. Schooling is the principal human capital asset considered. Physical assets, such as land, could be added to the list.

Migration decisions will certainly depend on the levels of nominal wages or earnings (the latter being standardized according to hours worked) that a potential migrant would expect to receive in various locations. These expected earnings levels will differ according to the potential migrant's age, sex, and education. Key consumer prices, such as the prices of staples, will also figure in migration decisions and are included as separate items in the table. In some African countries, these prices exhibit considerable locational variation arising from transport costs and subsidies. Table 6.1 also includes measures of (urban) rents and direct measures of transport costs; the list could be expanded to encompass the prices of services such as electricity and water supply, as well as access to educational and health services.

A statistical framework

Building on the insights of Harris and Todaro, suitably modified to include the locational characteristics represented in Table 6.1, we now turn to a model of migration that is amenable to statistical analysis. The empirical model discussed here was originally put forward by Schultz (1982). We shall introduce the model in this section and return subsequently to consider it in more depth.

Consider a person who lives in location 1 at a point in time. The net benefit attached to that location is expressed as:

$$U_1 = \omega_1 + \varepsilon_1 \qquad (3)$$

where ω_1 represents the level of real expected earnings, and the disturbance term ε_1 embodies other unmeasured and idiosyncratic factors. We regard ω_1 as being determined by a host of economic variables, including the nominal wage w_1 the person expects to command, other features (for example, unemployment rates u_1) of the local labor market, the prices of housing, food, and other location-specific goods p_1, and infrastructural

Table 6.1: Exogenous explanatory variables for migration analyses

Human capital assets
- Own schooling
- Age
- Sex

Factor markets[a]
- Local wage rates (male and female, specific for levels of schooling and type of location)
- Local rates of unemployment and labor force participation (male and female separately by levels of schooling and type of location)

Product markets[a]
- Major own-enterprise product prices
- Major consumption item prices
  Basic staples prices
  Other food prices
  Rents and housing prices
  Transport prices
  Other consumption prices
  Health services prices
  Education prices (monetary and time)
- Financial market prices (formal and informal interest rates)

Infrastructure[a]
- Education
  Schooling/training availability
  Schooling/training quality
- Health and family planning clinics

a. Derived from community surveys or aggregated individual responses from household surveys.

variables z_1,

$$\omega_1 = \beta_1 w_1 + \beta_2 u_1 + \beta_3 p_1 + \beta_4 z_1 \qquad (4)$$

The β coefficients in (4) should be interpreted as weights that, when applied to the nominal wage, unemployment, prices, and infrastructure, produce a real standard-of-living index ω.

For the potential migrant who resides in location 1, an alternate location j holds out the possibility of a net benefit equal to:

$$U_j = \omega_j - c_{1j} + \varepsilon_j \qquad (5)$$

where ω_j is the real earnings level in j (dependent on w_j, u_j, p_j, and z_j), and ε_j is the disturbance term for location j. The factor c_{1j} represents the relocation costs that must be borne to move from location 1 to j. These costs may depend on the migrant's age, sex, and education, on the distance or travel time between locations, and on informational factors and the like. Thus, equation (5) gives the benefit to a move with relocation costs netted out.

The potential migrant confronts an array of locational options, including the possibility of remaining in her origin location 1, with each option being characterized by an expected payoff:

$$U_1 = \omega_1 + \varepsilon_1$$
$$\vdots$$
$$U_j = \omega_j + c_{1j} + \varepsilon_j$$
$$\vdots$$
$$U_K = \omega_K + c_{1K} + \varepsilon_K \qquad (6)$$

The location promising greatest net benefit is selected from among these possibilities.

Under suitable assumptions regarding the disturbance terms ε (see Ben-Akiva and Lerman 1985), the probability that the optimal choice is to remain in the origin location 1 is:

$$P_{11} = \frac{e^{\omega_1}}{\sum_{k=1}^{K} e^{\omega_k - c_{1k}}} \qquad (7)$$

whereas the probability of a move from location 1 to j is given by:

$$P_{1j} = \frac{e^{\omega_j - c_{1j}}}{\sum_{k=1}^{K} e^{\omega_k - c_{1k}}} \qquad (8)$$

Note that in the expressions above the characteristics of *all* potential locational alternatives affect decisions to stay or to move. The greater the net benefit index $\omega_j - c_{1j}$ associated with a particular alternative j, the greater the likelihood that it will be chosen. Equations (7) and (8) are choice probabilities corresponding to the *logit* choice model.

In the form presented here, the underlying parameters of the logit model can be estimated only by iterative and computationally difficult techniques. Yet as Schultz (1982) has noted, there is a way of viewing the model that renders estimation straightforward. Suppose that there exist N_1 potential migrants in the index location 1. Then the ratio of movers N_{1j} from location 1 to j to stayers N_{11} is:

$$\frac{N_{1j}}{N_{11}} = \frac{N_1 P_{1j}}{N_1 P_{11}} = e^{\omega_j - c_{1j} - \omega_1} \qquad (9)$$

Two features of equation (9) bear emphasis. First, although in principle all locations enter a potential migrant's calculations, the ratio shown in (9) contains only the net benefits for locations 1 and j.[5] Second, provided $N_{11} > 0$ and $N_{1j} > 0$, the equation is linear in logarithms, which facilitates estimation by ordinary regression methods. We shall employ this relationship below to develop a simple regression model that can uncover the influences of wages, prices, and other variables on migration decisions.

Analysis of migration data from household surveys

The data collected in many household surveys furnish what might be termed "partial" histories of individual migrations. Before we turn to the details of the analysis plan, a digression is in order regarding the merits and limitations of such histories.

Migration histories and construction of dependent variables

In many household surveys, questions permit only a partial reconstruction of an individual's sequence of locations. Figure 6.1 shows the portions of the full migration histories that can be reconstituted with the data typically at hand. For simplicity, let us restrict attention to three potential locations—labeled in the figure as rural (R), city 1 ($C1$), and city 2 ($C2$). Figure 6.1(a) depicts an individual who has lived in rural location R since birth. She is surveyed in R at age a_s. In Figure 6.1(c) a one-time migrant is shown; this person was born in city 1 and resided there until age a_1, at which point she moved to R, remaining there until the date of interview. Even with only a partial coverage of the individual's experience, the survey will identify her migration history in full. Likewise, the history of the person depicted in Figure 6.1(e), who was born in R, left for city 2, and then returned, will be fully recovered if the survey makes allowance for two episodes of migration.

By contrast, the migration histories depicted in Figures 6.1 (b),(d), and (f) will not be recovered in full in a typical household survey. The very short-term migrant shown in 6.1(b), whose sojourn away from R lasted less than a year, might not be distinguished from her counterpart in 6.1(a), who has never moved. For the cyclical migrant depicted in 6.1(d), we may know the age a_1 at which she first left her birthplace R and the age a_3 of the most recent out-migration from R, but may lack information on intervening events. Similarly, the

early portions of the migration history for the person in 6.1(f) may not be accessible through the sequence of migration questions giving only partial histories.

Migration window

With this background, let us consider the construction of a dependent variable for the analysis of migration. The dependent variable M will be binary in nature, taking the value "1" if the individual changed location in a pre-specified window of time prior to the survey, and taking the value "0" if no such move occurred. The essentials of the analysis are sketched in Figure 6.2. Suppose that a window of time of two years' length has been selected as the basis for the analysis. The individual shown in Figure 6.2 was surveyed in city 1 at age a_s, but two years previously had lived in rural area R. Among the influences that figure into locational decisions are:
- Individual characteristics such as age, sex, and education, summarized in the vector X;
- The prices and infrastructure variables (w_R, u_R, p_R, z_R) of origin area R; and
- Similar characteristics for city 1 (including its distance d_{RC1} from R) and alternative locations.

The task of the empirical analysis is to determine the effects of these individual, origin, and destination characteristics on migration decisions.

A first consideration in such an analysis is the appropriate length of the migration window. Consider Figure 6.3. In the cases depicted in 6.3(a) and 6.3(b), the migration window begins two years prior to the survey, when the person is age $a_s - 2$, and ends at the survey date. The person shown in 6.3(a) did not move within this two-year window; hence his or her $M = 0$. The person shown in 6.3(b) did change location, yielding $M = 1$. Suppose now that the window had been extended to cover five years prior to the survey, as indicated in Figures 6.3(c) and 6.3(d). The person shown in 6.3(c) would now be counted as a migrant, and the person in 6.3(d) would have moved twice in the interval, rather than once. Unless the survey elicits a full migration history, the questions posed in the migration questions would probably not reveal person (d)'s location as of age $a_s - 5$.

Thus, two consequences follow from the extension of the migration window: (i) a longer window will inevitably catch more changes of location; but (ii) the longer the window, the less likely we are to possess information about the person's initial

Figure 6.1: Representative individual migration histories
(R = rural area, C1 = city 1, C2 = city 2)

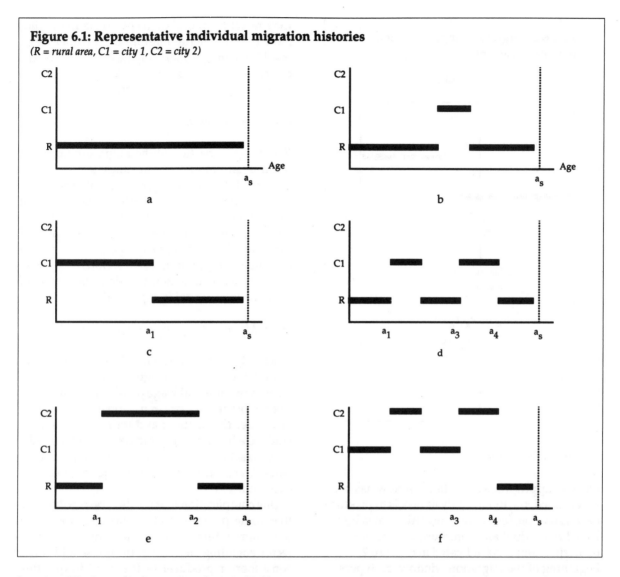

location. The loss of information about initial location is serious. It means that we cannot link information about prices and infrastructure in the initial location with subsequent migration decisions. Moreover, the longer the window, the less informative are economic conditions (w, u, p, z) prevailing at the survey date for analyses of migration preceding the survey date.

What then is the appropriate window length? The answer must depend on the nature of migration, a country-specific matter that cannot be resolved here. A one-year window may capture too few migrations for some African countries; and yet a five-year window may not allow enough initial locations to be identified. A compromise must be struck regarding window length on the basis of an examination of the survey data and related secondary sources. We note that a standard question in population censuses concerns residence at a point one year or five years prior to the census. If tabulations of such census information are available, they may help in determining the frequency of migration and hence the appropriate window length.

Empirical analysis

We now turn to the empirical analysis itself. A typical analysis proceeds in three stages. First, out-migration profiles by age, sex, and initial location are constructed and compared with other published information. In the second stage of the investigation, a multivariate analysis of out-migration is undertaken. Finally, a multivariate study of origin-destination pairs is conducted, following the approach of Schultz (1982).

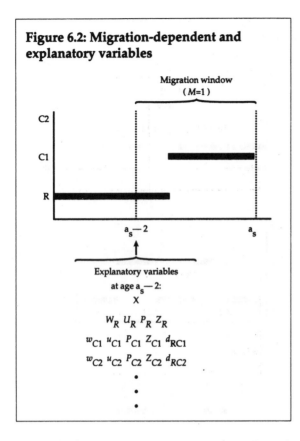

Figure 6.2: Migration-dependent and explanatory variables

Migration window
$(M=1)$

C2

C1

R

$a_s - 2$ a_s

Explanatory variables
at age $a_s - 2$:
X

w_R u_R p_R z_R

w_{C1} u_{C1} p_{C1} z_{C1} d_{RC1}

w_{C2} u_{C2} p_{C2} z_{C2} d_{RC2}

•

•

•

Out-migration profiles

Once an appropriate migration window has been determined, the initial analysis task is to produce descriptive profiles of out-migration rates by selected individual and community characteristics of origin regions. As indicated in Figure 6.2, at the beginning of the migration window, each person in the sample is characterized by an initial location; these locations might be classified as rural or urban, and the degree of "urban-ness" may also be of interest. The individual's sex and age at the beginning of the window are available. Educational attainment may be taken as given, at least for potential migrants of an age such that further education is improbable. For each combination of location, age, sex, and education, the probability of migration ($M=1$) is then determined from sample tabulations.

These descriptive profiles can be compared to other country-specific sources of migration information. They may also be assessed against the model migration profiles developed by demographers (Rogers 1975; Zachariah and Condé 1981), which exhibit considerable regularity with respect to age pattern. Any deviations from such established patterns can be investigated to determine if

they result from omissions or errors in the data. Note that the model migration schedules developed by demographers rely heavily on non-African data; deviations from the schedules need not signal the presence of data errors.

Out-migration models

Following inspection of the migration profiles, a multivariate model of out-migration should be estimated. In such an approach, only the origin-specific prices, wages, and infrastructure are considered in the estimation, in addition to individual variables such as age, sex, and education. A logit model is again appropriate for this analysis, although for preliminary descriptive purposes ordinary least squares regression will often suffice. The logit model is expressed as,

$$\text{logit } M_i = \alpha_0 + \alpha_1 w_0 + \alpha_2 u_0 + \alpha_3 p_0 + \alpha_4 z_0 + X_i \gamma \quad (10)$$

where M_i is the individual indicator of migration (0 or 1 for person i); origin-level characteristics such as the nominal wage or level of earnings w_0, unemployment u_0, prices p_0, and infrastructure z_0 also enter the relation; and individual traits, including education, age, and sex, are subsumed in X_i. Interactions between the individual characteristics X_i and the economic variables might also be explored.

One complication that needs to be considered is that some prices—notably, those for foods and other agricultural goods—may have different effects depending on whether the household is a net consumer or producer of the good in question. Clearly, if a good such as rice is produced in rural areas and consumed in both urban and rural areas, a single α coefficient cannot capture the effects of a change in rice prices on both urban and rural well-being. For some goods, equation (10) should be amended to include interactions between locational characteristics (that is, urban-rural dummy variables; dummies for regions that possess natural advantages in the production of certain crops) and prices. This would allow rice prices to have a different net impact in urban and rural areas, and between rural areas where rice production is feasible and others where rice growing is difficult.

A note on explanatory variables

The explanatory variables w_0, u_0, and p_0 should *not* be constructed from person i's data record, in

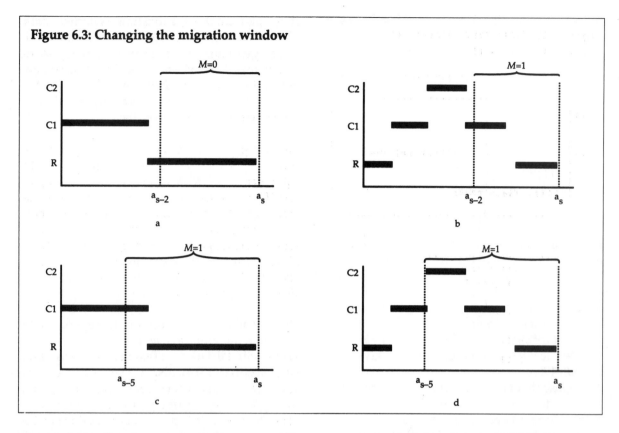

Figure 6.3: Changing the migration window

general, but rather from one of two sources: (i) community-level data gathered in a supplementary community questionnaire (where applicable); and (ii) aggregated individual data, where the basis for the aggregation consists of individuals similar to person *i* in respect to age, sex, education, and initial location. Why this extra layer of complication? First, the use of an individual's own nominal wages, own experience of unemployment, and the like, raises issues of selectivity that are difficult to resolve.[6] Moreover, the individual data collected in a survey typically pertain to the survey date, not to the earlier period corresponding to the beginning of the migration window. For instance, an individual's current experience with unemployment may be a *consequence* of a move occurring earlier within the migration window, rather than a cause of that migration. These concerns argue for the use of community or aggregated data in preference to individual data.

The construction of community data on wages, prices, and infrastructure poses its own problems. A household survey sampling frame cannot include all communities and market areas in a country. Some surveyed individuals will be found to have migrated from communities outside the sampling frame. It will not generally be possible, at least in the initial stages of data gathering, to

reconstruct the key economic variables (w_0, u_0, p_0, z_0) for these communities of origin. (Note that cross-national migrants present such problems in the extreme.) We have little alternative but to exclude such migrants from consideration.

Assessing the effects of structural adjustment

How do the estimated out-migration coefficients α in equation (10) shed light on structural adjustment and labor mobility? At first glance, the interpretation of out-migration coefficients seems to be straightforward. Consider the coefficient α_1 attached to the origin-area nominal wage w_0. We expect to find $\alpha_1 < 0$; that is, higher nominal wages in the origin area should inhibit out-migration, other things being equal. If an adjustment program increases nominal wages in community A and reduces them in community B, we anticipate less out-migration from A and greater out-migration from B.

Yet complications can arise, and it is entirely possible that the estimated α_1 will be found to be positive rather than negative. This seemingly perverse result—suggesting that higher wages encourage out-migration—can be explained as a consequence of including only the origin variables in the migration equation. Consider again the potential migrant's decision options. He or she chooses from a list of locations offering utility levels:

$$U_1 = \omega_1 + \varepsilon_1$$
$$\cdot$$
$$\cdot$$
$$U_j = \omega_j + c_{1j} + \varepsilon_j$$
$$\cdot$$
$$U_K = \omega_K + c_{1K} + \varepsilon_K \qquad (11)$$

where location "1" is the origin area and the ω_i variables depend on location i's wages, prices, and infrastructure. The probability of out-migration is the probability that the utility yielded by the best locational alternative in the set $(2,...,K)$ exceeds the utility derived from remaining in origin location 1. Therefore, the out-migration logit coefficients should be interpreted as giving the effects of changes in origin variables *relative to* the best locational alternative (Ben-Akiva and Lerman 1985).

Suppose that an adjustment program tends to increase nominal wages in origin community A but produces an even greater increase in the best alternative location, community B. Then an increase in origin wages would tend to be positively correlated with an increase in wage levels elsewhere, and in the sample as a whole higher origin wages could well exhibit a positive correlation with higher rates of out-migration, giving a misleading estimate $\alpha_1 > 0$. The statistical problem is essentially one of omitted variables. Migration decisions depend on the potential migrant's comparison of levels of well-being in his origin location relative to elsewhere, and yet equation (10) omits all such indicators of well-being for locations other than the origin. Thus, while out-migration equations are straightforward to estimate, and exploit the richness of individual-level data, any policy conclusions based on such equations must be advanced with caution.

Models for origin-destination pairs

These concerns motivate an exploration of origin-destination pairs, a mode of analysis that provides a much firmer base for policy inference. As noted, a full origin-destination analysis is demanding from the computational point of view. Schultz (1982) proposes a simplified approach, using aggregated data, which should prove adequate for our purposes. (More refined approaches can

be explored.) Box 6.1 illustrates selected results from Shultz's analysis. Recall an important result from equation (9). It was shown that if origin-area 1 contains N_1 individuals of a given age, sex, and education, N_{11} of whom did not change location and N_{1j} of whom moved to location j, then the ratio of movers to stayers is given by:

$$\frac{N_{ij}}{N_{11}} = \frac{N_1 P_{1j}}{N_1 P_{11}} = e^{\omega_j \cdot c_{ij} \cdot \omega_1} \qquad (12)$$

where, as earlier, the ω_1 and c_{1j} are represented as,

$$\omega_1 = \beta_1 w_1 + \beta_2 u_1 + \beta_3 p_1 + \beta_4 z_1$$
$$\omega_j = \beta_1 w_j + \beta_2 u_j + \beta_3 p_j + \beta_4 z_j$$
$$c_{1j} = \beta_0 + \beta_5 d_{1j} + \beta_6 a + \beta_7 e \qquad (13)$$

and we allow moving costs c_{1j} to depend on the potential migrant's age (a) and educational level (e) as well as distance d_{1j}. Taking logarithms of (12) and inserting (13) yields,

$$\log \frac{N_{1j}}{N_{11}} = -\beta_0 + \beta_1 (w_j - w_1) + \beta_2 (u_j - u_1)$$
$$+ \beta_3 (p_j - p_1) + \beta_4 (z_j - z_1) - \beta_5 d_{1j}$$
$$- \beta_6 a - \beta_7 e \qquad (14)$$

a linear equation that can be estimated by ordinary regression methods. Note that the explanatory economic variables on the right-hand side are the locational *differences* in nominal wages, unemployment levels, prices, and infrastructure.

To implement the regression approach, it is first necessary to aggregate the individual data contained in the survey into categories defined by origin and destination areas, age, sex, and education. The aggregation is required in order to ensure that $N_{1j} > 0$; otherwise, equation (12) cannot be converted to linear form. Just as in the out-migration analysis, the labor market and price data are constructed from community surveys or aggregated individual records; a typical specification will include interactions of prices and locational characteristics. The use of aggregate rather than individual data introduces some imprecision in the results, but for our purposes this need not be a serious drawback.[7]

Policy implications

Priority questions for policy involve the impacts of earnings, prices, and infrastructure on rural-to-urban migration; migration to secondary cities;

Box 6.1: Understanding the determinants of migration: Do unemployment rates matter?

T. P. Schultz (1982) has considered the issue of whether unemployment rates are important determinants of migration for men, using census data on regions in Venezuela. The issue is of concern to employment policy in the African context.

The data: Population census data from 1961 on 20 Venezuelan states, augmented by data from labor market surveys. Only men are considered in the analysis.

Methods: Schultz uses a variation of the origin-destination logit models discussed in the body of this chapter, in which to explain migration from state i to state j, the explanatory variables X are specified in terms of differences $X_j - X_i$. The sample is divided according to the level of (male) education, so as to study whether the determinants of migration vary in direction or strength across various educational groups. The following explanatory variables are among those examined:

E_i	The proportion employed of all males in the civilian labor force, state i, 1961
W_i	The estimated monthly wage rate for wage and salary workers, specific to education, state i, 1961
U_i	The proportion of state i's population in urban areas, 1961
D_{ij}	The distance, in kilometers, between the capital cities of states i and j

Selected results

Exogenous variables	Men without schooling (N=379)	Men with some secondary schooling (N=378)
$W_j - W_i$	2.69**	4.49**
$E_j - E_i$	0.32	4.58**
$U_j - U_i$	1.54**	2.48**
D_{ij}	-1.59**	-0.91**

** Statistically significant at 0.01 level.
Source: Schultz 1982, Table 2.

Interpretation: The analysis both confirms and challenges the influential theory of migration advanced by Todaro (1969).

As would be expected, the results show that (i) higher-wage states attract migrants (see positive coefficients on $W_j - W_i$); (ii) more-urbanized states also attract migrants; and (iii) the greater the distance between any pair of states, the smaller is the rate of migration. It appears that better-educated men are more responsive to wage differences and to differences in urbanization levels in choosing among alternative locations (the estimated coefficients are larger for men with secondary education), and are less deterred by distance (this coefficient is smaller). Thus, to understand the spatial flows of the labor force, it is necessary to disaggregate the labor force according to levels of education.

The challenge to Todaro's views is evident in the coefficient on the male employment rates. According to Todaro, potential migrants consider both the probability of finding employment (here indexed by the employment rate E) and the wage level W in choosing among locations. But the results show that Venezuelan men without schooling are insensitive to location-specific employment rates: The coefficient on $E_j - E_i$ is small and statistically insignificant. By contrast, men with secondary schooling are attracted to states with high employment rates and will tend to leave areas with low employment rates.

These results are plausible if one considers that men with no education are unlikely to possess the resources to go very long without work. A new migrant may take any offered employment, even at low wages, perhaps while continuing to search for better work. Open unemployment is not feasible for men in this category of education; thus, unemployment rates (or their complements, employment rates) do not figure into migration decisions. For men with secondary schooling, however, open unemployment is a possible job-search strategy, and therefore unemployment rates have relevance to migration decisions.

This finding reconfirms the payoff to stratifying an analysis by schooling levels. Suppose that a policymaker armed with these results notes an increase in unemployment rates in a particular region. The policymaker would predict a reduction in net in-migration for better-educated migrants (all else being held constant) but would predict little change in net flows for less-educated migrants. Over time, the skill composition of the labor force in the affected region would tend to shift toward the less-educated.

and rural-to-rural movements. By affecting prices, earnings, and the provision of infrastructure, structural adjustment can influence the economic determinants of spontaneous migration flows. How can the results of the analyses sketched here be put to use as one input into regional development planning?

Migration, adjustment, and regional planning

Suppose that the β coefficients of equation (14) have been estimated. Further suppose that an adjust-

ment program can be associated with a particular locational configuration of wages, prices, and the like (w', u', p', z'), which differs from the pre-adjustment configuration by location (w, u, p, z). Consider a group of individuals in location 1, where location 1 is perhaps a rural region that has been targeted by policymakers for a set of agricultural investments and interventions. Initially, location 1 contains N_1 potential migrants. Under the pre-adjustment configuration of infrastructure and prices, we could expect N_{11} of these to remain in location 1 over a period corresponding to the migration window, N_{1j} to migrate to migrate to location j, N_{1k} to location k, and so on, where we calculate the N_{1n} using:

$$N_{1n} = N_1 P_{1n}(w, u, p, z) \qquad (15)$$

with P_{1n} being the migration probability from area 1 to area n implied by the initial set of wages, prices, and infrastructure, as indicated in equations (7) and (8).

To understand the full implications of the change in (w, u, p, z) for regional development, we want to account not only for migration out of the target location 1, but also for migration into that location from all other locations. This can be done[8] by forming a matrix of migration probabilities P_{ij} and applying the probabilities to the initial distribution of potential migrants:

$$\begin{bmatrix} P_{11} & P_{21} & P_{31} & \cdot & \cdot \\ P_{12} & P_{22} & P_{32} & \cdot & \cdot \\ P_{13} & P_{23} & P_{33} & \cdot & \cdot \\ \cdot & \cdot & \cdot & & \\ \cdot & \cdot & \cdot & & \end{bmatrix} \begin{bmatrix} N_1 \\ N_2 \\ N_3 \\ \cdot \\ \cdot \end{bmatrix} = \begin{bmatrix} N_1^* \\ N_2^* \\ N_3^* \\ \cdot \\ \cdot \end{bmatrix}$$

$$(16)$$

The matrix multiplication on the left-hand side of (16) summarizes the spatial redistribution of the initial labor force $(N_1, N_2, N_3, ...)$ through both in- and out-migration over a period equal in length to the migration window. This circulation culminates in a new distribution $(N_1^*, N_2^*, N_3^*, ...)$.

The new distribution N^* is first calculated using the pre-adjustment configuration of wages, prices, and infrastructure. It is then recalculated using the set of wages, prices, and infrastructure (w', u', p', z') that characterize the economy undergoing adjustment. The differences in the two calculations of N^* will reveal the extent to which structural adjustment sets in place new economic incentives that attract or discourage migrants in net terms.

Suppose that an agricultural investment program increases the real price p_k of an agricultural good k in the target rural location 1; by increasing marginal value products, the program also increases earnings levels w in the target rural location and perhaps in others specializing in the production of good k. These changes in prices and earnings presumably contribute positively to the well-being of rural dwellers, but may have a negative impact on urban dwellers facing higher prices

for that agricultural good. The β coefficients of equation (14) are of interest because they help to summarize the impact of such price and earnings changes on the magnitude of net migration.

The logic of these analyses is similar when considering rural-to-urban migration or migration to and from secondary cities. In each instance, one selects a target location or set of locations and examines the implications of adjustment-related changes in (w, u, p, z) for net migration. The technique described is a type of short-term projection of population, where the population of interest comprises potential migrants. For planning purposes, one may also require projections of *total* population by location, which would involve estimates of natural increase as well as migration. The techniques involved in such projections are described in detail in Rogers (1975).

The consequences of labor mobility go beyond the labor market as such. As noted earlier, African policymakers have been greatly concerned with rural-to-urban migration, a concern that has its roots in the demands placed on public sector resources by urban growth (Linn 1982; Montgomery and Brown 1990). Expenditures on transport, housing, and delivery of water, electricity, and waste disposal services put considerable stress on public management and revenue-raising abilities. A knowledge of the way in which prices, labor market conditions, and infrastructure guide migration decisions can be critical to public investment strategies and revenue planning.

Longer-run issues

This discussion has emphasized the links between initial market conditions (as indicated in wages, prices, and so on) and migration outcomes. Yet the other side of the relationship, whereby labor supply affects wages and prices, should not be ignored in moving from estimation to policy conclusions. Wages affect individual labor supply; but in the aggregate, labor supply also affects wages. Urban unemployment and land rents affect migration in the short term; but over the longer term migration is one factor affecting unemployment and rents. Such relationships are admittedly difficult to quantify on the basis of a single round of cross-sectional data collection. One should not project the spatial allocation of labor very far into the future, using (16), under an assumption of constancy in prices, wages, unemployment, and infrastructure. Feedback among interrelated markets is central to the process by which an economy achieves its new equilibrium growth path over the course of structural adjustment.

Conclusion

Given the concerns of African policymakers regarding urban population growth and regional development, there are advantages in considering jointly the two sources of population growth by location, that is, natural increase and increase by way of migration. Perhaps half of African urban growth is attributable to natural increase. Thus, even in countries where overall rates of population growth are not thought to pose difficulties, the connection of urban growth to natural increase provides one powerful rationale for assessing the impacts on fertility of urban-oriented investments in educational and health infrastructure and family planning service delivery. Migration-induced urban growth can be addressed by considering how changes in economic variables alter migrant flows among the largest and the secondary tier of cities and from rural to urban areas. For regional planning purposes, it may be important to draw together projections of fertility and migration based on the economic models described here.

It may be useful to conclude with a consideration of some interactions between the various responses of the household, especially those between fertility and migration.[9] Household decisions in a variety of dimensions, encompassing fertility, migration, and the education and health of children, can be considered as being jointly influenced by a common set of exogenous meso-level economic variables (prices and availability of infrastructure) and macro-level policies. To appreciate the impacts of structural adjustment on household welfare, it will be important to consider the full array of household responses.[10] It is more informative, for instance, to know that adjustment-induced income growth in region A has reduced fertility *and* increased levels of child schooling, than to know only the fertility impact. The longer-term impact of income growth in region A is put in deeper perspective when one knows that its increased levels of schooling will likely encourage out-migration from region A to other regions where the economic returns to school-

ing are higher. Such interconnections at the household level may not be immediately apparent in any single empirical analysis, but are highlighted and clarified when the results of several analyses are considered jointly.

Notes

1. There is enormous variation in the definition of urban areas across African countries; this suggests caution in making any cross-country comparisons.

2. The discussion here centers on an individualistic model of migration. Yet in Sub-Saharan Africa, migration may be viewed as an economic strategy pursued by families to improve levels of consumption and reduce risk (see Stark and Lucas 1988). A full analysis of migration from this perspective would take us well beyond the scope of this chapter; issues such as remittances and income transfers among family members would require detailed consideration.

3. In some contrast to the view prevailing in the early literature, there is now considerable doubt regarding urban wage rigidity (see Squire 1981).

4. In deriving (2), Harris and Todaro assume that the turnover rate in the urban sector is unity. A more general case is given as,

$$u^e = \delta \left[1 - \frac{w_R}{w_U} \right]$$

where δ is the turnover rate (see Mincer 1976).

5. This result follows from the "independence of irrelevant alternatives" property of the logit model (Ben-Akiva and Lerman 1985).

6. One difficult statistical problem is that individual earnings in a particular location are observed only for those individuals who have chosen to move to or remain in that location. Ben-Akiva and Lerman (1985) discuss how this aspect of selectivity can be dealt with in the logit choice model.

7. The need for aggregation is reduced if a computer software package such as GLIM (Baker and Nelder 1978; Healy 1988) is available. We note that GLIM will estimate log-linear models of the form given in equation (12) without requiring $N_{1j} > 0$. GLIM is widely available and can be taught on a personal computer with a minimum of instruction.

8. See Rogers (1975) for examples of this type of multi-regional analysis.

9. See also the discussion in Chapter 10.

10. See Rosenzweig (1982), Levy (1985), Wolfe and Behrman (1986), and Rosenzweig and Schultz (1987) for illustrative empirical analyses.

7

Analyzing human resource effects: Education

Jere Behrman

Education takes many forms. Usually the emphasis is on formal education through schools because this is one of the most important forms of education, one more easily observed than many others, and one that is thought to be particularly affected directly by policy. For such reasons this chapter focuses on education through formal schooling. But it will give some attention to other forms of education—for example, formal and on-the-job training and preschool and outside-of-school education in the household.

The policy issues

Adjustment policy may have effects on education through both supply and demand factors. In some cases, these effects may be fairly direct and perhaps obvious. In others, they may be more indirect and less obvious since they reflect the filtering of adjustment policy through many types of institutions in the economy—firms, farms, governmental organizations, private and public schools and training programs, and households. These institutions, in turn, may be affected by adjustment policy through direct policies—such as reductions in school subsidies, increases in school user fees, or increased rationing of school places—or more indirectly, such as through the impact of reduced fiscal deficits on household income and thus on the consumption and time use choices of households. Generally, members of poorer households, although not necessarily the poorest households in particular, are most vulnerable to such effects.

Because of such complexities, the impact of adjustment policy on education cannot be considered in isolation. Other concerns discussed in this volume—for example, the determinants of poverty, of employment and earnings, of health and nutrition, and of the role of women—all have important implications for education.[1] And, perhaps with a lag, education will have important implications for all these other outcomes. All these social dimensions that may be affected by adjustment are also affected by the overall macro developments and structural shifts in economic activities engendered by adjustment policy. And all these effects have an important time dimension, with longer-run outcomes perhaps differing substantially from short-run effects, in magnitude, and possibly in direction.

Given the importance of education in attaining a number of society's goals, it is useful to sort out the probable impact of adjustment policies on education. This chapter attempts to indicate how this task might be approached. The loci of the proximate determinants of education are various micro institutions, such as households, farms, firms, and schools. In this chapter we explain how to analyze the impact of adjustment policy on education through such proximate determinants. But before examining this micro behavior, we need to consider the macro-meso setting in which it occurs. To motivate the whole analysis, it is useful to indicate the main policy preoccupations pertaining to adjustment policy and education. Because these are dependent on the time horizon, it is useful to distinguish between the short run and the longer run for this purpose.

Policy interventions likely to influence education in the short run

The most obvious of these policy interventions are those that directly affect the supply of formal schooling and training programs. Adjustment policy usually involves short-run cuts in governmental expenditures in order to reduce fiscal deficits.

The general cuts in governmental expenditures may include cuts in subsidies for formal education and training, which in turn may cause increased efficiency in the use of resources for such purposes, reduction in the *quality* of education, reduction in the non-educational amenities associated with education (for example, school lunches), reduction of the *quantity* of education (perhaps accompanied by increased rationing of such education), and/or increases in user charges or prices for such education. Increased efficiency of the use of resources used in the production of education may occur without any reduction in the quantity and quality of education. Such efficiency may be attained within a given schooling type, or by reallocating resources across schooling types. The latter may occur at the same time that user charges are increased. All of the other changes are likely to cause a reduction in the quantity of education, the quality of education, or both.

Who is affected depends on the exact nature of the policy changes. But in most societies the poor are politically less able to protect themselves against such changes than are those who are better off. While most of these changes are likely to be negative, some may be positive on the supply side due to adjustment policy. For example, if firms that have training programs with a long gestation perceive that their medium- and long-run prospects are improved by the adoption of adjustment policies, either because of expected sectoral shifts or because of expected macroeconomic improvements, they may act to increase the supply of training even in the short run.

The demand for education also is likely to be affected substantially by adjustment policy. The major effect in the short run is usually presumed to be a reduced demand for schooling because of a short-run reduction in income. To what extent reduced income affects the demand for schooling, of course, depends upon whose income is reduced. The strongest effects occur if those at the margin of schooling continuation decisions experience income reductions.

Reduced demand for schooling may result from a deterioration in the health and nutrition of children, who then are less able to gain from attending school or training programs. There also may be reduced demand for education because of time allocation decisions, so that the opportunity cost of children's time spent in school increases relatively because of the increased importance of their time spent in either economic or household activities. For example, if women spend more time in labor market activities to offset reductions in household income from reduced employment of men, older children (particularly girls) may be called upon to perform various household activities instead of going to school. But the same example also points to the possibility of the opposite effect if women spend less time in economic activities due to reduced employment options or if children have less attractive employment options.

On the demand side, as on the supply side, there may be a short-run beneficial effect if the adjustment policy increases the expected private rate of return to education because of expected improvements in the medium- and longer-run prospects of the economy if the adjustment program is successful. Explicit policy reforms that might have such effects through the demand side include any adjustment policies that affect employment, wages, and relative prices faced by the household. This means, effectively, that virtually all adjustment policies may have such effects, from devaluation to fiscal restraint to price and wage policies.

Policy interventions likely to affect education in the longer run

Longer-run effects depend very much on the degree of success of the adjustment policy. The more successful it is, compared with the situation that would have prevailed without the adjustment program, probably the greater will be the private returns to education of most types and the supplies of resources to be used for education, but the opportunity cost of time spent in education rather than in productive activities also is likely to be greater. Generally, the former effect is expected to dominate, though it is far from obvious that it will in all cases. The whole set of adjustment policies will be relevant once again, since what counts are realizations (that condition future expectations) for the economy as a whole.

The macro-meso setting for the impact of adjustment policy on education

The micro-level behavior that determines the supply and demand for education occurs within a larger macro context that is affected by adjustment policy. The meso setting includes the conduit mechanisms that transfer the effects of adjustment policy at the macro level to the proximate determinants of the micro-household and other relevant micro-institutional behaviors that directly determine education.

On a general level, the meso setting is likely to be affected by adjustment policies in two major respects: by altering the markets in which micro entities function, and by changing the infrastructure in which they operate. The major adjustment policies likely to affect education through these meso variables are currency devaluation, fiscal and monetary restraint, and international and domestic price liberalization.

A discussion of the impacts of such policies on general macro aggregates is not within the scope of this chapter.[2] Such effects may be complex, depending on the combination of expenditure switching (through relative price changes), expenditure reduction (through income effects), and changes in expenditure composition that either occur as part of the adjustment policy itself or are induced by that policy.

Again, these effects all have an important time dimension so that, for example, the immediate aggregate effects may be contractionary, but the longer-run ones expansionary if the adjustment program is successful. These two broad conduits for the transmission of adjustment policy to these meso institutions (markets and infrastructure) are now considered.

Markets

Markets can be characterized in a number of ways. For the present case we will distinguish between factor, product, and financial markets, recognizing that each of these types of markets may be more or less formal (in the sense of being subject to explicit contracts and governmental regulations).

Factor markets are important in at least three respects. First, for the many poor who work as employees, they are the major source of income,

and a major determinant of at least some forms of education, including formal schooling (Chapter 5). If adjustment policies change wage rates or employment options in such markets, these may lead to changes in the demand for education. If the initial stage of adjustment involves retrenchment, these effects initially may be negative. If the adjustment program is successful, they are presumed eventually to be positive.

Second, changed wages may have a price effect on the demand for education in addition to the income effect just described. One dimension of the price effect is the opportunity cost of time spent in education instead of in the labor force. If adjustment policy results in an initial decline in labor market demand and in real-wage rates, the opportunity cost of time devoted to education declines, although it increases eventually if the adjustment policy is successful. Another dimension of the price effect is the expected return to investment in education in terms of labor market rewards. These presumably reflect expectations about labor market developments after education, and thus may refer to some time in the future. If the adjustment policy is perceived to have some reasonable probability of improving the economy over what it otherwise would have been, then expected returns on educational investments will likely increase. However, this effect may be dampened by any initial negative impact on labor markets since, typically, current experiences enter into the formation of expectations about future outcomes.

Third, factor market changes also may affect the supply side of education. If initial restrictive policies result in an initial reduction in the real wages of more-educated individuals, for example, there may be an initial reduction in the cost of the most important (at least in financial terms) input for supplying education. With a successful adjustment policy, over time increasing demand for more-educated labor will probably reverse this effect.[3]

Product markets have at least four important possible dimensions for the concern of this chapter.

• In most developing countries, a number of the relatively poor generate income primarily as small producers in agriculture or in the informal sector. The product prices such producers face are an important determinant of their income. Adjustment policy is likely to have a negative effect on these incomes initially (probably reversed in the longer run if adjustment is successful) if there is a reduction in overall aggregate demand and if reduced demand in other parts of the economy causes laborers to shift into these types of self-employment. But that is not the only effect. For certain important segments of this part of the economy—for example, those involved in the production of tradables, including basic agricultural staples—the aggregate price effect favoring tradables due to devaluation and trade liberalization is likely to work in the opposite direction, and may more than offset any adjustment- policy-induced decrease in aggregate demand even in the short run.

• There is also a price effect for such self-employed that affects both the opportunity cost of their time devoted to education and expectations about the returns to education.

• A major factor affecting the household real income of the poor and, therefore, the demand for education is the relative prices of consumption items. These prices are likely to decline initially because of the overall reduction in aggregate demand, though the price effect of devaluation works in the opposite direction for tradables, some of which (basic staples) may be very important in the consumption basket of the poor.

• The product price of education is directly relevant. The impact on this price is not immediately obvious. For formal education, adjustment policy often involves a reduction in subsidies; and it sometimes involves the introduction of (or increases in) user fees, and increased rationing of positions in public schools (both of which may be equivalent to price increases, broadly defined). But at least in the short run, the possible reductions in the costs of the budgetarily most important input in the educational process (more-educated persons), greater efficiencies, and possibly expanded scholarship and loan programs may result in a decline in the real product price for education.

Financial markets may have important effects by facilitating income generation and investment in education on the demand side as well as the supply of education services on the other side of the market. Typically, adjustment policy attempts to make such markets more efficient by increasing real interest rates and reducing rationing in the formal credit markets. The rise in real interest rates would seem to discourage investment in education (as well as other forms of investment), other things being equal. But generally, the poor have had limited access to such capital markets, particularly for investments in education. So the effects depend substantially on the extent to which adjustment policy in the formal credit markets spills over into informal markets and to which there is fungibility in household resources (under the assumption that even in the informal credit market, loans explicitly for education are rare).

Once again, the net effects are hardly obvious. Prior to adjustment, even if real interest rates were low (and credit rationed) in the formal credit market, interest rates may have been quite high in the more relevant informal market. Efforts to rationalize credit markets may cause a reduction in interest rates in the informal markets, and any short-run restraint in aggregate demand may induce a fall in interest rates as well.

Infrastructure

Infrastructure, used here to refer to publicly provided physical capital and services, can be broadly subdivided into social and economic infrastructure.

The most important *social infrastructure* that affects the determination of education is that used directly in education, particularly publicly provided formal schooling and training. The availability and quality of both the capital stock and the current inputs (most important, the staff) are critical determinants of the amount of education and of its quality.

The current inputs can be altered fairly quickly by budgetary stringencies, which can cause shortages of material inputs such as books and of personnel inputs such as teachers. Even when civil service regulations preclude the rapid dismissal of teachers, for example, normal attrition without replacement can reduce their numbers (often quite capriciously from the micro point of view of individual schools), and turnover with less-qualified replacements can reduce their quality. Reduced real wages and salaries for teachers and other staff as part of budgetary stringency may tend to increase personal attrition and turnover. But these effects may not be so large in the short run because overall macro stringency probably diminishes the immediate attractiveness of alternative employment for such individuals.

Even if real-wage declines cause no exodus of experienced teachers in the short run, they may cause morale problems or encourage moonlighting that reduces teachers' short-run efforts. They also may cause a longer-run exodus of experienced teachers and reduce success in attracting higher-quality new recruits. If the adjustment policy is reasonably successful from an aggregate perspective, other opportunities for relatively well-educated individuals will improve, particularly if real wages for teachers do not increase rapidly enough.

Though the immediate impact of any budgetary stringencies is likely to be mostly on current material inputs and on staff, there may be some important effects on physical stock even in the short run. Schools and training institutions may be closed, which may appear to be a sensible rationalization from an overall point of view, but this imposes at least a time and transportation cost on those who would have used such facilities. Maintenance often is reduced in such circumstances, and this may have a delayed, but substantial, impact on the provision of educational infrastructure. There are sometimes threshold effects with regard to maintenance of such capital stock, so that the cost of delays may be considerable in the longer run.

Though educational infrastructure is the most obvious part of the social infrastructure affecting educational investments, it is not necessarily the only part that is relevant. Reductions in other social services may have a negative impact on education, either because these services are provided in conjunction with education or because they work through households to affect the demand for education. Examples of the former include food and nutrition programs provided through the educational system, such as subsidized or free school meals. Reductions in such programs in themselves may reduce the attractiveness of sending children to school because these transfers to households are tied to school attendance.

But reductions in nutrition and health programs may have a negative impact on schooling attendance even if the programs are not tied to school attendance, both by reducing the real income of former recipient households and by increasing the effective prices they pay in money and/or time for health and nutrition inputs, which in itself may reduce the productivity of time that children spend in school and lessen their incentive for being in school.[4] Reductions in other social infrastructure, such as in more general welfare provisions, will likely have a similar income effect on the demand for education, though not a particularly important price effect.

Changes in *economic infrastructure* due to adjustment policies may also have indirect effects on education. In the short run, these are likely to be three:

• Reduced maintenance and reduced expansion of transportation and communication systems as part of efforts to reduce fiscal deficits may increase the time and monetary costs of travel to educational institutions and thus effectively increase the price of attendance to actual and potential users.

• These infrastructure reductions are likely to reduce the demand for laborers, leading to reduced household income and reduced demand for education through the labor market.

• The adjustment policy may affect the expected longer-run quality of the economic infrastructure, thereby altering expectations about general economic development and about the economic returns to education. It is hard to know the direction in which this effect is likely to work since it might be reasonable to expect an initial deterioration in economic infrastructure due to short-run fiscal stringency but eventual improvements relative to what it would have been without the adjustment policy.

In the longer run, adjustment policy can have similar indirect price and income effects on the demand for education, depending crucially on the degree of success of the policy.

Assessing empirical links between macro adjustment policy and the meso setting for the determination of education

There are seven main reasons why it is difficult to assess empirically the links between macro adjustment policy and the meso setting for the determination of education.

• Several of the effects of adjustment policy on the meso setting described previously work their way through the complexities of the overall economy to affect factor, product, and credit markets.

• Some of the effects work through altering expectations about returns to educational investments, and such expectations usually are not well known by policymakers and analysts.

• There is a time dimension to the effects, with substantial differences and possibly even reversals in effects over time.

• Some of the important changes in the meso setting may be quality rather than quantity changes, which usually are not observed well empirically.

- Some of the changes may occur through rationing rather than price changes, and the former may be harder to observe or to control in the estimates than the latter.

- The evaluation should be made in comparison with what would have occurred without the adjustment policy, not in comparison with some ideal or unsustainable situation.

- In many cases, previously existing analytical studies and tools, such as applicable economy-wide models, are limited or non-existent.

Nevertheless, one should analyze as effectively as one can the relations between adjustment policy and the meso setting for the determination of education. The evaluation requires an economy-wide perspective and the capacity to control for the counterfactual situation—what would have happened without the adjustment policy. If the country experienced a commodity boom or bust in its major primary commodity exports at the time it was undertaking the adjustment policy, for example, it would be misleading to look at the impact on the meso variables for the determination of education without controlling for changed world commodity markets.

Ideally, one would like an evaluation of the effects for each major meso variable suggested in Frame 7.1.[5] This evaluation should also be for each of the major types of household that are likely to be of primary concern because their location in the income distribution means that their decisions regarding educational investments are likely to be particularly at risk because of adjustment.

To evaluate the impact of adjustment policy on the meso variables related to the determination of education, ideally one would use an economy-wide model that includes explicit details of the adjustment policy, controls for other shocks, and determines endogenously the meso variables of interest. Such an evaluation can be made easier if there are usable and sensible economy-wide models that incorporate all or most of the explicit policy changes that are part of the adjustment policy package, other primary sources of macroeconomic shocks (example, changes in the international terms of trade), and endogenous determination of the major relevant meso variables.

With such a tool, one can conduct counterfactual experiments to evaluate the impact of the adjustment policy on the major relevant meso variables. In the best of all cases, such models may be available to determine *some* of the variables of interest. The models in Dervis, de Melo,

Frame 7.1: Suggestive list of meso variables for analysis of education

1. Markets
1.1 Factors
Labor
- Wage rates (low-skilled; higher-skilled as bases for expected returns to education; teachers, trainers; by sex, region, experience)
- Employment/unemployment by skill

Non-labor
- Inputs for small-scale own-enterprise (prices and availabilities)
- Inputs for education (prices and availabilities)

1.2 Products
Education
- Schooling prices and availabilities (including admissions examination success rates and other indicators of rationing)
- Training prices and availabilities

Major consumption items
- Staple and other food prices
- Nonfood prices (such as clothing, housing, health inputs)

Major products of small enterprises—prices

1.3 Financial
Formal: interest rates, terms, availabilities
Informal: interest rates, terms, availabilities

2. Infrastructure
2.1 Social
Education
- Schooling: quantity and quality (such as teacher-student ratios; education of teachers; books and other teaching materials per student)
- Training: quantity and quality

Non-education: quantity and quality of health and welfare services

2.2 Economic—current and longer-run expenditures and staff
Transportation
Communication
Employment-related
Extension (agricultural, other)

---

and Robinson (1982) and Adelman and Robinson (1988) generate some of the important variables regarding income distribution and factor and product markets.

If such models are available, they should be used to estimate the impact of adjustment policy on as many as possible of the variables in Frame 7.1. But even in the best of all cases, the available models do not permit estimation of the impact of adjustment policy on *all* of these variables, and in most cases, models of this type are not readily available. Since the construction of such models or the adaptation of existing ones is likely to require resources far beyond those available for the study of the impact of adjustment policy on education, alternative approaches are generally required to estimate the impact of adjustment policy on the relevant meso variables.

In the absence of such tools, two modes of analysis are recommended as components of a second-best approach.

First, for the meso variables of interest, one should undertake estimates of the deviations from the secular trends during the adjustment period. The relevant questions to ask are: are there significant deviations from the underlying secular trends; and if so, do they have a pattern that suggests that the deviations may have been caused by the adjustment policies instead of by other macro shocks? Simple regressions of these variables (or of their logarithms) on time trends and on dichotomous variables for the structural adjustment period provide a means of evaluating whether there have been significant deviations from the underlying trends during the period of the adjustment effort.[6]

This procedure enables us to separate from ongoing trends events that at least coincide with the adjustment policy. It lessens the possibility of misinterpreting, for example, any ongoing deterioration in meso variables due to the previous situation that called for the adjustment effort as being caused by the adjustment policy. By incorporating information about a longer time period, it also lessens the possibility of mis-attributing an impact to the adjustment policy, if there is a one-year change in the reported value of some relevant meso variable (from the period immediately before the adoption of the adjustment policy to the first period of the adjustment policy).[7]

While this procedure is likely to be much more systematic and satisfactory than merely selectively inspecting the available data, it has its limitations. The presumed counterfactual is a continuation of the secular trends, which in some sense could not have been maintained for long since the previous situation was not sustainable; for this reason, the procedure uses a counterfactual that (at least eventually) is too optimistic about what the situation would have been otherwise and thus too pessimistic about the impact of the adjustment program. While the bias toward excessive optimism (at least eventually) about the counterfactual situation seems likely if indeed there is a need for the adjustment policy, it does not follow that the counterfactual contains such a bias for the initial part of the adjustment period.

If employment was high prior to the adjustment policy because of unsustainable governmental deficits, for example, then eventually—but not necessarily at the start of the adjustment policy—this high employment probably could not have been sustained. At most, this procedure indicates association, not causality, and even understanding the association may be difficult if there are lags in the impact of adjustment policy.

But despite these limitations, in many contexts looking at the deviations from the secular trends of the relevant meso variables may be a cost-effective way to evaluate the impact of adjustment policy on such meso variables and to avoid errors that can easily occur from selective inspection of the data or from proceeding on the basis of theoretical suppositions.[8] The results of such an investigation indicate whether the changes in the meso variables were significant during the adjustment period. If they were significant, these estimates also indicate the size of the associated change, which could be used with the micro estimates discussed later to estimate the impact on education.

Second, for some of the meso variables, there might a priori seem to be especially strong links with particular elements of the adjustment program. For example, reductions in real central governmental educational expenditures plausibly might have a direct impact on the available indicators of educational infrastructure, such as those suggested in Frame 7.1. But at the same time, an x percent reduction in government expenditures is unlikely to have an x percent impact on the indicators of educational infrastructure because some internal efficiencies may be implemented, because relative prices may change, and because there may be substitution among inputs in the "production" of education.

Reduced government educational expenditures probably affect various types of households differently, and these are of interest because of their different locations and use of different components of the educational infrastructure. It may be useful to estimate reduced-form relations with the available indicators of educational infrastructure as the dependent variables and with government expenditures on education and other important indicators of adjustment policy as the right-side variables. Such relations may provide a useful basis with which to explore the possible impact of actual and alternative patterns of changes of government educational expenditures and other policies on education.

Meso-micro analysis of the impact of adjustment policy on education

The previous section suggests several hypotheses about the impact of adjustment policy on education, as transmitted through the market and infrastructure conduits of the meso setting.

• *Hypothesis 1*: The income effect, reflecting developments in both factor and product markets, is likely to lead to a short-run decline in the demand for education, other things being equal, for households whose incomes decline because of budgetary stringencies or dependence on production of nontradables (for example, many urban labor and informal sector households). However, even in the short run, there may be the opposite effect for households that depend on tradable production for their income (such as smallholders and rural labor households that depend on production of tradable staples for their income). In the longer run, if the adjustment policy is successful, the generally increased income is likely to lead to increased demand for education for most households, others things being equal.

• *Hypothesis 2*: The direct educational price effect related to the cost side is likely to be negative for many households, but ambiguous for other households. In the short run, the time and monetary costs of education are likely to increase generally due to reduced educational and transportation infrastructure, increased user charges for formal schooling and training, and increased rationing of positions in public schools and training programs. Though all these effects reflect budgetary stringency, some may be lessened with more time if the adjustment policy is successful. Households and individuals that face *increased* demands for their labor in the short run (smallholders and rural labor households that depend on tradable production of staples for their income) and in the longer run (probably most households if the adjustment policy is successful) have the negative price/cost effect reinforced through the higher opportunity cost of their time in terms of economic activities.

On the other hand, in the short run a number of poor households are likely to face *reduced* opportunity costs of time devoted to education because of the lessened overall aggregate demand, reinforced by shifts in the composition of demand due to relative price shifts for those involved in production of nontradables. The opportunity-cost-of-time dimension of educational prices/costs is

likely to be in the opposite direction from the income effect.

• *Hypothesis 3*: The price effect directly related to the expected rate of return on educational investments is likely to be generally positive if there are expectations that the adjustment policy will be successful in improving overall economic prospects. The exceptions to this general statement seem limited to some specialized form of training for occupations in production activities in sectors likely to decline, because the expected negative price effects due to the adjustment policy outweigh the expected positive income effects if adjustment policy is successful in the longer run. Casual observation suggests that specialized training for such declining sectors is not likely to be widespread.

This section is the heart of this chapter: how to analyze the impact of adjustment policy, through the induced changes on the meso setting, on the micro determination of schooling and how to test the resulting hypotheses. At the micro level, there are both demand and supply sides of the determination of education. But to the extent that much of the supply side is determined by governmental policy (as for formal public schooling and training), important and perhaps predominant components of the supply determinants have already been discussed with regard to the meso setting. These basically affect the infrastructure faced by the household. So this section focuses on the demand for education, though such demand is conditional on supply considerations and there is some discussion of supply considerations. Since the locus of demand decisions concerning education is usually centered in individuals who share a number of resources within a household, the household is the focal unit of analysis.

The household's role in the determination of education

The household plays a major role in determining its members' demand for education. With a broad definition of education (not limited to its formal components), the household is also a major supplier of some forms of education. Parents, relatives, and older siblings, for example, help to educate younger children. And probably the adults receive important education from the children as well, though the generations may have different perceptions about the relative importance of the flows in the two directions. If the household is the locus of a family farm/firm, further education accompanies the employment of household members in that enterprise. Sometimes, particularly in agriculture, such education about the local micro environment seems to be important in determining the productivity of the household enterprise.

The standard economic concept of household behavior includes a set of allocation rules, household production functions, budget constraints, predetermined assets of the household, and exogenous prices and infrastructure. An example of an allocation rule would be to maximize the satisfaction of household preferences or to engage in bargaining among household members to determine the allocation of resources and of time uses among them.

An example of a household production function would be that the health of a child is "produced" by the food, water, and health care that the child receives, the child's genetic endowments, the household and community environments, the health-care skills that the child's mother has (reflecting both her formal education and the habits and knowledge she has acquired), and the time that she devotes to health care for the child.

The budget constraint is a "full income" constraint that indicates that the total available household resources (including the time of household members, as well as physical and financial resources and transfers to the household) must equal or exceed the household's total use of such resources (purchases at market prices, time uses, including those related to education and to economic activities and household production and leisure, and transfers from the household). The predetermined assets of the household include physical and financial assets and human resource assets, which in turn reflect previous formal education and training and usually unobserved endowments due to factors such as genetics and the childhood environment of current adults.

Application of the relevant resource allocation rule leads to reduced-form demand relations for each of the variables determined by the household, including the time uses of all household members, and among them the time spent investing in education. These left-side variables may be continuous, such as the time spent in education, or test scores. They also may be limited dependent variables, such as admission to a given schooling level or to a given type of schooling at that level (for example, public or private secondary schools). The right-side variables in these relations are the variables given (or predetermined or exogenous) from the point of view of the household: assets, prices, and infrastructure:[9]

$$Z_{ij} = f(A, P, I) \qquad (1)$$

where Z_{ij} is the jth outcome determined by the household affecting the ith individual in the household (important examples for this chapter are the time and other resource uses of individuals in educational investments, examination performances, and admissions to various types of schools);[10] A is a vector of all of the predetermined assets of the household for the period of relevance (physical, financial, human resources, genetic, and other endowments); P is a vector of all the relevant product and factor market prices that the household faces; and I is a vector of all of the relevant infrastructure that the household faces.

The basic *research strategy* has the following four steps:

• Prepare data from the household survey and from other sources that permit estimation of a set of relations of the general form of equation (1) for all of a number of outcomes related to education observed in the survey.

• Estimate relation (1) from these data for all of the relevant outcomes.

• Estimate the changes in the right-side meso price and infrastructure variables due to the adjustment policy for a given duration of that policy by relating the changes in the variables used to estimate the alternative versions of equation (1) to the estimates of the changes in the meso setting induced by the adjustment policy. These were discussed in the previous section.

• Use the following differenced form of equation (1) and the estimated changes in the right-side meso variables from the third step to estimate the impact of adjustment policy of a given duration on various outcomes related to the determination of education:

$$\Delta Z_{ij} = f(\Delta P, \Delta I) \qquad (2)$$

where Δ is the difference operator for the relevant duration of the adjustment policy under consideration.

Most of the rest of this section is devoted to developing these four steps. But before turning to those details, it is useful to emphasize five important features of relations (1) and (2).

First, both relations refer to an outcome for a specific individual, but both include on the right side predetermined characteristics of all individuals in the household. To determine the time invested in the education of small children or the probability of admission to different schooling levels, the schooling and other human resource endowments of all household members are included. This is the case because if any of these predetermined human resources were different, that difference would cause a change in total household resources and a reallocation of household resources that in general might affect the time invested in the education of small children or the probability of admission to different schooling levels, together with all other outcomes determined by the household.

This means that for the exploration of the impact of adjustment policy over a given duration on a number of different dimensions of educational investments by a household (such as education of small children, admission to levels of education for which there is rationing, apprenticeships of older children, training of young adults), the right-side variables should be the same even though the outcomes differ.

Second, for similar reasons the prices include all relevant product and factor market prices and the infrastructure variables include all relevant social and economic infrastructure. That is, the prices include not only the direct prices of education, but all product and factor prices affecting the household. These include the prices of all important consumption products and services faced by the household, including the prices of the opportunity costs of time of household members. If the household has a family farm or enterprise, all the relevant product and factor prices for that activity should be included.[11] Likewise, the infrastructure should include the social infrastructure directly related to education, the social infrastructure relating to health and other outcomes, and the economic infrastructure. Changes in the health infrastructure due to adjustment policy, for example, may affect household resources and resource allocation (including the time for investment in education) whether or not they affect the health of the individual of concern regarding a particular educational investment.

Third, income is not included explicitly in either relation. However, income is included implicitly because income is the return on assets (including time) and both the assets and their returns are included. This treatment avoids the estimation and interpretation problems that would occur if an income measure were included that reflected the endogenous choices of the household, such as the number of hours worked in economic activities. It also allows us, insofar as the data permit, to represent the possibility that the income effects vary depending on who in the household receives such income. For example, some analysts conjecture that the income impact on children's education will be greater if mothers receive such income than if fathers receive it. If so, an increment in the mother's education, other things being equal, might have greater impact on children's schooling than an increment in the father's education that results in an identical increase in family income.

Fourth, any given estimate is for a specific period. As the period lengthens, the changes in the right-side variables in equation (2) also differ. The time pattern of such changes presumably depends critically on the time pattern and the success of the adjustment policy. If budgetary stringency causes deterioration in infrastructure and reduced real wages initially, but adjustment policy eventually leads to better infrastructure and higher real wages than would have prevailed without it, then the short- and the longer-run impact of adjustment policy must be considered separately.

Fifth, the exclusion of any of the right-side variables at the estimation stage may cause omitted variable biases if such variables are correlated with observed (and included) right-side variables. Important examples of right-side variables that are difficult to observe include the abilities and motivations of different household members and rationing rules, both of which may cause biases, for example, in the estimated coefficients of household assets or income.[12] The suggestion here to include among the outcomes admissions examination performance and admission success is motivated in part by the desire to deal directly with rationing, though this exploration will be free of bias only if such examinations are the only basis for rationing. If there are other bases for rationing in particular countries, the researchers should collect information on the rationing procedures so that there can be control for such rationing in the estimation.

STEP ONE: SELECT VARIABLES TO BE USED IN THE MICRO ANALYSIS OF HOUSEHOLD DEMAND FOR EDUCATION, AND PRELIMINARY TABULATIONS. We now turn to details concerning the variables represented at a high level of abstraction in equations (1) and (2). Of course, exact representations of the concepts underlying many of the variables are not available in many cases. However, often one or more indicators of the desired variable are available. If there are several such indicators for a particular variable, it generally will be desirable to explore the empirical implications of the alternative indicators since each may be measuring imperfectly the phenomenon of interest. In some cases, good indicators for the relevant variables exist in household survey data. In other cases, some manipulation of the household survey will be required. In yet other cases—particularly with regard to data on test scores or other variables used to ration public school places—we strongly recommend supplementing the household survey with community surveys and other approaches to obtain the necessary information. Each of the relevant variables should first be examined to see if the distributions are plausible since errors can easily creep into statistical analysis. Questions should be asked, for example, about whether the ranges of variables are sensible. If some seven-year-old children are reported to have completed five grades of schooling, for instance, there probably are problems in the underlying data that need to be corrected before proceeding.

This initial examination of the data for errors (and also for outliers) should be followed by the preparation of a selection of tabulations. These will serve both to assist the analyst in defining the relevant variables (both dependent and explanatory) and to provide some initial findings that may guide policy. A summary of the types of variables that should be be selected for such tabulations is given in Frame 7.2.

INDICATORS OF RECENT EDUCATIONAL INVESTMENTS AND OTHER RELATED OUTCOMES. Recent educational investments and other related outcomes (such as admission to public school at different school levels) are of particular interest because they reflect recent developments. The single most useful variable for measuring recent education outcomes is whether the respondent (in a household survey) attended school during the reference period (say, over the past 12 months). The advantage of this variable over others is that it refers to the recent experience on which the other household and community survey data focus. However, since whether or not a particular individual attended school in the past year is likely to be heavily dependent on whether that individual attended school the previous year, in a sense this variable still reflects the impact of more distant past conditions.[13] Because rationing of school

places is important in many contexts, especially for post-primary schooling, it would be desirable to supplement this variable with information on the outcomes of such rationing. For example, if rationing is by scores on examinations, it would be useful to know if each child sat for such examinations in the past year and if they did, what scores they obtained (or at least, whether they were successful in obtaining admission).[14] Because schooling attendance varies enormously across different children and with differing conditions related to child health and participation in income-generating activities, it would also be useful to collect information on days absent from school for children who were enrolled in school in the past year.

Since schooling attendance and examination sitting and performance are all highly age-dependent and perhaps sex-dependent, the first step in the analysis should be to summarize the sample data, controlling for age and sex. Frame 7.2 provides a useful design for an initial summary of a number of relevant variables by age and sex. Age is indicated by year in this table, rather than by a more aggregated grouping, since there often are significant differences in schooling attendance and examination performance between two adjacent years of age, particularly for ages that are the transitions between one schooling level and the next schooling level. Examination of these data will provide the basis for making several decisions about subsequent analysis.

First, this examination will be a critical input into the decision as to which ages to concentrate on. The ages of most interest for the present purposes are the ages at which there is substantial variation in schooling attendance and at which decisions are made about continuation of schooling to subsequent levels, perhaps in part through some rationing mechanism such as admissions examination performance. If because of compulsory schooling attendance regulations, almost everyone attends the initial grades of schooling, for example, then the ages associated with those grades are not of much interest for the proposed analysis, and the same logic applies if no one continues into tertiary schooling. What is of interest are the ages for which there is substantial variation in schooling attendance and substantial changes in schooling attendance.

Second, this summary of the data will give insight into whether other variables are of interest for differing age-sex groups. For example,

Frame 7.2: Summary of schooling characteristics derived from a household survey: Range, median, mean, standard deviation, and number of observations for variables by age and sex

General education
- Ever attended school
- Highest grade
- Highest diploma
- Examination performance [a] and time of examinations (for admissions and for achievement) particularly for past year, but also for earlier years if possible

Past 12 months [b]
- School/college attendance
- Grade enrolled in
- Whether in school one year earlier and, if so, in what grade
- Time going to and from school
- If in school in past year, number of days absent from school

Educational expenses (past 12 months)
- School and registration fees
- Contributions to parent associations
- Uniforms and sports clothes
- Books and school supplies
- Transportation to school
- Food, board, and lodging
- Other expenses (clubs, extra classes)
- Other in-kind expenses
- Who paid?
- Scholarship?
- Value of scholarship

Characteristics of main occupation in past 12 months
- Training in present job?
- Training duration
- Hours per week in training
- Who paid for training?
- Salary lower during training?
- How much salary lower?

Characteristics of secondary job in past 12 months
- Training?
- Training duration

Curriculum
Primary
- Highest grade
- Interruption?
- Length of interruption
- Repeat grade?
- Number of repeats
- Public/private
- Certificate?

Secondary
- Ever attended, type
- Highest grade
- Repeat grade?
- Number of repeats
- Highest certificate
- Private/public

Technical
- Ever attended
- Highest grade
- Highest certificate
- Private/public

Tertiary
- Ever attended
- Years
- Institution type
- Highest diploma

Apprenticeship
- Ever been?
- How long?
- Main trade
- Fees?
- Free room and board?

Training courses
- Ever attended
- Months attended
- Main subject

Note: For dichotomous variables or variables with relatively few categories, percentage distributions across categories are preferred. Some of the questions are not applicable for some ages (for example, those on secondary schooling for seven-year-olds).
a. If examination scores are not available, information about passing versus failing admissions examinations will be useful.
b. This information is particularly relevant since it is for past 12 months, about which much other information is available.

scholarships may be of relevance only for certain age ranges or schooling levels.

Third, these data will give an indication of whether there are sex differentials in schooling attendance, highest grade completed, total expenses, scholarships, payment for schooling expenses, schooling interruptions, repeating grades, days absent from school, sitting for admissions examinations, success on admissions examinations, and cognitive achievement. In light of the often hypothesized high returns to female schooling and the frequent apparent differences in the educational options for males versus females (see

Schultz 1988b), asking systematically whether there are such differences is useful (see Box 11.7 in Chapter 11). Careful examination of the version of Frame 7.2 for males versus that for females should be enlightening in this regard. Quite possibly such differences are small in certain age ranges (probably the younger ones), but may be larger and favor males in other age ranges. Such an examination should be sensitive to possible changes in sex differentials with age. Beyond examining these data, it will be useful to test for statistical differences between the sexes for different variables.[15]

Frame 7.3: School enrollment ratios by age, sex, and region, Ghana, 1988

(percent)

Age-group	Accra		Other urban		Rural		All areas		
	M	F	M	F	M	F	M	F	All
6-11	91.4	87.3	84.7	70.6	71.7	54.6	75.8	61.3	68.7
12-15	90.0	75.0	83.7	61.4	71.1	54.9	75.3	58.1	67.3
16-18	66.7	52.2	62.9	47.8	59.2	31.9	60.8	37.6	49.7
19-25	31.4	17.8	27.7	5.4	23.3	4.7	25.2	6.1	14.6
All	73.0	60.4	67.0	49.9	60.4	38.1	62.9	42.8	52.9

Source: Data from the 1988 Ghana Living Standards Survey.

Fourth, these data will provide useful background for the multivariate analysis in the second step in other respects. For example, there is a question about how dependent the schooling attendance decision for the past year is on whether a particular individual attended school in the previous year. The information summarized in this frame regarding attendance proportions by age and schooling interruptions should help explain whether for given age ranges almost everyone attends school (so for such an age range there is not a problem regarding past experience) and whether schooling interruptions are common (in which case whether an individual attended school the year before last is less relevant in the decision about attendance in the past year).

The starting point for most analysts will be the tabulation of the gross and net education enrollment rates[16] by age, sex, and region. An illustration of this is given in Frame 7.3.

The age disaggregation is based on the primary, lower secondary, upper secondary, and tertiary education levels. However, a more detailed age disaggregation may be called for, even tabulating enrollment rates for each single year. Similarly, the regional disaggregation is only illustrative and will obviously vary by country.

Frame 7.3 shows how such tabulations can be helpful both in themselves and as a guide to further (multivariate) analysis. While primary enrollment rates for urban areas are high, there is clear evidence of gender bias for this group, with female rates being significantly lower than those for males. In rural areas, this disparity is even more marked. Female enrollment rates are particularly low in rural areas for upper secondary levels (ages category 19-25), with only around 5 percent of females typically being enrolled at that level. In short, the frame shows interesting variations in enrollment at all levels of education; it reveals that the gender variable is likely to be

significant in further analysis and that enrollment rates vary significantly across the regions. The frame does not reveal whether the variations in enrollment are due to differences in the regional availability of education services or to differences in the demand for education, arising from variations in living standards. For this, multivariate analysis is essential.

After such examination of the data, the dependent variables should be defined. But how does one treat age and sex differences in the definition? A consideration of Frame 7.2 in most cases should narrow considerably the relevant age ranges for independent variables of interest, and examination of sex differences may limit the relevant sex differences. But in most cases there will remain a number of ages of interest and some evidence of sex differences in schooling attendance and related variables. At least two strategies are possible for dealing with these. First, the dependent variable can be defined relative to that for other individuals of the same age (and possibly sex) by subtracting the mean experience for the relevant reference group defined by age and sex. Such a procedure has the advantage of controlling for age and possibly sex in a manner that makes it possible to combine observations across individuals in the multivariate analysis discussed without further concern in the estimation for age and sex differences, but at the cost of assuming that once there is this control there are no other age-sex differences in the coefficients of relation (1). Subtracting the reference mean for the same age and possibly sex seems to be the preferred way of modifying the dependent variable to control for age and possibly for sex. Alternatively, some or all of the estimated coefficients can be allowed to differ across age and sex with the untransformed variables used as the dependent variables. This has the advantage of allowing for greater flexibility in accounting for differential effects in the coefficients of relation (1) by age and sex, but at the cost of estimating, presenting, and interpreting more relations. This cost is, of course, less if the initial examination of Frame 7.2 leads to a limited number of ages of interest. The second alternative is preferable unless the difficulties of estimation are very large (so that there is a great advantage to undertaking fewer estimates) or the sample is very small (so that there is a great advantage to combining observations across age and sex groups).

The first part of Frame 7.4 gives the dependent variables of interest and indicates their probable priority. The first-priority variables refer to the education experience of the past 12 months, for which there is considerable information for the right-side variables. The second- and third-priority variables are of interest, but are measured for any time in the past (not just the last year) so the indicators for the right-side variables have much more measurement error given that they change over time.

The second part of Frame 7.4 gives similar information for the right-side variables that represent the predetermined household assets, the time and money prices, and the infrastructure. The major general point about these variables is that the last two groups depend much more on community than on household characteristics, and so are more likely to be obtained from community surveys, though by averaging across household variables in a given community one also can obtain information about the nature of the community markets and infrastructure. The priorities are meant to be roughly suggestive of what variables might tend to be most important for the purpose of this analysis, but of course there may be substantial variations across countries, regions within countries, and household types.

The following variable-specific point should be noted. For the predetermined adult education in the household, education for parents is indicated as first priority. But others may play a major role in the determination of children's schooling. If examining Frame 7.2 leads to the conclusion that others within the household often are important, the schooling of other adults in the household should be treated as first-priority variables rather than as second-priority variables as indicated in Frame 7.4.

STEP TWO: ESTIMATE RELATIONS FOR DETERMINING THE EDUCATION INDICATORS. Once the variables in Frame 7.4 are ready, relations of the form of equation (1) can be estimated with the alternative indicators of education listed in the frame as dependent variables and with the right-side variables listed in the lower half of the frame. The natural starting point would seem to be estimates of the form of relation (1) in which all of the right-side variables enter in additively. Several points about this estimation merit emphasis.

First, all the estimates should be multivariate estimates to control for the other observed determinants when obtaining the estimated impact of each individual determinant. In fact, it is only to control for such possibilities that the A variables should be included in equation (1), since in the differenced version in equation (2) they disappear. That is, it is only because some A variables are likely to be correlated with P and I variables that it is necessary to include the A variables in the estimation of equation (1). Parental schooling, for example, is likely to be associated with the quality of local schooling in I; therefore, if the former were excluded, the estimated impact of the latter probably would be biased upwards.

Second, ordinary least squares (OLS) procedures should be used first for estimation. These are relatively easy and quick to undertake and relatively robust to problems in the underlying assumptions. In the present context, there should be no problems due to simultaneity and fewer than the usual problems with omitted variable biases.[17] However, some of the proposed dependent variables are limited rather than continuous. The assumptions underlying the OLS estimates are then not satisfied and OLS estimates may be misleading. Examples of limited dependent variables are the dichotomous ones for whether one was in school in the past year, whether one has had training, whether one sat for admissions examinations for particular schooling levels last year, and whether one was admitted to particular schooling levels last year. For the relations for which such variables are the dependent variables, it would be desirable to use some limited dependent variables estimators such as probit, logit, or tobit to see how robust the estimated effects are to the OLS violation in the underlying distributional assumptions.

This is particularly likely to be important for variables for which the means are far from 0.5, such as the proportions of children at higher ages who attended school in the past year. In some cases, there are more than two possibilities—for example, whether one was admitted to a public school, admitted to a private school, or not

Frame 7.4: Regression variables for analyzing education outcomes

	Probable priorities		
	1	2	3
Dependent variables (Z_{ij})			
School/college attendance last 12 months	x		
Grade in which enrolled in last 12 months	x		
Private versus public schooling			x
Ever attended school [a]		x	
Highest grade completed [a]		x	
Highest diploma obtained [a]			x
Vocational/technical [a]			x
Highest vocational/technical grade [a]			x
Literacy (read short text) [a]			x
Literacy (write letter) [a]			x
Written calculations [a]			x
Ever taken literacy course [a]			x
Ever apprentice [a]			x
How long apprentice [a]			x
Ever taken short training course [a]			x
Months in short training course [a]			x
Training in primary occupation [a]			x
Training duration in primary occupation [a]			x
Training in secondary occupation [a]			x
Training duration in secondary occupation			x
Whether sat for admissions examination for various schooling levels in past 12 months	x		
Performance on admissions examination	x		
If enrolled in school in past year, number of days absent	x		
Cognitive achievement test scores	x		
Right-side variables			
Predetermined household assets (A)			
Human assets			
Mother's schooling [b]	x		
Father's schooling [b]	x		
Other co-resident adult's schooling [b]		x	
Mother in household	x		
Father in household	x		
Other adult co-residents		x	
Physical assets			
Housing characteristics			
Rooms per occupant		x	
Type of dwelling	x		
Occupancy status		x	
Drinking water source [c]			x
Lighting type [c]		x	
Cooking energy [c]			x
Garbage disposal [c]			x
Toilet type [c]		x	
Outside walls material [c]	x		

admitted. For these cases, multinomial estimates should be made with all of the possibilities considered in one system of estimates.

Third, for a given dependent variable there is the question of how aggregate the estimates should be with regard to age, sex, and household type. This issue was discussed at some length with regard to age and sex, and we concluded that it is probably preferable to undertake separate estimates by age and sex in order to explore whether the coefficients differ across age and/or sex. There is the possibility that different types of households (smallholders versus rural labor households versus urban labor households ver-

| | Probable priorities | | |
	1	2	3
Floor material [c]		x	
Roof material		x	
Area per occupant	x		
Production assets (total value of agricultural or other enterprise assets) [d,e]	x		

Factor, product, and financial markets—money and time prices (P)

Factor markets			
Local wage rates (male, female) [f,i]	x		
Expected wage rate increases for relevant level of schooling [l]		x	
Inputs for own enterprise [g]			x
Major consumption item prices			
Basic staples prices [i]	x		
Other food prices [i]		x	
Other consumption prices [i]			x
Health services [j]		x	
Major own-enterprise product prices [e]	x		
Education prices			
Monetary costs [h]	x		
Time costs [h]	x		
Financial market prices			
Interest rates (formal and informal)			x

Infrastructure [k] (I)

Social			
Education			
Schooling/training availability [m]	x		
Schooling/training quality (e.g., teachers/student, qualification of teachers, books/student)	x		
Non-education (e.g., health clinics)		x	
Economic			
Transportation (monetary and time costs to regional center)	x		
Communication			x
Employment-related			x
Extension		x	

a. Only for those < 25 years of age.
b. Zero if no information. Control with next set of variables.
c. Data will have to be examined to determine a relatively small number of relevant categories, each of which will be represented by a dichotomous 0-1 variable.
d. It may be desirable to use physical measures of specific assets, such as agricultural land area.
e. The inclusion of this variable may depend on separating households by major income sources.
f. From a community survey or averaging household survey results for adults in same community with same schooling level (possibly with control for receipt of such wages).
g. For example, fertilizer for smallholders.
h. From a community survey, or average over households in community.
i. Need to be careful regarding seasonal fluctuations.
j. Ideally from composite community health-care price index from health analysis.
k. From a community questionnaire.
l. For example, the relative increase in wage rates in the local community due to the schooling/training level in question.
m. For appropriate schooling/training level given age. This may include, for example, the proportion of students in the community of a given age and sex who sat for particular admissions examinations and their average performance.

sus small-scale household enterprises) may face different demand conditions beyond the ways indicated by the observed right-side variables. For the OLS estimates, covariance analysis (sometimes called Chow tests) permit systematic evaluation of whether sub-samples should be combined, and such tests should be undertaken. If the tests indicate that the restriction that the coefficient estimates across such sub-samples are equated is not rejected, then the relevant sub-samples should be combined.

Fourth, there is an issue about exactly what sub-sample should be used for a particular estimate to avoid selectivity bias. This results when there is a selection rule for a sub-sample based on unobserved characteristics that play a role in the estimation for which the sub-sample is used but are not controlled in that sub-sample.[18] Empirical evidence suggests that selectivity bias may cause substantial misunderstanding of empirical micro relations related to human resources in developing countries (see the surveys in Schultz 1988b and Behrman 1990). Selectivity bias can be avoided by controlling for the selection rule in the estimates if a sub-sample is used or by formulating the question so that the estimates do not depend on a selected sub-sample.

In this context, the upper secondary schooling admissions decision provides an illustration. Those who are admitted to upper secondary school typically are very selected: they entered and graduated from primary school, they entered (perhaps after some examination or other rationing procedure) and graduated from lower secondary school, and in many cases they sat for and passed the upper secondary school admissions examination. If one attempted to estimate whether they were admitted to upper secondary school only with the sub-sample of individuals who graduated from lower secondary school or who passed the upper secondary admissions examination (as in Appleton, Collier, and Horsnell 1990 for Côte d'Ivoire), one could not interpret the estimates with confidence because the failure to control for the previous selection rules would likely cause selectivity bias in those estimates.

To avoid such biases, one of two options needs to be followed:

• The previous selection rules can be controlled in the estimation of the outcome of interest. One way of controlling for such rules is to include in the relation of interest a variable constructed from the estimated probability that each individual in the sub-sample would have been selected by the selection rules; that is, in the example regarding upper secondary school admission, to include a variable constructed from the estimated probability that each individual in the sub-sample had entered and completed primary and lower secondary school and had sat for and passed successfully the admissions examination for upper secondary school. However, to follow such a procedure, the selection rules must be identified. There must be variables that determine the selection process but do not enter into the decision of interest.[19] In the case being discussed, this requires variables that affected entering and completing primary and lower secondary school and sitting for and successfully passing the upper

secondary school admissions exams, but that do not have an impact on the decision to enter upper secondary schooling. One is unlikely to find variables that satisfy such conditions except through arbitrary exclusion restrictions in the data.[20]

• The question can be posed in such a way that the use of a selected sub-sample is avoided. For example, rather than estimate whether an individual who successfully passed the upper secondary school examination enters upper secondary school from the selected sub-sample of individuals who successfully completed that examination, one could estimate for the *entire* sample of 14-year-olds what determines whether they enter upper secondary school.[21] This may have the apparent disadvantage of lumping together those who do not enter upper secondary school for a diverse set of reasons (ranging from never entering primary school to deciding not to enter upper secondary school despite having passed the entrance examination). But it has the offsetting advantage of avoiding the selectivity bias that would result if the sub-sample were limited to some group such as those who sat for the upper secondary school entrance examination. This general approach is recommended unless there is a possibility of controlling directly for the selectivity rules (which is relatively rare).

Fifth, a number of additional issues might merit exploration for some countries:

• *Interaction effects* may be important, say, between parental schooling and infrastructure (for example, Schultz 1988a and 1988b; Behrman 1990). Some have argued that parental schooling effectively substitutes for schooling infrastructure, and others that it complements such infrastructure. Such possibilities could be explored by seeing what the sign of any significant interaction terms between parental schooling and observed indicators of schooling quality are if such terms are added to the linear form of relation (1).[22]

• *Exogenous income components* may be explored instead of the assumption that all income is endogenous. Typically in empirical studies, for example, it is assumed that "unearned" income (income other than from labor income) is exogenous. This assumption is problematic since such income often reflects current labor time-use decisions in own farm/firm activities or past labor time-use decisions that led to current returns to past savings in the form of physical and/or financial assets. But it may be desirable in some studies to test for the endogeneity of such unearned income by using the standard Wu-Hausman endogeneity test.[23]

• *Who controls income*, not just the amount of household income, is thought by some to be important. One hypothesis states that income controlled by women is more likely to lead to increased investment in child schooling (and to other forms of investment in children) than is income controlled by men. This may be important in assessing the impact of adjustment policy on education if such policy affects men and women differentially, as well it might because of occupational segregation by sex. It is difficult to explore such possibilities empirically, however, because of the same problem of the endogeneity of income; this is an even clearer and more widely recognized problem if the income of interest is labor income, reflecting not only unobserved characteristics relating to wage-rate determination but also those relating to labor supply. The basic proposed estimates will give some insight into this question if it is possible to include wage rates among the prices.[24] Beyond that, it may be possible to explore the impact of non-labor income through the transfers received by different household members if such transfers are sufficiently common, although the endogeneity issue remains.

• The *time period* may be relevant, if there are adjustment lags in various decisions. Any given estimates are for a particular time period, so that the estimates may change over time. Generally, the available data do not permit much exploration of this possibility at the household reduced-form estimation stage, though there is some possibility of dealing with it at the next stage of the analysis in which relation (2) is used.

Given the nature of the available data, it seems that at the regression estimation stage the only question is what assets are assumed to be fixed in A. The longer the time period, the more such assets can be affected by savings/dissavings and further training and education even for adults. In some cases, it may be useful to explore to what extent the estimates of the coefficients of the prices and infrastructure change if the set of variables in A is reduced by eliminating those that would seem to change most rapidly (for example, measures of consumer and producer durables). In those cases in which there are panel data, some further estimates can investigate the lag structure (or at least a simple possible form of it) by including the lagged dependent variables in the relations. The coefficient of the lagged dependent

variables can be interpreted as an adjustment coefficient within the following simple model:

$$X_{ijt} = a\,X_{ijt-1} + b\,(X^d_{ijt} - X_{ijt-1}) \qquad (3)$$

where the t and $t-1$ subscripts refer to the time period, and X^d_{ijt} is the desired long-run level of X_{ijt} that is determined by observed variables as in relation (1) and toward which there is adjustment each period to cover b of the gap between the current desired long-run level and actual level for the previous period.

As an example of some of the issues that are raised in analyzing education performance, Box 7.1 summarizes the results of a recent study on Ghana.

STEP THREE: ESTIMATE THE IMPACT OF ADJUSTMENT POLICY ON THE PRICE AND INFRASTRUCTURE VARIABLES THAT DETERMINE HOUSEHOLD EDUCATIONAL DECISIONS. The next task is to estimate the changes in the prices and infrastructural variables that enter into the right side of relation (1) because of the adjustment policy. Such changes are likely to be very dependent on the duration of the adjustment policy, and may differ over time in magnitude and possibly even in sign. One should obtain sets of estimates of the impact of such changes for different time periods: the first year of the adjustment policy, a medium-term perspective of several years, and a long-run perspective. Of course, the longer the time perspective, the more speculative are such estimates. But one needs to keep these different perspectives in mind to assess fully the impact of the adjustment policy. For example, suppose that the immediate impact of adjustment is to reduce economic options and the quality and the quantity of the infrastructure due to budgetary stringency, but that in the longer run it successfully turns around a stagnant economy and improves economic options and the infrastructure. In such a case, an evaluation that considered only the short-run effects probably would undervalue the gains from the adjustment policy, just as one that considered only the longer-run effects would overstate them.

The meso variables considered in the discussion of macro-meso interactions and those used in the estimates of relation (1) discussed in this section generally will not be identical. Therefore, some links will have to be established. It will probably not be possible to estimate linking regressions for such links since the necessary data are not likely

Box 7.1: Analysis of the impact of health on schooling achievement: The importance of simultaneity

The problem: Common sense and casual observation suggest that extremely poor child health limits schooling achievement. But does this mean that most children in African societies would improve their schooling achievement if their health were better? The authors of a number of studies for developing countries claim that the answer is yes. They present ordinary least squares estimates of the determinants of different measures of schooling attendance and achievement with health indicators among the right-side variables, and claim that the significance of the coefficient estimates for the health indicators in such relations supports the conclusion that better health generally improves schooling achievement.

However, such estimates assume that child health is determined independent of child schooling, not simultaneously with it. On the basis of economic models of household behavior or casual observation, it appears that child health might be determined simultaneously with child schooling. If so, the standard estimates show *association* between child health and child schooling, but *not* causality. Parents with more interest in their children or more unobserved skills (that is, unobserved by social scientists and outside observers, though perhaps clear to participants) in raising their children may invest more in both their children's health and their schooling, in which case the standard estimates *overstate* the effect of child health on child schooling. But different parents may face different unobserved relative prices for child health versus child schooling or have different preferences for investing in child health versus child schooling or attempt to compensate for unobserved learning endowments by investing more in child health. In any of these cases, the failure to treat child health as simultaneously determined in relations for schooling achievement results in *downward* biases in the estimated impact of child health on child schooling achievement.

There is no reason to expect these biases in opposite directions to cancel out. But because of them, standard estimates of the effect of child health on child schooling may be misleading guides to the true impact of child health on schooling, and thus distort understanding and policy formulation.

The data: Ghana Living Standards Survey (GLSS).

The estimates: Cognitive achievement production functions are estimated for advanced reading tests with child health represented by child height (standardized by international experience controlling for age and gender) (see table below). In the first case, child health is treated as predetermined, as in the standard estimates. In the second case, child health is treated as simultaneously determined, with a number of family background and community school and health characteristics used in the first-stage estimates (similar to the estimates in Box 11.7, but with a more extensive set of variables). In both cases, grades of schooling are treated as choices, and thus simultaneous estimates are used for schooling.

Interpretation of the estimates: The first regression suggests that child health has a significant positive effect on child cognitive achievement. But the second estimate suggests that the standard procedure underestimates this impact by a factor of over two and a half due to the failure to control for the simultaneous determination of child health with child schooling. Apparently, because of unobserved relative prices or preferences, parents tend to invest more in the health of children with fewer unobserved learning endowments, so the standard estimates are biased downward substantially. The much larger estimated effect with control for simultaneity means that policies that positively affect child health have a much larger impact on child schooling achievement than would appear in the standard estimates without such simultaneity control.

Impact of child health on cognitive achievement for Ghanaian children age 10-18

Variable	Health assumed predetermined		Health simultaneous	
	Coefficient	T-ratio	Coefficient	T-ratio
Constant	-7.40	-6.6	-6.70	-5.7
Father's schooling	-0.06	2.0	0.06	2.0
Mother's schooling	-0.01	-0.2	-0.02	-0.3
Father-mother schooling[a]	0.01	3.2	0.01	3.0
Child, male	0.50	2.2	0.82	3.2
Child age	0.02	2.3	0.02	2.6
Child ability	0.28	10.3	0.25	8.5
Child schooling	0.25*	2.2	0.29*	2.5
Child height (Z score)	0.38	4.0	1.04*	4.2

a. Treated as simultaneously determined.
Source: Behrman and Lavy 1991.

to be available. The researchers will have to use judgment to determine to what extent the more aggregate changes measured under macro-meso analysis affect the disaggregated variables used in the estimation of relation (2). For example, if the real government resources for primary education decline by 10 percent in the first year of an adjustment program, what impact is that likely to have on the schooling infrastructural variables used in the regression estimates?

In making such judgments, one must keep in mind that some increased efficiencies may be induced by the restriction in resources; that there may be induced shifts in the composition of inputs into the educational production process by the induced changes in prices and scarcities due to adjustment policy; that prices may go down considerably for some important inputs (particularly staff); and that some of the resources for local education come from sources other than the central government. All these considerations imply that the probable declines in the indicators of local schooling infrastructure used in relation (1) are likely to be less than in the more aggregate measures discussed under macro-meso linkages. Given the inherent uncertainties in making such judgments, however, it should be best to make a range of estimates under alternative assumptions about the extent to which such intervening factors mitigate the impact of adjustment policy on the meso variables observed at the household level.

STEP FOUR: ESTIMATE THE IMPACT OF ADJUSTMENT POLICY ON EDUCATIONAL INDICATORS. This last step is straightforward. Use the estimates of the changes in the meso variables from step 3 and of the parameters of relation (2) from step 2 to estimate the impact of adjustment policy on the range of educational indicators included in the dependent variables (Z_{ij}) of Frame 7.4 for alternative time periods and for alternative assumptions concerning the extent to which observed more aggregate changes affect the indicators of the meso setting used to estimate relation (1). For any given outcome, this will lead to a set of estimates. For example, there will be a set of estimates regarding ranges of possible induced changes in school attendance for primary-age boys for the first year of the adjustment policy, for the medium run, and for the long run.

Policy implications

Obviously, the policy implications for any specific case depend on the details of that case. But this chapter has indicated an approach to quantify the impact of some adjustment-policy-related choices on educational investment, and thus inform better policy choices. This section provides some general principles on which such policy inferences may be drawn and presents appropriate illustrations.

The first general policy principle is the need to place the education sector in a larger perspective. The effects of adjustment policy on education have to be assessed in terms of the tradeoffs elsewhere. If a given reduction in government resources devoted to education would cause a 10 percent reduction in lower secondary schooling enrollments in the first year of an adjustment program, what is the tradeoff in terms of other objectives? To lessen this reduction to, say, 5 percent, how much deterioration would one have to accept in child health, the balance of payments, the rate of inflation, or other indicators of the success of the economy? Although the type of analysis laid out in this chapter is partial equilibrium in nature, and the broader issues of tradeoff are economy-wide, the indicated analysis (together with similar analysis for other parts of the economy) can help to give some quantitative insight that can be used to improve policy formulation.

The second principle is the importance of the time dimension. The impacts of adjustment policy on education and on other outcomes of interest have an important time dimension to them. Policy evaluation needs to consider both the immediate impact and the longer-run impact. Otherwise, the chances of inappropriate evaluation increase substantially. Of course, it is difficult to know what the time paths are likely to be for all of the different outcomes of interest. But using the approach taken in this chapter, one can gain some quantitative sense of the impact of adjustment policies on education over different time periods. With the use of similar approaches for other sectors, one can get a clearer view of the policy perspective over time with inherent tradeoffs to give a better basis for policy.

The third principle is that there may be considerable substitution within the household regarding the demand for education and related outcomes. This is one important reason that changes in government resources directed toward education may not result in simple proportional changes in education. The household making the education decisions is operating in a meso setting of multiple markets and social and economic infrastructure, all of which are likely to change in response to adjustment policy. Changes in household income due to changes in labor markets may have greater impact on educational investments than do changes in educational infrastructure.

Only by viewing the household as making educational decisions within this larger context and by allowing for internal substitution within the household can the analyst estimate the probable effects of changes in the educational infrastructure due to adjustment policy on household educational decisions.

The fourth principle is that disaggregation may be very important in understanding the impact of adjustment policy on education. The impact may be much different for males than for females, for primary schooling than for secondary schooling, for schooling versus training, for smallholders versus labor households, and so on. Examination of the aggregate effects may miss many of these details. For example, if aggregate schooling attendance declined in the short run by only 3 percent, it would be wrong to conclude that there were not some important deleterious effects if at the same time primary schooling attendance by girls in poor rural households declined by 15 percent, given both distributional goals and the high apparent total returns to schooling for females. The approach outlined in this chapter permits some quantitative assessment of such differential effects.

The fifth principle is that there also may be important choices that can be made regarding the impact of macro changes in government educational expenditures. For a given central educational budget, there is a range of combinations of subsidies, user charges, scholarships, and direct provision of educational services that the ministry of education can provide. Different combinations may have different implications for the education of different groups in society. The general approach outlined in this chapter, particularly if supplemented by more analysis of the "production" of education from the supply side, can help illuminate some of the tradeoffs in determining the composition of educational policy given various educational goals.

Notes

1. Other chapters provide insights into the analysis of the impact of structural adjustment on the returns to education in labor markets, own-enterprises, and household production. Changes in those expected returns, in turn, feed back on the demand for education.

2. Such a general discussion as in World Bank (1991b) provides part of the background for this book. Related references are Addison and Demery (1985), Behrman (1988a),

Behrman and Deolalikar (1988b and 1990), and Demery and Addison (1987b).

3. Prices of other inputs might also be expected to increase. Examples would include imported inputs, such as specialized instructors and equipment that are not available in very elastic supply from domestic sources (at least in the short run). Such cases are likely to be relevant relatively rarely except for specialized advanced education. The impact on the cost (price) of education abroad is a related, and probably more relevant, phenomenon.

4. See Behrman (1990) for a review of empirical studies of the impact of health and nutrition on child school performance in developing countries. These studies are suggestive, but not persuasive because of the failure to control for simultaneous determination of health and nutrition.

5. The variables in Frame 7.1 are suggested by the discussion in this chapter. They are meant to be suggestive only, with considerable variations across countries with regard to what is available. This suggestive list will be helpful not only as a checklist, but also as a means to encourage investigators for each country to think of other relevant indicators for the particular situation under study.

6. The statistical question is whether the dichotomous (sometimes called "dummy") variables have significant coefficient estimates according to standard t-tests and, if so, what their signs are.

7. Such errors are likely to be common in the conditions prior to the adjustment program, particularly if these involved considerable inflation, relative price changes, and government efforts to play down the extent of the economic crisis. For examples in which deviations from longer-run trends indicate much different patterns of what happened during a structural adjustment effort than just examining the change from the year before to the first year of the adjustment effort in an explicit case, see Behrman and Deolalikar (1990) or consider the underlying studies of Behrman and Deolalikar (1988b), Boyd (1988), and Cornia and Stewart (1987).

8. For examples of the problems with the latter approach, see Note 7.

9. This relation is for the jth outcome determined by the household for the ith individual in the fth family in the hth household in the tth time period. To avoid a plethora of subscripts, household and time period subscripts are not indicated. Chapter 8 shows a formal derivation of reduced-form demand relations.

10. Not all the outcomes determined by the household are individual- or even family-specific. Variables that are not do not have the i subscript, but just the family and/or the household subscript.

11. This assumes, as probably is appropriate, that the income generation and consumption decisions of the household are interconnected rather than the former determining the latter recursively without feedback. Such interconnection or

simultaneity may be due to incomplete markets, to consumption decisions through health and nutrition affecting productivity in a range of activities, and to farm/firm selling prices differing from buying prices because of transaction costs. For more extensive discussion of these issues, see Singh, Squire, and Strauss (1986a), Behrman and Deolalikar (1988a), and Alderman (1987).

12. Some examples of the former are given in Behrman and Birdsall (1983), Behrman and Deolalikar (1988c), Behrman and Sussangkarn (1989), Behrman and Wolfe (1984b), Birdsall and Behrman (1984), and Boissiere, Knight, and Sabot (1985). Also see the survey in Behrman (1990).

13. It would be useful if the household survey also asked whether each individual had attended school in the year before the reference year. With the answer to such a question it would be possible to investigate whether the observed right-side variables during the past year caused a change in schooling attendance between the year before last and the last year. This approach effectively would control for conditions before the past year.

14. Though such information is most useful for the past year, it would also be desirable to obtain retrospective information about sitting for examinations and examination scores for previous years. Here the focus is on admissions examination performance. If such examinations are used to decide on admission, their results (at least at the level of whether or not admission was granted) should be available at low cost. It also would be useful to have the results of cognitive achievement tests for all household members, as for the Ghanaian LSMS, as indicators of schooling performance. The costs of administering standardized tests, however, are likely to be substantial, so such measures are not emphasized in what follows.

15. There are standard procedures for such tests. For qualitative variables (whether attending school currently, whether or not successful on admissions tests for a particular schooling level), chi-squared tests are appropriate. For continuous variables (how many grades of schooling completed, examination scores), t-tests for the differences in the means are appropriate. Such tests can also be conducted by estimating a simple regression with the dependent variable being the variable of interest and the right-side variable being a dichotomous ("dummy") variable with a value of one if the individual is a male and a value of zero otherwise; the estimated coefficient of such a dichotomous variable is the estimated mean difference between the sexes for this variable, and the t-test for this estimate is a test for the significance between the sexes.

16. The gross enrollment rate (say, for primary schooling) is defined as the total number of children regularly attending primary school during the current school year divided by the total number of children of primary school age. The net enrollment rate for the primary level is defined as the number of children of primary school age regularly attending school, divided by the total number of children of primary school age.

The gross enrollment rate may exceed unity if there are significant numbers above primary school age attending primary school.

17. There should not be simultaneity problems because the relations are reduced-form demand relations, so the right-side variables are predetermined or exogenous from the point of view of the household. The omitted variable problem is less than usual because omitted variable bias often apparently results in overestimation of the impact of parental schooling because of the failure to control for unobserved parental abilities, motivation, and so on (see Behrman 1990). But in the present context the impact of parental schooling as such is not of interest since it is only important to include it as a control in relation (1); the resulting estimates of parental schooling do not enter into relation (2) if A enters into relation (1) additively. It is not troublesome if parental schooling represents in part the effects of such unobserved parental characteristics; in fact, the more it picks them up the better, since that lessens the probability that the coefficient estimates of the other variables are biased because of failure to control for such unobserved variables.

18. These selectivity issues are not limited to the analysis of education decisions. They are pervasive in much socioeconomic analysis. Perhaps the most emphasized case is in estimating the determinants of wage rates, given that there is a selectivity rule pertaining to who participates in the labor force. Another example concerns the selection of type of health-care provider, given the selection processes regarding who considers themselves to be sick.

19. This is an exclusion criterion for identification. There are other means of identification, such as by functional form, but such approaches are not very satisfactory in the present context since there are no persuasive reasons for the choices of functional forms.

20. If there were panel data, there would be more possibility of finding such identifying variables because some of the selection processes occurred at earlier times when conditions differed.

21. The sample would be separated by sex since that is not an individual or household choice variable and since the relations may well differ by sex. Other questions could also be explored for the sample, such as whether they had completed primary school, completed lower secondary school, sat for the upper secondary school admissions examination, and successfully completed the upper secondary school admissions examination. The critical point is that the *entire* sample of 14-year-olds would be used for the estimates for each question, *not* just the ones who had passed some previous selection rule.

22. Note that if relation (1) has such interactions, relation (2) becomes more complicated by including, in addition to the explicit terms indicated above, $DX_1 * X_2$ and $X_1 * D X_2$, where X_1 and X_2 are the two variables that interact in relation (1).

23. If the unearned income component to be explored is the net revenue (or profit) from household enterprises, for example, such net revenue is estimated as dependent on the

exogenous assets and prices that affect the enterprise production, the residuals are calculated from that relation, the variant of relation (1) is estimated in which net revenue is included instead of the exogenous production-side prices and assets, but in addition the estimated residual from the net revenue function is included, and a t-test for the significance of the coefficient estimate of the residual net revenue indicates whether there is a simultaneity problem with such income. For a detailed discussion of applications of this exogeneity test, see Pitt and Rosenzweig (1985) and any recent basic econometrics text, such as Maddala (1988).

24. Of course, individual wage rates will not be observed for every individual. In fact, the same selectivity problem is likely to be very important in determining what wage rates are observed. If they are to be used in the analysis, it is important to control for such selectivity in estimating wage rates.

8

Analyzing human resource effects: Health

Mark Pitt

Health is an important objective of households and governments in developing countries. To households in low-income societies living near subsistence levels, small changes in household budgets or health program provision can critically affect physical well-being. In addition to its direct importance to individual welfare, health indirectly affects welfare through its influence on the productivity of work and on the efficiency of human capital accumulation.

The policy issues

Considerable public resources in low-income countries are devoted to programs that enhance health—providing medical and family planning services, building and maintaining sanitation and clean water facilities, controlling parasitic diseases, and subsidizing foods. Public health technologies have dramatically improved life expectancy in developing countries without the improvements in nutrition, hygiene, housing, and income that coincided with reduction in mortality in Europe and North America. The World Bank (1980) estimates that life expectancy in developing countries in 1970 would have been eight years less without the contribution of new and inexpensive public health technologies such as those based on pesticides and vaccinations.

In Africa, the disease reduction role of centralized agencies that rely on public expenditure is probably greater than in any other part of the world because of contagious disease and diseases spread by parasites and water. Reducing the prevalence of these diseases requires continued improvements in control and monitoring services, immunization and sanitation, and public health education. Household purchasing power is low and so is the ability to purchase privately procured health inputs—most significantly, food. In an uncertain environment prone to calamitous drought and political upheaval, households, unable to smooth consumption through insurance or borrowing, are subject to catastrophic illness and hunger in the absence of outside intervention.

Structural adjustment may influence health by altering expenditure on programs that provide medical and public health services (and the fees charged for these services), by reducing real incomes, by altering wages and farm profitability, and by changing the prices of market goods. Not all households will be equally affected by structural adjustment. The relative impact depends on the nature of state intervention before adjustment and the timing, magnitude, and distribution of policy alterations that constitute the adjustment package. For example, producers of export crops may benefit from devaluation or the dissolution of state marketing boards. Food producers may benefit from the end of policies that artificially kept food prices down. Workers in state subsidized enterprises may become unemployed, and the destitute poor may suffer from reductions in transfers from the state, food-for-work, and other relief programs.

Much of the recent economics literature on health in the developing countries has shown a clear microeconomic focus; making use of newly available micro data sets to evaluate the impact of various interventions—prices and programs—on health, and the influence of health on labor productivity, human capital accumulation, fertility, and intra-household resource allocation.[1] Fortunately, the methods and results of this new literature are of direct relevance to the use of household survey data in the analysis of structural adjustment in Africa. As the literature demonstrates, the analysis of these issues is complex both theoretically and empirically. Unobserved (by the investigator) determinants of health specific to individuals (inherent healthiness, referred to here as the individual health endowment) and to the locale in which the individual resides (the health environment) require specifications and statistical methods that pay attention to heterogeneity and the bias it can impart. Health is difficult to measure, and measurement error in empirical work must be assessed. The accurate measurement of the effect of health program placement on health outcomes is of direct concern in the evaluation of structural adjustment. If the spatial placement of health programs is responsive to the health attributes of targeted populations not measured by the household survey data at hand, simple measured associations between programs and program outcomes will not provide correct estimates of program effects. These considerations make study of the determinants of health, and consequently of the impact of structural adjustment on health, complex and challenging.

The macro-meso setting

In the framework used throughout this book (see Chapter 1), households are affected by adjustment policy through two broad conduits, infrastructure and the markets in which they trade. Food nutrients are inputs into the production of health, and their prices and distribution have been the targets of government policy in almost every developing country. Food prices are affected by direct government subsidy and (much less often) by tax policy, exchange rate policy, aid distribution, marketing, and other supply restrictions and direct rationed allocation to consumers. Alteration of all these interventions is likely to be part of a comprehensive structural adjustment. This topic is discussed in Chapter 9.

Structural adjustment will typically move an economy toward freer markets and away from quantitative regulation (rationing, import licens-

ing, and price control) and large-scale intervention in markets. Given the levels of price distortion prevailing in much of Africa, the movements in relative prices in the aftermath of a structural adjustment may be very large. How households alter their consumption pattern in response to changes in relative prices, and how this change in relative prices maps into changes in individual health is the key empirical question, addressed at length here. Of course, not all changes in price can be attributed to structural adjustment. Even with a stable policy regime, prices of many goods—certainly of foods—tend to move over time in response to other shocks, such as weather, crop failures, war, and prices in world markets. The large seasonal variation in prices in many areas of Africa shows the lack of storage and transportation infrastructure. Transport costs and lags as well as informational deficiencies are of such importance in much of Africa that even in a completely laissez-faire economy one might expect that the intertemporal variance in domestic prices for internationally traded agricultural goods would far exceed the variance in international prices. The implication is that the entire change in prices in the aftermath of adjustment cannot be attributable to adjustment.

The health effects of price changes depend on the price of goods whose prices have been affected, and the household's ability to substitute given its preferences and the biological health technology. Since most food price changes are likely to alter the composition and level of nutrient intake, increasing the intake of some nutrients while reducing consumption of others, even complete knowledge of the full matrix of food and nonfood own- and cross-price elasticities is not sufficient to judge the health effects of price changes. Indeed, of the nine food prices considered by Pitt (1983) in Bangladesh, variations in seven had both positive and negative effects on the intake of the nine nutrients considered.[2] Of 11 food prices considered by Pitt and Rosenzweig (1985), only one unambiguously affected the demand for all nine nutrients in one direction. Growing evidence suggests that the poorest households are the most price sensitive, and are likely to substitute more than richer households. There is substantial intercountry difference in substitution elasticities: the evidence on this from Africa is particularly sketchy.[3]

There is some evidence that for the poor changes in income have relatively small effects on nutrient consumption. Behrman and Deolalikar (1987) suggest that income elasticities of demand for poor households in semi-arid India are very low, implying that reductions in income result in much less than proportionate changes in the intake of calories. Africa-specific evidence is sparse, and recent evidence from Brazil (Strauss and Thomas 1989) suggests that these findings may be sensitive to specification. In any case, nutrition is but one set of inputs into health, and substitution between nutrients and nonfood inputs, such as those provided by public health measures, may be small. While good nutrition may reduce the impact of malaria, diarrhea, and other debilitating diseases, it is a poor substitute for disease control programs and medical intervention.

Studies of the determinants of household-level nutrient consumption provide no information on how a change in the aggregate diet of a household affects the nutritional intake or status of *individuals*. If interest in aggregate (family-level) consumption or overall nutritional "availability" in low-income households is mainly derived from concern about the nutrition or health status of members of such households, understanding how household aggregates map into the well-being and health of individuals, and how the household distributes its resources among members, is critical. Indeed, there is evidence that the intrahousehold distribution of resources is not equal across family members (Behrman 1988b and 1988c; Pitt and Rosenzweig forthcoming; Pitt, Rosenzweig, and Hassan 1990; Rosenzweig and Schultz 1982).

One aspect of the distribution of foods in low-income settings has caught the attention of many social scientists: the disparity in nutrients received by women compared to men. One hypothesis is that gender-based inequality reflects disparities in labor market opportunities across men and women in these settings, with the pecuniary returns to a household from the allocation of food to women being less than those for men. Some evidence supporting this hypothesis is the relationship between sex differences in infant mortality rates and differences in labor market participation rates between men and women in South Asia (Rosenzweig and Schultz 1982).

Although attention has mainly focused on gender inequality in food allocations, if the relationship between healthiness and productivity differs across occupations and activities, the distribution of activities across individuals within gender classes should also be related to the intrahousehold distribution of foods, preventive medical care, and other health inputs. Pitt, Rosenzweig, and Hassan (1990), analyzing individual and household data from Bangladesh, found a pecuniary return to health and effort in the labor market, and that work activity distributions substantially influence the intrahousehold distribution of food. They also found that energy-intensive effort tends to reduce health as measured by weight for height and that there is substantial calorie reinforcement for those best able to alter the energy intensity of effort—adult males (age 12 and above) and male and female children (age 6-12).[4]

Not all the costs of ill health are borne by the individual whose health is temporarily or permanently impaired. Within a household, the ill health of one person is likely to evoke resource adjustments by other persons, perhaps differentiated by gender. Estimates of the direct effects of changes in health policy will be underestimates of their true impact to the extent that these resource adjustments reduce schooling or labor market experience of other household members. For example, Pitt and Rosenzweig (forthcoming) found that existing sex-based differences in the division of time between household care, schooling, and labor force activities in Indonesia are worsened among teenagers where child morbidity is at a higher level. In particular, teenaged daughters were significantly more likely to increase their participation in household care activities, to decrease their participation in market activities, and to drop out of school compared to teenaged sons, in response to increases in infant morbidity. Considering these "third-party" costs of ill health will result in better estimates of the effects of policy changes that affect health and a greater awareness of the differentiated effects of such interventions.

Besides prices for market goods, food prices being important among them, changes in the supply of health services and the cost to users for these services are the policy interventions most likely to affect health outcomes in the short run. In most developing countries, user fees for medical services are very low or zero. The largest costs of using medical services are direct travel costs and the opportunity cost of time spent in travel and queuing. Thus, the market for medical service is rationed by these costs rather than by user fees. Structural adjustment may result in user fees sufficiently high to ration the market, resulting in a very different allocation of service provision across individuals. Unfortunately, very little work has been done on how the demand for medical services responds to user fees, travel and queuing time, quality of service, informational constraints, and the prices of other goods. An exception is the work of Gertler and van der Gaag (1990), who estimate own-price and income elasticities of demand for medical services in Côte d'Ivoire and Peru. They find that the demand for medical care is price sensitive, that the poor are more price sensitive than the rich, and that child care is more price elastic than adult care.

Structural adjustment may involve reductions in government expenditure. Clearly, reductions in expenditure on health and health-related programs are of greatest concern.[5] To the extent that public health provision is funded or directly provided by donor agencies, focusing on government budgets may provide a misleading index of total government expenditure on health programs. Reductions in health programs may be accompanied by renewed efforts to target programs to those whose health is thought to be at greatest risk, or by increases in user fees for non-poor users. Efforts at targeting can be enhanced by microeconometric investigation of the demand for health and related services and of the efficacy of service provision in augmenting health.

Meso-micro analysis

Analyzing the main determinants of the health of household members involves three sets of issues. First, the underlying model of household behavior must be defined; second, reduced-form demand equations for health are then derived; and finally, appropriate estimation techniques are applied to the household data set.

A model of household behavior

In this section, a model of household behavior is outlined to depict the major linkages between sets of policy variables, biological factors, and the health of individual household members. Health status is viewed as purposeful behavior conditioned by costs and resource availability, tastes, and stochastic and non-stochastic environmental factors. The model's presentation is informal. A formal economic presentation of the same ideas is presented in the accompanying boxes. Although the informal presentation conveys the basic implications of the model of household behavior, the reader is strongly urged to also read through the more formal presentation.

The basic conceptual framework is an integrated model of a multi-member household in which consumption and production decisions are made. In this framework, health is a good produced by the household for each individual member, using nutrients derived from foods, as well as other health inputs. It is useful to disaggregate health inputs into those that are individual-specific, such as food consumption or vaccinations, those shared by all members of the household, such as water quality, sanitation facilities, and housing quality, and those shared by all individuals and households in the region in which the household resides, such as temperature, humidity, altitude, and propensity to parasitic infestation. It is further useful to divide all health inputs into those measured and observed, and those not known by the investigator. If one were to statistically estimate the health production function using regression techniques having only observed health inputs as regressors, the regression residual would contain the effects of unmeasured (unobserved by the investigator) health inputs on health. This residual may also contain a purely random component—random in the sense that it is not known or predicted by the household or individual.[6]

The technology governing the production of health—the health production function—is a purely *biological* technology and not an economic behavior. The household's choice of health input quantities given this technology is, on the other hand, behavioral rather than technological. This biological technology (production function) may differ across types of individuals defined by age, sex, and pregnancy or lactation status. Even individuals of the same "type" (age and sex) receiving identical sets of health inputs may have differing health status[7] because of differences in their *health endowment*—the innate healthiness of an individual inclusive of genetic endowments but excluding the innate healthiness of the region of residence—which affects health but cannot be influenced by the household. The health production function (Box 8.1) thus depicts how health is affected by food consumption, nonfood health inputs, and factors beyond the household's or individual's control, the health environment.

The household maximizes a utility function that includes as arguments the health of individual members and foods. It is sensible to include both health and food consumption directly in the utility function since health is desirable in itself and because foods are consumed for reasons other than their nutritional value. The utility function also includes the leisure of individual household members, their consumption of non-foods, and their work effort, the latter being a *bad* (utility-decreasing) rather than a *good* (utility-augmenting). This formulation is very general in that it permits households to assign different *weights* to the consumption by every individual of each good, including health. Allowing for the possibility of discrimination in the allocation of resources (including health) among members and types on the basis of sex and age is prudent in general but especially significant in Africa.

Health may affect the productivity of labor time and hence income. If markets recognize and reward health-related productivity differentials, then the wage for an individual is a function of his or her health, the strenuousness (energy intensity) of effort required by the individual's occupation, and the personal characteristics of the individual, such as schooling. In farm households, health status may directly affect agricultural productivity in addition to productivity in the wage labor market. The implication of these productivity effects is that they tend to reduce the net cost of attaining any level of health since increased health results in increased income through the productivity effect. In addition, to the extent that the pecuniary returns to increased health differ across member types (age and sex), the household will have an incentive to allocate more health inputs, such as food, to those individuals whose value of work time is most sensitive to increases in health. In the case of a farm household, the marginal product of work time may depend on the level of other farm inputs used in production.[8] Marginal products of labor for any given labor allocation will be higher for households with large quantities of land or farm animals, for example. Thus, the productivity returns to health will also depend on the level of all farm inputs.

Households maximize household utility subject to the health production function, a time constraint that specifies that the total time available to an individual in any time period can be allocated to work, leisure, and the household care activities (childcare, household chores), and an income constraint that includes the return to household farm activities. The process of constrained household utility maximization is formalized in Box 8.2.

Reduced-form demand equations for health

Explicitly setting out the structural relations that underlie household behavior informs us of the full set of policy variables that may affect health and the mechanism by which they work. This household maximization problem leads to a set of *demand* equations for all household choices as functions of all the exogenous (non-household-choice) variables—known as the *reduced-form* demand equation. In its most general form, the household's demand for health for household members of any type (age/sex) is a function of all

Box 8.2: Constrained utility maximization

Formally, the household, consisting of T individuals, maximizes a utility function of the form:

$$U = U(H^i, L^i, C^i, Z^i, e^i) \qquad i = 1, \ldots, T \quad (2)$$

which includes as arguments the health of the individual members as well as foods (C^i).* It is sensible to include both health and food consumption directly in the utility function since health is desirable in itself and because foods are consumed for reasons other than their nutritional value. The utility function also includes the leisure of individual household members (L^i), their consumption of nonfoods (Z^i),** and their work effort (e^i).

The total time available to an individual household member i (Ω^i) can be allocated to market (wage) work (J^i), household care activities (T^i), leisure (L^i), and, in farm households, to activities associated with crop production and processing (F^i). Thus, the time budget is:

$$\Omega^i = F^i + T^i + J^i + L^i \quad (3)$$

Health may affect the productivity of labor time. If markets recognize and reward health-related productivity differentials, then the wage for individual i is a function of his or her health, the strenuousness (energy intensity) of effort required by the individual's occupation (e^i), and the personal characteristics (d^i) of the individual, such as schooling:

$$W^i = W^i(H^i, e^i, d^i) \quad (4)$$

In farm households, health status may directly affect agricultural productivity in addition to productivity in the wage labor market. The farm production function is described by:

$$Q = Q(F, F^h, X, A, K, H, y, u) \quad (5)$$

where Q is farm output, F is on-farm family labor, F^h is hired agricultural labor, X is a vector of agricultural inputs, A is land under cultivation, K is a vector of capital inputs, and H and y are vectors of health status and personal characteristics of family members, respectively.

Households maximize the household utility function (2) subject to the health production function (1), the time budget constraint (3), the wage function (4), the farm production function (5), and a (full) income constraint that restricts them to spending no more on goods and health inputs than they earn in the labor market and in household farm production:

$$\sum_{i=1}^{T} W^i \Omega^i + V + \Pi = \sum_{k=1}^{K} P_k \left(\sum_{i=1}^{T} C_k^i \right) + P_z \sum_{i=1}^{T} z^i + P_Y \sum_{i=1}^{T} Y^i$$

$$+ \sum_{i=1}^{T} W^i (L^i + T^i) \quad (6)$$

where Π is farm profit, and

$$\Pi = P_Q Q - P_x X - \sum_{i=1}^{T} W^i F^i - W^h F^h \quad (7)$$

where V is non-earnings income (non-labor and non-farm income), W^h is the wage paid hired workers, P_z is the price of good Z (the nonfood consumption good), P_Q is the price of the farm output Q, P_X is the price of farm material inputs, and P_k is the price of food k.

---

* If all human nutrition came from foods, the health production function (1) could have been written with foods C^i as inputs instead of the nutrients N^i. To complete the formulation with nutrients as inputs, an expression converting nutrients into foods can be added. However, this additional equation adds nothing to the discussion in this section.

** There are many distinct nonfoods consumed by households so that consumption of nonfoods by individual i, Z^i, is a vector of goods as are foods C^i. However, because of the key role played by food in the production of health, the individual elements of the vector C^i will be made explicit by the use of summations over vector elements in the equations that follow. For notational simplicity, Z^i and other vectors of goods to be introduced below are not so treated.

It does not matter for our household model whether the household utility function represents the preference of an altruistic family dictator, is a unified set of preferences among household members, or is the result of a bargaining process. The list of arguments that appear in the (reduced-form) equations to be estimated are unaffected by the derivation of the household utility function. If, for example, it is found that mothers' wages have a bigger effect than husbands' wages on the allocation of health resources devoted to daughters, and the reverse is true for health allocations to sons, one cannot claim that this unambiguously establishes the validity of a bargaining model in which higher wages give one more bargaining power and parents "prefer" offspring of the same sex. Such an outcome is also possible with non-bargaining models.

---

the exogenous variables: the prices of all goods (including time) in the utility function, the health production function, and the farm production function; the health endowment or innate healthiness of each member of the household; the region-specific health environment; the gender and other (exogenous) personal characteristics of every household member;[9] and the quantities of land, capital, and unobserved factors that affect farm output. The reduced-form demand equation for health is presented in Box 8.3.

The following comments apply to the health reduced-form demand equation: First, by including the actual quantities of land and productive capital rather than prices, we are assuming that these *quantities* can be considered fixed, in that they are not choice variables (at least in the medium term) to the household.

Second, in practice, the housing quality goods (the G goods) can also be treated as fixed to the household so that their (typically unmeasured) prices (P_G) can be replaced with a set of variables that measure the quantity of these goods consumed by the household.

Third, the individual health endowments (μ^i), the regional health environment (λ), and unobserved factors that affect farm productivity (the cultivation endowment u) are unobserved by the researcher, but presumed known to some extent by the household. These are unknown to us, and will form a part of the regression residual when the demand equation is estimated.

Fourth, if markets are sufficiently well functioning, the farm household can be thought of as solving its farm production and utility maximization problems recursively (in sequence). It will first act to maximize farm profits in its choice of farm inputs, and then maximize utility given these profits. This recursive structure—known as *separability*—means that the prices of farm output (P_Q), the hired labor wage (W^h), prices of material inputs (such as fertilizer) (P_X), quantities of land and capital (A and K), and the unobserved characteristics (u) of the cultivator can all be dropped from the demand equation (8) and replaced simply by measured farm profits (Π). The reasonableness of the separability assumption will certainly vary across regions in Africa. Separability seems reasonable for cash crop farmers, such as cocoa or tobacco cultivators, but less so for food crop cultivators for whom market sales and purchases of agricultural output or agricultural wage labor are rare (subsistence farmers).[10]

Fifth, of very direct concern, the prices of the nonfood health inputs (P_Y) are typically not available or, if available, are not economically relevant in that these do not represent true (private) opportunity costs. For example, even if inoculations are "free" in that no fee is collected from the person inoculated at the time of inoculation, the opportunity cost to the household of an inoculation may not be zero. It is possible that not everyone who wants an inoculation gets one. This may be because there is an insufficient supply (excess demand exists). The true "price" of an inoculation includes important pecuniary and nonpecuniary costs to the household in addition to any inoculation charge. These costs may include the cost in time and money of getting to an inoculation center, a cost that may not be inconsequential in many areas of Africa. In addition, there is the "cost" of acquiring information. An individual who is not well informed about the benefits of inoculations or how to go about getting them will behave like one who confronts a high price—he or she will not get inoculated even if no fee is levied. Similar reasoning applies to other public health programs and interventions such as public health clinics, family planning clinics, and the like. Other types of public health initiatives by their nature do not involve a fee for service because of the *public goods* nature of the services provided—malaria control and the spraying or draining of the breeding places of waterborne parasites and other disease-carrying organisms are examples. If it is true (as is assumed by most researchers) that health program placement is exogenous in the estimation of individual-level health reduced-form demand equations, then the availability of (or traveling distance to) public health programs and facilities can be used as regressors in lieu of prices. Unfortunately, considering the

---

Box 8.3: The reduced-form demand equation for health

Formally, the reduced form is:

$$H^i = D^{Hi}(P_1,...,P_K, W^1,...,W^T, P_Z, P_G, P_Y,$$
$$\mu^1,...,\mu^T, \lambda, P_Q, P_X, W^h, d^1, ..., d^T, A, K, u) \quad (8)$$

In this reduced-form demand equation, the demand for health of person type i depends on the prices of all K food goods (P_1 through P_k), the wages (time prices) of all T household members (W^1 through W^T), the prices of nonfood goods (P_Z), the price of health inputs that do not provide utility directly (P_Y, the "medical inputs"), the price of household "public" resources that affect health

(for example, housing and water quality, sanitation facilities of the household), the health endowment or innate healthiness of each of the T members of the household (μ^1 through μ^T), the region-specific health environment (λ), the price of the (farm) output produced by the household (P_Q), the prices of all purchased inputs into producing this good (P_X), the wage rate paid hired workers (W^h), the gender and other (exogenous) personal characteristics of every household member (d^1 through d^T), the quantities of land available for cultivation (A), productive capital (K), and the unobserved characteristics of the land and cultivator that affect productivity (u).

possibility that programs are likely to be placed by a government in response to observed regional health deficiencies, the correct statistical measurement of health program effects on health becomes problematical. Adjustment policies often result in significant changes in public health program budgets, so that it is important that this research obtain an accurate measure of the influence of public health program availability and placement on individual health. Alternative methods of estimating the effects of public health program placement on individual health will be addressed at greater length later. For now, we will treat public health program placement as exogenous and thus replace the price of health programs (P_Y) with measures of availability or distance (γ).

Sixth, it is difficult to determine theoretically appropriate functional forms for the reduced-form demand equation ($D^H(\bullet)$). By choosing a functional form for the utility function (equation 2)—such as the Stone-Geary utility function that underlies the simple Linear Expenditure System (LES) or a quadratic utility function—and a functional form for the health production function, one cannot (in general) analytically solve for the health reduced-form demand equation. The demand equations are not LES (even if the utility function is of the LES (Stone-Geary) form) because the maximization problem of a household that must produce one or more of the goods it consumes (health) differs from the usual problem of utility maximization subject only to a budget constraint. Treating health as a utility-augmenting good produced in the household implies that its demand equation is a combination of the demand for health from the utility function and the supply of health from the health production function. For example, consider the impact of a compensated increase in the price of a food on the demand for health. As both food and health are goods in the utility function, the magnitude of the price effect depends on the extent to which they are substitutes or complements in preferences. But as food is also a source of nutrients used to produce health, the increased price of food will also increase the price (or cost) of achieving any level of health. The size of the increase in this implicit (shadow) price of health depends on the nutrient content of the foods, and the marginal rates of substitution in health production among all health inputs. So the total (reduced-form) effect of a food price increase on the demand for health includes influences from both preferences and the biological health production function. Because of this complication, the usual strategy is to assume a linear functional form for all the reduced-form demand equations. The unobserved health endowments μ^i are assumed to enter additively. We can think of the residual (ε^H) of the linear reduced-form demand equation for health as containing the own- (δ^{ii}) and cross-effects (δ^{ij}) of health endowments on the health of individual i, in addition to all other sources of unexplained variation (η^H):

$$\varepsilon^H = \delta^{ii}\mu^i + \sum_{j \neq i} \delta^{ij}\mu^j + \eta^H \qquad (9)$$

With these points in mind, the estimable reduced-form demand for health equation can then be written (suppressing the superscript i):

$$H = \alpha_0^H + \sum_{j=1}^{K} \alpha_j^H P_j + \sum_{j=1}^{T} \beta^{Hj} W^j + \sum_{j=1}^{T} \gamma^{Hj} d^j$$

$$+ \theta^H G + \psi^H P_Y + \phi^H \Pi + \rho^H V + \varepsilon^H \qquad (10)$$

where the Greek letters in equation (10) (except Π and ε) refer to parameters to be estimated, and the superscript H on these parameters refers to the fact that they are the parameters of the health reduced-form rather than the reduced-form of another household choice variable. Note that this version assumes that the health reduced-form demand equations for every member type are identical except for the sets of $d^1, ..., d^T$ personal characteristic variables (age, sex). Alternatively, one could estimate separate health reduced-form demand equations such as (10) for sets of individuals defined by age and sex.

Reduced-form demand equations for all contemporaneously determined household choice variables (necessarily) have the same set of right-hand-side variables (regressors) as the health reduced-form. There may be some interest in studying the effects of structural adjustment on the demand for health inputs as well as on health outcomes. The analysis of the demand for food and food nutrients (which are important health inputs) is discussed in Chapter 9. For example, the reduced-form demand equations for nonfood health inputs Y^i are (suppressing the superscript i):

$$Y = \alpha_0^Y + \sum_{j=1}^{K} \alpha_j^Y P_j + \sum_{j=1}^{T} \beta^{Yj} W^j + \sum_{j=1}^{T} \gamma^{Yj} d^j$$

$$+ \theta^Y G + \psi^Y P_Y + \phi^Y \Pi + \rho^Y V + \varepsilon^Y \qquad (11)$$

Variables in the reduced-form for health

MEASURES OF HEALTH. Four types of data on health status are assumed to be available to the researcher: the self-reporting of respondents as to whether they had suffered an illness, the effect of any illness on the performance of customary activities, the anthropometric measurement of height and weight of children five years and under, and information on miscarriages, stillbirths, and infant deaths for pregnancies within the past 12 months. Anthropometric measurement is less likely to suffer from measurement error than the two self-reported health status measures. Of particular concern for the self-reported indicators of health status is the possibility that the propensity to consider one's state of health as being "ill" versus "not ill" may be correlated with individual and household characteristics such as education, age, and (full) income. Pitt and Rosenzweig (1985) used self-reported illness (whether the respondent was sick in the previous week and whether he or she was sick in bed) as the dependent variable in estimating separate reduced-form health equations for 2,347 farm household heads and wives from Indonesia. They interpreted the positive relationship between respondents' schooling (in years) and the probability of reported illness as resulting from systematic self-reporting measurement bias.[11] The other self-reported indicator of health status, whether illness has altered the usual activities of the respondent, is also likely to suffer from measurement error, which is correlated with some actual determinants of (unobserved) "true" health—the opportunity cost of time, and the marginal utility of health and income. This problem is probably more acute for another measure of health status sought in some household survey questionnaires: whether the respondent stayed in a hospital or health center and for how many nights. Clearly, this measure of health is likely to be strongly related to the socioeconomic status.

There is some evidence that other health data frequently available, miscarriages, stillbirths, and the death of young infants, tend to be underreported by households in similar surveys. It is likely that the probability of not reporting such an event is related to household attributes and the economic environment.

As the preferred anthropometric data are available for persons age five and under, the measurement error in self-reported indicators of health is of consequence in analyzing the effects of structural adjustment on the health of most respondents. It would be a mistake to ignore this subpopulation or to think that self-reported health indicators do not contain useful information on health in spite of the measurement problem. Although it is likely that the reduced-form coefficients associated with age, education, wealth, and wage rates of household members will be estimated with bias in an equation having self-reported health status as a dependent variable, it is likely that many of the regressors in the health reduced-form are not correlated with self-reporting measurement error, and consistent estimates of their effects on health can be obtained. In particular, all the market- and region-specific variables, such as prices and health program availability, are unlikely to be highly correlated with self-reporting error or with the individual- or household-specific variables correlated with self-reporting measurement error. It is still likely then that the effects of the exogenous determinants of health most directly affected by structural adjustment will be reasonably well measured. Nevertheless, anthropometric measurement of health status, in particular weight and height, are still to be greatly preferred in an analysis of the economic determinants of health and the impact of structural adjustment on health.

A more satisfactory measure of self-reported health status would use a list of reported health symptoms, such as fever, diarrhea, skin outbreak, and the like. In areas where certain types of disease are known to be widespread, symptoms associated with these diseases can be itemized in the questionnaire. This type of measure may actually be more informative in some respects than weight and height, although more likely to suffer from self-reporting bias.

REDUCED-FORM DETERMINANTS OF HEALTH. The regressors of the health reduced-form suggested by the conceptual model described and assumed to be available in household surveys include:

• *Prices* (P_j): prices of foods (see also community-level data)
• *Wages* (W^i): predicted wage rates of head of household and spouse
• *Individual attributes* (d^i): gender and possibly age, ethnicity, or religion of respondent
• *Household "public" goods* (G): sources of drinking water for the household, nature of rubbish disposal, type of toilet, physical attributes of

household dwelling (type of dwelling, number of rooms, whether dwelling shared, source of lighting, main fuel used for cooking, construction materials used in outside wall, flooring and roof), age and education of head of household and head's spouse

• *Prices of nonfood health inputs (P_v):* measure of availability and accessibility of public health and fertility control programs (from community-level data)

• *Unearned income, farm profits, and wealth (Π and V):* measures of wealth including land ownership, value of livestock, value of agricultural equipment, assets of non-farm enterprises, nonearnings income and farm profits.[12]

Prices. These should be derived from the community-level survey rather than by calculating unit values by dividing the reported value of consumption or expenditure by a household by the physical quantity. Calculating household-specific prices by the unit value method imparts bias if individual food categories consist of items of varying quality. Higher-quality food has a higher unit price than lower-quality food, and since taste for quality is a normal good, price and income effects are confounded.[13] This quality bias problem is more likely to be a problem for heterogeneous goods such as "beef" and "fish and shellfish" than for more (locally) homogeneous goods such as kerosene or salt. If independent measures of prices for constant-quality foods are not available from the community questionnaire, much of the quality bias problem of using unit prices can be eliminated by using the average unit price in a locality (village) for each food category.

Wages. Wage rates can also be derived as "unit values" from the household questionnaire or from a community survey, the latter being preferred. If the household questionnaire is used, it is necessary to calculate the average wage for each gender by schooling level and season. A more sophisticated approach would estimate selectivity-corrected wage equations by gender and use these wage equations to predict wage rates. But in most African contexts there would likely be little return for the effort required.

Household public goods. Most of these are categorical variables in typical survey questionnaires. Depending on the distribution of outcomes and

sample size, it may be necessary to aggregate some categorical outcomes. For example, 12 choices for source of drinking water would require 11 binary (0-1) variables. Some of these may be empty (never chosen) in the data or be chosen by such a small number of households that reasonably precise estimation of their health effects is impossible. Investigators should then use their judgment to aggregate categories. Some other regressors are probably of only second-order importance as determinants of health or are highly correlated with each other. Not including as regressors the full set of variables describing the construction of the dwelling will probably not have a consequential impact on the estimated parameters of interest.

Prices of nonfood health inputs. Measures of the availability and/or distance to providers of health and related services obtained by the community survey will act as proxies for the prices of these services. Investigators should be careful not to use as regressors the information on actual use of health services and the cost of travel to the service location provided by the household questionnaire. The primary problem is that use of health services is a household choice, a dependent variable rather than an exogenous independent variable. Obvious "simultaneous equations bias" would result from using as regressors the survey information on whether an individual had consulted a health practitioner or visited a health center or consulted anyone about an illness. We would expect that visits to a health practitioner and health would be inversely correlated but would certainly not conclude from this that visits to a health practitioner cause poor health. The same problem exists even for the use of preventive medical care—the poorer a person's inherent healthiness (the less their health endowment), the more likely it is that person will seek preventive medical care, other things being equal.

Unearned income, farm profits, and wealth. It would be useful to create a variable for the total value of assets from the data available. The exogeneity of all sources of non-earnings income is problematic. Transfers that are not "regular" may in fact be a reflection of the ill health of household members or other household outcomes that reflect household choices. One can make the case that even "regular" transfers represent past consumption, investment, and migration decisions of households that are correlated with unobserved determinants of health, hence resulting in biased coefficients. To the extent that non-earnings income is unimportant or zero for most households, this issue may be moot. In some African countries, however, remittances from household members who work and live away from their immediate family members may be an important source of non-earnings income to the sample household. If the remitters reside outside the sampled households' village or town, it may be useful to treat this as exogenous non-earnings income—included in the reduced form.

Estimation methods

TABULAR ANALYSIS. The first step should always be simple tabular analysis. Creating some simple tables is a quick and easy way of getting a "feel" for the data and will indicate whether the range and variation in variables of interest are sufficient to use in regression analysis and if outliers or coding errors are present. The first table to be produced should be a table of means, standard deviations, and minima and maxima for all the variables described.

After this table of descriptive statistics has been prepared, a set of cross-tabulations should be undertaken to examine patterns in the data. Health outcomes should be tabulated against gender and age, region of residence (or ethnicity), measures of wealth and income, education of household head and spouse, and availability of important public health and family planning programs and medical providers. A more sophisticated cross-tabulation might attempt to control for an important correlate of health status, such as age, while tabulating against community access to important public health programs (see, for example, Frame 8.1).

Conditioning on age, as in Frame 8.1, may uncover the effects of health programs that primarily affect the health (as measured by weight for height) of infants (age less than two years) rather than older children. Cross-tabulations such as these help researchers uncover "stylized facts" about the association between health interventions and health outcomes. However, cross-tabulations necessarily involve only a subset of the variables that prior analysis had indicated as behavioral determinants of health. Cross-tabulations thus only provide partial associations and may be misleading. For example, a variable

chosen for cross-tabulation with a health outcome may be highly correlated with a variable not in the same cross-tabulation, and may be picking up the effect of the omitted variable as well as its own effect. Research with this type of data indicates that this omitted variable bias can be severe. For this reason, a regression that controls for all reduced form-determinants of health is the preferred method of analysis.

REGRESSION ANALYSIS. Estimation of the health reduced-forms using an anthropometric measure of health as dependent variable is accomplished by ordinary least squares regression. Estimation of the health reduced-forms that use binary indicators of health, such as self-reported illness, should use probit or logit estimation methods. These procedures are found in many popular econometric software packages. There are some problems with the reported t-statistics when ordinary least squares regression (or probit or logit) are applied to these data. A more technical discussion of this issue is presented in Box 8.4. The reader is strongly encouraged to read this material, which suggests a variety of econometric specifications that are useful and are not difficult to implement.

The interpretation of the regression coefficients is straightforward in a reduced-form. In the case of linear regression (without interactions), the coefficients are the effects of a unit change in each regressor on the dependent variable. For example, the coefficient on the price of milk in a weight-for-height reduced-form is the effect of a unit change in the price of milk on the weight for height of a child. If milk prices are in currency units per liter, and if it is known that structural adjustment resulted in an increase in the price of milk of 10 currency units per liter, then the effect of this increase in price on weight for height is simply the regression coefficient times 10. If natural logarithms are taken of the dependent variable and all (continuous and nonzero) regressors,

Frame 8.1: Weight for height of children by age and program availability

(100 grams/cm)

	Health program present in community	Health program not present in community
Ages less than 2		
Ages 2 and 3		
Ages 4 and 5		

Box 8.4: Technical issues in regression analysis

While ordinary least squares regression provides consistent parameter estimates under fairly general circumstances, with household survey data it may tend to give estimates of the standard errors of regression parameters biased downwards—that is, the reported t-values will be biased upwards. This bias occurs when the regression residuals are not independent. This lack of independence can be the result of the following (in order of magnitude):

• An individual appears more than once in the estimation sample because he or she was sampled at more than one survey round and multiple survey rounds were pooled for estimation. As the regression residual includes time-invariant individual health endowments, the residuals for an individual are likely to be correlated across time periods.

• More than one individual in a household appears in the estimation sample (even in a single cross-section). Members of a household are not only likely to have individual endowments (μ^i) that are correlated, in part representing unobserved household-specific determinants of health, but also they share a common health environment (λ), many of the attributes of which are unobserved by the investigator.

• More than one individual from a region appears in the estimation sample. Again, their regression residual will be correlated because of thier common incompletely observed (measured) regional health environment (λ). Note that in the case of multiple survey rounds, individuals measured in a common survey round will have correlated residuals if there are time-specific factors, such as season, prevalence of contagious disease, or other natural phenomena, that importantly affect measured health.

Consistent estimates of the standard errors of coefficients can be obtained by estimating a random- or fixed-effects model. Random-effects estimation is a form of generalized least squares that uses the information that the residuals have a correlation structure (random-effects estimation also requires the assumption that the random effects—the components of the residuals that are not independent across observations, in this case, endowments—are not correlated with the regressors, which is the assumption made about residuals in all reduced-form estimation). Many common statistical packages have random-effects estimation built in. Fixed-effects estimation treats the commonality among sample observations essentially as a fixed parameter. For example, if an individual is sampled at more than one point in time, all time-invariant (observed and unobserved) characteristics can be captured by a (binary) dummy variable specific to the individual. For even small samples, this results in a relatively large number of extra parameters that need to be estimated. This problem of too many parameters is eliminated by differencing across time periods—a procedure that results in the same parameter estimates as explicitly including dummy variables. Eliminating unobservables common to all household members by household fixed-effects entails differencing the regressors for each individual from the average for all household members. An example of this approach to studying the intrahousehold distribution of health and food is Pitt, Rosenzweig, and Hassan (1990). A consequence of household fixed-effects is that the effects of household-specific determinants of health (including the household public goods G) cannot be identified. Note that the fixed-effects model precludes the estimation of the effects of time-invariant factors (for example, gender and household characteristics such as drinking water source) on health.

When estimating health reduced-form equations for persons over the age of five, self-reported illness must be used as the dependent variable. Because the dependent variable is dichotomous, logit or probit models should be estimated. Unfortunately, correlated errors are likely to be a problem too difficult to deal with computationally when the dependent variable is not continuous.

then the coefficients have the familiar elasticity interpretation. In the case of prices and program availabilities, these elasticities are the direct effect of a percentage increase in each price and program on the health outcome.

The interpretation of coefficients is only slightly more complicated in the case of a probit or logit regression. Partial derivatives, which have the same interpretation as a linear regression coefficient, and elasticities are often output from computer packages that estimate these models.

Other problems

HEALTH PROGRAM PLACEMENT. There remains the issue of whether the reduced-form estimation strategies described accurately measure the effect of public programs on health outcomes. A fundamental problem in program evaluation is that the location of programs and the timing of program initiatives—program placement—is not likely to be random to the extent that government decision rules are responsive to unmeasured attributes (regional health endowments) of targeted populations. Simple measured associations between health programs and health outcomes may not provide correct estimates of program effects and thus may mis-estimate the effects of structural adjustment on health.

In any country, at a point in time, program efforts vary widely across areas, even if the programs are funded and controlled by the central government. Access to public health clinics, hospitals, maternity clinics, and fertility control programs varies considerably from region to region. Given the limited resource capacities of the central public agency, program allocations must be rationed. The placement of programs is thus likely to depend on the expected location-specific returns to the program, which will vary across areas according to, among other attributes, physical and demographic characteristics (endowments). If program placement is attentive to location-specific endowments, and such endowments influence outcomes of interest to policymakers, it is important in program evaluation to have information on endowments. It is inevitable, however, that not all exogenous locational characteristics are measured or are measurable. This is surely the case in African countries.

For example, consider the case of a country with areas having environmental features favorable for the propagation of geographically concentrated debilitating diseases, such as malaria, river blindness (onchocerciasis), trypanosomiasis (sleeping sickness), or schistosomiasis (bilharzia). The central government, knowing this, places a disproportionate level of health programs in these regions relative to regions in which these diseases are less frequent. The correlation between frequency of illness or weight for height and health program availability based upon household data that rely on spatial variation may then be positive. It would be incorrect to conclude from this negative coefficient that health program investments *caused* ill health; rather, health programs were placed where health endowments were lowest. The result of this "reverse" causation is to underestimate the effects of health programs on health outcomes when the latter is regressed on the former.

Data on the spatial distribution of health programs and outcomes at more than one point in time, expected to be available in the household survey, can be used to identify program effects consistently. Fixed-effects estimation (see Box 8.4), which estimates how *changes* in local programs affect *changes* in the health of the local population, is free from the contamination of areal heterogeneity bias. Note that if the points in time are too "close," it will be difficult to get good estimates of program effects since health program availability will have hardly changed at all. However, if a structural adjustment program importantly affects the ability of the government to maintain health programs, significant changes in health program availability will be found in the aftermath of structural adjustment.[14] If there is in fact little change in health program availability after structural adjustment, then there is likely to be little change in health outcomes as a consequence of changes in health program availability, so that the measurement of health program effects becomes unimportant.

FUNCTIONAL FORM AND SAMPLE DISAGGREGATION. The reduced-form demand equations for health and health inputs presented in equations (10) and (11) are written as linear forms because of the computational simplicity of working with linear-in-the-parameters estimating equations. If degrees of freedom are adequate, investigators may wish to allow for interactions among variables where it seems such interactions are justified by some information about behavior.[15] For example, it would be sensible to interact program variables with mothers' education if there is reason to believe that the effect of certain program interventions on the health of children depends on mothers' education. There may be also be policy reasons to estimate models that permit an analysis of the incidence of structural adjustment among variously defined groups. If there is reason to believe that the healthiness of these groups (or demand for health inputs) may respond differently to changes in reduced-form determinants, the investigator may introduce a variable that defines groups (rural/urban location, region) with reduced-form regressors or break the sample and estimate separate reduced-forms for each group of interest. Statistical tests (Chow tests, F tests) can be used to determine whether such disaggregation or interaction is statistically valid.

MORTALITY AND FERTILITY SELECTION. Drawing inferences about the effect of health interventions (including food prices) on children from studies based solely on samples of *surviving* children may lead to an incorrect assessment of program effects if the effects of programs on survival and fertility probabilities are ignored. In many African countries, infant mortality rates are very high, and health programs that affect child health (as measured by height and weight, for example) also affect the probability of survival for children. It is not enough to consider the impact of health programs and goods prices on child mortality in addition to their impact on health. Estimating the reduced-form determinants of child health is further complicated because changes in mortality induced by changes in programs that affect health (due perhaps to structural adjustment) may alter the average health of the surviving population by causing those with higher inherent probabilities of illness (those with low health endowments μ^i and λ) to not survive. It might be expected that the likelihood of infant death will be importantly related to this health endowment. Consider, hypothetically, a health program that predominately affects survival but not the health status of those who survive (oral rehydration). Such a health program may actually *reduce* the average health status of the surviving population (and have a negative coefficient in a reduced-form for health) by permitting the survival of some low-endowment children who would otherwise die, while not appreciably augmenting the health of those who would otherwise survive. Only if infant mortality were uncorrelated with health endowments would there be no survival selection since the average endowments of survivors and nonsurvivors would be equal. Only in this limiting case does finding that a program has no effect on the average health of survivors imply that the health of those who would otherwise survive is not enhanced. Thus, knowing only a program's influence on the average health of surviving children may be dangerously inadequate in evaluating its effectiveness and the effect of changes in program availability on health.[16]

Unfortunately, correcting for the selective effects of mortality is difficult. It is necessary (but not sufficient) to know the effects of programs and prices on the rate of survival *and* the average health of survivors. Knowing the former requires information on mortality during a (common) reference period. The survey questionnaire may only provide this information for infants born in the 12 months before the survey date. Considering that mortality rates are highest in the first year of life, this is still useful information. It would be better to record information on all child deaths in each woman's reproductive life, and the year, sex, and birth order of all live births and whether they resulted in surviving infants (at the time of the survey) or deaths (and when death occurred). Statistical methods exist (and are available in some "canned" statistical packages) that measure and correct for the selection bias imparted by non-random mortality. A simple two-stage method first estimates the reduced-form determinants of mortality using the same set of regressors as equation (10).[17] This estimation stage is valuable by itself since infant mortality is an important health outcome and the effects of structural adjustment on mortality as well as anthropometric measures

of health on living children need to be studied.

Another source of sample selection—more subtle but potentially as important as mortality selection—is fertility selection. Health programs (and food prices and wages) not only affect which infants are alive to be surveyed but also the fertility decisions of households—whether pregnancy occurs or not. As with mortality, changes in programs and prices resulting from structural adjustment may alter the fertility decisions of households. The additional children born, or whose birth is averted, may have non-random health characteristics. Pitt and Rosenzweig (1989) examined the effect of fertility selection on the estimated parameters of reduced-form health demands for infants in Malaysia and found fertility selection to be significant. Ignoring it resulted in large mismeasurement of program effects on health. Like the case of mortality selection, correcting for the effects of fertility selection requires the estimation of a reduced-form having the same regressors as the health reduced-form (10) (with the exception of the gender of the child, as this is not known to the household at the time the fertility decision is made). The measure of fertility to be used as dependent variable should be the number of pregnancies over a reference period. In the household survey envisioned here, anthropometric data are available for surviving children up to a specific age, so that it would be most useful to have information on all pregnancies that could have resulted in a child in that age range.

Reduced-form demand for health inputs

The reduced-form determinants of all (contemporaneously determined) household choice variables have the same set of regressors as the health reduced-form. A linear formulation of reduced-form demands for health inputs is given by equation (11). Most health inputs typically included in household surveys are measured as binary or polychotomous variables that require the use of binary probit, binary logit, and multinomial logit estimation methods. The caveats associated with estimating and interpreting the health outcome reduced-forms described apply equally for health input reduced-forms. A set of health inputs likely to be measured in the survey includes:

• Consulted health practitioner for checkup
• Consulted health practitioner for illness
• Consulted health practitioner for prenatal care
• Consulted health practitioner for postnatal care

- Frequency of postnatal care
- Choice of health practitioner for illness
- Child vaccinations by type
- Place of vaccination
- Duration of breastfeeding of children
- Participation in community feeding program
- Frequency of prenatal care in past pregnancies
  - Source of prenatal care
  - Household food consumption (see Chapter 9).

It is not necessary that econometric estimation be carried out for all these health inputs. Investigators should single out a health input for intensive study if simple tabulations of the data show that its use has importantly changed in the aftermath of structural adjustment, if they are aware of significant budgetary changes affecting the ability of public health facilities to provide services, or if they are aware of significant changes in fee schedules. Data limitations can also make tabulation a useful alternative. For example, if the community-level information available is only a count of public health facilities in each region that provides a particular health service without regard to the quality of service provided and other attributes such as queuing time, a policy shift that keeps the count of facilities unchanged but reduces service flows and quality will not be uncovered by regression analysis of the community-level data. If information on budgets, staffing, or other indicators of quality and service flows is available from other sources, even anecdotal information, investigators would do well to link this information with information on changes in use derived from the household surveys.

Estimating the willingness to pay for medical care

It is unlikely that user fees for medical services ration the market. The opportunity cost of travel time has been found to be an important and significant determinant of medical care demand in almost all studies of the demand for medical care in developing countries. If the community or household questionnaire provides information on the distance or travel time to different types of medical care providers, it is possible to impute a price to medical care. Using the observed or imputed wage of an individual as the opportunity cost of time, the price of medical care provided by a specified type of provider is the fee charged by that provider plus the product of travel time and the wage. Wages can be imputed either by estimating selectivity-corrected wage regressions based upon the sub-sample of individuals who would report market wages and hours or, more simply in the case of rural areas, by averaging wage rates (by gender) within each village. Within village and gender groups, individual variation in wages is likely to be small. For children, who are typically accompanied by an adult to the health-care provider, the price of medical care can be taken as the price of adult time for the gender that most often accompanies children (women) plus any return to child time that can be imputed.

Estimating the price elasticity of medical care is accomplished as described (reduced-form demand for health inputs). The imputed prices for medical care should be added to the list of regressors. Indeed, if these prices are calculated, they can also be added to the list of regressors for inclusion in the reduced-form demand equation for health. Their regression coefficient has the interpretation of the effect of a change in the medical care price on a measure of health outcome.

An econometric issue to consider in estimating models of medical provider choice is the appropriate estimation sub-sample. For example, household questionnaires provide information on the health practitioner visited for illness, for prenatal care, and for children's vaccinations. The former two questions provide information on provider choice *conditional* on a previous endogenous (household choice) event—being ill or pregnant.[18] No one seeks "prenatal" care who is not pregnant, or seeks treatment for illness who is not ill. But it is likely that the existence of pregnancy or illness is related to the observed and unobserved determinants of provider choice. As a result, estimating a model of health practitioner choice when ill using only the sub-sample of those individuals who report themselves ill will result in "selectivity bias." The appropriate procedure is to estimate a polychotomous variable model having as dependent variables a set of indicators for choice of provider if ill (or pregnant) but also for the outcome "not ill" (or "not pregnant").

The efficacy of health inputs: Estimating the health production function

The health outcome and health input reduced-form demand equations described tell us how social and economic factors influence health behaviors. As the model presented makes clear, the reduced-form is not the effect of health behaviors (health inputs) themselves on health, but rather the combination of the effect of health behaviors and the determinants of that behavior. The reduced-form regression coefficients thus reflect the preferences, beliefs, perceptions, and information of the household, and not solely the effect of health behaviors. However, the health production function, which provides the direct biological effect of health inputs on health, can be estimated and is of policy interest in assessing the potential efficacy and cost-effectiveness of health program interventions.

Ideally, estimation of the health production function requires information at the level of the individual for all inputs that affect health. Information on food consumption at the individual level is not usually available in household questionnaires. As food intake is likely to be a primary determinant of individual health, estimation of the health production function is problematic. One solution adopted by Pitt and Rosenzweig (1985) is to estimate the health production function using household data: the dependent variable is the proportion of household ill and the independent variables are household aggregates of health inputs. This approach is valid if the individual health technologies are linear and identical (except for intercept shifters) across household member types (age/gender). Irrespective of the data used, health production function estimation requires instrumental variable estimation methods (such as two-stage least squares) since the health inputs are presumed to be endogenous. The instrumental variables are the reduced-form determinants of health listed. Identification requires that the number of reduced-form determinants of health in that list that are not included in the specified health production function exceed the number of endogenous health inputs. Two-stage least squares estimation is commonly included in standard econometrics software packages.

Principles of analysis and policy implications

The preceding discussion suggests that an analysis of the relationship between government policy interventions, health, and other household behaviors has stiff data requirements. Health is multi-dimensional and difficult to measure—anthropometric measures, although expensive to collect, offer important benefits. The importance of unobservables in the determination of health implies that longitudinal data will also aid in economic analysis. Panel data allow the analyst

to estimate the effect of changes in government programs without the bias that non-random program placement can impart. Finally, the selective effects of mortality and fertility can seriously affect the accuracy of the reduced-form determinants of health. Correcting for these sources of selection requires data on the health status of the (surviving) sampled population and on mortality, and a complete pregnancy roster of all women.

Using nutrient intake as an indicator of welfare or health has serious drawbacks. Nutrient intake itself cannot be considered an argument in the utility function or even a good indicator of welfare. The focus on nutrients derives from their importance as an *input* into the production of health and the common absence of adequate data on health. Knowledge of how nutrient intake maps into health is important for policy analysis. Even complete knowledge of the matrix of food price elasticities may not lead to conclusions about the effects of price interventions if price changes do not unambiguously result in a rise or fall in the intake of all important nutrients. To the extent that households that have greater access to health services or live in less sanitary environments also face higher or lower food costs (for example, rural versus urban areas), cross-sectional estimates of food price effects that ignore the health infrastructure may lead to misleading conclusions about the consequences of food price interventions.

Studies of the determinants of nutrient intake are necessarily at the household level. It is likely that households do not allocate resources equally among their members, and so the implications of policy for the well-being of certain classes of individuals (women, children) are not identified. Health data are at the individual level so that reduced-form demand equations for health directly provide the effect on the health of the individual by type of changes in policy interventions (prices and programs).

Changes in individual health have implications for labor productivity, wages, fertility, and human capital investment. These are particularly difficult issues to measure, but ignoring them may lead to serious underestimation of the returns to investing in health.

Notes

1. For an excellent and comprehensive review of this literature, see Behrman and Deolalikar (1988a).

2. This result pertains to uncompensated price elastici-

ties for households whose food expenditures were greater than those of 75 percent of all households. For households in the 90th percentile, six of nine price elasticities had non-identical signs across the nine nutrients.

3. On the importance of substitution elasticities for the evaluation of nutrition-based food policy, see Timmer (1981), Timmer, Falcon, and Pearson (1983), and Pitt (1983). For an African case study, see Strauss (1984).

4. The relationship between productivity, wages, and health or nutrient consumption has been confirmed by Strauss (1986) using data for farm households in Sierra Leone, Deolalikar (1988) using Indian data, and Sahn and Alderman (1988) for Sri Lanka.

5. In examining cuts in real government expenditure in 37 developing countries, Hicks and Kubisch (1984) found that social expenditure was the most protected among the five categories of government expenditure defined, especially in the lowest-income countries. For a thorough examination of the evidence on the impact of economic adjustment on health and nutrition, see Behrman (1988a).

6. Discussion of issues surrounding the measurement of health will be deferred to later sections.

7. The importance of this purely random component to health depends on how health is measured. For example, this random component will be relatively larger if the measure of health is a dichotomous indicator of whether an individual is sick on any given day than if the measure is the height of an individual. Although individuals may have differing propensities to become ill (their μ^i), whether one is sick in a short reference period depends more on purely random events than does height, the result of a lifetime of health behaviors and endowment. As will be made clear, this random component to health differs from the terms μ^i and λ in that while all three are unknown to the researcher and thus contribute to the error term in statistically related relationships, the μ^i and λ terms are *not* random events to the household.

8. The discussion here refers to household farm activities for clarity of presentation but applies equally to any household production of goods and services for the market, such as weaving, crafts, processing, and other small cottage industries, as well as trading, transportation services, and other services produced by household members.

9. Typically, the schooling and age of the head of the household and his or her spouse are treated as exogenous variables to be included in the reduced-form demand equations. The age and schooling of children are often not considered exogenous as they reflect recent fertility and human capital decisions by the household, which are not independent from the health input decisions of households. Indeed, the education analysis represented in Chapter 7 explicitly considers the schooling of children as a choice variable of the household affected by structural adjustment.

10. Explicit statistical tests of the separability hypothesis in developing country agriculture have been performed by Pitt and Rosenzweig (1986) and Benjamin (1988), both studies using data from Indonesia and both not able to reject separability. The Pitt and Rosenzweig paper is of particular relevance here since it used information on the health of cultivators to test the separability hypothesis. The test was based on the following implication of separability: if perfect markets exist for the services provided by farm family cultivators, then the healthiness of any of them (which was demonstrated to significantly affect labor supply) should not affect farm profit, as market substitutes are available. Benjamin's separability test was based on a related implication: household size and composition should affect family labor supply but not affect farm profits if labor markets are well functioning.

11. A similar conclusion about self-reported health is drawn by Wolfe and Behrman (1984).

12. Farm or non-farm enterprise profits should be replaced by the reduced-form determinants of profits—prices of inputs (including labor) and outputs, as well as quantities of land, capital, and other fixed factors—if it is believed that household production decisions are not separable from consumption decisions.

13. On the treatment of this problem, see Deaton (1988).

14. However, this change in the availability of health services may not be captured by all measures.

15. Interaction is meant to include not just the products of regressors with other regressors but also the product of a regressor with itself (quadratic terms).

16. An example much more applicable to developed countries concerns measuring the effect of neonatal intensive care facilities on some measure of the health of a sample of (living) infants. As is well known, a primary result of neonatal intensive care has been a dramatically increased rate of survival of very premature infants. It is also well established that premature infants are significantly more prone to health problems during their life than infants carried to full term. Neonatal intensive care is likely to have little impact on the health of most full-term infants. A regression having a measure of infant health as a dependent variable and the accessibility of neonatal intensive care facilities as a regressor is likely to show that neonatal intensive care facilities have a detrimental effect on infant health. The negative regression coefficient reflects the influence of neonatal intensive care on the survival of low-endowment infants. These, by surviving, reduce the average healthiness of the sampled (surviving) population. It is clear that these facilities can only improve the health of any infant conditional on its survival. The negative sign simply reflects the selective effects of mortality on inclusion in the regression sample—surviving infants.

17. Since the dependent variable is binary in this case (infant survives, infant dies), a probit or logit regression is appropriate.

18. Strictly speaking, the choice of children's vaccination

provider is conditional on there being a child in the household, which should also be considered an endogenous choice of households.

9

Household food security and nutrition

Graham Eele, Roger Hay, and John Hoddinot

Food security issues are high on the agendas of many African countries engaged in policy reform. This chapter provides a framework for analyzing the impact of structural adjustment on household food security and nutrition. It seeks to acquaint researchers with the tools required to carry out such an analysis. Household food consumption patterns and individual nutritional achievements are viewed as functions of household characteristics and external factors, notably prices and infrastructural variables. Hypotheses are formulated regarding changes in meso-level variables arising from structural adjustment, and approaches to the estimation of the resulting food security and nutritional effects are proposed.

The key unit for food security analysis is the household (although the meaning of individual-level food security is explored here), whereas for an evaluation of nutritional status it is the individual. The purposes of analyses at the household level are to identify households whose food security is at risk, understand the factors that affect food security, and attempt to quantify the underlying relationships. The nutritional status of individual household members (for example, young children) is similarly explained in terms of household-level variables. The main concern is to identify how changes in household incomes, the relative prices of basic food and other commodities, and key household and community characteristics affect the level and variability of expenditures on food, nutrient intake, and other measures of food security. Specifying and estimating these

relationships will allow key parameters, elasticities, and other factors that indicate how changes in the independent variables affect measured outcomes to be calculated. These parameters can be used to indicate the effect of past policies and to simulate the impact of future interventions.

Given the wealth of analytical possibilities, it is important to understand the limitations operating on the analysis of food security and nutrition during a process of structural adjustment. At the national level, it may be possible to predict the impact of policy changes on outcomes such as the level and variability of national food supply. As the level of analysis is disaggregated, the relationships being examined become more complex. At the level of individuals, many different factors affect food intake and nutritional status and it may be difficult to detect the effect of specific macro policy changes.

The analysis proposed can be used in a number of ways. These include:

• Predicting the impact of policy reform on the food security of the nation and of different household groups. This requires an understanding of the household economy, the relationship between households and markets, and the responses of households to public policy reforms.

• Assessing the impact of past policy changes on food security. Here, we emphasize the impact of policy changes on food-insecure target groups. It will be difficult to separate the impact of adjustment policies from the underlying conditions that lead to the adjustment package.

• Monitoring food security and nutrition in a period of policy reform. Given resource constraints, this may be achieved by focusing on selected household groups and indices sensitive to declines in the well-being of these households.

• Assessing the costs and benefits of policy revision or of additional policies that might be introduced to improve food security. These include policies that might ameliorate the transitory effects of the adjustment process on particular population groups. This is the most important and difficult type of analysis.

This chapter begins with an overview of issues facing the food security analyst, including a clarification of the levels and time frames of analysis; it develops a detailed guide to the analysis of household-level food security in the adjustment context; and it examines the effects of structural adjustment on the nutrition of individuals.

Issues in food security analysis

Food security can be defined in a number of different ways. In this chapter, we will take the definition put forward by Reutlinger and Selowsky (1976). Food security is thus defined as access by all people at all times to enough food for an active, healthy life. There are two dimensions to the analysis of food security. The first concerns the level of analysis. Food security can be examined at the national, regional, community, household, or individual level. Much of the analysis in the context of structural adjustment will focus on the impact of national policy reform on households and on individuals. We will be particularly interested in those households that are food-insecure and those whose food security is threatened by the adjustment process.

The second dimension relates to the time frame. For example, households may be unable to gain sufficient access to food all the time. This is termed *chronic food insecurity*. Here, analysis focuses on the level of food consumption and the factors that determine this. Alternatively, access to food may be adequate on average but variations result in access to food being inadequate some of the time. This is termed *transitory food insecurity*. It may result from regularly occurring events, such as dry seasons, or irregular events, such as droughts. The emphasis here is on the variability in food consumption and its consequences. A working definition of food security exists only when the level and time frame of the desired analysis are specified.

Food security at the national level

Food security at the national level is a major policy goal for almost all Sub-Saharan African countries. National food security may be defined as a satisfactory balance between aggregate food demand and food supply at prices that do not exclude poor households from access to food. Alternative definitions compare some aggregation of theoretical food needs with total supply. While this approach has some superficial appeal, in practice it has a number of drawbacks. First, the translation of food needs in terms of nutrients into quantities of food commodities is complex. Second, it generally ignores the role of prices and incomes as determinants of demand and the effects of price changes and policy reforms as factors influencing supply.

Nations are chronically food-insecure when, over a series of accounting periods, food supply (which includes domestic production, commercial imports, food aid, and changes in stocks) is insufficient to meet food demand at reasonable prices. Transitory insecurity will result when, from time to time, supply falls short of demand. Food prices will rise and the poor will be forced out of the market. In general, policies related to improving national food security tend to concentrate on the stabilization and increase of food supply. Almost all Sub-Saharan African countries have national policies designed to increase the level of food supply, especially that component derived from the national production of basic food staples. The achievement of national self-sufficiency in basic staples (which is rarely defined precisely) is seen as a key national objective. The achievement of national food security, however, presupposes both adequate and stable supplies (obtained through an appropriate combination of domestic production and trade) and sufficient demand or purchasing power to guarantee adequate access to food. The demand-side analysis of food security has to be carried out at the household level, where individual food consumption is determined. An assessment of the level and the variability in the availability of food from all sources, and of food needs, is required. The latter calls for the use of normative measures of nutritional requirements.

Food security at the household level

A conceptual framework for analysis at the household level is provided by Sen's (1981) theory of exchange entitlements. Households can be considered as having a set of entitlements. These are defined by the economic, social, legal, and agro-economic environment in which the households live. They include entitlements to own production, to trade, to the labor of the household members, and to a variety of transfers, including social security payments, food aid distribution, and other mechanisms. Households can choose to use their entitlements in many different ways; they can choose between using household labor to produce food and other agricultural commodities and seeking employment and purchasing food from the income they obtain. What they choose to do will, in part, be determined by the exchange rate or price at which the entitlements can be exchanged for food and other goods and services. The set of exchange entitlements is the set of food and other commodities that can be obtained with all possible combinations of entitlements at given prices.

A household is food-insecure when its set of exchange entitlements is insufficient to meet the food needs of the household members, taking into account that food is only one of the basic needs of the household. If the exchange entitlement set is insufficient to meet food needs all of the time, then the household will suffer from chronic food insecurity. This is a function of poverty. Transitory food insecurity occurs with a temporary decline in the exchange entitlements set. This may result from a regularly occurring set of events, such as seasonal variation, or it may be the result of factors such as drought or other environmental calamity or the impact of macro policy change and structural adjustment.

The exchange entitlement concept implies that food insecurity at the household level is a result of inadequate demand for food. Total household income, including the value of own production, transfers, and all other income sources, is not sufficient to provide the household with enough food to meet its needs at the prices the household faces. To paraphrase Sen, household food insecurity is the phenomenon of households not having enough food to eat; it is not the fact of there not being enough food. In the context of structural adjustment, the analysis of household food security needs to be concerned with the impact of adjustment policies on the entitlement set of different types of households and on the prices these households face.

Investigation of these issues raises theoretical and practical problems. Even though household budget and consumption surveys in most countries are a complex and wide-ranging data collection exercise, they will not be able to capture all the subtle and detailed aspects of household food security. For example, in an African context, household entitlements may include assets and incomes that households can claim from kinsfolk and the state when income shortfalls are experienced. These will include traditional links with other households, which imply transfers in times of need, as well as officially organized relief programs. These transfers will only be directly observable in times of crisis, but omitting them will lead to an overstatement of household food insecurity.[1] As already indicated, food security has a time dimension that is difficult to capture in a single cross-sectional survey. While countries will be encouraged to repeat household surveys at regular intervals, in many places this will not be possible. The analyst will need to realize the limitations of the data and ensure that the details of the data do not obscure the wider picture.

Individual food security and nutrition

In a similar fashion, food security at the level of the individual can be defined as continuing access to adequate food for an active and healthy life. As analysis shifts from the household to the individual, however, food security is affected by an increasing number of factors. Individual food security can be viewed as an individual's claim on household food resources in relation to the needs for growth, work, and the maintenance of essential body functions. A "food-secure" household environment is clearly an important determinant of individual food security, but it is neither a necessary nor a sufficient condition. An important factor determining individual food security is the relationship between household members. Food security at the level of the household does not necessarily mean that all household members will receive sufficient food to meet their needs. Alternatively, food-insecure households may restrain the consumption of some members of the household to protect the vulnerable individuals, or they may distribute food in accordance with power and status, thereby compromising the food security of weaker members. The mechanisms that determine how food and other resources are distributed among household members are complex and difficult to measure in large-scale surveys. In the analysis of the social dimensions of structural adjustment, the main emphasis will be on those mechanisms that are likely to be directly affected by adjustment measures. These may well include changes not only in levels of income, but also in who actually earns the income. These issues are discussed in more detail in Chapter 11.

At the level of the individual, much of the analysis will focus on nutrition and, in particular, on measures of the physical impact of inadequate food consumption. In part this is because of the problems associated with the accurate measurement of individual food and nutrient intakes, but good nutrition is an important policy objective in its own right. Household food security is related to nutritional status, but it is not the only factor involved. For young children, on whom much of the analysis will concentrate, protein-energy malnutrition is related to three main factors: the incidence of disease and infection; childcare practices; and the ability of the household to maintain its food security. The analysis of nutrition in the context of food security, therefore, must be closely related to the analysis of health (Chapter 8).

The emphasis on the nutritional status of young children is justified because this group of the population is most vulnerable to inadequate food intake. Insufficient calories and protein for young children will result in poor physical and mental development and may well be a major cause of mortality. In many African countries, malnutrition is thought to be a major cause of, or an important contributory factor to, many infant and young-child deaths. The indication of malnutrition through anthropometric measurement is a well-developed technique that can also be relatively easily applied in household surveys. Measures of the nutritional status of adults can be developed; the use of these techniques is discussed further in the next section.

In the context of food security, protein-energy malnutrition (PEM) is the most important nutrition problem faced by African countries (Latham 1984). Other nutrition problems do exist; for example, vitamin A deficiency, iodine deficiency, and anemia. In a number of countries, their incidence and severity have spurred the establishment of major public health programs. Structural adjustment may well have an impact on these types of malnutrition, but the main mechanism will be through the changes imposed on the operation of health services. The effects of adjustment on these components of nutrition, therefore, are considered in Chapter 8.

An approach to the analysis

Policy analysis that will promote needed actions must identify the nature of food insecurity in the country; specify who is food-insecure and identify the main characteristics of the households and individuals who suffer from food insecurity; and establish the causal factors and mechanisms related to food security. The emphasis in this final step will be on specifying the relationships between the macro-adjustment measures and food insecurity at the household and individual levels.

The analysis of both household and individual food security is a demanding task. The approach adopted throughout this chapter is to undertake the simpler analytical steps first, then build on these using more sophisticated techniques. While the order of the presentation emphasizes the estimation of consumption parameters, the analyst is strongly advised to start with a detailed examination of basic tables and descriptive statistics. The mechanical application of econometric techniques, without a thorough understanding of the data and the context, can easily yield misleading results and wrong policy conclusions.

The analysis of household food security

As households operate in an economic environment determined, at least partly, by public policy, this section is divided into two parts reflecting that fact. Linkages are developed between adjustment policies, the household economy, and food security. The discussion then turns to methods for analyzing household food security and nutrition. The focus is particularly on the estimation of income elasticities of food expenditure, the estimation of demand systems, and the identification of target groups for food policy interventions.

The household economy, adjustment, and food security

Households become food-insecure when the acquisition of food falls below what is required for all members to live "active and healthy" lives. Accordingly, for a household to be "food-secure," the following balance should hold:

$$Ac \geq R \qquad (1)$$

where $Ac = B + O + G + A + \Delta St$, and Ac is household acquisition of food expressed in nutrient units; R is the sum of individual nutrient requirements; B is food bought; O is household food production retained for consumption; G is food received as private gifts; A is food aid received as wages or gifts; and ΔSt is the net change in household food stocks.

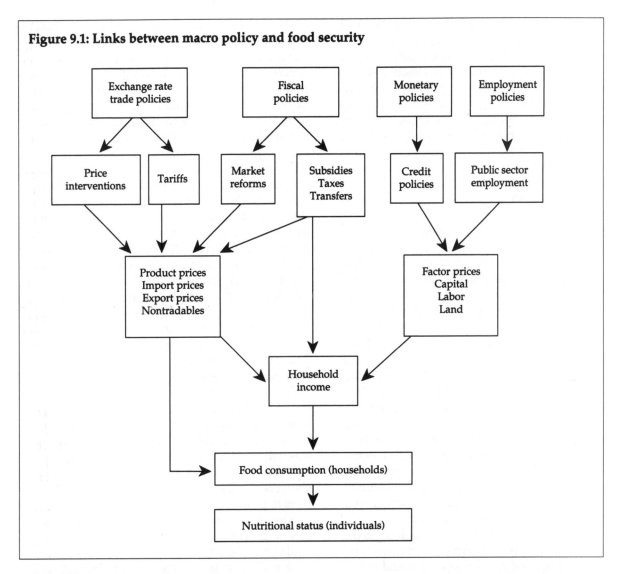

Figure 9.1: Links between macro policy and food security

This food balance equation highlights the fact that households use their entitlements to acquire food in a number of ways, and that households may be both producers and consumers. It is important to be aware of this feature when assessing the impact of structural adjustment on household food security. For example, raising food prices might worsen food security by increasing the cost of food. However, it also increases household income, which, other things being equal, should improve food security. Before going on to a discussion of the impact of adjustment policies, it is useful to summarize the relevant literature in this area. See also Chapters 7 and 8 and World Bank (1990b).

Empirical and theoretical work on the (rural) household economy has been summarized in a volume edited by Singh, Squire, and Strauss (1986a). The authors develop a feasible way to model household responses to policy changes likely to affect food security, one that allows the analyst to incorporate both production and consumption behavior in the same framework.

Their approach can be summarized as follows. Households are assumed to have a utility function consisting of three arguments: an agricultural staple; a market-purchased good; and leisure. Utility is maximized subject to cash, time, and technology constraints. Consequently, households make decisions in three areas: production, consumption, and labor supply. With respect to production, it is assumed that households will seek to maximize profits by setting marginal costs equal to marginal returns. Provided the household knows the existing wage rate, it can determine the optimal level of labor input. It does not need to decide how much food it will consume nor how much labor it will supply itself. Thus, production decisions can be made independent of consumption and labor supply. However, consumption and labor supply decisions are not independent of production decisions, which depend on both prices and incomes. Although prices can be taken as given, incomes are partly affected by production decisions. Thus, consumption decisions are not independent of production decisions. This is termed the profit effect and is incorporated into analyses of the effect of price changes on consumption.

This model assumes a competitive market for labor in rural areas (not the case in many parts of Sub-Saharan Africa) and ignores the fact that production and expenditures may be differentiated by gender. It is also difficult to incorporate risk and seasonality effects. Production and consumption decisions are not separable where health or nutrient intake affect labor productivity. Where separability does not hold, it is necessary to replace net farm profits with input prices and quantities.

Within the context of the model, adjustment policies affect household food security by changing prices, incomes, and the institutional structure in which households operate. The linkages between policy shifts and the household economy are illustrated in Figure 9.1. Discussion here is limited to policy changes that directly affect household food security. The net effects will be specific to different income groups, to net producers and consumers, and to different regions, particularly where markets are poorly integrated.

A typical outcome of adjustment policies is the liberalization of product markets, including food markets. The removal of regulations and subsidies from domestic markets will affect the relative prices between farm inputs and outputs, and between producer and consumer prices. The reduction in regulation of external trade, together with exchange rate liberalization and fiscal constraints, will affect the cost of imported farm inputs and food in both nominal and real terms. Liberalization of financial markets will affect the cost and availability of formal sector sources of capital.[2] Labor markets, particularly in urban areas, are also likely to undergo changes during the adjustment process. Fiscal austerity and institutional reforms often reduce public sector employment. Wage rate regulations may also be changed. This may lead to increased unemployment and reduced income for many urban households. It will also have consequences for households in rural areas, where remittances constitute an important source of income.

The net effect of structural adjustment on rural household entitlements will depend on several factors. Incomes will rise if additional revenues derived from producer prices are not offset by higher input costs or reductions in remittance income. Where households can switch resources from less remunerative activities to those receiving increased prices, further gains in income will accrue. Should these offset the reduction in welfare associated with higher consumer prices, household food security will improve. However, food-deficit households will be made worse off if they cannot increase production and if they are unable to increase their non-agricultural incomes. Finally, the benefits will be region-specific. Food producers in remote areas will almost certainly experience a rise in input costs. Output prices may fall despite an overall increase in nominal producer prices. Food producers closer to entry points and centers of demand are more likely to enjoy a relative improvement in their trading position. The methodology for analyzing the relative strengths of these effects is now outlined.

Entitlements of urban households will be affected by changes in incomes through the effects of structural adjustment in the labor market. They will also be affected by changes in prices, though this will partly depend on the households' previous access to food at subsidized prices and on changes in supply brought about by price incentives to producers and trade liberalization.

When examining the effects of adjustment policies on households, the analyst should pay particular attention to two interlinked features: the time scale and household groups. Households whose food security is likely to be threatened by these changes during the transitional period include rural families depending on rural labor markets, the families of state sector employees made redundant, and low-income urban families facing declining wage rates relative to food prices. As the length of the "transitional period" is unknown, it is not appropriate to assume that these short-run changes will disappear quickly or automatically. In the long run, adjustment policies should increase household income in relation to food prices and therefore improve food security. Producers should gain from adjustment policy reforms, particularly if they produce export crops and have access to inputs and markets for their products. This suggests that a major objective of the analysis should be to identify and, if possible, predict which groups of households are likely to gain and which are likely to lose from adjustment policies, concentrating particularly on those whose food security may be threatened. The methodology for doing so is discussed in the section on the identification of food-insecure households.

Household-level data analysis

Household-level food security analysis typically involves a number of steps. We propose that analysts (a) examine the relationship between measures of food consumption and economic factors largely operating at the meso level, starting with an assessment of the relationship between food (and nutrient) intake and income, including the estimation of expenditure and calorie elasticities; (b) extend the analysis to incorporate prices and the estimation of price elasticities; (c) develop the analysis to include the general economic and social environment in which households live through the specification and estimation of household models; and (d) use the results of this analysis to identify food-insecure households. The results of these activities lead to an examination of the policy implications, and recommendations for the development of data collection systems.

ESTIMATING THE INCOME ELASTICITY OF THE DEMAND FOR FOOD. The discussion of household food security noted several conduits through which households obtained food. In analyzing the relationship between income and food consumption, emphasis is placed on explaining how changes in the former affect the latter (how income changes in light of structural adjustment programs has been discussed earlier). This is accomplished by estimating the elasticity of demand for food with respect to income. As this is relatively straightforward, the method of doing so is outlined first. In the next section, the analysis is extended to include prices.

Existing studies differ substantially in their estimates of income-food expenditure and income-calorie elasticities. The former range from 0.01 to 1.18, depending on the commodity in question, on differences in estimation procedures, and on the extent to which food groups were disaggregated. (See Bouis and Haddad 1988 and Behrman and Deolalikar 1988a for a detailed summary of estimates.) Income-calorie elasticities appear to be generally rather lower for reasons relevant to survey analysis (see Bouis and Haddad 1988 and Behrman 1990). Recent evidence suggests that even when low-income households face a decline in the value of their income, they are able to maintain calorie acquisition by switching to lower-quality or otherwise cheaper foodstuffs, reducing waste, and entertaining less. These "adjustments" show up in lower income-calorie elasticities—that is, when income falls, calorie acquisition falls less than food expenditure. Finally, Strauss and Thomas (1989) have suggested that the calorie-expenditure curve is kinked. Their Brazilian data suggest a positive relationship between nutrient intake and expenditures for poor households. The curve kinks between 2,500 and 3,000 per capita calories per day and is flatter at higher expenditure levels.

The first stage in examining the relationship between income and calorie acquisition should be a descriptive analysis of the data, to include the calculation of means, standard deviations, coefficients of variation, and maximum and minimum values. Data analysis identifies potential problems and errors and indicates specific hypotheses for further investigation. Different derived variables can be assessed for their potential use in the analysis.

Frequency distributions and cross-tabulations are also useful at the preliminary stage. But correlation between two variables does not imply causation. Variables chosen for a cross-tabulation may be correlated with variables not included. A high degree of correlation between two variables may actually reflect the omitted variable. A sample cross-tabulation is shown in Box 9.1.

The next stage is the econometric estimation of the calorie acquisition–income relationship. In general terms, this can be expressed as:

$$C = c\,(X, Z) \qquad (2)$$

where C is a measure of food or calorie acquisition; X is a measure of income or expenditure; and Z is a vector of other household characteristics.

Before estimating this model, one must specify a functional form for this relationship. There are a number of possibilities, and a useful theoretical review is available in Deaton and Muellbauer (1980) and Blundell (1988). A functional form suggested by Deaton (1987b) is:

$$w_i = a_i + b_i \ln(x/n) + c \ln(n) + \sum_j (d_j z_j) + u_i \quad (3)$$

where w_i is the budget share of the ith commodity ($= (p_i\,q_i)/x$); p_i is the price of good i; q_i is the quantity of good i purchased; x is total household expenditure; n is household size; z_j is a vector of other relevant variables; u_i is the error term; and a_i, b_i, c, d_i are parameters to be estimated.

Although there are alternative functional forms, such as the semi-logarithmic ($p_i q_i = a + b \ln(x)$) and log reciprocal ($\ln(p_i q_i) = a - b \, x^{-1}$), use of the specification outlined above is preferable. An important requirement of any system of Engel curves (of which this is an example) is that they satisfy the adding-up property. That is, if they are estimated for all goods, the predicted budget shares will sum to unity. Here, this is satisfied where the following conditions hold (Deaton and Case 1987):

$$\Sigma \, a_i = 1 \text{ and } \Sigma \, b_i = 0 \qquad (4)$$

Finally, it is easy to compute elasticities using:

$$e_i = 1 + (b_i / w_i) \qquad (5)$$

where w_i is evaluated at the sample mean.

The dependent variable, household food expenditure, can be measured in several ways. Ideally, individual consumption of food should be measured to compute calorie and protein intake as this minimizes measurement error and hence estimator bias.[3] The main problem is in measuring this variable. Accurate estimation requires weighing food that is actually eaten, which implies a considerable degree of intrusion by the enumerator, as well as a great deal of time, highly skilled enumerators, and a high degree of cooperation by respondents. Alternatively, measurements can be obtained on a recall basis by interviewing the individual responsible for preparing and distributing food—but this method may greatly increase the time required to complete the interviews.

Alternatively, food consumption can be assessed in terms of food acquisition, including consumption from own production; purchases; payment for labor in food (as opposed to cash); net food transfers to individuals not resident in the household; food consumed away from the household; and free (or subsidized) distribution by the government through food aid projects, programs (for example, school meal programs, food-for-work projects), and gifts. It should be noted that food acquisition is not exactly equivalent to food consumption. Differences between them can be ascribed to changes in foodstocks held in the household; waste in preparation and after eating; the net difference between the amount of food provided to non-household members and the amount provided to members of this household by other households; and changes in food composition arising from preparation and cooking.

To measure food acquisition, a number of factors need to be specified. These include:

• *The time period*. Food acquisition refers to a specified period of time, usually one to two weeks, depending on the design of the survey that underlies the analysis. It is important to note where the visits fall with respect to the agricultural production cycle. Household food acquisition is often related to seasonal considerations. Some commodities are purchased in bulk, infrequently. Households reporting no expenditures may purchase food, but not during the reference period of the questionnaire.

• *The unit of measurement*. Food acquisition can be expressed in either per capita value terms, as a share of the household budget, or in nutritional units. It may be necessary to value commodities that have not passed through the market and do not have a price associated with them. One possibility is the consumer price prevailing in the locality at the time of the transaction. This may be

---

Box 9.1: Cross-tabulation of total food expenditure by expenditure group

The data: The Ghana Living Standards Survey (GLSS 1987/88).

The problem: To see how household expenditure on food changes as other household social and economic variables change. At this stage, the analysis is only descriptive. The aim is to see which variables may be related to food expenditure with a view to including them in more complex analysis later. For example, we may expect that food expenditure may well be related to the total expenditure (or income) of the household, although not necessarily linearly. Households are grouped into five quintiles representing different levels of total expenditure. As expected, the data show that the share of food expenditures decreases among better-off households.

Total expenditures and expenditures on food, by expenditure group, Ghana, 1987/88
(thousands of 1988 cedis per annum)

Expenditure group	Total	Food	Percentage on food
1	175.8	122.7	69.8
2	274.0	189.4	69.1
3	321.6	219.9	68.4
4	387.4	255.6	66.0
5	379.3	234.3	61.8
All	307.6	204.4	66.4

Source: Republic of Ghana 1988.

obtained from a community questionnaire, or possibly by averaging over prices recorded for the same commodities that have passed through the market. However, different households in the same community may face different prices. For example, poorer households, which purchase food in small quantities, may pay a higher unit price than wealthier households purchasing larger amounts. Expressing food acquisition in nutritional terms requires data on the nutrient composition of food items. Both WHO and FAO have published such data for the main commodities consumed in Sub-Saharan Africa. Commodities should be disaggregated as far as possible before calculating calorie and nutrient values. Failure to do so may generate misleading estimates of the impact of changes in independent variables on food acquisition. Behrman (1990) and Behrman and Wolfe (1984b) suggest that nutrient-income elasticities may be overestimated when fixed conversion factors are applied to aggregate food groups.

A recent paper that illustrates many of these problems is Bouis and Haddad (1988). Although their work is based on data from the Philippines, their analysis is applicable to data for African countries. In one version of the model that they estimate, calorie availability is used as the dependent variable. This is calculated by applying calorie conversion factors to foods consumed by households in the previous seven days. To accomplish this, food is disaggregated into 50 categories. The figure is then calculated net of meals given to workers or as gifts. The independent variables used include total expenditure or income, average age of household members, number of adult equivalents, education of head and spouse, and the retail price of maize and rice.

Bouis and Haddad use a number of estimation procedures, including ordinary least squares and two-stage least squares and a quadratic relationship between calorie acquisition and income/expenditure. They find that OLS tends to overestimate the elasticity, particularly when income is used as the regressor. Expenditure performs better as a regressor. They also note that using calorie availability as the dependent variable leads to estimates biased upward. The analyst should be aware of variation in parameters provided by different estimation procedures, as it is likely that this will be the variable available for analysis.

A key independent variable is some measure of income. While it is possible to compute income from most household surveys, this is not recom-

mended here for several reasons. First, income is not exogenous as it reflects decisions regarding the amount of labor supplied by the household. Second, nutrient intake may affect labor produtivity (see Strauss 1986 and Behrman and Deolalikar 1989b). If this is the case, the estimated impact of income will be biased upward. Finally, estimates of income may be liable to under-reporting by respondents and may reflect large short-run volatility.

Given the difficulties associated with the use of household income as a regressor, it is necessary to use a proxy variable. One possibility is total household per capita expenditure. This variable is less likely to have measurement errors, is subject to fewer short-term variations, and can be considered exogenous. However, there are several disadvantages in using it as a regressor. It weakens the link between policy changes, household income, and demand for calories, and does not permit the analyst to examine the effects of control of income on household expenditures. See Chapter 11 for a discussion of this issue.[4]

It has been argued recently (Alderman 1990) that, in the context of the producer-consumer model of household behavior, per capita expenditures are a choice variable. Including this variable as a regressor will lead to biased estimates. This problem can be overcome by using two-stage least squares estimation. Initially, household per capita expenditures are regressed on variables reflecting household demographic composition and assets. The predicted per capita expenditures are then included as regressors in least squares estimation of the function describing the determinants of malnutrition. However, within the existing literature, there is no consensus on this last point. For example, the studies by Behrman and Wolfe (1984b) and Deaton (1987a) use per capita expenditures, whereas Alderman (1990) uses instruments for them through the method described here. The analyst may wish to use both methods to see whether they lead to significantly different results.

Other characteristics to be included in the analysis will depend on local requirements. Among the variables commonly included in studies of this type are:

• *Household structure.* Other things being equal, larger households will tend to consume more food than smaller households. To compare consumption levels and composition between households, one must account for differences in household size. This can be done in a number of ways. A simple method is a "head count" of the number of members of the household. However, this does not take into account variations in household composition. A household with six adults is likely to have different consumption characteristics than one with one adult and five young children. An alternative procedure is to weight individuals in the household using a weighting factor to calculate the number of adult equivalents or the number of consumption units. It may also be useful to include the age and sex of the household head in estimation equations.

- *Education levels.* Education will affect food acquisition by promoting a greater awareness of the importance of good nutrition. Women's education is particularly important in this regard. It also proxies for greater productivity in market and household activities and, for women, increased bargaining power within the household (Behrman and Wolfe 1984b).

Box 9.2: Expenditure elasticities of foods in Ghana

The data: The Ghana Living Standards Survey (GLSS 1987/88).

The problem: To estimate expenditure elasticities of various food commodities in rural and urban Ghana. The elasticities are estimated using a budget share model as outlined in the text (equation 3). The independent variable is the predicted natural logarithm of per capita total household expenditures. Separate models have been estimated for rural and urban areas.

Estimated elasticities of selected food commodities, Ghana, 1987/88

	Elasticities	
Food	Rural areas	Urban areas
Cereals	0.69	0.91
Maize/kenkey	0.60	0.79
Rice	1.27	1.20
Millet/sorghum	0.70	0.50
Wheat flour/pasta	1.35	1.48
Root crops/plantains	0.90	1.09
Cassava/gari/fufu	0.88	1.03
Plantain	0.49	1.10
Meats/dairy	0.97	0.90
Beef	2.62	1.31
Poultry	2.62	1.31
Fish	0.66	0.60
Dairy products	1.86	1.74
All food	0.91	0.94

Source: Alderman 1990.

- *Other variables.* These include household location (urban or rural).

A selection from Alderman's (1990) estimates of expenditure elasticities for Ghana is given in Box 9.2. In addition to the approach used by Bouis and Haddad outlined above, the analyst may find it useful to consult other recent studies, including Behrman and Deolalikar (1987), Edirisinghe (1987), Alderman (1987), Behrman and Wolfe (1984b), and Ward and Sanders (1980).

ESTIMATING PRICE-FOOD EXPENDITURE ELASTICITIES. We have previously highlighted the consequences of changes in household income, proxied by total expenditure, on the demand for food. We now extend the analysis by introducing prices.

The simplest approach is to include a set of prices in the general model of the demand for food, that is:

$$C = c\,(X, P, Z) \qquad (6)$$

where C is a measure of food or calorie acquisition; X is a measure of income or expenditure; P is a vector of prices; and Z is a vector of other household characteristics.

The relationship between food consumption, income, and prices can be expressed in a number of ways. See Deaton and Muellbauer (1980) and Blundell (1988) for a detailed discussion of the properties of these models. Perhaps the simplest functional form is the double logarithmic, that is:[5]

$$\ln(q_i) = a_i + b_i \ln(x/n) + \sum_j \{c_{ij} \ln(p_j)\} + \sum_j \{d_{ij} Z_k\} \quad (7)$$

where q_i is the quantity of food i consumed; x is the value of total household expenditures; p_j is the price of the jth food; Z_k is a set of characteristics of household k; and a_i, b_i, c_{ij}, and d_{ij} are parameters to be estimated. The own-price elasticity of demand for food i is the parameter c_{ii}. Cross-price elasticities are c_{ij}.

The measurement of x and Z_k has already been discussed. Price information is not usually collected as part of the household surveys but is available from other sources. The dependent variable q_i can be obtained by dividing household expenditures by the cluster-level prices.

While this approach is straightforward computationally, there are two drawbacks to its use. The first arises from the method used to obtain quantities. Deaton (1988) has shown that when quantities are obtained by dividing expenditures by cluster prices, the resulting price elasticities will be biased. There are two reasons for this, illustrated by Deaton's discussion on estimating the price elasticity of "meat." First, meat is not a homogeneous good, but rather a set of goods. Each of these will have different income elasticities. For example, prime cuts of beef are likely to have a higher income elasticity than does mutton. Consequently, the price paid for a unit of meat will reflect household characteristics such as income. Regressing the quantity of meat on its price is essentially a regression of one choice variable on another. This leads to problems of simultaneity bias. Second, changes in prices will affect not only the quantities purchased but also their quality. A rise in the price of beef may cause households to substitute cheaper sources of calories and protein, leaving the acquisition of calories and protein relatively unchanged. Consequently, the price elasticity will be exaggerated. Deaton goes on to develop an alternative approach that corrects for these difficulties. (The analyst is referred to Deaton 1988 for a detailed discussion of the estimation procedure.)

The second drawback arises where households are both producers and consumers of food. The price variable appears twice: as an argument itself, and indirectly through the profit effect. Consequently, it is necessary to add a term reflecting this indirect effect to the general model of the demand for food noted above:

$$C = c\,(X, P, Z, Y^*) \qquad (8)$$

where Y^* is household full income.

Household full income reflects two components: net farm profits and the total value of household time. Time can be valued at the prevailing wage in the cluster or by estimating wage equations using data on individual characteristics. Chapter 5 contains a discussion of this point.[6]

The next step is to specify a functional form. A relatively straightforward possibility is the linear expenditure system (LES). This has the advantage of using expenditures as the dependent variable. Consequently, it avoids the difficulties associated with dividing expenditures by cluster prices. For example, if the demand parameters for two foods are to be estimated, the LES would be:

food 1

$$p_1 q_1 = p_1\,(a_1 + t_1) + w_1\,[Y^* - p_1\,(a_3 + t_1) - p_2\,(a_4 + t_2)]$$

and food 2

$$p_2 q_2 = p_1\,(a_2 + t_2) + w_2\,[Y^* - p_1\,(a_5 + t_1) - p_2\,(a_6 + t_2)] \qquad (9)$$

where t_1, t_2 are taken as linear functions of household demographic characteristics; and $a_1 - a_6$ are parameters to be estimated.

The LES equations are estimated using least squares regression. If there are many zero entries for a dependent variable, indicating non-purchase of an item, then least squares will produce biased parameter estimates. This difficulty can be overcome using a Tobit estimation procedure. Strauss (1984) provides an example of this.

The price elasticity of the demand for food 1 is calculated by differentiating the LES with respect to the price of food 1. As the exact functional form is partly dependent on the manner in which farm profits are calculated, the general form is presented here:

$$(dq_1/dp_1) = (dq_1/dp_1) + (dq_1/dY^*)(dY^*/dp_1) \qquad (10)$$

The first term on the right-hand side captures the ordinary effect of prices on demand and will be negative. The second term captures the profit effect. This illustrates a key feature of the household producer-consumer model. For households that are producers of food, estimates of price elasticities of demand that omit the profit effect will be overstated. Indeed, inclusion of the profit effect may cause demand-price elasticities to be positive. Illustration of this is provided in Box 9.3.

In this discussion, the dependent variable has been the level of expenditures on food items. It is possible to express these in nutritional terms. This is useful where the policy question relates to the acquisition of calories rather than expenditures on food.

THE IDENTIFICATION OF FOOD-INSECURE HOUSEHOLDS. A basic aim of the analysis of food security and nutrition is to identify who the food-insecure are, what the prevalence of malnutrition is, and where it occurs. This is a key step in translating the results of the analysis into action, both for the review and development of policy and for the development of more refined data collection systems.

Food security is closely related to poverty. Not only are the poor likely to be chronically food-insecure, they are also at much greater risk of transitory low levels of food consumption. The starting point for the analysis of food security, therefore, will be the analysis of poverty as outlined in the poverty profile in Chapter 4. Although comparisons with the non-poor are important, much of the rest of the analysis in this section is concerned with the food consumption characteristics of households below the poverty line and with the variables associated with the symptoms of food insecurity.

An important first step is to examine household expenditure patterns and to classify households by the budget share devoted to food commodities. As a rough rule of thumb, households spending more than 70 percent of their expenditures on food (including the estimated value of own production consumed by the household) can be expected to be food-insecure. More detailed analysis can be carried out by looking at the food commodities households consume. Bennett's law states that the proportion of calories derived from starchy

staples declines with increasing incomes. Food-insecure households are likely to spend a greater proportion of their income on basic staples than those with higher incomes.

The estimation of income elasticities for food commodities also helps identify the food-insecure. It is expected that food-insecure households will have a high propensity to spend extra income on food. They are also likely to consume those commodities that are not preferred by the better-off. It is important to identify which foods are inferior goods and at what level of income. Commodities largely consumed by the poor that are important in providing calories—and on which expenditure declines as income increases—could be used to provide targeted food subsidies (Timmer, Falcon, and Pearson 1983).

An important next step is to consider sources of food, particularly for the poor and those households identified as potentially food-insecure. A key distinction is between those households (mostly rural) who provide most of their basic food from own production and possibly even sell surpluses—the net producers—and those who purchase most of their food from the market—the net purchasers. It is important for policy purposes to know whether most of the food-insecure are producers or purchasers as there are direct implications for pricing policy. In many countries, the assumption is that urban households are net purchasers and rural households are net producers. Analysis of the evidence from a number of African countries, however, suggests that many of the rural poor are generally dependent on the market for their food supplies (Pinstrup-Andersen 1989) and that price rises for basic staples may well be working to the disadvantage of the food-insecure, at least in the short term.

Relative prices will be much more important for the poor than for the better-off. The fact that consumers are poor and that their food security is threatened means that they have to be responsive to changes in incomes and relative prices. Indeed, Timmer, Falcon, and Pearson (1983) suggest that if there is no evidence of high own- and cross-price elasticities for basic staples among the poor, then there may be a relatively low incidence of food insecurity. It will be important here, however, to distinguish between net producers and net food consumers.

The next step is to compare the food security classification with certain identifiable household characteristics through cross-tabulations. Relevant household characteristics include:

- Level of household income
- Structure of income and the degree of diversification
- Household demographic structure (ages and number of males and females)
- Sex of household head
- Asset holdings, for example, total assets or the holdings of consumer durables
- Geographical location.

The aim is to identify characteristics that are correlated with food insecurity and that can be used for targeting interventions. For example, "concentration" diagrams can be constructed that allow policymakers to focus on areas that might be examined more closely or made the target of area-based interventions. Other factors for targeting could include households with a specific demographic structure, for example, female-headed households.

IMPLICATIONS FOR POLICY. An important application of this analysis is in the design of programs that enhance or preserve household food security during adjustment.[7] These include:
- Indirect income transfers in the form of general or commodity-specific food subsidies
- Use of public employment schemes
- Use of direct income transfers (in the form of food aid, cash, or food stamps or ration cards entitling the holder to free or subsidized food) to targeted groups.

A useful classification of food and nutrition interventions is provided by Timmer, Falcon, and Pearson (1983), who distinguish between targeted and non-targeted and between nutrition and food interventions. Nutrition interventions are considered to be those that affect the nutritional status of the target group without involving an overall increase in food intake. Food interventions include the possibility of increasing food intake among the food-insecure.

The estimates of income and price elasticities for the target groups can be used to determine the effects of different interventions. In addition, it may be possible to identify commodities suitable for price subsidization because they are self-targeting in the sense that are mostly consumed by the poor and food-insecure.

To be effective, these interventions require criteria for identifying target households that are amenable to administrative selection processes. One advantage of the analysis outlined here is that it establishes links between risks of food insecurity and easily identifiable household characteristics that can be used as selection criteria. For example, dwelling structure can be used as a wealth proxy and can be related to levels of food insecurity.

The identification of correlations between household characteristics and food insecurity has one further important practical use: to monitor changes in household food security as adjustment programs are implemented. It is likely to be too costly to make repeated observations of household food consumption. The best chance of establishing a feasible monitoring strategy is to focus on changes in the economic environment in which vulnerable households operate—notably their access to different markets, and the prices they face. Perhaps the most crucial monitoring indicator is some expression of household terms of trade with respect to food, such as an index of food prices compared with wage rates or product prices.[8] This can be constructed by comparing the cost of a basket of food commodities and the value of household income. The key variables to be observed are producer prices, wage rates, and consumer food prices.

This approach is especially valuable if it can be repeated at regular intervals, allowing changes in household terms of trade to be monitored. Concerning producer prices, it is important to observe both annual and seasonal variations in all the major producing-area markets and for all main crops. It is also necessary to observe prices offered by different marketing agents together with credit arrangements that may affect the prices offered. Any delay in payment after purchase should be used to discount the price offered. Finally, nominal producer price movements should take into account prices of inputs (material inputs and labor primarily) and changes in exchange rates. From this it should be possible to calculate indices representing producer terms of trade. This will provide an important indicator of the sum of different effects on producers.

With respect to wage rates, some choice will need to be made about the most important wages to monitor. Those most accessible and most significant include minimum wage rates, agricultural wages, and unskilled urban wage rates. Wages and producer prices should be compared with cost of living indices. It is unlikely that fully calculated cost of living indices will be able to keep pace with continuous devaluations and changes in the prices of consumer goods, much less be available regularly for the consumption basket of various groups of households whose consumption patterns are significantly different. Nevertheless, producer prices and wage rates need to be compared with consumer prices in order to express them in real terms. An alternative is to make comparisons with food prices (and possibly additional important non-food items) weighted according to the composition of consumption by low-income rural and urban groups. Where food purchases account for the largest share of total expenditures, an index of "food terms of trade" may be an acceptable approximation. If costs of accommodation and transport (in urban areas) and a few important manufactured items are added, a fair indication of trends in the purchasing power of poor families may be obtained.

Analysis at the individual level

Food security at the household level (as measured by a satisfactory balance between acquisition and needs) does not guarantee reliable and adequate individual access to food. This section outlines how food security can be analyzed at the individual level.

Assessing the nature and extent of malnutrition

The most satisfactory measure of individual food security is individual food intake, but this information is not obtained in household surveys. Instead, anthropometric measures of children aged between 3 and 60 months have been recommended as proxies. Studies conducted in different parts of the world indicate that well-nourished children tend to grow at the same rate everywhere. Certainly, it has been shown that well-nourished children in Africa grow at about the same rate as their counterparts in developed countries.[9] Children who exhibit poor growth, measured by either height or weight, are likely to be malnourished. The incidence of malnutrition can be shown by comparing the growth of children in the study with a reference population of children known to be well nourished.

Household surveys often collect data on the age, sex, weight in kilograms, and height (or length for children below 24 months) in centimeters for all children (say, between 3 and 60 months). These data can be used to construct anthropometric measures, including:

• Height (or length) for age, comparing the heights of children with the median height of children of the same age from the reference population

• Weight for height (or length), comparing the weight of the child with the median weight of a child from the reference population with the same height

• Weight for age, calculating the weight of a child as a percentage of the median of the weights of children of the same age from the reference population.

Tables of weights, heights, and lengths for boys and girls of stated ages in a reference population and of weights for stated heights and lengths have been published by WHO (1983). The most widely used reference population is that observed by the National Child Center for Health Statistics (NCHS), referred to as the NCHS standard.

Height for age is considered to be a measure of nutritional history. A child who is short for his or her age is considered to be *stunted*. Mindful of the caveats outlined later, height for age can be considered a proxy for long-term food security. If a child is thin given his or her height, he or she is considered to be *wasted*. Weight for height is a measure of wasting and is thought to reflect the current nutritional status. Height for age and weight for height, therefore, measure different aspects of nutritional status and can be considered to be more or less independent. Weight for age is a composite measure that incorporates aspects of both stunting and wasting. Analysis of household data will benefit the most from using height for age and weight for height indices. Box 9.4 illustrates how to estimate measures of nutritional status.

In addition to the tables of reference data referred to above, algorithms have been developed describing the slopes of normal growth curves. These have been written into software packages for the calculation of anthropometric indices, as percentiles, percentage of median values, and standard deviation scores (see Box 9.4).

Children's anthropometric status is a function of many variables. The quality and quantity of food consumed in relation to needs for growth, activity, and body maintenance is certainly one determinant of body size and mass. However, growth faltering is also a consequence of impaired health. For example, childeren suffering from diarrhea will obtain fewer nutrients and calories from a given quantity of food than healthy children. The health environment—for example, access to clean water and health facilities—will also affect children's growth. Genetic endowments have also been shown to be an important determinant of nutritional status (see Kennedy and Cogill 1987 for evidence from Kenya, and Sahn 1990 for Côte d'Ivoire).

Children's anthropometric status also reflects the manner in which households manage childcare. There are two components to this measure. First, it reflects the ability of households to provide care. For example, Thomas, Strauss, and Hendriques (1988), Strauss (1990), and Barrera (1990) have indicated that anthropometric status improves as mothers' education increases, reflecting better knowledge regarding childcare practices. Other aspects of care that have been shown to affect anthropometric status include weaning age and duration of breastfeeding. Second, time constraints may impinge on the ability of mothers to provide care. For example, in rural areas, these may be particularly acute during periods of peak agricultural activities. To some extent, this may be made up for by care provided by older siblings (Sahn 1990).

Finally, anthropometric status will also reflect parental preferences. Again, there are two issues to consider. It may be that parents seek to equalize the anthropometric measures of their children. Alternatively, they may value additional improvements equally, independent of their distribution among their offspring. Behrman (1988b) provides a useful methodology for examining this issue. Related to this is the issue of sex bias. It has been argued, for example by Sen (1984) and Sen and Sengupta (1983), that in some regions of South Asia, boys are favored over girls in the allocation of nutrients. However, studies in Africa (Svedberg 1988; Strauss 1990) have failed to find similar biases. Preferences may differ between adult members of the household. In particular, it has been argued that mothers place greater weight on children's welfare. Behrman and Wolfe (1984b) and Horton and Miller (1987) present evidence consistent with this view.

The foregoing indicates that anthropometric status is a function not only of food intake, but also of health, genetic background, childcare, and parental preferences. Accordingly, assuming that poor nutrition is a result solely of inadequate food security is incorrect. The analyst must be mindful of this when analyzing individual food security issues using household-level data.

Analyzing the determinants of malnutrition

The simplest level of analysis of these data involves tabular analysis of individual, household, and community characteristics and anthropometric measures. These characteristics are described here. Analysis should include means, standard deviations, minima, and maxima. This can be followed by cross-tabulations of measures of anthropometric status with variables of interest, such as age, gender, household wealth, and location. Such tabulations are particularly well suited for presenting information to decision-makers who are not well versed in the analysis of nutritional data. They are also useful in suggesting whether health interventions, rather than food policy changes, will have a greater impact on anthropometric status. Another common use for seeking associations between nutritional indices and household characteristics is to establish selection criteria for targeted interventions. When developing and presenting these results, however, the analyst should be mindful of the caveats noted earlier.

Consider the cross-tabulation of the percentages of children stunted against mother's education and income derived from a survey in Côte d'Ivoire and reported in Table 9.1. The percentage of children stunted in rural areas of Côte d'Ivoire is cross-tabulated against household per capita expenditure and mother's education. There is no clear linear relationship between the prevalence of malnutrition among children and expenditure, but this may be due to the effects of other factors not included here. Note that for all expenditure groups, the prevalence of malnutrition is less in households where mothers have some education and that this effect appears to be greatest in the two lowest expenditure quintiles.

A second type of analysis uses econometric techniques. An important advantage of this approach is that it allows the analyst to control for the omitted variable problem associated with cross-tabulations. Here, it is useful to express the dependent variable in actual terms, rather than in relation to cutoff points described in Box 9.4. The independent variables are derived from a model in which households maximize a utility function subject to cash, time, and technology constraints described earlier (Singh, Squire, and Strauss 1986a). There are five types of independent variables (Strauss 1988): individual attributes, such as age and gender; parental characteristics, including education, age, and height; household characteristics that appear in the farm production function (such as land and capital); variables reflecting community attributes, such as drinking water supply and health facilities; and the prices of consumption goods, including food, nonfood items, and leisure.

Table 9.1: Percentage of children stunted, by expenditure group and mother's education, Côte d'Ivoire, 1985

Per capita expenditure quintile	Mother's education	
	None	Some elementary
1	24.1	10.7
2	20.7	10.9
3	17.6	8.3
4	19.4	16.8
5	23.3	15.1
All	21.1	12.9

Source: Sahn 1990, Table 5.

If the prices used by the analyst were collected on a cluster basis, there would be no price variation within the cluster. Using prices under these circumstances will tend to bias downward estimated standard errors. This can be overcome by using an estimation procedure known as fixed effects. References for this are Hausman and Taylor (1981), Hsiao (1986), and Chapter 8 in this volume. While this approach is necessary to generate unbiased standard errors, it does not permit direct measurement of the effect of price changes on nutritional status.

A second issue concerns the inclusion of some measure of individual nutrient intake. This would appear desirable given that the emphasis here is on the linkage between acquisition of food and nutritional status. But these data are difficult to collect. In the context of the producer-consumer model of household behavior, household expenditures on food are a choice variable. As such, including this variable as a regressor will lead to biased estimates. This problem can be overcome through the use of an instrumental variables technique. For example, household expenditures on food are regressed on variables reflecting household demographic composition, assets, and location.

These considerations indicate that the following two-stage strategy is appropriate. In the first stage, per capita food expenditures are regressed on the variables noted in the previous paragraph, using a fixed-effects estimation procedure. It may be advantageous to transform the dependent variable into natural logarithms as this will reduce heteroskedasticity. The independent variables will include:

• *Household demographic composition.* This includes the number of males and females by age-group.

• *Household assets.* This includes wealth held in the form of human capital—specifically, levels of educational attainment of adult males and females; and non-human wealth, including the size of landholdings, the value of household capital in the form of liquid assets and machinery, and the value of consumer durables.

• *Household location.* At the least, this will include urban or rural locales. In countries with differing agro-climatic zones, it may be useful to take this into account through the inclusion of appropriate regional dummy variables.

Multiplying the estimated coefficients by the value of these variables for each household

Box 9.5: Estimating the determinants of anthropometric status in Ghana

The method: This example is taken from a paper by Alderman (1990), based on the Ghana Living Standards Survey (GLSS). The approach taken by Alderman is comparable to that described in the text. Initially, he estimates the determinants of the log of per capita expenditures and also of illness. The former is a function of the following variables:

- Number of males and females by age-group
- Number of males and females by level of education
- Value of livestock
- Value of vehicles
- Value of other capital
- Area of land owned in different ecological zones
- Cocoa area
- Age of household head.

Various dummy variables were used to indicate where the household lived and whether the head of the household was female.

The predicted per capita expenditures are included in the least squares regressions taking children's height for age and weight for height as dependent variables. Other independent variables in the estimation equation are:

- Age of the child in months
- Age of the child squared
- Household size
- Number of older siblings
- Number of younger siblings
- Dummy variables for location
- Dummy variables to indicate the education level of the mother
- Interaction terms between age and location
- Sex of the child.

The results: Alderman obtains the following results. Height for age falls with the age of the child, indicating that chronic malnutrition is cumulative. Mother's height has a strong and positive influence on gender height for age. However, the coefficient for mother's education is not significant. No gender bias is found, nor is the dummy variable for urban locations significant. Children with younger siblings are significantly shorter than those without. Higher per capita expenditures significantly improve height for age.

Similar results are found when weight for height is used as the dependent variable, though the variable for per capita expenditures is not significant. This regression does not perform as satisfactorily as height for age. This is not entirely surprising, given that weight for height is a short-term variable, and hence liable to greater random fluctuations.

---

independent variables is assumed, then the equation to be estimated using ordinary least squares becomes:

$$N_{if} = a_0 + a_1 X_{if} + a_2 PXHT + a_3 X_{pf} + e_{if} \quad (11)$$

where N_{if} is the nutritional status of the ith child in family f; X_{if} is a vector of characteristics of child i in family f; $PXHT$ is the predicted per capita expenditure on food; X_{pf} is a vector of parental characteristics of family f; e_{if} is an error term; and a_0, a_1, a_2, and a_3 are parameters to be estimated.

Before discussing the regressors to be used, it is worth noting that several important variables are not available from the household surveys. These include mother's height, weaning ages, and past breastfeeding practices. Independent variables that are available and should be included are:

- *Individual characteristics.* These include age, sex, birth order, and immunization record.
- *Parental characteristics.* These include education of father and mother and mother's age at birth of child.

Box 9.5 outlines an example of this type of analysis. The analyst may find it useful to consult other examples, including Knudsen and Scandizzo (1982), Kennedy and Cogill (1987), Sahn (1990), Barrera (1990), Strauss (1988), Pitt, Rosenzweig, and Hassan (1990), Thomas, Strauss, and Hendriques (1988), and Horton (1988).

Thus far, the role of community attributes such as health facilities has been excluded (but see Chapter 8). Direct inclusion of community variables, such as access to drinking water and health services, will lead to biased standard errors because they are common to all households within the cluster. This can be overcome through the use of fixed-effects estimation, but this causes these variables to drop out of the estimated equation. One way of getting around this, as suggested by Strauss (1988), is to use interaction terms such as distance to doctors by mother's education. Since these vary by household, the problem with bias disappears.

Conclusion

The analysis presented in this chapter is designed to identify the factors that affect food security at the household and individual levels, to quantify these relationships, and to identify those at risk from food insecurity. Structural adjustment programs affect the prices, the incomes, and the

---

generates predicted per capita expenditure on food. This is then included in the estimation of the relationship between anthropometric status and individual and parental attributes. If a linear relationship between anthropometric status and the

institutional framework within which households operate. Consequently, the analysis of food security is necessary for the assessment of the impact of past policy reforms, for predicting the impact of future policy changes, for monitoring the well-being of vulnerable households during structural adjustment, and for assessing the costs and benefits of policy revisions, including those designed to ameliorate the impact of adjustment. As noted, it is necessary to specify the level of analysis and the time frame when undertaking such an analysis.

Household survey data are not especially suited for examining national-level food security issues. However, they offer a wealth of analytical possibilities at the household and individual levels. In particular, it is possible to estimate the impact of changes in incomes and prices on the acquisition of food. Comparing this against a normative measurement of requirements indicates how a household's food security is affected by policy reform. These results can also be used to inform decisions regarding the monitoring of groups vulnerable to food insecurity and regarding policies designed to ameliorate the transitional effects of adjustment.

Notes

1. Devereux and Hay (1987) refer to these claims as "latent income."

2. However, few smallholder producers have access to formal credit markets (Collier and Lal 1986), and it is unclear what happens in informal credit markets when interest rates are raised or a credit squeeze is imposed on formal sector markets.

3. See Bouis and Haddad (1988) for a detailed discussion of this point.

4. Studies that indicate that the distribution of income within the household affects the pattern of demand for food and other goods include von Braun, Hotchkiss, and Immink (1989) on Guatemala, Horton and Miller (1987) on Jamaica, von Braun (1988) on the Gambia, and Kumar (1979) on India.

5. It should be noted that this functional form is not appropriate when the estimation of the demand for all goods is being attempted as it violates the condition that the b_i's sum to zero. See Deaton and Muellbauer (1980) for a discussion.

6. Note that if production and consumption decisions are not separable, it is necessary to include the prices of food, nonfood items, wages, and crop input prices in the estimation of the demand equation. The analysis plan on health (Chapter 8) provides a further discussion of this.

7. These temporary expedients should not be unduly costly nor should they become permanent welfare transfers at the expense of vigorous income and employment policies.

8. This is also discussed in Chapters 5 and 12.

9. Because the standard deviation for the reference population increases with age, this measure, which is not age-dependent, is more accurate than the cutoffs of 80 percent for weight for height and 90 percent for height for age.

10

Effects of structural adjustment on fertility

Mark Montgomery

The fundamental changes in the economic circumstances of households during structural adjustment inevitably lead to demographic responses. Some of these are beyond the control of the household (such as increased mortality resulting from reduced incomes and reduced availability of health care services), and some are part of the household's coping mechanisms (for example, changing decisions about family size and location). These *endogenous* responses on the part of the household to *exogenous* economic circumstances are part of a range of responses to structural adjustment. One should view fertility, investments in children's health and education, and the migration of adult household members as distinct dimensions along which the household responds as its economic environment changes. This perspective implies a common conceptual framework, as indicated in Figure 10.1, in which the various response variables are seen as being jointly determined by exogenous prices, infrastructure, and household assets. Rosenzweig (1982), Levy (1985), Wolfe and Behrman (1986), and Rosenzweig and Schultz (1987) have pursued such a joint approach in a series of illuminating empirical analyses.

This chapter focuses on one important component of these endogenous responses—fertility. At issue is whether the new economic incentives that accompany adjustment, and that influence human capital investments in the health and schooling of children, also influence family size. Among the questions to be considered are the following.

Do economic contractions, felt with particular severity in African cities, encourage postponement of childbearing and lower lifetime fertility? Could structural adjustment produce a pro-natalist response in rural areas and an anti-natalist response in urban areas? How might public investments in health care, education, and family planning influence fertility? The methodology proposed in this chapter will enable us to explore these and related questions.

The African context

Fertility levels are among the principal determinants of rates of labor force growth, the age structure of the labor force, and the growth and structure of national populations. As is well known, fertility rates in Sub-Saharan Africa are exceedingly high; recent figures (van de Walle and Foster 1990) suggest a range of 5.0 to 8.25 births per woman. There are indications of recent fertility declines in Zimbabwe, Botswana, and Kenya, but elsewhere the level of fertility has remained virtually unchanged for decades. Indeed, the evidence suggests an increase in fertility in some African countries in the 1970s, in marked contrast to the fertility declines in most of the developing world.

African fertility levels yield rates of labor force growth in the neighborhood of 2.1 percent per year, rates of overall population growth as high as 3.4 percent (for Kenya), and population age structures in which, typically, nearly one of every two persons is under age 15 (World Bank 1981). For

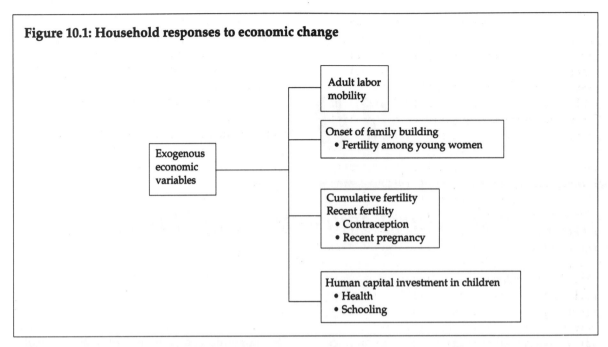

Figure 10.1: Household responses to economic change

Exogenous economic variables

Adult labor mobility

Onset of family building
- Fertility among young women

Cumulative fertility
Recent fertility
- Contraception
- Recent pregnancy

Human capital investment in children
- Health
- Schooling

Nigeria, a country of some 107 million people in 1987, a history of high fertility will all but guarantee a doubling of total population in the next 25 years. At such extremes, fertility levels must have a profound influence on the character of economic development in Sub-Saharan Africa.

Three features of current African fertility patterns are of interest. First, except in Zimbabwe, Botswana, and perhaps Kenya, current use of modern contraceptive methods remains low. Second, fertility is restrained from reaching even higher levels by traditional birth-spacing practices that include long periods of breastfeeding and post-partum sexual abstinence (Bongaarts, Frank, and Lesthaeghe 1990). Third, use of contraception is widely regarded as an acceptable means of spacing births and containing extra-marital fertility (Oni and McCarthy 1988). Thus, even though current levels of contraceptive use are low, evidence suggests a latent demand for family planning services to improve birth spacing and infant and maternal health.

Less well understood is the potential for family planning service delivery to encourage fertility decline in Sub-Saharan Africa. A key issue here is the extent of unwanted fertility. If levels of unwanted fertility are high, as some contend, public investments in family planning may yield significant fertility reductions even if wanted family sizes remain constant. This issue is sometimes discussed in terms of a "KAP-gap."[1] The KAP-gap has to do with the proportions of women who say

they want no more children and yet, perhaps because of the limitations of fledgling African family planning programs, do not avail themselves of modern contraception. Westoff (1990) has argued that the KAP-gap is relatively small in Africa, leaving little scope for program intervention so long as levels of desired family size resist change.

Economic determinants of fertility

Although there may be disagreement about the levels of unwanted fertility, it is clear that levels of *wanted* fertility are high in Sub-Saharan Africa (McCarthy and Oni 1987). Much of the rationale for high fertility can be traced to fundamental economic factors. Some aspects of culture and religion are also important to maintaining high fertility. Caldwell and Caldwell (1987) make a strong case for the uniqueness of the African high-fertility regime, giving emphasis to the role of lineage, fears of barrenness or sterility, and the risks courted by a low-fertility family in what remains a high-mortality environment. Yet as van de Walle and Foster (1990) note, similar features characterized a number of traditional Asian societies that nevertheless went on to experience rapid fertility declines. This raises the question of how economic rewards and constraints associated with childbearing lend support to high fertility (World Bank 1984; Birdsall 1988) and how such economic factors may be influenced by structural adjustment.

In traditional societies, children make significant contributions to the household labor force, and may give value both in agriculture and in urban enterprises (Mueller 1976). A family's access to land may be secured by a large household labor force (Frank and McNicoll 1987). Furthermore, adult offspring provide their parents with an assurance of care in old age, and may function as "embodied savings" in an economic milieu that circumscribes possibilities for savings through formal capital or asset markets (Hammer 1986). A large family with several adult children may tap a network of relatives for support in times of hardship or when special needs arise, thereby blending the savings and insurance motivations for childbearing (Cain 1983).

In short, the existence and penetration of formal markets, prices, and the availability of infrastructure all figure into household fertility decisions. How does the traditional high-fertility regime give way under new economic and social pressures?

The quantity-quality tradeoff

A central theme in this chapter is the link between fertility and human capital investment in children, as captured in the concept of a "quantity-quality" tradeoff. As societies develop, they tend to undergo transition from relatively large family sizes (high "quantity") with low levels of human capital investment per child (low "quality") to smaller families characterized by higher levels of investment per child (Birdsall 1988). This demographic transition, by reducing rates of labor force growth and increasing the human capital with which the labor force is equipped, provides a base for continued economic development.

In formerly traditional societies that have experienced modernization and significant fertility decline (for Thailand, see Knodel, Chamratrithirong, and Debavalya 1987; Knodel, Havanon, and Sittitra 1990), it seems that a key element in the transition has been the growing appreciation among parents of the value of a child's education. As employment opportunities open up that offer significant economic returns to schooling, parents may come to regard schooling as the key to a better life for their children, and as a human capital investment that may eventually provide benefits to the parents themselves. Yet education is costly in terms of both direct costs and opportunity costs of forgone child labor; it generally remains too costly for parents to give each child schooling *and* continue

to bear the number of children that is appropriate in traditional settings. Some aspect of household expenditures must give way, and, typically, fertility falls as household investments in education per child increase.

Note that the quantity-quality tradeoff is of potential significance at both the micro and meso levels. At the micro or household level, fertility decline frees private resources that can be invested in children's human capital (King 1987). At the meso level of markets, infrastructure, and policy, a decrease in the size and growth of the school-age population frees public resources that can be redeployed in improving the quality of schooling (Schultz 1987).

Effects of policy interventions

Public policy has the potential to influence fertility levels in two ways: directly, by providing family planning and health programs; and indirectly, by providing opportunities for parents to invest in the human capital of their children. By removing constraints to investment in child quality, public policy can indirectly encourage decreases in quantity, that is, in levels of fertility. At the same time, induced changes in the structure of economic incentives can lead to changes in employment opportunities for children and for women of childbearing ages. These in turn may influence fertility decisions.

As regards structural adjustment and fertility, four questions merit investigation in the context of this volume:

• What is the relationship between household income per adult and levels of household fertility?

• What is the relationship between adult educational levels and levels of household fertility?

• Do investments in educational, health, and family planning infrastructure and services affect fertility levels? How do the prices associated with such services influence fertility decisions?

• At what ages does fertility appear most responsive to economic variables? In particular, what policy-related variables seem to influence fertility among young women?

Income and fertility

The first question asks whether the number of children can be regarded as being a "normal good," in the sense of being related positively to the level of household income. The strength of income effects is of interest in Africa, because it bears on the extent to which income contractions accompanying structural adjustment may be expressed in postponed or lower lifetime fertility.

Lesthaeghe (1989) has speculated that the economic reversals of the 1980s in Sub-Saharan Africa may induce a "crisis-led" demographic transition. Urban families in particular have experienced dramatic increases in the prices of imports and foods, and often in fees for health care and schooling. The pressure on family budgets may have been severe enough to render acceptable, for the first time, the notion of family limitation. Once the innovative concept of family limitation becomes widely acceptable, so the argument goes, it undermines the traditional rationale for high fertility, so that fertility decline may well continue even as economic conditions begin to improve. Thus, an economic crisis provides the thin edge of the wedge that eventually topples the high-fertility regime. The crux of Lesthaeghe's argument is a transformation in the relationship between fertility and income, such that fertility, a normal good in traditional settings, becomes inferior in respect to income in the course of transition. We return to this issue in connection with the tradeoff between child quantity and quality.

Income effects produced by changes in prices may differ in important ways across economic sectors. Consider an increase in the real price of foodstuffs. For urban consumers, who prior to adjustment might have enjoyed a degree of subsidy, a food price increase may be felt first as a contraction of the household budget. Urban households may react by postponing fertility; existing resources may be stretched simply to cover the needs of children already born. But for rural food producers, the price change may signal an increase in the value of the marginal product of child farm labor. The net impact could well be pronatalist in the rural sector, and anti-natalist in the urban (as may have occurred in China following the agricultural reforms of the late 1970s and early 1980s).

Adult education and fertility

A number of studies (Cochrane 1979; Ainsworth 1989; Schultz 1989) have suggested that while income effects on fertility may be positive, the effects of female education are strongly negative. Thus, as economic development proceeds, a tension emerges between income and education

effects. Increases with development in income per adult may have a pro-natalist influence, while increases in female schooling tend to exert an anti-natalist influence. Precisely why female education has an anti-natalist effect in Africa is unclear. The conventional interpretation runs as follows. Better-educated women receive higher wages or earnings. If child-rearing and employment represent competing claims on a woman's time, then the opportunity cost of child-rearing is measured by the woman's wage. With other things equal, better-educated women should tend to have fewer children.

It is doubtful that this conventional explanation applies to the situation in Sub-Saharan Africa. Empirical investigations of time use tend to show little direct conflict between working and child-rearing in African settings. Indeed, young children often accompany their mothers to work, and other family members can supply childcare at negligible cost. The relationship between mother's schooling and fertility must depend on other factors, not yet well understood. One possibility is that better-educated mothers have higher aspirations for the education of their children, and therefore tend to have fewer children. The investigations of Ainsworth (1989) and Schultz (1989) show that, in the absence of gains in female educational attainment, increases in household incomes alone would be expected to increase fertility.

In the view of some authors (Cochrane 1979; Bongaarts, Frank, and Lesthaeghe 1990), the effect of female education on fertility is non-linear. Simple tabulations show that African women with one to three years of primary schooling tend to have more children, on average, than do women without schooling. If the anti-natalist effect comes into play only at the late primary or secondary level of schooling, countries wishing to reduce fertility rates might consider placing a greater share of educational resources into these schooling levels. Thus, it is important to assess any non-linearities in the schooling-fertility relationship for the analysis of the income redistributive effects of structural adjustment.

Child schooling, health, and family planning

In Sub-Saharan Africa, family planning programs remain in their early stages in most countries (Cochrane, Sai, and Nassim 1990). However, vigorous efforts have been mounted in Kenya, Zimbabwe, and Botswana. In the 1980s, these countries exhibited marked increases in contraceptive use, accompanied by modest declines in fertility (see van de Walle and Foster 1990). A number of Sub-Saharan countries are characterized by active private sector involvement in family planning, often occurring well in advance of concerted public sector efforts. Even in countries with little or no public involvement, then, it may be possible to assess the effects of family planning activities on fertility.

The indirect effects of public investments in schooling on fertility are also of considerable interest. There are indications that changes in school costs, coupled with a high demand for education, may be responsible in part for the ongoing fertility decline in Kenya. A body of micro-level research outside Africa has indicated the potential for public investments in education to generate spillover benefits in terms of fertility reduction; Birdsall (1980), King (1987), Levy (1985), Duraisamy and Malathy (1990), Rosenzweig (1982 and 1988), and Rosenzweig and Schultz (1987) provide examples of this kind of analysis. Health programs may also induce a tradeoff between fertility and child schooling, by lowering child mortality and thereby raising the returns to early child investments. These relationships, while potentially of great significance, remain poorly understood and have not been investigated in empirical depth for any African country.

Several important policy questions need to be explored. How much movement along the fertility-schooling tradeoff can be expected from increases in public educational investments alone? How much movement can be expected from investments in health and family planning programs alone? Are investments in education and health/family planning complementary in respect to their influence on fertility decline?

Fertility at young ages

The demographic implications of reductions in fertility at young ages have often gone unappreciated by policymakers. Such delays can exert a powerful influence on population rates of growth even if fertility over the lifetime is unaffected. The reason is that the timing of fertility within the reproductive lifecycle affects population growth rates net of the level of fertility. The level of fertility determines the size of one generation relative to the previous generation; the timing of fertility determines the speed with which one

generation succeeds the previous one. Timing effects can be surprisingly powerful, as Bongaarts and Greenhalgh (1985) demonstrate for the case of China.

More important perhaps are the links between fertility at young ages, and the health and economic status of women. Early marriage and birth are among the most important risk factors implicated in studies of maternal mortality in Africa (Maine and others 1990). A woman's autonomy and decisionmaking authority within the household may be enhanced if she is relatively mature upon marriage; this in turn may affect the level and nature of health resources devoted to children and, consequently, their survival. Furthermore, economic factors that delay marriage—in particular, female schooling and employment conditions for women—may continue to exert downward pressure on lifetime marital fertility levels. If economic factors influence rates of marriage—and it is reasonable to suppose that levels of earnings, unemployment, housing rents, and other prices do make a difference—then by working through such economic variables, structural adjustment can influence the timing of fertility, levels of fertility and mortality, and rates of population growth.

An empirical analysis of fertility

With these considerations in mind, we now turn to the central concern of this chapter: how an analysis of household data can improve our understanding of the relationship between fertility behavior and structural adjustment. Our first task is to define the dependent variable.

Cumulative fertility

The dependent variable defined for the analysis that follows is the number of children ever born (CEB). The analysis proposed assumes that such information is available in the household survey used for the analysis.[2] A list of potential explanatory variables, to be discussed in more detail, is provided in Table 10.1. These variables are taken to be *exogenous* to fertility decisions; they represent aspects of the economic and social environment that affect fertility, but are not themselves affected by fertility decisions.[3]

Note, for instance, that characteristics of the husband (age, education, and the like) are *not* included in the table. The links between marital status and fertility are exceedingly complex in

Africa, given high levels of pre-marital fertility and high rates of marital dissolution in a number of countries (Acsadi and Johnson-Acsadi 1990). Furthermore, infertility or difficulties in conception may precipitate separation or divorce, so that the causation between marital status and fertility runs both ways. All this suggests that marital status should be viewed as an *endogenous* variable in respect to fertility and that analyses conditioned on marital status can be misleading.

Data quality and descriptive analyses

To assess the quality of the fertility data on children ever born, preliminary tabulations should be prepared that describe mean levels of cumulative fertility by age. The common practice in demographic work is to divide age into the following five-year groups: 10-14, 15-19, 20-24, 25-29, 30-34, 35-39, 40-44, and 45-49. Many Sub-Saharan countries will have had a World Fertility Survey or, more recently, a Demographic and Health Survey—these surveys provide a useful point of reference for the fertility analyses.

Once the quality of the data has been established, useful additional information can be gleaned from cross-tabulations of cumulative fertility by education, region, urban-rural location, and ethnic group. In such cross-tabulations, one regards current age as being a kind of control

Table 10.1: Exogenous explanatory variables for fertility analyses

Individual and family characteristics
Female schooling
Female age
Household income per adult (permanent, current, non-labor)
Ethnicity

Selected community characteristics
Region
Urbanization
Prices[a]
   Local wage rates
   Basic staples prices
   Other food prices
   Major own-enterprise product prices
   Formal and informal interest rates

Infrastructure and service delivery[a]
Health services (access, type, fees)
Family planning (access, fees)
Education (access, fees, indicators of quality)

---

a. Derived from a community survey or from aggregated individual responses from a household survey.

variable, not necessarily of intrinsic interest, whose influence must be netted out so that the effects of socioeconomic characteristics on fertility can be seen with greater clarity. Thus, each cross-tabulation should include current age and one of the characteristics listed.

Statistical analyses

The cross-tabulations prepare the ground for a statistical analysis of cumulative fertility, in which the influence of economic and social factors is of fundamental interest. The analysis is concerned in general with an equation such as the following:

$$F_i = f(X_i, W_i, Z_i, \varepsilon_i) \qquad (1)$$

where F_i represents the number of children ever born to woman i, and the variables influencing fertility include X_i, a group of individual and family-specific covariates (the woman's age, education, family income); W_i, representing community characteristics (for example, region, level of urbanization, prices); Z_i, referring to measures of health infrastructure, availability of family planning services, and availability and quality of primary and secondary schooling; and ε_i, an error term that summarizes all unmeasured influences on fertility.

To illustrate the general approach, consider the regression equation:

$$F = \alpha_0 + \alpha_1 P_F + \alpha_2 P_s + \alpha_3 Y + \alpha_4 P_s Y + \varepsilon_F \qquad (2)$$

where for the moment we ignore all influences on fertility other than household permanent income per adult Y, the price or access cost of schooling P_S, and the costs of access to family planning or related health services P_F.

In this illustrative equation, the direct effects of family planning/health policies on fertility are expressed in the coefficient α_1. If P_F measures the costs of access to services, then reductions in P_F should encourage reductions in fertility, that is, $\alpha_1 > 0$. The indirect effects of policy appear in the coefficients α_2 and α_4 associated with educational infrastructure and services. If child quantity and quality are substitutes, then educational investments that lower the costs of access to schooling P_S may produce lower fertility levels (as indicated in the coefficient α_2).

We also expect important interactions to exist between the effects of household income Y and P_S

on fertility levels. When schooling is expensive and access difficult (high P_S), fertility may tend to increase with the level of permanent income. That is, with high P_S, fertility may appear to be a "normal good." But as access to schooling improves (lower P_S), parents may increasingly substitute quality for quantity (Knodel, Chamratrithirong, and Debavalya 1987; Knodel, Havanon, and Sittitra 1990). Thus, the level of fertility may respond positively to income when it is difficult to send children to school, but may exhibit a negative relation to income as access becomes less costly to the household.[4]

Definition of dependent and explanatory variables

Table 10.1 lists the individual- and community-level covariates that can be considered in a regression model of the type described here. Three different specifications of household income per adult should be considered in the analyses (Ainsworth 1989). Household *permanent income* is measured by the level of consumption per adult. Consumption includes annual consumption expenditures plus the value of home production consumed and the imputed value of services derived from durable goods. Consumption is taken as a proxy for permanent income because it tends to fluctuate less over the life cycle than does annual income, and therefore better represents long-run access to economic resources. *Current income* is the sum of income from wages, home production, the value of services from durable goods (including imputed rents for home owners), receipt of transfers, and any residual sources of income. Finally, *non-labor income* includes the value of services from durables, transfer income, income from property rentals and from financial assets, and all other income not derived from the household supply of labor. Depending on the nature of the public programs, social security income may or may not be classified as non-labor income; income from pensions, which depends on previous labor supply, should be excluded from current non-labor income.

Both permanent income and current income depend, in part, on the earnings and labor supply of women in the household. To the extent that labor supply and cumulative fertility are related, it is possible that the income measures and the regression error term ε_F will be correlated. Thus, it may be necessary to use instrumental-variables methods to purge permanent and current income of their correlation with the error term. One possibility is to use community-level price data (see Table 10.1) to predict the level of income per adult among households in the community. Another possibility is to use household non-labor income as an additional instrument, or to use non-labor income in the place of permanent or current income.[5] For further discussion and an assessment of alternative techniques in the context of the Côte d'Ivoire living standards survey, see Ainsworth (1989).

The adult schooling variable of interest is the woman's schooling. (Note that including the husband's schooling would implicitly introduce current marital status in the regression specification, which we have argued is inappropriate.) The remaining variables in Table 10.1 concern community characteristics (presence of primary or secondary schools, availability of health and family planning clinics). As noted in connection with equation (2), the regression specification should consider such community variables together with interactions between these variables and the woman's schooling and household income.

Two issues deserve mention regarding the construction of the dependent variable, children ever born. It is awkward to treat children ever born as a variable that is continuous in nature, as would be the usual practice in a regression analysis. A measure of children ever born cannot take negative or non-integer values, and its range is restricted to values between 0 and an upper bound of perhaps 15 in most surveys. Strictly speaking, then, one should not regard the error term ε_F of equation (2) as being normally distributed.[6] These concerns have led some investigators to consider statistical models for integer or count data in fertility analyses; Ainsworth (1989) applies such models in her study of Côte d'Ivoire, and her analysis is summarized in Box 10.1. The results show few important differences between ordinary regression models and more elaborate statistical models, even though the latter are, at least in principle, more appropriate to fertility data. It seems that for the purposes of the initial analyses, ordinary regression estimates of equation (2) may well suffice.

Finally, the role of the woman's age in these analyses deserves further mention. Age is an indicator of a woman's progress through her reproductive years; with all else equal, the influence of age on cumulative fertility should be non-negative. To control adequately for such influences, it is usually necessary to include age, age squared, and age cubed in the regression specification, or to use a set of dummy variables indexing age.[7]

Box 10.1: Understanding the determinants of fertility: The case of Côte d'Ivoire

Household data have been used to explain variations in children ever born in Côte d'Ivoire (Ainsworth 1989). Reduced-form specifications highlight the important role played by permanent income and education in determining fertility, and the need to stratify the sample in estimating the relationship.

The data: 1985 Côte d'Ivoire Living Standards Survey. All women over the age of 15 years are included in the sample used for the analysis.

The method: First, ordinary least squares (OLS) estimates were derived. However (as discussed in the text), the dependent variable—children ever born (CEB)—is not a continuous variable, as required by the OLS model. It is censored in that only positive integer values can be observed. Therefore, Ainsworth uses two alternative estimation methods: Maximum Likelihood Tobit and the Poisson Count Model. The former allows for negative values of CEB, thus correcting for the censoring of the dependent variable, but it does not correct for the integer feature of CEB. The Poisson Count Model takes into account both censored and integer aspects of the dependent variable (see Ainsworth 1989, p. 21-24, for details). As the results do not differ greatly between these estimation models, for convenience only the OLS results are reported here (see table below).

The interpretation: Ideally, income used as an explanatory variable should be confined to non-labor income, since labor income cannot be considered exogenous. This is because household labor income will include the woman's own earnings, which are themselves clearly dependent on fertility. Because of the number of households reporting no non-labor income, Ainsworth was obliged to use a proxy for permanent income (the log of total household expenditure per adult). This variable is not strictly exogenous since it includes the influence of the woman's labor income.

The results highlight the need to stratify the analysis by rural and urban areas. The differences observed in the results for the sub-samples indicate that the use of the rural/urban intercept dummy is not sufficient. The differences in the fertility function between rural and urban areas are quite striking. The negative influence of years of schooling on fertility seems to apply mainly to the urban sample. However, the poor performance of education in explaining rural fertility may simply be due to the small number of observations of women with higher levels of schooling. On the other hand, the positive influence of income on fertility is statistically significant only for the rural sample. Moreover, the size of the coefficients (and the point elasticities calculated at means) also vary between rural and urban areas. For example, the estimated point elasticity of fertility with respect to years of schooling is -0.11 for the urban sample and only -0.01 for rural women. Ainsworth also shows that the results differ when the sample is stratified by age-groups: for example, the schooling variable is not significant for older females, and is particularly important in explaining fertility variations in the 15-24 age category.

Determinants of fertility
(OLS estimates; dependent variable: children ever born)

Exogenous variables	All women	Urban women	Rural women
Age	0.4296**	0.4891**	0.4106**
	(0.0218)	(0.0308)	(0.0285)
Age squared	-0.0038**	-0.0046**	-0.0036**
	(0.0003)	(0.0004)	(0.0003)
Years of schooling	-0.1113**	-0.0990**	-0.0633~
	(0.0158)	(0.0168)	(0.0391)
Urban dummy	-0.4467**		
	(0.1606)		
Ln permanent income per adult	0.3215**	-0.0842	0.5827**
	(0.1015)	(0.1286)	(0.1444)
R^2	0.44	0.53	0.37
N	1444	597	847

** Significant at 0.01 level; * significant at 0.05; ~ significant at 0.10.
Source: Ainsworth 1989, p. 27.

To focus on the fertility of young women, one can select a sample of women whose age at survey is below some cutoff (say, age 25) and run equation (2) separately for such women. Alternatively, one can interact age with other variables in the regression equation (for example, income) to determine whether the covariates have a differential effect on the fertility of young women.

Ainsworth (1989) provides examples of such analyses.

Recent fertility and contraceptive usage

Analyses of the socioeconomic determinants of cumulative fertility will be valuable, given the scarcity of such studies for Sub-Saharan Africa, but will necessarily suffer from one important limitation: economic measures derived from a household survey refer to the survey year, whereas cumulative fertility is influenced by socioeconomic factors over all reproductive years prior to the survey. To achieve a better match between fertility and its economic determinants, we should supplement the cumulative fertility analyses discussed here with an investigation of recent fertility and recent contraceptive use. Household surveys can be designed to obtain information on pregnancy and contraceptive use. With questions on pregnancy, the dependent variable would be $P=1$ to indicate that a pregnancy occurred in the reference period (usually 12 months preceding the survey) and $P=0$ if no pregnancy occurred. Another dependent variable might be constructed from household data—$C=1$ if the woman (or her husband/partner) currently employs a form of contraception and $C=0$ if they do not use contraception.[8]

Descriptive analysis

The first task regarding the description of these data is to produce plots of pregnancy and contraceptive usage by age and socioeconomic status, where the latter is defined by measures of household income and the woman's schooling. As with the cumulative fertility data, these summary plots should be assessed against recent information drawn from the Demographic and Health Surveys and earlier World Fertility Surveys. The graphs of pregnancy rates by age can be easily summarized in terms of period-specific total fertility rates (TFRs).[9] Of particular interest in the descriptive analysis are the proportions of women who are of prime reproductive age, who are not pregnant, and who use no modern contraceptive method. These women are candidates for the "KAP-gap" already discussed.[10]

Statistical analysis

Since recent pregnancy P and contraceptive use C are binary (yes/no) dependent variables, it is inappropriate to use ordinary regression methods in modeling the effects of covariates on P and C. In this context, a logit model provides a convenient framework for the multivariate analysis of pregnancy and method use. As an illustration, we can specify:

$$\text{logit } F_i = \alpha_0 + \alpha_1 P_F + \alpha_2 P_S + \alpha_3 Y + \alpha_4 P_S Y \qquad (3)$$

where F, the dependent variable, refers either to the pregnancy indicator P or to the contraception indicator C.[11]

As was the case in the cumulative fertility analyses, the *direct* effects of the health/family planning access variables P_F are of interest, as are the *indirect* influences of access to schooling on fertility decisions. In fleshing out the empirical specification, the individual and community variables of Table 10.1 should again be employed.

An empirical implementation of equation (3) should *not* include the number of children already born as a covariate, even though cumulative fertility is clearly related to motivations for current contraceptive use. The reason has to do with statistical endogeneity. Cumulative fertility reflects a host of measured and unmeasured traits, including abilities to conceive. It can be regarded as a summation, over the portion of a woman's reproductive lifetime ending at the survey, of lagged versions of the variables under examination, that is, lagged versions of recent pregnancy and current contraceptive use. If cumulative fertility is inserted into equation (3) as an explanatory variable, the coefficients of all socioeconomic variables become vulnerable to selectivity bias.

An analysis of pregnancy and contraceptive use among young women parallels the analysis for all women. One can select for study only those women who fall below an age cutoff, or one can interact selected covariates with age at survey in equation (3) to determine whether the covariates exert a differential influence on fertility and contraceptive usage by age. The analysis of contraception can be pursued in greater depth than suggested by equation (3). Frequently, surveys obtain information on the type of method used, ranging from no method used, to use of folk or traditional methods, including abstinence, and to various modern methods. The division of responses between no use, use of ineffective/traditional methods, and use of effective methods may be of interest. Each category can be singled out in a logit analysis paralleling the one discussed; a multinomial logit approach (Ben-Akiva and Lerman 1985) can also be investigated.

Conclusion

The analyses described are directed at several fundamental issues. One aim is to determine the relationship between income and fertility; this is central to charting the influence of structural adjustment and income growth on the future path of fertility. In examining the effects of income on fertility, allowance must be made for interactions between income and other covariates. The discussion emphasized interactions between income and the costs of child schooling, but other interactions also merit investigation. The key point is that fertility need not be a normal good under all circumstances; service delivery in the areas of family planning and education has the potential to transform the relationship between income and fertility.

Another area of importance is the indirect influence of educational and health infrastructure on fertility. These indirect effects underlie the tradeoff between child quantity and quality, which has proven to be integral to demographic transitions outside Africa. Educational and health investments may complement or substitute for investments in family planning service delivery, responsibility for which has fallen largely to the private sector in most Sub-Saharan countries. For countries in which it is possible to estimate the direct effects of family planning programs, an effort should be made to assess the effectiveness of these direct interventions relative to the indirect influences of education and health investments.

Young women are an important target group in these analyses. As noted earlier, interventions that have the effect of delaying fertility can exert a significant influence on population growth rates, and reductions in fertility at young ages may translate into lower lifetime fertility levels. Thus, the analyses described here should be carried out separately for young women, or if the data for young and older women are pooled, emphasis should be given to exploring interactions with age.

Notes

1. KAP refers to "knowledge, attitudes, and practice" regarding contraception and family limitation.

2. This information is sometimes available in surveys that are not specifically designed to measure and explain fertility, such as the World Bank's LSMS survey and the SDA Integrated Survey.

3. The question of statistical exogeneity is taken up later in the text.

4. Gary Becker's seminal writings on the quantity-quality model distinguish between the empirical or observed effects of income on fertility, often negative in sign, and the hypothetically positive effects of income that might be observed if the level of child quality (schooling) could somehow be held constant.

5. The theoretically appropriate concept of income in household economic models is *full* income, which is determined by exogenous household "endowments" of time and abilities, wage rates, own-production possibilities, and non-labor income. Non-labor income is only one component of full income.

6. Recall that unbiased and consistent estimates of the regression coefficients α are obtained even if the error term ε is not normally distributed, so long as all right-hand-side variables X are uncorrelated with ε, that is, $E [\varepsilon \mid X] = 0$. The normality assumption itself is not crucial; at issue is whether a normally distributed ε could be uncorrelated with X given the bounded nature of the dependent variable F.

7. Note that age at survey also indexes birth cohort, and may serve as a proxy for historical time trends in fertility. This affects the interpretation of the age coefficients in the regression model. If time trends in fertility are important, one should not interpret the age coefficients as representing only the effects of age itself on cumulative fertility. Especially for those Central African countries in which fertility may have risen in the 1970s, age coefficients should be interpreted carefully.

8. The base for the analysis of contraceptive use should exclude women who report a current pregnancy, since these women are not at risk of conception.

9. The total fertility rate (TFR) indicates the average number of children ever born to a woman who faces a given set of age-specific fertility rates, if the rates are constant over her reproductive lifetime and the woman survives through her reproductive years. If the age-specific rates are expressed in terms of single years of age, the TFR equals the sum of the single-year rates. To translate age-specific pregnancy rates to age-specific fertility rates, one needs an estimate of the proportions of pregnancies that do not end in live births.

10. A breakdown of such women according to current marital status would be informative.

11. The expression logit $F = f(X)$, where F is a binary zero-one variable and X represents all right-hand-side variables such as in equation (3), means that the log of the ratio Prob $(F=1)$/Prob $(F=0)$ equals $f(X)$.

11

The impact of adjustment on women

Paul Collier

There is an important difference between the analysis in this chapter, on the role of women, and other analyses, such as those on health. Health, as an objective of development, is of direct policy concern. Gender is one of many ways in which data can be disaggregated, and the rationale for doing so is twofold. First, in earning income, women often face different constraints than men. Since structural adjustment is largely about changing constraints, if those facing women and men are sufficiently different, it is illuminating to treat the genders as distinct groups rather than studying gender-undifferentiated averages. Second, women and men often have radically different propensities to consume particular public services, and so budgetary changes can have powerfully gender-differentiated effects. This chapter will give examples of how gender disaggregation can add to our understanding of particular topics, such as health. It should be stressed that gender is not a topic in itself but rather a possible disaggregation to be borne in mind when studying a topic. The art of analysis is to keep disaggregation to a minimum so that it is possible to see the wood for the trees. Sometimes gender disaggregation will not add enough to be worthwhile. However, for some topics it will turn out to be useful and for others essential. With properly set-up survey data, the cost of seeing whether gender disaggregation is going to be informative is usually very low.

The next section sets gender in the context of other disaggregations important for the analysis of structural adjustment. We discuss the symptoms of gender-differentiated constraints on the generation of income. We then move from the symptoms to the constraints themselves. Finally, we explicitly relate gender to a series of public policies. Throughout, examples of how African survey data have been and can be used are presented in boxes.

Choosing the level of aggregation

Perhaps the most fundamental step in economic analysis is the choice of aggregation of activities and of agents. Although gender issues concern disaggregation between agents, it is useful to begin with activities. At a minimum, the new macroeconomics of structural adjustment usually distinguishes between the six activities shown in Figure 11.1. First, a distinction is made between marketed and non-marketed goods and services because only for the former can resources be allocated through the price mechanism. Second, within marketed activities, distinctions are drawn between capital and consumer goods, and between tradables and nontradables. Finally, within tradables, a distinction is made between protected and unprotected (or disprotected) activities. (For a further discussion of the new macroeconomics of structural adjustment, see World Bank 1991b.)

However, there is no equivalent consensus as to the appropriate disaggregation of agents. The key determinant of this choice is whether we are concerned primarily with the processes by which living standards are determined, or only with the outcome of those processes—that is, whether we are concerned with production or only with

Figure 11.1: Disaggregation of activities in the new macroeconomics of adjustment

consumption. If the latter, then the appropriate unit of observation is self-evidently the individual person. However, in Africa (although such information is useful for the improved targeting of services and transfers), of greater policy concern is the process whereby living standards are generated. A part of poverty is due to constraints on the generation of income that can be alleviated by appropriate changes in policy. The primary purpose of the analysis of survey data is to help identify such policy changes.

This implies a radically different disaggregation of agents. The criterion for disaggregation now becomes the decision problem of the agent: only where decision problems differ significantly is it necessary to distinguish between agents. On this criterion three disaggregations at once suggest themselves and are commonly used: (a) by the activity or activities in which the agent is engaged (see Figure 11.1); (b) by the location of the agent (rural/urban); and (c) by the extent of the decisionmaking problem encountered by the agent as an organization, namely:

- Individual person (none)
- Household (cooperative conflict)
- Firm (hierarchy).

In this chapter, we suggest that on the same criterion a fourth disaggregation, by gender, is often appropriate since the constraints, and hence the decision problem, are likely to differ substantially by gender.

A corollary of this rationale for an analysis that distinguishes between women and men is that, generally, there is not a small, self-contained set of "women's issues" that can be appended to an otherwise unaltered analysis. Rather, many standard issues in resource allocation become better illuminated when the analysis is disaggregated by gender. When added to the three-way disaggregation of agents, we arrive at a potential disaggregation of six activities by two locations, by three organizational forms, and by two genders, which is 72 classes of agents. Even this understates the potential number of agents since many agents will be engaged in multiple activities rather than just one. Six activities give rise to 64 different combinations of activities (ranging from doing none to doing all six). Clearly, the scope for analytically meaningful disaggregations rapidly leads us into unmanageably large numbers of different groups. The answer to this problem is to check with the data which among these groups is sufficiently large or poor to be important from a policy perspective. Box 11.1 gives an example from a survey of Central Province, Kenya, of how 64 different combinations of activities can be reduced with little loss to around nine combinations.

In summary, to understand the processes that generate income, we must base our disaggregation upon analytically purposive distinctions as to how income is acquired. Since there are many such distinctions, we must scrutinize the survey data to see which distinctions are important.

If, however, we seek to improve the targeting of public consumption services, then our disaggregations are differently motivated. We should make those distinctions that help decisionmakers and administrators design the delivery of services to reach those most in need. The most readily identifiable distinctions between people are age, location, and gender. Age and location are continuous variables: that is, we can go on making finer and finer distinctions and so the question will usually be at what point it is sensible to stop. There are, of course, no such problems with gender: the question is simply whether the distinction is worth making. As with all disaggregations, the test is empirical. However, since the gender disaggregation is so simple, it will always be worth making. Box 11.2 uses data from Tanzania to show that the addition of gender disaggregation makes age-group and symptom disaggregations more revealing in identifying differences in the incidence of illness, and thus the targeting of curative and preventive health services. The scope for useful descriptive statistics on well-being is considerable. However, since the use of such statistics is fairly straightforward,

Box 11.1: Using survey data to reaggregate

The data: Survey of rural households in Central Province, Kenya, 1982.

The problem: It is believed that the minimum analytic distinctions between activities are three types of farm income —food crops, nonfood crops, and livestock—and three types of non-farm income—business, wages, and remittances. Since households undertake multiple activities, this gives potentially 64 different combinations. The impact of price changes on households will differ between these combinations. The problem is to identify which are important.

The criteria: Two criteria can be used to cut down the range of combinations. First, we can eliminate those in which less than 5 percent of the sample is engaged. Second, we may wish to revise this on inspecting information about mean incomes. A combination with less than 5 percent of the sample may still be important for policy purposes if mean income is well below average. Note, however, that if the cell size is too small, then the observed mean income is probably spurious as a guide to the characteristics of the wider population.

Box Table 1 shows the distribution of the households over the 64 possible combinations of activities. From this table we find that only seven combinations meet the 5 percent cutoff. These seven account for 66.4 percent of all households. Box Table 2 calculates mean per capita income. Scrutinizing it suggests that the combination of food crops + livestock, which just misses the 5 percent cutoff, should still be included because the income of this group is little more than half that for the whole sample. This group is a sizable component of the poor. Hence, we arrive at eight meaningful combinations plus a residual "all other combinations" that accounts for around 29 percent of households.

Table 1: Distribution of households by activity
(percent)

| | | | | Non-farm | | | | |
Farm	None	Own business only	Wage only	Remittances only	Own business + wages	Own business + remittances	Remittances + wages	All types non-farm	Total
None	0.9	0.0	10.8	0.3	0.0	0.0	1.2	0.0	13.2
Food crops only	1.8	0.4	8.2	0.9	1.4	0.0	1.2	0.0	13.7
Cash crops only	0.6	0.1	0.0	0.1	0.0	0.0	0.0	0.0	0.9
Livestock only	0.2	0.2	0.1	0.0	0.0	0.0	0.0	0.0	0.5
Food and cash crops	2.6	0.0	1.2	10.0	0.6	0.0	0.4	0.0	5.9
Food crops and livestock	4.9	1.6	5.8	3.2	1.0	0.0	2.9	0.1	19.5
Cash crops and livestock	0.7	0.0	0.0	0.0	0.0	0.0	0.0	0.3	0.4
All types of farm income	16.5	1.4	9.5	9.2	0.7	1.7	6.0	0.3	45.7
Total	28.6	3.8	35.6	14.8	3.6	1.7	11.6	0.4	100.0

Table 2: Mean household per capita income by activity mix
(Shillings)

| | | | | Non-farm | | | | |
Farm	None	Own business only	Wage only	Remittances only	Own business + wages	Own business + remittances	Remittances + wages	All types non-farm	Total
None	0.0	-	1,634.5	240.0	-	-	2,343.5	-	1,506.4
Food crops only	340.9	824.5	1,772.7	792.1	4,318.0	-	1,252.9	-	1,923.0
Cash crops only	-106.8	9,799.4	-	732.9	-	-	-	-	2,135.3
Livestock only	40.0	970.0	1,171.0	-	-	-	-	-	945.5
Food and cash crops	484.6	-	655.9	1,170.8	4,034.5	-	2,763.4	1,889.2	1,247.7
Food crops and livestock	1,024.1	1,479.5	1,657.1	1,894.1	3,838.8	-	3,318.4	1,889.2	1,913.3
Cash crops and livestock	163.1	-	-	-	-	-	-	-	163.1
All types of farm income	1,301.2	2,257.5	1,675.8	1,623.1	1,683.3	2,526.7	1,825.6	1,696.7	1,599.9
Total	1,106.2	1,926.8	1,627.3	1,615.5	3,681.7	2,526.7	2,132.6	1,725.6	1,662.6

Source: Bevan and others 1989, Tables 2.7 and 2.8.

the rest of this chapter will concentrate on the process of income generation. This is more complex, and probably more important.

Symptoms of gender-differentiated constraints

This section discusses how to use survey data to determine whether constraints on economic decisions are likely to be significantly different for men and women. If they face different constraints, two phenomena should be identifiable, one static and the other dynamic. First, female-controlled resources should, as a consequence, be distributed over economic activities very differently than male-controlled resources. This is because, faced with a common set of incentives

The data: Survey of households in rural Tanzania, 1983 —information on illness during the past three months.

The problem: To identify groups of the population most prone to illness.

The table below divides the population into four age-groups and by gender and distinguishes between five symptoms of illness. Here the three distinctions, age/gender/symptom, reinforce each other. If we fail to make the age and symptom distinctions, then there is little difference between the genders: 18.1 percent of the men and 19.4 percent of the women have been ill. Adding the breakdown by age, however, we find a strong and revealing gender difference. Women age 16-49 are 33 percent more likely to be ill than men. This suggests the hypothesis that childbearing places a physical strain on women that adversely affects their general health. Adding the breakdown by symptom, the gender differences become larger. Women age 16-49 are 43 percent more likely than men to suffer from fever, diarrhea, or vomiting, but less likely to suffer from chest-based illnesses (perhaps because they smoke less). In this example, the gender distinction makes the age and symptom distinctions more informative.

Percentage of population ill, by age, sex, and symptom

	Age-group				
Symptom	*0-4*	*5-15*	*16-49*	*50 +*	*Total*
Males					
F	14.8	9.6	9.1	20.2	11.5
DV	4.8	1.7	1.3	1.8	2.0
FDV	2.2	1.3	1.1	5.0	1.8
C	4.8	2.7	2.6	4.6	3.2
CB	0.9	0.2	0.3	2.3	0.6
Percentage ill[a]	25.7	14.8	13.7	32.1	18.1
Females					
F	16.7	11.9	13.0	15.4	13.4
DV	5.4	2.6	1.9	1.1	2.6
FDV	3.9	1.3	1.5	2.3	1.9
C	3.5	2.1	2.3	4.0	2.6
CB	0.4	0.5	0.4	1.1	0.5
Percentage ill[a]	27.2	16.5	18.2	22.9	19.4

F indicates fever.

D indicates diarrhea.

V indicates vomiting.

C indicates cough.

B indicates blood in sputum.

a. Percentage ill is less than the sum of the corresponding symptom percentages since some individuals suffer more than one symptom.

Source: Bevan and others 1989, Table 14A6.

of supply response will differ systematically. Both phenomena are of the essence for structural adjustment.

Adjustment is about resource movements between activities. Changing the incentive structure is merely a necessary means by which such movements are induced. Assisting the process of adjustment therefore means identifying the types of agents who control resources in the activities that should contract, and discovering how policy changes can ease the impediments to the reallocation of those resources to other activities. If women and men are allocated very differently among sectors, then a given change in the structure of incentives will imply different requirements for them to be mobile. But the differing constraints may also imply that women have less capacity to be mobile than men. For example, women might be disproportionately located in sectors that need to contract and at the same time have less capacity than men to reallocate resources to sectors that should expand.

The major resource women control is their *labor* (although, as we will see, women may often not be in full control of their labor time). A simple and instructive starting point in the gender-disaggregated analysis of survey data is to compare the allocation of male and female labor. Referring back to our discussion of disaggregation, it is meaningful to do this in several different ways. First, we distinguish between farm work, wage work, own business, family, education, and health-related time. Box 11.3 shows that on this basis there are large differences between the genders in the allocation of time. Women spend far more time working on the family farm, somewhat more time working on other farms, and far less time on their own businesses and in wage employment. They spend overwhelmingly more time fetching water and wood. Box 11.3 investigates this further by distinguishing between female heads of household and wives in male-headed households. Wives' time is even more skewed toward the farm and fetching water and wood, and less time is devoted to business and wage employment. The box also distinguishes between women with and without education: educated women spend substantially more time in business and non-agricultural wage employment without spending less time on other forms of work. Finally, it compares boys and girls in the age-group 6-15, the prime school-age-group. Girls spend nearly three times as long working as do boys. This surely raises the question whether the

and differential constraints, maximizing agents will allocate their resources differently. Second, when the structure of incentives change, so that it is optimal to reallocate resources, the process

work they do is detrimental to their performance at school.

The other important basis for disaggregating the allocation of work time is the macroeconomic sectors identified in Figure 11.1. Of the six activities previously identified, in most of Africa domestic production of tradable capital goods is sufficiently minor for the activity to be aggregated in with the rest of manufacturing as a "protected tradable" (tradable capital goods are an important category in the macroeconomics of expenditure but not of production). The task for the analyst of survey data is now to assign the activities reported in the survey to the five remaining analytic activities. This task will entail a series of choices that will differ between countries to some extent. However, in much of Africa, as a first approximation the activities can be proxied as set out in Frame 11.1.

Of these, food production is the most problematic to allocate since it can potentially be part of either the protected or the unprotected tradable sector instead of being nontradable. This is a crucial decision for the investigator: women are heavily specialized in food production and so whether, overall, women are disproportionately in the protected tradables, unprotected tradables, or nontradables sectors largely depends upon it. The designation as between tradable and nontradable depends upon transport costs: often these are sufficiently high for broad self-sufficiency to be cost-minimizing in a normal year, in which case food is appropriately regarded as nontradable. If food is traded internationally, then it can be classified between protected and unprotected on the basis of the relationship of the producer price to the world price. If food is exported, then the question is whether the producer price is broadly equal to the world price minus domestic transport costs. If the producer price is substantially above this level, then food is a protected tradable. If food is imported, then (since at the margin domestic transport costs have to be paid on imported food) the investigator should select among the locations supplied by imported food the one with the highest transport costs. The key comparison is then between the actual producer price of food and the price that, together with the cost of transporting it to this location, would equal the cost of imported food including its transport costs. If the two prices are broadly equal, then food is unprotected. If the actual producer price is substantially the higher of the two, then food is a protected tradable. Having made these assign-

Box 11.3: Gender differences in the allocation of labor time

The data: Survey of Central Province, Kenya, 1982.
The problem: To identify differences in time allocation between and within the genders.

Panel (a) in the table below identifies 12 non-leisure uses of time. Women spend far more time working on the farm, fetching water and wood, and being ill. Men spend far more time in off-farm work, in education, and as outpatients. Panel (b) in the table below focuses on seven of these uses of time. It first compares women who are household heads with those who are wives. It then compares women with different levels of education. Finally, it compares boys with girls. Women who have the autonomy of being household heads spend more time in non-farm employment and less time fetching water and wood. Educated women spend far more time in non-farm wage employment, but not at the expense of other activities. Girls spend nearly three times as many hours in these activities as boys.

Non-leisure-time use, 1982

(a)	Hours per year	
Type of work	Males	Females
Own farm	227	361
Off-farm wage work	105	35
Own business	47	19
Work on estates	4	3
Work on other small farms	38	45
Fetching water	28	209
Fetching wood	21	187
Education	376	345
Outpatient time	8	4
Accompanying outpatient	1	5
Inpatient time	1	1
Other illness-related time	21	30

(b)	Females only					
Type of work	House- hold heads	Wives	No edu- cation	Com- pleted pri- mary	Boys	Girls
Own farm	830	897	407	408	26	54
Off-farm wage work	109	63	5	58	0	0
Own business	105	37	15	27	0	0
Work on estates	0	9	7	0	0	0
Work on other small farms	119	94	59	40	1	2
Fetching water	405	507	230	292	20	63
Fetching wood	405	470	210	210	15	47
Total					62	166

Source: Bevan and others 1989, Tables 14E1, 2, and 3.

ments, a further feasible and important disaggregation is the contractual mode by which labor is allocated to the sector: through the labor market, through the household, or through the individual.

**Frame 11.1: Relating macroeconomic sectors
to activities identified in surveys**

Concept	Survey proxy
Consumer goods	
Tradable	
Protected	Manufacturing
Unprotected	Export crop agriculture
Nontradable	Food agriculture
	Services, trade
Capital goods	
Nontradable	Construction
Non-marketed goods and services	Public sector employment

Two descriptive statistics are useful: the percentage of the female labor force engaged in each sector (by contractual mode), and the percentage of the total labor force in each such category that is female. Such an arrangement of survey data is portrayed in Box 11.4, which shows both an "ideal" disaggregation and a more limited example of what has been done on Kenyan data. The Kenyan example demonstrates that there are large gender differences in labor allocation between the sectors derived from macroeconomic analysis. The protected tradables sector and the nonfood nontradables sector are overwhelmingly male. The food sector and small-farm export agriculture are predominantly female.

In practice, it is not usually possible to distinguish between labor whose allocation is household-controlled and that which is individually controlled. However, at least as far as gender is concerned, a good proxy for this is whether the household is male- or female-headed. Whether this disaggregation of household allocation is worthwhile probably varies considerably within Africa. In parts of West Africa, very few households are reported as being female-headed; in parts of East Africa, around 40 percent of households are female-headed, and the distinction is extremely important.

Box 11.4 tells us both where the labor force is by gender and the relations of production by which it is there. We might find, for example:

• That women are skewed toward the nontradable sector (where they predominate)

• That women are skewed away from market allocation of labor

• That within household allocation, female-headed household labor is more skewed toward nontradables than that of male-headed households.

What might these findings suggest? Structural adjustment involves a reallocation of resources from the nontradable to the tradable sector. If women predominate in the nontradable sector, this tells us that resource reallocation will primarily concern females. If, additionally, women's labor is allocated by the household, this tells us that we cannot rely upon the labor market to achieve this reallocation. If, within household allocation, female-headed households are skewed toward nontradables, and if such households are numerous, this suggests that the gender of the household head may significantly influence accessibility to tradable activities.

A useful supplement to Box 11.4 is the mean wage rate in each sector (Frame 11.2). The wage rate is some guide to the marginal product of labor. Pronounced differences in wage rates between sectors indicate either differential endowments of human capital or differential barriers to entry. This is of interest for gender issues if the hierarchy of wage rates by sector tends to correspond to the concentration of female labor in each sector. For example, we might find that women tend to be concentrated in those sectors in which mean wage rates are lowest. This implies either that women have differentially lower rates of accumulation of human capital, or that they face differentially higher entry barriers to the more remunerative sectors (or both).

A further supplement is to disaggregate wage rate information by gender (where sample sizes permit). Controlling for human capital, differences in wage rates by gender seem to be rather small relative to the very large gender differences in labor allocation by sector. However, this remains uncertain, and so it is worth getting direct evidence on it where this can be achieved at low cost. The two supplementary analyses are summarized in Frame 11.2.

Box 11.4 and Frame 11.2 take us quite a long way in determining whether gender is likely to be a significant issue in structural adjustment (from the viewpoint of production). For example, they might between them suggest:

• That most of the labor that must reallocate from nontradables is female

• That this labor is not allocated through the market

• That this labor appears to be locked into the sector where it already has typically low earnings; and that the problem (if any) in the labor market appears to be one of differential access rather than of differential earnings once in the market.

Box 11.4: Distribution of the labor force by macroeconomically meaningful sectors

The problem: To estimate the differing gender compositions of the sectors identified in the macroeconomic analysis.

Since this work would be new, there is no good example with which to illustrate it. Hence, an "ideal" presentation of survey data is suggested below (box Frame 1), followed by a more limited example for Kenya (box Table 1).

The Kenyan example utilized both household survey data and employment and earnings survey data. The latter, being an establishment-based survey, misses informal and subsistence activities but is likely to be more accurate for formal sector wage employment. Note the very large differences in the gender compositions of the various sectors. In Kenya, food was judged to be nontradable in that in a normal year the country would be self-sufficient.

Frame 1: An "ideal" portrayal of the data

| | Mode of contract | | | |
| | Household | | | |
Sector	Female-headed	Male-headed	Wage labor	Total
Protected tradables	X Y	X Y	X Y	X Y
Unprotected tradables	X Y	X Y	X Y	X Y
Nontradable consumer goods	X Y	X Y	X Y	X Y
Nontradable capital goods	X Y	X Y	X Y	X Y
Public services	X Y	X Y	X Y	X Y

X indicates percentage of total female labor force in category.
Y indicates percentage of labor force in category that is female.

Table 1: An actual example for Kenya, 1981

| | Percentage of labor force | |
Sector	Female	Male
Unprotected tradables		
Wage labor on estates	24	76
Smallholder labor	58	42
Protected tradables	12	88
Nontradables		
Food	63	37
Capital goods	4	96
Private service (wage labor)	21	79
Non-market (public services)	19	81

Source: Collier 1989, Table 2.

The construction of the tables should be feasible on many sets of survey data. The only disaggregation that will sometimes be problematic is

Frame 11.2: Mean wage rates by sector and gender

Sector	Female	Male	All
Protected tradables	-	-	-
Unprotected tradables	-	-	-
Nontradable consumer goods	-	-	-
Nontradable capital goods	-	-	-
Public services	-	-	-
Total	-	-	-

the allocation of labor by gender between food and export crop agriculture. In cases where surveys do not record labor allocation by crop, a proxy can still be achieved by investigating, separately for male- and female-headed households, whether there is a correlation between the proportion of crop output that is export crops and the proportion of the household labor force that is female. A useful technique for investigating this sort of question is a regression. In this case, the regression would be:

$$y_i = a + b x_i$$

where y_i is the proportion (by value) of farm output attributable to export crops in household i, and x_i is the proportion of the household i labor force that is female.

Two things should be stressed about this regression. First, it is a "reduced form." It investigates something that is the outcome of a more complex, but unmodelled, process. Activity choices can be presumed to reflect considerations of factor endowments other than labor, such as land and credit, and also considerations of risk. Potentially, the regression can be expanded to include such influences. Second, much choice remains open to the analyst: for example, how to define the labor force, and whether to use gross output or net income.

Non-labor factors of production are usually more difficult to disaggregate by gender from survey data. As an approximation, the agent who controls the allocation of land between food and export crops can be taken to be the head of the household, although the extent to which this is inaccurate will need to be checked from nonsurvey sources. In this case, the relevant gender disaggregation for land is between male- and female-headed households, as shown in Frame 11.3.

Control of capital disaggregated by sector and gender is not usually identifiable from survey data.

So far the analysis has concerned the static picture of resource allocation. We now advance to the analysis of *resource mobility*. A particularly interesting aspect of resource mobility from the viewpoint of gender is the process of entry into economic activities that the agent has not previously undertaken. This is likely to be of importance where women are heavily concentrated in those activities that need to decline relatively. In much of Africa, the central process of resource allocation is the expansion of export agriculture. We first give an example that suggests that there can be a substantial, gender-related problem in this expansion. The example concerns tea growing in Kenya.

Recent work on the adoption of tea in tea-growing parts of Kenya during 1975-82 has compared male- and female-headed households. Tea is arguably the most important export activity with potential for expansion in Kenya, since, unlike coffee, it is not subject to international quotas. Hence, in investigating the determinants of tea adoption, we are at the heart of impediments to appropriate resource mobility. The study found that female-headed households had only half the propensity of male-headed households to adopt tea. Since in Kenya around a third of rural households are female-headed, this diminished propensity is in aggregate substantial. Further, the case of Kenyan tea is particularly revealing because most of the tea picking is done by females. This is reflected in the effects of the household labor endowment on the propensity to adopt tea. Holding other household characteristics constant, extra male labor has no effect on the propensity to adopt tea whereas extra female labor leads to a statistically significant increase. An additional female adult in an otherwise average household raises the propensity to adopt by around a quarter. Thus, in Kenya, the key sector of tea is characterized by three apparently incompatible facts. Women do most of the work on tea, households with more women are more likely to adopt the crop, yet households headed by women are far less likely to do so. The implication is that female-headed households face some severe constraints, additional to those faced by male-headed households, that prevent them from entering what would otherwise be a natural activity for female-headed households.

How can the policy analyst study this sort of phenomenon? The most straightforward technique is tabular, and this is the technique that we have relied on so far. Box 11.5 shows how tables might be used to investigate gender effects in tea adoption. However, the difficulty with using tables for this sort of question is that several different influences need to be disentangled. Tea adoption is, by hypothesis, influenced by the gender of the household head, by the male and female labor endowments, and probably by other factors, such as the age of the head. Each time an influence is added, a further breakdown of the sample is needed. This rapidly exhausts the sample size because the number of observations remaining in each cell becomes too few to be a reliable guide. Hence, economists tend to use more powerful techniques than tables when confronted by more than a few potential influences. Two highly useful techniques are regressions and logits. Regressions are appropriate where the phenomenon to be explained can potentially take on any value (such as income). Logits are appropriate where the phenomenon to be explained can only take on two or three values. For example, in the present case there can only be two possible outcomes: the household does or does not adopt tea. The appropriate technique is therefore a logit rather than a regression, although a regression can be used if no software is available to run a logit. Regression software is universal, and the results are straightforward to interpret. Logit results are more difficult to interpret. Box 11.6 sets out a logit analysis of tea adoption using Kenyan data.

Logit analysis is appropriate wherever the dependent variable can only take two or three values. However, some economic processes are a mixture of both discrete and continuous variables. An important example is earnings in the labor market. Such earnings reflect two interrelated processes: gaining access to a wage job and getting a particular wage rate in that job. To analyze gender issues in the labor market, these two processes are best investigated simultaneously. The appropriate methodology is tobit analysis, which combines the discrete outcomes

Frame 11.3: The allocation of land by sector and gender

	Male-headed households	Female-headed households
Food crops	X	X
Export crops	X	X
Other uses	X	X

X indicates percentages of land used for this purpose.

Box 11.5: Investigating gender influences on tea adoption using tables: A hypothetical example

The problem: To investigate by tabular means whether gender is a significant influence on the adoption of tea.

The limitation of using tables is that there are likely to be several influences on tea adoption.

Suppose we start with the hypothesis that the age and gender of the household head are likely to matter, as are the household's endowments of male and female labor. Tables can then be used to see whether there are substantial differences in the proportion of households adopting tea, by breaking the sample down into "cells" within which households have the same age-group and gender as the head, and the same male labor endowments. With three age-groups, two genders, three male labor groups, and three female labor groups, there are therefore 3 x 2 x 3 x 3 = 54 cells.

We then compare the proportion of households adopting tea in these cells. The tabular approach rapidly hits the limits of sample size if there are several influences to be investigated, as in the present example.

The four influences can only be handled together by breaking the sample down into 54 cells, but then there must be enough observations in each cell for a proportion of adopters to be a meaningful figure. For samples in the 1,000 to 2,000 range, breaking the sample down much beyond 50 cells is unlikely to yield reliable information. Hence, in this example, if there were more than four important influences on tea adoption, it would be difficult to investigate the effects of gender using only tables.

The alternative approach in such a situation is discussed in Box 11.6.

An example of a tabular approach to tea adoption

Age-group of head	Under 30	30-49	50+
Male labor endowment 1 adult or less			
Female labor endowment 1 adult or less			
Male-headed	X	X	X
Female-headed	X	X	X
Female labor endowment 2 or 3			
Male-headed	X	X	X
Female-headed	X	X	X
Female labor endowment more than 3			
Male-headed	X	X	X
Female-headed	X	X	X
Male labor endowment 2 or 3 adults			
Female labor endowment 1 adult or less			
Male-headed	X	X	X
Female-headed	X	X	X
Female labor endowment 2 or 3			
Male-headed	X	X	X
Female-headed	X	X	X
Female labor endowment more than 3			
Male-headed	X	X	X
Female-headed	X	X	X
Male labor endowment more than 3 adults			
Female labor endowment 1 adult or less			
Male-headed	X	X	X
Female-headed	X	X	X
Female labor endowment 2 or 3			
Male-headed	X	X	X
Female-headed	X	X	X
Female labor endowment more than 3			
Male-headed	X	X	X
Female-headed	X	X	X

X indicates percentage of those households that were not growing tea in 1975 and adopted it during 1975-82.

---

modelled by a logit with the more common continuous dependent variable regression analysis. For an example of such a gender-focused analysis for Côte d'Ivoire, see Appleton, Collier, and Horsnell (1990). That analysis found that, once in the labor market, women received the same wages as men, controlling for their educational characteristics, but that even among those already in the labor force, women were far less likely than men to enter wage employment, and that their participation was far more sensitive to wage rates.

In some respects, the ideal outcome of a gender-focused analysis is that, as other explanatory variables are added, gender gradually ceases to be a significant disaggregation. The hypothesis is not that women and men have intrinsically different economic attitudes but that they tend to face different constraints. Hence, if we were able to get satisfactory empirical measures of these different constraints, for example, better access on the part of men to credit, we would then be able to account fully for the observed differences in behav-

ior. In practice, however, our measures of differential constraints are unlikely to be sufficient to account fully for the effect of gender. This stage of the analysis can primarily establish whether the symptoms of gender-differentiated constraints are present and important. If they are, there is a case for investigating likely constraints and how policies bear on them. This is taken up in the next section.

Four gender-differentiated processes

At least four distinct processes account for why women face differential constraints on economic activity. First, women may *encounter discrimination outside the household*. In developed countries, the most emphasized example has probably been differential wage rates. In developing countries, however, discrimination in the labor market appears more to take the form of differential access to wage employment. For example, in rural Tanzania (where formal sector employment is an

Box 11.6: Gender effects on tea adoption: The logit approach

Where there are several influences on tea adoption, the tabular approach encounters its limits and more powerful techniques are needed. When the phenomenon to be explained can take many values, the normal technique is regression. Tea adoption, however, is not like this: we are investigating only two states, adoption or non-adoption. The technique that deals with such a problem is termed a logit, and it is available in many statistical software packages. Here we explain how to use it and how to interpret the results. We illustrate with Kenyan data.

The data: Rural Kenya, 1982.

The hypothesis: Tea adoption is influenced by the age and gender of the household head, the male and female labor endowments of the household, the proportion of neighboring households adopting tea, and whether the household is already growing coffee.

The results:

Variable	Coefficient	T-ratio
Household head		
Gender	-1.03	2.15
Age	-0.05	1.47
Age squared	0.0004	1.06
Labor endowment		
Males	0.10	0.57
Females	0.42	2.05
Neighboring households	4.20	4.55
Already growing coffee	-0.88	2.15

Interpreting the results: The coefficients show the effect of gender and other variables on the likelihood that the household adopts tea. In total, 47 percent of the sample adopted tea during the period, so for the average household the probability is 0.47. To interpret the coefficients, it is neces-sary to allow for the transformations that this probability goes through in a logit. First, the probability of adoption can only vary between 0 and 1, but for statistical purposes it is better for the "dependent variable" to be able to vary between $-$ infinity and $+$ infinity. A logit achieves this by explaining not the probability, P, but $P/(1-P)$. For the average household in our Kenyan sample, this was $0.47/0.53 = 0.89$. Second, a logit works with logarithms, so for the average household, the dependent variable is the logarithm of 0.89, which is -0.12. Now we are ready to interpret the gender coefficient. From the results column we see that this is -1.03. This tells us that for a household with otherwise average characteristics, if it is female-headed instead of male-headed, $\ln[P(1-P)]$, instead of being -0.12, will be reduced by 1.03—that is, it will be -1.15. We now work back to the probability of adoption that this implies. First, we move from the logarithm $P/(1-P)$ back to $P/(1-P)$. The antilog of -1.15 is 0.31. Second, we move back from $P/(1-P)$ to P. Since $P/(1-P)$ is 0.31, P is 0.24. This tells us that in otherwise average households, female headedness lowers the likelihood of adoption of tea from 47 percent to 24 percent, a dramatic reduction. The effect of adding one more female adult to the average household is to raise $\ln[P/(1-P)]$ by 0.42, so it rises from -0.12 to $+0.30$. The antilog of 0.30 is 1.35; so with $P/(1-P) = 1.35$, $P = 0.57$. The extra female adult thus increases the likelihood of adoption of tea from 47 percent to 57 percent. Both effects are statistically significant, as can be seen from the t-ratios. By contrast, the endowment of male labor has no effect on adoption (the t-ratio is insignificant).

The logit approach is a much more sophisticated procedure than tabular analysis. It requires better software and more thought, but it is justified when there are too many important influences to incorporate into tabular break-downs.

---

elite occupation), men with secondary education had a three-in-four chance of such a job, whereas women with the same education had only half that chance (Collier, Radwan, and Wangwe 1986). Often a more important instance of discrimination is the credit market. Because women usually do not own marketable land rights and, as subordinates in the household, cannot establish reputations for creditworthiness, they tend to have markedly worse access to credit. This is especially severe in economies subject to financial repression, where credit markets are rationed by risk-bearing ability.

The second process, which also operates outside the household, is the different directions in which the *tendency to imitate or copy role models* attracts men and women. The tendency to let decisions be influenced by what other similar or admired agents have chosen is a universal feature of human behavior. It is a key way in which innovations spread over the population. There is now some evidence that role models are gender-specific: girls copy women, boys copy men. For example, in urban Côte d'Ivoire, people have been found much more likely to enter formal wage employment if their parents had been so occupied (controlling for other characteristics), but there is some indication that each tended to copy the parent of his or her own gender. An implication of this is that if some new economic opportunity is initially taken up by men, it may automatically be diffused over the male population by a mechanism that will not transmit it to the female population (Appleton, Collier, and Horsnell 1990).

The third process is that within the household there are *asymmetric rights and obligations.*

For example, in rural Africa, women incur obligations to grow food crops for subsistence, to gather fuel and water, to cook, and to rear children. In return, men meet certain cash needs of the household and usually are responsible for the allocation of land. This pattern of reciprocal obligations is often unequal. In rural Africa, women work for considerably longer hours than men. Part of this work is on holdings whose output is controlled by men. This gives rise to a classic "principal-agent" problem: the woman has little incentive to work well. For example, Ongaro (1988) used a recent Kenyan sample survey to compare the effectiveness of weeding (a female obligation) on maize yields in male- and female-headed households. He specified a regression of maize yields per hectare in which the number of weedings was one of the explanatory variables and then fitted the regression separately for male- and female-headed households. In both types of household there were two weedings per season and each weeding significantly raised yields. However, whereas in female-headed households these weedings raised yields by 56 percent, in male-headed households the increase in yield was only 15 percent. Since other differences were controlled for, the most likely explanation is a systematic difference in effort due to differential incentives. To put this in perspective, if Ongaro's sample is representative of rural Kenya, the national maize loss from this disincentive effect is about equal to the maize gain from the application of phosphate and nitrogen fertilizers.

The fourth process is the *burden of reproduction.* Because there is a phase during mid-life in which women's time is pre-committed, certain activities are precluded. Skills decline, and long-term contracts such as are common in the labor market are terminated. The physical demands of childbearing and breastfeeding strain health: recent studies (Bevan and others 1989) show that female health relative to male health goes through a trough in the child-rearing years. This health deterioration rebounds upon income-earning opportunities, especially because of the uncertain discontinuities in the availability of labor. Women become confined to a range of economic activities in which such discontinuities are relatively unimportant.

Between them, these four differences from men tend to skew women's labor allocation to different sectors than men's, and to impair female mobility between sectors—the symptoms suggested earlier.

Public policies

There is a case for skewing the provision of certain public services toward women, because private substitutes tend to be skewed against them. However, public provision itself often tends to be skewed against women. In several key processes, private market and non-market access mechanisms tend to favor men over women, and these differences are reinforced by public allocation. Women of childbearing age have a markedly higher incidence of illness than men, yet a markedly lower propensity to use public health facilities. In their work on the adoption of new activities, Bevan and others (1989) found a powerful local copying effect: households imitate what others are doing. If each gender tends to follow its own role models, women have fewer opportunities to learn through imitation since the new activities are primarily the preserve of men. Yet the public extension service is usually directed mainly toward men. The propensity of parents to pay for the private secondary education of daughters appears to be substantially less than that for sons. Yet the majority of public secondary school places are allocated to boys. We will explain how to quantify the effect on the private demand for secondary school places of a marginal reallocation of public places from boys to girls. Turning from the distribution of goods and services to inputs, women work markedly longer hours than men and yet bear the primary obligation to provide common-use inputs to the household (water and fuel). This obligation can be extremely time-consuming: whether it is depends heavily on public infrastructure policies. Women, lacking autonomy and land rights, face greater difficulty in building creditworthiness reputations and in offering collateral. They are at a disadvantage in private credit markets. Yet public credit programs tend to be oriented toward men.

The generalization from these examples is that a key distinction as to service provision is between those services that are in rationed supply (generally public) and those that are cleared by the market. Secondary education, information about techniques, health care, water supplies, and credit are all partly rationed and partly provided privately. The analysis needs to identify the gender-specific determinants of access to services, both the direct determinants of rationed and nonrationed access, and the interactions between rationed and unrationed provision.

Extension services and copying of techniques

Only some farmers have access to individual extension visits, but most farmers have the chance to attend group demonstrations (which involve significant time and transport costs) and to copy their neighbors. The determinants of access to each information channel can be investigated independently and, more important, their interactions can be studied. The public information channel of extension needs to be investigated in conjunction with the private information channel—the copying of other households—which is probably more powerful. Ideally, surveys on rural households should provide both subjective and objective information on learning from the extension service and from neighbors. Subjective information can be gathered on the respondents' stated sources of the information on which changes in agricultural techniques were based. Objective data are available on contacts with the extension agents. It is also possible to use the cluster feature of samples to investigate the effects of neighbors, a cluster being a contiguous group. Hence, it is possible to use information on other households in the cluster to investigate copying of neighbors.

It is then possible to analyze whether there are gender biases in the processes of information acquisition. If there are, the biases in private and in public processes can be compared.

Health services

The location of households relative to health clinics varies so that some households will face prohibitive costs of access. Public and private clinics also coexist, with differences in user charges, time costs, and quality. With individual data on symptoms, actions (including treatment), user costs, and the duration of illness, it is possible to estimate gender-specific use of health service functions. It is also possible to investigate the determinants of child access to health care, in particular the effects of policy-dependent maternal characteristics. The immediate policy questions are:

• Are women less likely than men to make use of health services for a common level of sickness?

• If so, do policy variables such as distance to facility and the level of user charges have differential gender effects that would enable this bias against women to be offset?

• What are the interactions between health-care provision and other policies? For example, is child use of health services (girls/boys distinguished) increased more by a greater geographic density of health clinics or by a wider spread of female education?

Birth control

The burden of reproduction and child-rearing is usually measured in terms of the number of children in the household. However, it may also be a contingent liability. Households in which women of childbearing age do not have access to reliable methods of birth control face a probability distribution of the numbers and timing of future children. A potentially important contribution of birth control is that, by making these risks controllable, the household is freed from the need to guard against uncertain future liabilities. Hence, birth control, by reducing risk, can alter current investment strategies. Its effects can be immediate rather than being only long-term. For example, one such influence that has recently been investigated using African survey data has been the effect of future birth liabilities on the decision of the household to invest in the private secondary education of its current children. It was found that, controlling for the number of current children, the age of the husband, and household income, the future birth liabilities of the household powerfully reduced the willingness to invest in the education of children. Similar powerful effects may well influence other household investments, such as improved livestock, tree crops, or non-farm enterprises. These can be investigated along the same lines.

The expected future birth liabilities of the household are not directly observed in surveys but can be readily proxied by the age of the wife. It is possible to investigate this effect by using tables. Using the same technique as in Box 11.5, households can be grouped into those in which the wife is still of childbearing age and those in which the wife is above that age (in households with multiple wives, it is the age of the youngest that matters). These groups can then be further divided as in Box 11.5 by the age-group of the household head, labor endowments, and whatever else is considered to be important and feasible given the sample size. After the sample is split into groups that are comparable in respects other than childbearing, the effect of childbearing can be discerned from the different propensities to invest. More powerful techniques than tables can make the analysis more reliable and take it further.

Piped water

Some surveys have detailed information on wet and dry season water supplies. Some households have access to communal piped water, others to a private tap, and others only to traditional sources. Since piped water can have powerful consequences for both female labor supply and family health, its distribution is of some importance. While access to private piped water can be viewed as exogenous, access to communal piped water is to some extent determined by the household, although households will differ as to the time costs of access. The relative effects on use and time saved of differing piped water strategies constitute an important policy issue (use is measured in terms of both the time spent collecting water and the quantity of water consumed).

Credit

Few surveys include information on credit, and where they do, this information is usually at the household rather than the individual level. Gender issues can only be investigated through a comparison of female- and male-headed households. The information can be used to analyze the determinants of access to both private and public credit (and their interaction). Policy issues include:
  • Do female-headed households have differentially poor access to the private credit market?
  • Do they have differentially poor access to public credit?
  • What characteristics enable female-headed households to gain access to public credit, and what characteristics enable them to gain access to private credit? Are they the same, or is public credit being targeted to those shut out of the private credit market?

Education

National educational enrollment figures are usually available by gender, and these provide a starting point for the investigation of gender differences. However, they can be misleading. In contrast, household survey data can be particularly useful. Take access to primary schooling.

Data on school enrollments will typically show that boys outnumber girls but not by a wide margin. For example, in Côte d'Ivoire, about 44 percent of enrollments are girls, 56 percent boys. However, since most children go to school, these fairly small differences hide large gender differences in non-enrollment. Among those who never go to school, girls make up 66 percent and boys 34 percent. A 12 percent difference in enrollment rates hides a 32 percent difference in non-enrollment rates. Clearly, the policymaker concerned with extending educational access needs to focus on those children not going to school, and most of these are girls. The policymaker next needs to ask why these children are not going to school. A particularly important question is whether it is mainly a matter of low income, in which case the problem is part of the much wider one of poverty, or whether it is more specific. Since there are many influences on whether a child is enrolled, the tabular approach is not likely to prove useful. As with tea adoption, since the event we are analyzing is "discrete" (the child does, or does not, go to school), the appropriate technique is a logit. Box 11.7 shows how data for Côte d'Ivoire were analyzed using a logit and the results turned into a simple chart (Figure 11.2). The key result shown by the chart is that if incomes rise sufficiently, virtually all boys go to school but around a quarter of girls remain uneducated. The problem of uneducated children ends up being entirely one of gender as development proceeds. Since income was not going to solve the Ivorian problem of uneducated children, the government was probably right to make primary education compulsory (a decision made after this survey): otherwise, many girls would grow up to be uneducated mothers, which we now know has deleterious effects for their children.

Survey data can also be used to investigate the whole educational hierarchy. For example, in Côte d'Ivoire, there are also large differences in the chances of boys and girls who complete primary schooling to advance to government secondary school. Places are rationed by an examination. Appleton, Collier, and Horsnell (1990) split the problem of access into two stages: performance in the examination and being sent to school conditional upon examination performance. They found that the lower chances of girls were entirely explained by their worse performance in the examination. Knowing this, the policymaker would then need to find out why girls were

195

Box 11.7: Gender and access to primary schooling

The data: 1985 Côte d'Ivoire Living Standards Survey.

The problem: To investigate the different influences on access to primary schooling for boys and girls.

The technique: A logit analysis (see Box 11.6) was used. Because it was important to identify differences in how income affected the access of boys and girls, the sample of children was split into a sample of boys and a sample of girls and the logit estimated separately for each sample. The results are shown in the table below. Although the table contains valuable information, it is poorly presented: the coefficients cannot directly be interpreted and there is too much information for the policymaker to see what is important. Figure 11.2, however, represents part of the information in a much more useful way. It shows how the probability of non-enrollment is related to household income for each gender. It is calculated for the otherwise average child. That is, we set all other variables, such as the age of the household head, equal to the average for the sample, and vary only household income. The coefficients on household income are used (in the way described in Box 11.6) to calculate how the probability changes. As incomes rise, boys become almost certain to be sent to school. Girls from very low-income households have a 33 percent chance of not going to school. At very high income, this is reduced to about 22 percent, but beyond that it does not fall further (according to the data

it actually rises again, though the researcher can probably dismiss this as reflecting the few observations among very rich households). This tells us that income alone was not going to solve the Ivorian problem of uneducated children.

Logit estimates of determinants of enrolling in primary school for children age 11-18, by gender

Variable	Boys only Coefficient	Boys only T-ratio	Girls only Coefficient	Girls only T-ratio
Constant	-5.523	-1.464	-6.294	-1.988
Age	0.8410	1.633	0.8318	1.890
Age squared	-0.3003e-01	-1.692	-0.3113e-01	-2.056
Non-Ivorian	-1.765	-7.613	-1.005	-4.669
North	-1.314	-4.902	-1.544	-4.231
Urban	0.6507	3.264	0.3474	2.222
Mother educated	0.7456	1.194	1.659	3.105
Father educated	1.4733	4.350	1.593	1.524
Government job	15.6512	0.011	0.6835	2.673
Private job	-0.2379e-01	-0.070	0.6897	2.673
Income per capita	0.33153e-01	0.538	0.4998e-01	2.339
Squared	0.8316e-04	0.066	-0.5513e-03	-1.912
Cubed	-0.2304e-06	-0.030	-0.1626e-05	1.547
Livestock per capita	-0.6745e-02	-3.720	-0.2450e-02	-0.984

Source: Appleton, Collier, and Horsnell 1990, Table 3.5.

learning less in primary school than boys. The answer might be related to the school teaching system or it might be a problem at home. Recall from Box 11.3 that in Kenya school-age girls were spending far more time than boys contributing to household income.

Figure 11.2: Income and primary school non-enrollment

Probability of non-enrollment by gender

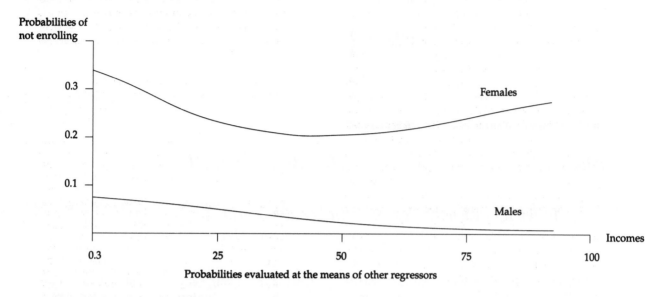

Probabilities evaluated at the means of other regressors

Ratio of girls' probability of non-enrollment to boys'

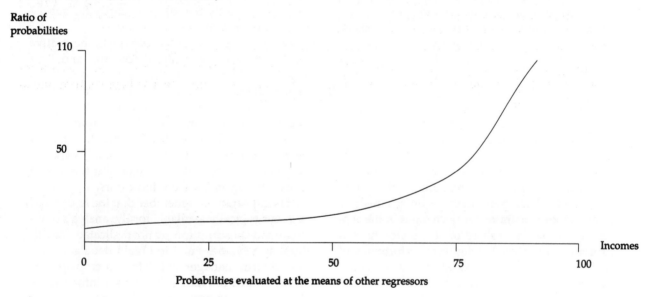

Probabilities evaluated at the means of other regressors

Source: Appleton, Collier, and Hornsnell 1990, Figure 3.1.

12

Smallholders and structural adjustment

Joseph Mullen and Richard Pearce, with Lemma Merid

In most countries in Sub-Saharan Africa, agricultural performance has, in recent years, been a source of concern to governments and to international institutions. The combination of inclement climate, fragile ecology, unstable world markets, and, in many cases, the negative effects of past policies has produced diminishing exports and escalating imports of agricultural commodities. In per capita terms, there has been an overall decline in production, and, in some instances, the proportion of marketed output has fallen.

The overwhelming majority of agricultural producers, and indeed most of the rural and total population, can be classified as smallholders, that is, peasants whose main resource is their own labor and whose plot sizes are determined by family labor constraints. Any changes in the economic and social welfare of this sector have a profound impact on the long-term performance of national economies. A special interest in smallholders is justified because they constitute the bulk of the poor in Africa and because of the potential significance of their contribution to successful adjustment through a supply response.

From a social dimensions of adjustment point of view, the broad analytical issues to be addressed in the smallholder context are unchanged relative to other groups. These issues include the effects of macro- and mesoeconomic changes on smallholders as producers, laborers, and consumers. The analysis of food consumption and nutrition and access to health care and education offered in other chapters in this book applies to smallholders, as does the poverty profile and the analysis developed in

Chapter 5 on wage employment and rural nonfarm household enterprises. However, smallholders are typically both producers and laborers, producing partly for sale and partly for subsistence consumption.

This chapter therefore focuses on (i) the relative contribution of agricultural (or crop and livestock) production activities and wage labor to household income and (ii) alterations in the allocation of time to on-farm and off-farm employment owing to labor, product, and input market changes associated with adjustment. Different responses in terms of the household's allocation of its labor resources naturally lead to differences in consumption and welfare indicators.

It is important to remember that the household surveys typically available for the analysis of income and consumption are not dedicated agricultural surveys designed to obtain detailed, year-round farm management data and crop-specific input-output (including labor use) information. They are not an appropriate source to study the agricultural supply response under adjustment. They do, however, often permit analysis of labor allocation between off-farm and aggregate on-farm employment, farm profit, the use of purchased inputs (an important predictor of agricultural productivity), and changes in assets and the subsistence ratio in response to appropriate household characteristics and mesoeconomic changes.

Macro-meso linkages

There is wide agreement today that the causes of

Africa's agricultural difficulties include inadequate price and institutional policies—the very problems structural adjustment programs seek to correct.[1] Agriculture is the main sector producing tradables in most African economies, in the form of export crops and food commodities partly for export and partly for import substitution. "Urban-biased" development policies aiming to promote industrial import substitution through trade restrictions tend to discriminate against agriculture. Indirect agricultural taxation associated with overvalued exchange rates in Africa has often been accompanied by high levels of foreign trade taxation in the form of export levies and monopsonistic, state-controlled procurement. The disincentive effects associated with these price policies have been reinforced by the low priority accorded agriculture in public investment policies, particularly in the areas of transport, appropriately scaled irrigation, and agricultural research and extension (see Krueger, Schiff and Valdés 1988).

Structural adjustment aims to depreciate the real exchange rate through reduction of import restrictions, nominal devaluation, and reduction of inflation. Devaluation and exchange unification are expected to help reduce the tax implicit in the exchange rate regime. Trade liberalization can be expected to lead to an increase in the availability of consumer or "incentive" goods. Adjustment may be considered a necessary condition to reverse the process of agricultural decline and to improve the income opportunities of smallholders. Of course, producers are negatively affected by devaluation-induced increases in the cost of imported inputs. Yet because of the low import content of their input mix, smallholders seem to benefit disproportionately from devaluation relative to larger farmers.

It is important to point out that adjustment in terms of the variables that affect the real exchange rate is far from sufficient for agricultural recovery and rural poverty alleviation. Adjustment must be accompanied by public investment in agriculture and the development of institutions capable of serving the needs of rural people in input distribution, credit, product marketing, and social services—all serving to provide an "enabling environment." These measures take time to implement. Hence a discussion of the short-run prospects of the rural poor under adjustment is also in order. It is appropriately developed with reference to rural labor markets, the degree of tradability of food crops, access to productive assets and infrastructure, market imperfections, and the factors that inhibit the adoption of high-return activities.

In the labor market, full- and part-time agricultural laborers are likely to gain in the medium to longer term as the demand for their labor (in the cultivation of tradable crops) increases. Rural labor may have a low supply elasticity in many African countries because of the relative absence of landless laborers. The real-wage effect of devaluation for rural wage earners would thus tend to be beneficial over the longer term. This is especially true where the adjustment program induces sustained agricultural growth.

In the short term, however, rural wage labor might suffer a real-wage fall. This will occur if estate production is slow to expand and/or if nominal wages rise less, in the short run, than the cost of key wage goods. The losses could be reinforced by an offsetting decline in labor demand in the nontradables sector.

In remote areas, food crops may be nontradable because of a lack of transport infrastructure or its lack of repair and maintenance following short-term fiscal retrenchment. The chronic poor in these areas who produce nontraded foods will see no change in their prices resulting from devaluation. As investments under adjustment improve the mesoeconomy in the medium to long term, remote regions will be drawn into national markets gradually. Local prices will increasingly be affected by national (and world) market conditions. As a result, nontradable foods will become more tradable in character, and the chronic poor should benefit from devaluation as producers, if they can market some surplus.

This assumes, of course, that the poor have access to land and that security of tenure remains intact. Securing the claims to ownership that poor people have over their assets is an important first step to ensuring that poorer rural groups benefit from an adjustment program (Chambers 1988, p. 3). Land rights are often tenuous, and the poor frequently have few channels for redressing their grievances. Unless policy reform is accompanied by measures ensuring the right to land of poor households, large estates growing mainly tradables and benefiting from policy reform start encroaching and hoarding land for speculative purposes. This will lead to a gradual diminution of land cultivated by the smallholder sector. So extending property rights to smallholder households, in addition to ensuring their subsistence, will raise their incentives to maintain and improve those assets. When land tenure interventions are made, care must be taken to protect the traditional rights of women to cultivate land for food. Such measures in the past have often designated men in the household as title holders, thus weakening the claims of women. The examples provided by Côte d'Ivoire, Ethiopia, Kenya, and Zimbabwe in giving women the right to inherit and own property should be emulated (World Bank 1986a, p. 40).[2]

Improving the access of poor groups to infrastructure can be as beneficial in many cases as increasing their productive assets. Infrastructure investments often bypass areas containing high concentrations of poor people. This makes their production costs relatively high, and acts as a barrier to gains from greater specialization. For example, while adjustment programs in Ghana and Kenya have sent clear signals for the expansion of tradable activities, many of the poorest farmers have faced difficulties in achieving this because of their location (Heller and others 1988, p. 20). In making new infrastructural investments, policymakers need to give more weight to actions that open access to and assist the poor. In many areas, transport infrastructure has broken down, so that some local markets are poorly integrated with the national market, leading to large regional price differences (Ahmed and Rustagi 1987, p. 109). This anomaly is further compounded by administrative restrictions on the flow of products. In designing a program of infrastructure, giving greater priority to areas ill served by transport infrastructure, but with a high concentration of poor people, could be economically and socially wise.

Another set of issues is raised when poor groups fail to benefit from adjustment because of weak price signals. In cases where this is due to weak marketing structures, the terms of trade facing poor farmers may be raised through improving the efficiency of official marketing organizations. In Asia, for example, 75 to 90 percent of the consumer price of food grains is paid to the farmer, while in Africa the proportion is only 35 to 60 percent (Ahmed and Rustagi 1987, p. 115). Nearly 30 percent of the difference in margins is attributable to the lower efficiency of African marketing organizations. In many countries, the growth of marketing costs has been as important as currency overvaluation in causing low producer prices (see Harvey 1988, p. 221, on Tanzania and Zambia, for example). Through the integration of smallholders into the mainstream, marketing reforms may now begin to benefit poor farmers. In Mali, for instance, a restructuring of the marketing system has shifted output and input prices in favor of farmers (Tuinenburg 1987, p. 503). Improvements in the efficiency of marketing organizations can reduce the conflict of interest that exists between poor food producers and poor consumers over food prices. One study found that, for a sample of African countries, reducing the marketing margin by 25 percent would result in a 49 percent increase in farm prices and a 13 percent fall in food prices, given reasonable assumptions about demand and supply elasticities (Ahmed and Rustagi 1987).

If smallholders produce nontradables, or if they make intensive use of imported intermediate inputs such as fertilizers (an unlikely event), they will be adversely affected by devaluation. The key to raising their incomes lies in creating alternative production patterns, which may require complementary policies, such as targeted extension services encouraging farmers to change crop mixes. It is possible that some smallholders fail to benefit from adjustment simply because they do not immediately switch production toward high-return activities. This may arise initially from a perception lag, as farmers may take time to observe relative price changes, and to believe that they will continue. Or the failure to change output patterns may be more deep-seated, arising from either ecological constraints or risk aversion. The participation of poor households in the most profitable cash crops is usually below average. Such participation is a strong determinant of income differences across households in most countries. In Tanzania, for example, the poorest 50 percent in the villages studied by Collier, Radwan, and Wangwe (1986, p. 75) were dependent on subsistence crops for 70 percent of their income—this is double the share for the better-off half. In Côte d'Ivoire, approximately 44 percent of the rural poor cultivate cocoa or coffee, compared with 65 percent of the rural population as a whole (Glewwe and de Tray 1987, p. 20). In Kenya, the probability of a household being poor falls if it grows tea and coffee—the main export crops (Greer and Thorbecke 1986). Although cotton is mainly grown by poor households in Côte d'Ivoire, their participation in other, more profitable, crops is lower (Glewwe and de Tray 1987, p. 14). Overall, female-headed households are less likely to cultivate cash crops because the allocation of the necessary land, credit, and inputs does not favor women. Altering the product-mix of female target groups will necessitate conscious effort and interventions in the supply of factors of production to them.

In summary, supporting cash cropping by farmers can increase their benefits from adjustment and growth. Recent studies have confirmed that export cropping can lead to significant gains (offsetting any unfavorable impacts) in smallholder income and nutrition (von Braun 1989; von Braun, Hotchkiss, and Immink 1989). Kennedy and Cogill (1989) have shown that agricultural commercialization in Kenya has had a favorable impact on landless agricultural workers, and has led to improved family nutrition and reduced hours of work for women though reductions in the food crop acreage and increases in family income. In some cases, investments in infrastructure and improvements in marketing may be adequate for target groups to raise their incomes sufficiently. In such instances, policy interventions clearly must be directed at the micro level. In other cases, a more comprehensive package of measures involving marketing and infrastructural services may be needed. Greater cash cropping may be dependent on access to productive assets being increased and on the extent to which the market infrastructure is developed to enable smallholders to change their perception.

We have identified the most likely situation to emerge from policy reform and the complementary policy measures required to safeguard the rural poor. But the extent to which these measures are likely to materialize is contingent upon political economy considerations that have not been dealt with. Where the political elite have a vested interest in the growth of the tradable-producing and estate sectors, and less of an interest in the nontradable food sector, land concentration may well emerge. The changes required in the distribution of fiscal resources and the employment creation capabilities of tradable agriculture are affected by pre-existing conditions and political economy considerations. Thus, a case can be made for policy modification or supplementation even though particular groups of smallholders are becoming better off under the policy reform. Where land is already scarce and the tendency toward concentration is high, it may be necessary to make a case for policy interventions specifically designed to stimulate employment-creating opportunities within the rural informal sector. Food and input subsidies may have to be removed gradually rather than abruptly, but will need to be much more targeted toward nontradable food producers.

Some compromise may need to be struck between the optimum economic policy and reform that takes into account political economy considerations and anti-poverty implications.

Meso-micro analysis

The foregoing discussion on the macro-meso interactions of relevance to smallholders has set the scene for the main concern of this chapter. This is to set out a plan of analysis of household data that will enhance the understanding of the effects on smallholders of mesoeconomic change.

The classification of smallholder households

The objective here is to define smallholders and to clarify how the rural population can be usefully divided into constituent sub-groups for policy purposes. In this pursuit, two interrelated criteria, based on labor use and size of holdings, are suggested. As a starting point, the sources of labor in farm production (family or hired) and the application of labor (on-farm or off-farm) are reasonable classification characteristics. Both affect the level of income, while the composition of income is influenced by on-farm/off-farm labor use decisions and crop choice.

Under circumstances of relatively inflexible factor proportions and unhindered access to land,[3] the quantity of labor available to the agricultural household will be a significant determinant of farm income. In many cases, the possibility of, and the necessity for, hiring outside labor exists, and consequently the opportunity to augment household income through hiring or selling labor. A relevant criterion in differentiating between groups of farmers could be the proportion of household labor to total labor used in production. Since smallholders are more disposed to supplement income through selling labor, rather than through labor hire, the relevant concept for defining a smallholder household is the net quantity of labor hired, that is, the hours of outside labor purchased by the household, minus the quantity of household labor sold off the farm. Taking this into account, a ratio of labor hired to labor sold could be computed. An agricultural household would have to register a value equal to, or less than, one to be included in the smallholder category.[4]

At the same time, net household labor use will largely determine the area of landholding. Thus, there will be close correlation between the net household labor and the farm size. Within the boundaries outlined here, the size of holding, together with average yield levels, typical cropping patterns, and price data, can provide a broad indicator of income. If a target farm income is hypothesized[5]—implying that all households that fail to realize this income merit concern in the form of policy assistance—then the holding size necessary to produce this income level can be calculated. The latter would provide the upper limit of the smallholder category as defined in terms of holding size.

This method of categorization is only valid for specific farming systems. Variations in the level of technology employed as well as in the agroclimatic conditions must also be taken into account if the area criterion is to be used effectively. For example, small-scale farms operating with a high degree of capital intensity may not always be usefully classified as smallholders,[6] and the minimum area necessary to provide "adequate" income may vary widely within countries because of different regional rainfall patterns and soil types. If there are regional variations in household size, holding size limits should be adjusted accordingly. Thus, although landholding size provides a promising basis for classification, the limitations alluded to here make the importance of wage labor a relatively better distinction criterion.

Alternatively, smallholders could be classified on the basis of uniform, operationally simple, unambiguous criteria, such as the composition of their income (the importance of wage relative to agricultural income) and the degree of market orientation.[7] An understanding of the extent of smallholders' dependence on the labor market for a livelihood has been sketched out here. Turning to market orientation, one should note that it can be manifested both voluntarily (by the decision to grow particular crops) and involuntarily (by a high proportion of household labor sale to make essential purchases). In any event, the proportion of income originating from farm and off-farm activities, as opposed to land size criteria, could provide a first yardstick of classification.

A useful distinction is between households that obtain the bulk (for example, more than 50 percent) of household income from off-farm activities (rural laborers), and those whose primary source of income is the family holding (smallholders proper).[8] Those falling in the latter category can be divided further into a subsistence-oriented group (subsistence farmers) and a market-oriented group. The market-oriented group grows tradable produce for export or for import substitution (export crop producers and producers of tradable food). The definition of the subsistence-oriented group is again arbitrary (for example, no tradable commodities produced; or less than 10 percent of total income derived from the sale of tradable commodities). It is worth recalling that all rural households are engaged in some form of exchange, including the sale of labor, and that there is no such phenomenon as a fully self-sufficient household.

In addition to rural households involved principally (the peasants) or marginally (the laborers) in agricultural production on the family farm, there are those who derive a large proportion of their income from non-agricultural non-wage labor activities.[9] The great majority of these are likely to be involved in mainly informal sector activities. Typically, these activities involve artisanal or trading skills, and generate production of both consumption and simple investment goods from locally produced or acquired raw materials, to meet locally expressed demands. (Blacksmiths who produce and repair the modest capital equipment essential to smallholder operations are an example.) Growth within this sector (induced by agricultural growth) is of crucial importance if adjustment measures are to stem rural-urban migration and, more broadly, if they are to activate intersectoral growth linkages.

The following classification of the smallholder population can thus be proposed (this is similar to proposals regarding the classification of the rural population made in Chapters 3 and 4):[10]

- Export crop producers
- Producers of tradable food (import substitution)
- Rural laborers
- Subsistence farmers
- Rural non-farming non-wage informal sector workers.

The aim of this classification is to gain an initial understanding of the constraints and opportunities facing various segments of the rural and smallholder population. A worksheet such as Frame 12.1 is a convenient starting point. Once the socioeconomic classification criteria are complete, analysts would start by studying class differences in incomes, expenditures, and standard of living indicators. Much can be learned from cross-tabulations and frequency distributions as well as means, standard deviations, and coefficients of variation of these "dependent" variables, such as the one suggested in Frame 12.2.

Frame 12.1: Worksheet for classification of households by major agricultural activity

| Household number | Share of income by source (percent) | | | Share of agricultural income by source (percent) | | | |
| | Wage | Agriculture | Other | Tradable products | | | Nontradable |
				Exportable	Importable	Total	
1							
2							
3							
...							
n							

Frame 12.2: Income and expenditures by household classification

| Smallholder group | Number of households | Average household (real) | | Share of food in total expenditures (percent) | Coefficient of variation | | | Share of income by source (percent) | | |
		Income	Expenditure		Income	Expenditure	Food share	Wage	Agriculture	Other
Exportable producers										
Importable producers										
Rural laborers										
Subsistence farmers										
Rural other										

Classification of products

Rural households, particularly smallholder households, will often be involved simultaneously in the production of tradables and nontradables. Nevertheless, a response eliciting a shift in emphasis between these categories is likely to occur sooner or later in the wake of adjustment. As a result, categorization of agricultural commodities into tradables and nontradables is a necessary first step in the analysis.

Theoretically, a tradable commodity is one that will be profitable to either import or export given (a) the current level of world prices, (b) the exchange rate, (c) domestic price levels, and (d) transport costs involved in internal distribution. Thus, a commodity is considered:

- Importable if $P > P^*(1 + t)$
- Exportable if $P < P^*/(1 + t)$
- Nontradable if $P^*/(1 + t) < P < P^*(1 + t)$

where P is the domestic price, P^* is its world price at the official exchange rate, and t is the transportation markup.[11]

This classification is extremely sensitive to each of the variables described. Apart from the obvious influence of transport costs, commodities may cross from one classification to the other in response to changes in world market prices (which are not under the control of national governments), and

in response to a variety of measures taken under adjustment programs, particularly movements in currency values or domestic price levels.

A further distinction can be made between protected and non-protected tradables, since following trade liberalization, the prices of imports, and therefore of import substitutes, can be expected to fall further if domestic prices were previously inflated by tariffs as well as by overvalued exchange rates. At the same time, given the importance of transport costs in these calculations, the analysis should take into account the locational disparities in classifications that may result, and the consequent differential influence that adjustment programs may have on household ability to respond to changes in the general pattern of incentives. Thus, a commodity can be an importable in regions close to a port, but become a nontradable in an interior town where domestic transport costs make imports non-viable. Those in remote areas will not have the same incentive to adapt their cropping or output pattern toward the types of commodity currently in favor elsewhere.

These circumstances can have considerable implications for the overall impact of adjustment programs. In countries where communications are very uneven, and where in consequence large numbers of rural producers remain isolated from international markets, a substantial proportion of

203

the population may not be able to take advantage of the potential benefits of adjustment. This problem is compounded if, as a result of expenditure cuts and other measures, the purchase price of both inputs and necessary household purchases rises more than proportionately in these remote areas.

A tabular presentation of the results illustrating the tradable/nontradable dichotomy, and the effect of transport costs on the classification process and the potential disadvantages faced by producers in the more remote locations, is useful. From this knowledge and using information on local cropping patterns/output patterns, a table can be constructed to illustrate the extent to which different household groups are involved in tradable or nontradable production, and the extent to which this varies by location.

It will be useful for policy purposes to note the extent to which the different groups of households are involved in producing tradable commodities. Although it is to be expected that, in general, the proportion will be higher among market-oriented producers, the extent may vary across regions, as may the proportion in each category of household. The inference to be drawn from this table is that the greater the proportion of tradable commodities in household production, the more potential benefit households will derive from the adjustment program. Of course, the information gained from a one-point survey will not take into account household responses, such as changes in cropping pattern. To have an understanding of the dynamic effects, measurement of supply response is required. Before such an endeavor, however, assessing nominal and real price differentials and levels of protection (taxation) is a necessary supplement to product classification.

Market intervention effects

In African economies, government intervention in product and factor markets has been pervasive. Direct and indirect interventions have been particularly widespread in agricultural product markets, generating significant price disparities across regions. Price disparities also arise from a lack of infrastructure. Policy reform and infrastructural development aim at unifying markets and reducing the inter- and intraregional disparities in farm-gate prices. To assess the progress made in this respect following policy reform, it will be useful to collect and monitor changes in farm-gate prices. A farm-gate price series should be constructed for different agro-climatic regions, which can then be compared with the average national producer price. Over-time divergences or narrowing of the gap between these series can serve as a measure of the extent to which markets have been unified and the extent to which macroeconomic policies have made an impact on regional economies. The interest in this exercise is in monitoring not only the absolute levels, but also relative prices and the direction of price changes resulting from policy reform. The sources of these price data are a published series and/or periodic community surveys.

Since price disparities can result from the lack of infrastructure, such price series can be used to indicate regional differences in the change of price signals. For example, any regional difference in price changes could be attributed to a change in the physical infrastructure, communications, and marketing, or to distributional arrangements associated with institutional reform. In general in Sub-Saharan Africa, costs associated with transport and distribution account for a disproportionately high part of the final price, and provide for very substantial locational disparities. Any variations in market access as a result of government expenditure policy or institutional reform will have a substantial impact on local prices—an impact that could be partly captured by monitoring changes in prices.

Thus, price data can be used in two ways: (a) to demonstrate the changes in local prices, and therefore price incentives, that have occurred following the introduction of the adjustment program; and (b) to allow for a comparison of price information across different locations and thus to study the extent to which programs designed to improve the infrastructure—or, conversely, cutbacks in government spending—have influenced regional price disparities.

Real price series should be calculated using appropriate deflators depending on the question the analyst wants to answer. Indices of consumer prices, prices of non-agricultural products, or prices of inputs can be used to reflect different aspects of the price study and to address different types of issues. In this effort, deflators reflecting rural conditions are the most appropriate. If these calculations are carried out for each commodity, an average for each household group can be estimated, weighted by the significance of each commodity in the respective production pattern. The results will give some indication of changes in local prices by household classification.

An important real price series that has long been the focal point of policy concern is the terms of trade between agricultural and non-agricultural products.

There are a number of possible measures of the terms of trade.[12] Of interest here are (a) the net barter, (b) the income, and (c) the household terms of trade. The net barter terms of trade are a ratio of two weighted price series P_a/P_m, such as prices for agricultural outputs and prices of non-agricultural products (for instance, manufactured goods). The denominator can describe a number of price series depending on the objectives of the researcher. The most commonly used are the weighted price of purchased inputs, to give the input-output terms of trade; and the weighted price of all purchased commodities to describe the full net barter terms of trade. Both measures are useful in the current context, the former to describe how price shifts have affected agricultural resource allocation and to highlight the differences in this respect between different groups of smallholders, and the latter to describe the shifts in the general price patterns facing rural households.

In calculating the numerator, however, the researcher must decide whether the weights used in averaging prices (for estimation of a price for a composite agricultural product) should refer to quantities produced or to quantities marketed. While the purchasing power of marketed output will, in reality, determine the volume of purchases, it is also likely that for some groups of smallholders, the quantities marketed will be very small and variable, being only that quantity "accidentally" surplus to household requirements. It is pertinent, therefore, to attach a market value to own consumption and include it in the calculations. Likewise, these commodities should be included in the composite index of purchased goods appearing in the denominator. If possible, terms-of-trade indices should be calculated and presented for each household category in each location. In making these calculations, it is useful to develop consumption profiles of the different household groups.

The income and household terms of trade are closely related. Conceptually, the two indices aim to introduce the quantity changes that accompany price changes. However, while the income terms of trade introduce the changes in the value of agricultural products resulting from both price and quantity changes, the household terms of trade extend the argument to include all income-generating activities in the numerator. By definition, the income terms of trade are a ratio of the index of the value of agricultural output (sales) to the index of non-agricultural prices. More formally, they are $(P_a Q_a)/P_m$. The household terms of trade, however, describe the ratio of a weighted index of all prices associated with household income, farm and wage income, and a weighted index of the prices of all expenditures. The household terms of trade provide a complete index of the net impact of price changes on household income, including imputed family labor income. Box 12.1 describes a simple method of assessing how changes in relative prices affect smallholders as both producers and consumers.

It is highly probable that regional wage differentials will be altered by adjustment programs, as areas most able to increase the supply of tradable commodities demonstrate an increase in demand for labor. While a one-point survey will not necessarily capture this, it may be possible to use other data sources to supplement the survey information and thus gain insight into the changes taking place.

The analysis of nominal prices explained here does not relay much information on the extent to which distortions, creating a wedge in domestic and international prices, have been removed. The various terms of trade measures also have similar weaknesses since they are only comparisons with domestic prices. The extent to which domestic prices have been aligned to international prices or the extent of adjustment required in the future can be captured by the calculation of crop-specific nominal rates of protection (NPC). NPC is the ratio of domestic prices to border prices minus one. More formally, and in its simplest form, NPC is computed as follows:

$$NPC = \frac{P_d}{P_d^*}$$

where P_d is the actual domestic farm-gate price and P_d^* is the international price (in domestic currency) at the farm-gate. For further details, the reader is referred to Tsakok (1990). A similar concept is the nominal rate of protection (NRP), which is simply NPC-1 (see Box 12.2).

The NPC[13] requires separate calculations using both official and shadow (or equilibrium) exchange rates—the difference between the two providing an indication of levels of implicit taxation resulting from exchange rate distortions. Similarly, the nominal rate of protection can be compared with the official tariff rate, the difference being attributable to quantitative restrictions. The interpretation of the NPC is simple. In general, NPC > 1 indicates that the product in question receives protection, and, therefore, other things being equal, its domestic production is encouraged; NPC < 1 indicates that the product is taxed and its domestic production discouraged. The extent of resource pull (or push), however, depends on the elasticities, the length of time that policy reform has been allowed to affect investment, resource reallocation, and the degree of protection afforded to inputs used in the production of the commodity. Box 12.2 describes the methodology and findings of a recently completed study on estimating NPCs (see Krueger, Schiff, and Valdés 1991).

A word of caution on the use of price indices: In many circumstances, the official prices of consumer and investment goods will have been largely irrelevant for many households, because supplies would not have been sufficient to meet demand at these prices. In many cases, local supplies may have been entirely absent and official prices meaningless. The consequent rationing of goods can distort analyses unless allowance is made for this phenomenon. This caveat is particularly relevant with regard to expenditures on non-agricultural products, agricultural inputs, and social services, supplies of which have frequently disappeared from rural areas before adjustment programs.

Box 12.1: Assessing real-income changes among poor smallholders

The effects of a structural adjustment program on smallholders' real income are complex, mainly because such groups typically earn their income from a variety of sources (see Chapter 4, Box 4.2) and spend their incomes on several products. Changes in relative prices will not only affect them as consumers, but also as producers and as wage earners in the rural labor market. To make an assessment of how a given change in relative prices is likely to change the incomes of smallholders, information is needed on their expenditure patterns and on their sources of income. Sahn and Sarris (1991) present a relatively simple method for making such an assessment. They assume that relative-price changes do not lead to quantity responses—either in production or in consumption. In this way, they estimate only the first-order (or impact) effects of relative-price changes on real incomes. Using a simple model of smallholder income determination, their approximation of real-income changes depends on the changes in relative producer and consumer prices, the patterns of expenditures, and the sources of income. To simplify the analysis, they distinguish the following producer and consumer prices:

Producer prices
- Agricultural exportables
- Tradable food staples
- Nontradable agricultural products

Consumer prices
- Tradable food staples
- Nontradable food products
- Non-agricultural products.

Estimates of real-income change are then obtained by combining changes in relative producer and consumer prices with income and expenditure shares, respectively. These are derived for poor smallholder households using household survey data (in Côte d'Ivoire, Ghana, Madagascar, Malawi, and Tanzania). Estimates of relative-price changes were derived from a variety of sources, illustrating the need for ingenuity in making such computations. For example, export prices for Côte d'Ivoire were computed as a weighted average of cocoa and coffee producer prices, with the weights, specified separately for the Forest and Savannah regions,

being given by income shares. The tradable staple food price index was a weighted average of maize and rice producer prices, while nontraded staple prices were represented by the producer prices of plantain, cassava, and yams. Similar procedures were followed for consumer price indices (weights based on expenditure shares) and for the other countries. The table below illustrates the results of the exercise for Tanzania.

Real-income effect of price changes in Tanzania

Year	P_x / P_f	P_x / P_n	Y
1980	120.0	87.0	154.1
1981	94.9	98.0	134.1
1982	93.9	97.8	134.1
1983	101.6	100.7	147.4
1984	78.6	85.8	133.9
1985	88.9	88.9	118.5
1986	100.0	100.0	100.0
1987	105.2	107.0	111.1
1988	116.8	120.7	91.6

P_x = export producer price.
P_f = tradable staple food producer price.
P_n = agricultural nontradables producer price.
Y = index of real income.
Indices are set equal to 100 in year of first World Bank structural adjustment loan.
Source: Sahn and Sarris 1991, Tables 4 and 6.

Interpreting these data involves two basic steps. First, the relative-price series must be understood in terms of policy interventions. So, although the formal structural adjustment program was not initiated until 1986, the relative-price series suggests that adjustment can be traced to 1984. Later, the tendency for the relative producer price of agricultural exportables to fall is clearly reversed. This suggests that the pre- and post-1984 periods should be distinguished in macro-meso analysis.

Second, how have these mesoeconomic relative-price changes influenced the real incomes of the poor—in this case, poor smallholders? Tanzanian smallholders derive their incomes mainly from traded and (especially) nontraded

Price analysis in its various forms, whether it includes official as well as parallel markets, is very partial and static in approach. To be of value for prescriptive purposes, it should be supplemented by elasticity estimates and should proceed from examining individual products to understanding the effect of policy on the enterprise—the smallholder household. The next section aims to incorporate the discussion regarding prices into household modeling.

Household models

The methods of analysis and presentation de-

food. Together, these provide 96 percent of poor smallholders' agricultural income (or 70 percent of their overall income). It is not surprising that the increase in the relative price of agricultural exportables after 1984 is associated with a deterioration in poor smallholders' real incomes. For food-producing smallholders in Tanzania, the relative-price signals produced through adjustment were generally unfavorable. The liberalization of the maize market, which led to a threefold increase in the price after 1984, did not benefit the smallholders. Although they derive 45 percent of their income from tradable food production, they are typically net purchasers of maize. So the maize price hike reduced their incomes during the second half of the 1980s. And these farmers did not benefit from the increase in exportables prices.

The key point about this simple method of analysis is that the real-income effects of relative-price changes are derived through the income and expenditure patterns of the target group selected. The use of some overall price index (like the CPI) would not yield useful results, because the expenditure weights used in calculating it may not reflect the expenditure behavior of the group.

These results tend to overstate income losses from producer price decreases and consumer price increases because they do not allow for production and consumption responses to relative-price changes. If poor smallholders could switch production into exportables (or reduce consumption of maize), their income losses would be less than those indicated. But the method has the advantages of being economical with data and relatively simple. The real-income estimates derived from the analysis give the first-order effects of relative-price changes on smallholders as producers and consumers. It would be possible to produce "counterfactual" relative-price time series (based perhaps on a more rigorous devaluation policy), and so generate counterfactual real-income series. The analysis illustrates the gains that can be obtained from aggregating commodities into meaningful groups for analytical purposes—in this case, agricultural exportables, tradable food staples, nontradable agricultural products, and nonagricultural goods.

scribed so far are useful for ex post description of a given incentive structure. Beyond this, however, it is often of interest to make predictions concerning household responses to policy changes. Given a household income and expenditure survey and some farm management and time-series data, it is possible to predict the future impact of adjustment programs on household incomes and production.

The analytical approach most appropriate in these circumstances is to model household activity. Household models account for the interrelationships of production, consumption, and labor use. The use of agricultural household models is well documented,[15] and there are a variety of examples for researchers to draw upon. This literature and the exposition of household models in previous chapters make it unnecesary to present a technical dicussion on these models here. However, it is useful to review the main strengths and limitations of agricultural household models in assessing the effects of policy reform.

The principal advantage of modeling is that it allows predictions to be made on the responses of the endogenous variables of policy interest to changes in the parameters, that is, in the policy variables such as output price or access to resources. An agricultural household model could therefore be used to predict:

• Changes in the economic well-being of households, as measured by the likely impact of policy shifts on consumption, profits, and leisure. For example, the response to a shift in output price consequent to depreciation of the exchange rate can be captured, and the implications for household resource use and consumption levels estimated.

• The implications for factor markets. For example, the consequences for labor demand and, therefore, wages can be predicted through estimating labor demand and supply elasticities.

• The consequences for rural input and output markets. For example, demand equations can be estimated for locally produced goods and services.

• The macroeconomic implications of policy changes, which can be estimated through aggregation of household responses. For example, the consequences for the foreign exchange position of an increase in the marketed surplus of an otherwise imported staple food can be assessed.

The main difficulty of modeling lies in specifying the model so that it properly reflects the country-specific circumstances under which smallholder households operate. As discussed earlier, government restrictions in factor and product markets affect the prices faced by economic decisionmakers to condition production and consumption behavior. For example, in the definition of a model, allowance has to be made for the role of state marketing agencies and quantity rationing, which have been a common phenomenon in many Sub-Saharan African countries in the recent past. In such cases, the ration level enters the model, together with the exogenously determined prices, and becomes an important policy instrument. Similarly, the frequently used assumption of perfect substitution between family and hired labor may not be tenable in countries where the labor market functions with many restrictions.

Input prices paid by smallholder households are often subsidized, and removal of these subsidies may be an important component of policy reform. Even if farmers are willing to pay higher

---

Box 12.2: Estimating direct and indirect effects of price intervention on smallholder agriculture

The problem: Changes in relative prices during periods of destabilization and policy reform are certain to influence the real incomes of smallholders, both as producers and as consumers. Box 12.1 illustrated how these effects can be assessed using a relatively simple methodology. However, this analysis reveals little about the extent to which price changes are the result of policy reform or of other factors (such as weather or world market price changes). Krueger, Schiff, and Valdés (1991) have suggested a methodology to isolate the effects of government policy interventions on agricultural prices and on value added in agricultural production. This method has been applied to several developing countries, including African countries. It may be used to assess how far policy reforms change smallholder producer prices and value added.

The method: The approach distinguishes the *direct* from the *indirect* effects of government policies. The former are the result of price interventions by the government that directly affect the producer price of the commodity concerned: this may be due to a tariff or an import restriction on an importable, an export tax or subsidy on an exportable, or simply price setting by a state marketing board. To assess the direct effects of government intervention, the analyst must compare the actual producer price with the price that would obtain in the absence of these direct interventions. This nonintervention price is calculated as the border price (the world price of the commodity valued at the official or actual nominal exchange rate) less transportation, processing, and marketing costs. This yields an estimate of the *border-equivalent producer price.* This is then compared with the actual producer price to obtain the *nominal rate of protection* (NRP) directly arising from price policy interventions for that commodity:

$$NRP = (\text{actual producer price/border-equivalent producer price}) - 1$$

The *indirect* effects of government policy arise from trade and exchange rate policies that distort the nominal exchange rate. For example, if import controls, tariffs, or export subsidies are imposed, the exchange rate would be *overvalued* compared with its free-trade value. The nominal exchange rate (E_0—defined as the foreign exchange price of the domestic currency) would be lower than the free-trade exchange rate (E^*). This overvaluation would, other things being equal, reduce producer prices of exportables and importables not benefiting from the trade restrictions.

Calculating the indirect effect of trade policy on agricultural prices therefore calls for an estimate of the overvaluation of the exchange rate relative to its free-trade value. This in itself is a major undertaking, involving assumptions about import and export price elasticities. The reader is referred to Kreuger, Schiff, and Valdés (1991) for further details. Given this estimate, the analyst can then assess the extent to which smallholder producer prices are indirectly penalized by trade and exchange rate policy. The method involves calculating what the producer price would be with no exchange rate overvaluation: this is simply the actual producer price times the ratio E^*/E_0. Actual producer prices are then compared with these adjusted producer prices to yield nominal rates of protection arising indirectly from the exchange rate distortion.

To calculate the total (direct and indirect) effects of policy interventions, actual producer prices are compared with border prices *valued at E^**, and suitably adjusted for transportation and marketing costs. The difference between the actual producer price and the border-equivalent producer price valued at E^* is then due to both the direct effect of price policy and the indirect effect of trade policy.

The results and their interpretation: This method of estimating the direct and indirect effects of government policy on agricultural prices was applied to Ghana (Stryker 1991) and Zambia (Jansen 1991). The data reported here do not cover periods of adjustment (which occurred mostly in the second half of the 1980s). Rather, they reflect policies associated with macroeconomic destabilization.

The table in this box summarizes how policy interventions directly and indirectly influenced the prices of two major commodities in each of the two countries from the mid-1960s to the mid-1980s. The second and fourth columns of the table show how government price policy has directly changed producer prices over time. In Ghana, producer prices of the commodities reflect the price-setting policies of the marketing boards concerned. Cocoa prices have been set below world market levels (valued at actual exchange rates), hence the negative signs on the nominal rates of protection. This effect has diminished over time. The producer price of maize, on the other hand, was generally set above world levels (again valued at E_0), thus giving maize producers positive nominal rates of protection. In the Zambian case, government price policy has tended to raise the producer price of Virginia tobacco,

prices, the amount of inputs that they can use is often determined exogenously. Under such conditions, the amount of fertilizer a farmer can use is no longer a choice variable, and instead becomes an exogenous variable in reduced-form equations in the model.

In general, in cases where the functioning of markets for factors and products is restricted and prices at which resources are transacted are not market-clearing, it would be desirable to use virtual (or shadow) prices. These prices should be estimated such that they induce the same impact as the ration but without the ration itself.

Finally, in many African countries, the smallholder sector operates in parallel with large-scale estate agriculture, the latter using modern technology and largely producing traded goods. The two sectors can be interdependent and/or

but to reduce the prices farmers receive for maize below border prices.

These estimates of the direct effects can be misleading, since they ignore the indirect effects of trade and exchange rate policy. The first column of the table shows the extent to which the actual nominal exchange rate was overvalued compared with its free-trade rate. In Ghana, the degree of overvaluation increased significantly during 1973-83, but has been corrected to some extent since. In Zambia, overvaluation has continued to increase throughout the period covered.

Given the overvaluation of the nominal exchange rates in both countries, the indirect effects of trade policy are certain to reduce producer prices below what they would have been under a free-trade policy regime. Combining the direct effects of price policy with the indirect effects of the overvalued exchange rate yields estimates of the total effect of government interventions on producer prices. This is reported in the third and fifth columns of the table. In some cases—cocoa in Ghana and maize in Zambia—the negative indirect effects of overval-

ued exchange rates reinforced the negative protection resulting directly from price policy. However, in the case of maize in Ghana and Virginia tobacco in Zambia, the direct effects are misleadingly positive, since negative nominal rates of protection are recorded once the effect of the overvalued exchange rates is taken into account. Virginia tobacco is included here to illustrate how negative indirect effects of trade policy can overwhelm positive direct effects. In fact, Virginia tobacco is grown mainly by large commerial farmers, and not generally by smallholders.

To assess the direct and indirect effects of policy interventions on *value added* in an activity, these calculations must be done for both the output price of the commodity concerned and the input prices. In this way, an estimate can be obtained of the *effective* rate of protection for the activity. See Krueger, Schiff, and Valdés (1991) for details of the method and its application.

Direct and indirect effects of government policy on selected agricultural commodities

		Nominal rates of protection (percent)			
	Nominal exchange rate adjustment [a] (E^*/E_o)	Direct effect [b]	Direct and indirect effects [c]	Direct effect [b]	Direct and indirect effects [c]
Ghana averages [d]		Cocoa		Maize	
1967-72	1.45	-54.0	-24.0	67.0	-7.0
1973-83	6.72	-48.0	-42.0	256.0	12.0
1984-85	2.71	-19.0	-59.0	177.0	-31.0
Zambia averages		Virginia tobacco		Maize	
1966-84	2.03	9.1	-26.0	-23.3	-48.0
1966-75	1.15	8.6	-7.3	-25.7	-36.3
1976-84	3.00	9.6	-46.9	-20.7	-61.0
1980-84	3.67	-	-49.7	-21.3 [e]	-65.9

a. Free-trade equilibrium nominal exchange rate (E^*) divided by actual nominal rate (E_o).

b. Nominal rate of protection: (producer price/border price) – 1. Calculated using official exchange rate (E_o).

c. Nominal rate of protection: [(producer price/Pna)/(border price x $E^*/P'na$)] – 1, where Pna is the GDP deflator (excluding mining and agriculture), and $P'na$ is the same deflator adjusted for the effects of the exchange rate overvaluation on the tradables component. Calculated using the free-trade equilibrium exchange rate (E^*).

d. Some years were excluded from the averages reported here because border prices at farm-gate equivalents were negative.

e. 1980-85.

Source: Ghana: Stryker 1991; Zambia: Jansen 1991.

competitive in factor and product markets. Since policy measures directed toward the estate sector affect the operations of the smallholder sector, it is necessary to study the two sectors concurrently.

Policy perspective

In reviewing the policy implications of adjustment programs, it is important for researchers to keep in mind the broad context in which the responses to policy reforms are taking place. Given the often radical nature of the programs, and the likelihood that they carry potential implications for almost all aspects of the social and economic life of many rural households, it is important that attention not be unduly focused on a minority of variables, resulting in only a partial view.

The first set of policy implications to be drawn stems from the ramifications of adjustment programs for households' capacity to generate income. The extent to which access to assets, inputs, and employment opportunities is influenced by policy changes will ultimately be a key determinant of success or failure, and therefore provide guidance to future policy. Thus, changes in access to credit facilities, the availability of and access to land, and developments regarding rural employment opportunities need to be monitored and appropriate policies initiated.

The second focus of attention is on the implications of policy changes for farm profit. The outcomes in this respect may vary considerably among the different smallholder categories, depending on (a) the extent to which the household is engaged in the production of tradable and non-tradable products, (b) the existence or absence of competition in export and domestic markets (the latter applying to import-substituting products), (c) output price adjustments and the ability to switch to more remunerative products, (d) use of non-labor purchased inputs, and (e) the extent to which the price of purchased inputs has been affected by subsidy removal and other policy reforms. It is possible that a locational dichotomy emerges, between regions where tradable production, particularly of exports, is feasible and regions suitable only for production of non-tradables or non-protected imports. It is equally possible that a proportion of households may be bypassed by policy reform.

A more complete indication of the impact of adjustment programs is provided by an assessment of modifications in household expenditure behavior. To this effect, indicators combining information on income generation with data on consumer prices and expenditure profiles provide a comprehensive means of evaluating the impact of the programs on various household categories. An essential part of any evaluation must include an estimate of the implications of the program for access to economic and social infrastructure. Easy and affordable access to markets and social services, such as education and health facilities, constitute an essential component of household income.

When interpreting the results of field surveys, researchers are encouraged to take into account the social and economic context that shapes household welfare. Concentration on the more easily quantifiable indicators to the exclusion of others may result in misleading conclusions. The notion of household income must be interpreted in its broadest sense if the full consequences of adjustment policy reforms are to be understood.

Notes

1. This section is based on a companion volume, World Bank (1991b, pp. 159-68).

2. Land reforms have not in general been associated with adjustment lending because their time frame has usually been longer than the adjustment program. An exception is their incorporation in structural adjustment loan agreements with Kenya, with the intention of giving land rights to squatters.

3. Although there are pockets of land scarcity in Sub-Saharan Africa, the major constraint to production is not access to land, but the availability of labor at the peak of the farming cycle. Any useful definition of the smallholder population must take into account this constraint to household income.

4. The danger in this definition, however, is that the labor needs of some groups of very poor households may be ignored. Such is the case where the household head is a woman and land preparation involves a substantial amount of heavy work that she is unable to undertake. Analysts should be aware of this possibility.

5. A target income would be based on the estimated value of an essential household consumption profile. Analysts should use their knowledge of local conditions and assumptions regarding per capita calorie and nutrient requirements (coupled with average family size data observed in household surveys) in deriving such an estimate.

6. Thus, a farmer operating a small area and employing little non-household labor, but at the same time using methods involving a high degree of mechanization and/or the

extensive use of purchased chemical inputs, is unlikely to be among the rural poor. (Data on farm equipment and purchased inputs are available from budget and expenditure surveys or farm management surveys.)

7. As is evident, the smallholder concept is at times rather loosely applied. In some sections, the discussion encompasses the rural sector at large, including farmers, laborers, livestock raisers, and non-farming, non-wage, rural, and informal labor under the general rubric of smallholder. Thus, the smallholder discussion should be put in a much broader context as and when necessary.

8. Livestock plays an integral part in the smallholder economy and is, in some areas, the principal focus of production. While pastoralists cannot be defined as smallholders in the conventional sense, they are frequently among the poorest of rural populations and possess many of the same broad characteristics with respect to their exiguous and fragile resource base and low levels of consumption. Local researchers must judge whether pastoralists should be treated as a separate group or subsumed under one or more of the other categories.

9. It is likely that the majority of rural households would meet the income criterion for inclusion among the rural poor. Nevertheless, there will be a minority of households—professionals, government employees, and those involved in large distribution and marketing activities—with which the analysis will not be concerned.

10. The list is tentative, and researchers may wish to extend or reduce the number of groups involved. It may be pertinent in some countries to create a sub-category of smallholders according to ethnic origin, especially when particular ethnic groups have restricted access to land.

11. It could represent import tariff or export subsidy (if $t > 0$) or export tax or import subsidy (if $t < 0$).

12. For a useful empirical review of appropriate techniques for calculating terms of trade, researchers are referred to FAO (1986).

13. Two articles that illustrate well both the usefulness and the potential pitfalls of NPCs are Westlake (1987) and Jaeger and Humphreys (1988).

14. The recent development in the concept and its empirical applications in many developing countries, including Ghana and Zambia in Sub-Saharan Africa, can be found in Krueger, Schiff, and Valdés (1991).

15. For a detailed outline of a basic agricultural household model and examples of the use of these models in practice, the researcher is referred to Singh, Squire, and Strauss (1986a). An early version of such models can be found in Barnum and Squire (1979a and 1979b). For a review of recent agricultural household models, see Singh, Squire, and Strauss (1986b).

Bibliography

Abumere, S. 1981. "Population Distribution Policies and Measures in Africa South of the Sahara." *Population and Development Review* 7:421-34.

Acsadi, G., and G. Johnson-Acsadi. 1990. "Effects of Timing of Marriage on Reproductive Health." In G. Acsadi, G. Johnson-Acsadi, and R. Bulatao, eds., *Population Growth and Reproduction in Sub-Saharan Africa*. Washington, D.C.: World Bank.

Addison, T. 1987. "Employment Policy and Economic Adjustment in The Gambia." Report for an ILO Preparatory Assistance Mission. ILO, Geneva (March).

Addison, T., and L. Demery. 1985. "Macro-Economic Stabilization, Income Distribution and Poverty: A Preliminary Survey." Overseas Development Institute, London.

Adelman, I., and S. Robinson. 1988. "Macroeconomic Adjustment and Income Distribution: Alternative Models Applied to Two Economies." *Journal of Development Economics* 29(1):23-44.

Adepoju, A. 1982. "Population Redistribution: A Review of Governmental Policies." In J. Clarke and L. Kosinski, eds., *Redistribution of Population in Africa*. London: Heinemann Press.

Ahmed, R., and N. Rustagi. 1987. "Marketing and Price Incentives in African and Asian Countries: A Comparison." In D. Elz, ed., *Agricultural Marketing Strategy and Pricing Policy*. Washington, D.C.: World Bank.

Ainsworth, M. 1989. *Socioeconomic Determinants of Fertility in Côte d'Ivoire*. Living Standards Measurement Study Working Paper 53. Washington, D.C.: World Bank.

Alderman, Harold. 1987. "Cooperative Dairy Development in Karnataka, India: An Assessment." International Food Policy Research Institute, Washington, D.C.

———. 1990. *Nutritional Status in Ghana and Its Determinants*. Social Dimensions of Adjustment in Sub-Saharan Africa Working Paper 3. Washington, D.C.: World Bank.

Alessie, R., P. Baker, R. Blundell, C. Heady, and C. Meghir. 1989. "The Working Behaviour of Young People in Rural Côte d'Ivoire: Evidence from the LSMS Panel." University College, London.

Appleton, S., P. Collier, and P.H. Horsnell. 1990. *Gender, Education, and Employment in Côte d'Ivoire*. Social Dimensions of Adjustment in Sub-Saharan Africa Working Paper 8. Washington, D.C.: World Bank.

Arida, P., and L. Taylor. 1989. "Short-Run Macroeconomics." In H. Chenery and T. Srinivasan, eds., *Handbook of Development Economics*. Vol. 2. Amsterdam: North-Holland.

Atkinson, A.B. 1987. "On the Measurement of Poverty." *Econometrica* 55:749-64.

Azam, J-P., and others. 1989. "The Impact of Macroeconomic Policies on the Rural Poor." UNDP Policy Discussion Paper. UNDP, New York.

Baker, R., and J. Nelder. 1978. *The GLIM System: Release 3. Generalized Linear Interactive Modelling*. Numerical Algorithms Group. Oxford: Royal Statistical Society.

Bardhan, P.K. 1984. *Land, Labor, and Rural Poverty*. New York: Columbia University Press.

Barnum, Howard N., and Lyn Squire. 1979a. "An Econometric Application of the Theory of Farm-Household." *Journal of Development Economics* 6(1):79-102.

——. 1979b. *A Model of an Agricultural Household: Theory and Evidence.* World Bank Staff Occasional Paper 27. Baltimore: Johns Hopkins University Press.

Barrera, A. 1990. "The Role of Maternal Schooling and Its Interactions with Public Health Programs in Child Health Production." *Journal of Development Economics* 32:69-92.

Becker, C., and A. Morrison. 1988. "The Determinants of Urban Population Growth in Sub-Saharan Africa." *Economic Development and Cultural Change* 36(2):259-78.

Becker, G. 1965. "A Theory of the Allocation of Time." *Economic Journal* 75:493-517.

Behrman, Jere R. 1988a. "The Impact of Economic Adjustment Programs on Health and Nutrition in Developing Countries." In David E. Bell and Michael R. Riech, eds., *Health, Nutrition and Economic Crises: Approaches to Policy in the Third World.* Dover, Mass.: Auburn House.

——. 1988b. "Intrahousehold Allocation of Nutrients and Gender Effects." In Siddig R. Osmani, ed., *Nutrition and Poverty.* Oxford: Oxford University Press.

——. 1988c. "Intrahousehold Allocation of Nutrients in Rural India: Are Boys Favored? Do Parents Exhibit Inequality Aversion?" *Oxford Economic Papers.*

——. 1990. *The Action of Human Resources and Poverty on One Another: What We Have Yet to Learn.* Living Standards Measurement Study Working Paper 4. Washington, D.C.: World Bank.

Behrman, Jere R., and Nancy Birdsall. 1983. "The Quality of Schooling: The Standard Focus on Quantity Alone Is Misleading." *American Economic Review* 73(December):928-46.

Behrman, Jere R., and Anil Deolalikar. 1987. "Will Developing Country Nutrition Improve with Income? A Case Study for Rural South India." *Journal of Political Economy* 95:108-38.

——. 1988a. "Health and Nutrition." In Hollis B. Chenery and T.N. Srinivasan, eds., *Handbook of Development Economics.* Vol. 1. Amsterdam: North-Holland.

——. 1988b. "Impact of Macro Economic Adjustment on the Poor and on Social Sectors in Jamaica." University of Pennsylvania, Philadelphia. (Prepared for World Bank, Operations Evaluation Department, Washington, D.C.)

——. 1988c. "Unobserved Household and Community Heterogeneity and the Labor Market Impact of Schooling: A Case Study for Indonesia." University of Pennsylvania, Philadelphia.

——. 1989a. "School Repetition, Dropouts and the Returns to Schooling: The Case of Indonesia." University of Pennsylvania, Philadelphia.

——. 1989b. "Wages and Labor Supply in Rural India: The Role of Health, Nutrition and Seasonality." In D. Sahn, ed., *Causes and Implications of Seasonal Variability in Household Food Security.* Baltimore: Johns Hopkins University Press.

——. 1990. "Health, Nutrition and Macroeconomic Adjustment with a Human Face: The Analytical Basis for the UNICEF Advocacy and a Case Comparison." In John Caldwell, ed., *Cultural, Social and Behavioral Determinants of Health: What Is the Evidence?* Canberra, Australia: Australian National University.

Behrman, Jere R., A. Deolalikar, and B. Wolfe. 1988. "Nutrients: Impacts and Determinants." *World Bank Economic Review* 2.

Behrman, Jere, and V. Lavy. 1991. "Child Health and Schooling Achievement: Association or Causality?" World Bank, Population and Human Resources Department, Washington, D.C.

Behrman, Jere R., and Chalongphob Sussangkarn. 1989. "Parental Schooling and Child Outcomes: Mother Versus Father, Schooling Quality, and Interactions." University of Pennsylvania, Philadelphia.

Behrman, Jere R., and Barbara L. Wolfe. 1984a. "More Evidence on Nutrition Demand: Income Seems Overrated and Women's Schooling Underemphasized." *Journal of Development Economics* 14.

——. 1984b. "The Socioeconomic Impact of Schooling in a Developing Country." *Review of Economics and Statistics* 66(2):296-303.

Ben-Akiva, M., and S. Lerman. 1985. *Discrete Choice Analysis: Theory and Applications to Predict Travel Demand.* Cambridge, Mass.: MIT Press.

Benjamin, Dwayne. 1988. "Household Composition and Labor Demand: A Test of Rural Labor Market Efficiency." Research Program in Development Studies, Discussion Paper 140. Woodrow Wilson School, Princeton University, Princeton, N.J. (November).

Berthélemy, J.C., and F. Gagey. 1987. "The Agricultural Supply Price Elasticity in Africa, A Note on Peasants' Rationality in Non-Walrasian

Context." *European Economics Review* 31(8).

Besley, T.J, and S.M.R. Kanbur. 1988. "Food Subsidies and Poverty Alleviation." *Economic Journal* 98.

Bevan, D.L., A. Bingsten, and P. Collier. 1987. "Peasant Supply Response in Rationed Economies." *World Development* 45(4).

Bevan, D., P. Collier, and J. Gunning, with A. Bigsten and P. Horsnell. 1989. *Peasants and Governments*. Oxford: Oxford University Press.

Binswanger, H. 1989. "How Agricultural Producers Respond to Prices and Government Investments." Paper presented at the First Annual World Bank Conference on Development Economics, April 27-28, Washington, D.C.

Birdsall, Nancy. 1980. "A Cost of Siblings: Child Schooling in Urban Colombia." *Research in Population Economics* 2:115-50.

———. 1985. "Public Inputs and Child Schooling in Brazil." *Journal of Development Economics* 18(1):67-86.

———. 1988. "Economic Approaches to Population Growth." In H. Chenery and T.N. Srinivasan, eds., *Handbook of Development Economics*. Amsterdam: North-Holland.

Birdsall, Nancy, and Jere R. Behrman. 1984. "Does Geographical Aggregation Cause Overestimates of the Returns to Schooling?" *Oxford Bulletin of Economics and Statistics* 46:55-72.

Blaug, M. 1974. "An Economic Analysis of Personal Earnings in Thailand." *Economic Development and Cultural Change* 23.

Blundell, R. 1988. "Consumer Behaviour: Theory and Empirical Evidence—A Survey." *Economic Journal* 98.

Blundell, R., and I. Walker. 1982. "Modelling the Joint Determination of Household Labour Supplies and Commodity Demands." *Economic Journal* 92:351-64.

Boateng, E.O., K. Ewusi, R. Kanbur, and A. McKay. 1990. *A Poverty Profile for Ghana, 1987-88*. Social Dimensions of Adjustment in Sub-Saharan Africa Working Paper 5. Washington, D.C.: World Bank.

Bongaarts, J., O. Frank, and R. Lesthaeghe. 1990. "The Proximate Determinants of Fertility." In G. Acsadi, G. Johnson-Acsadi, and R. Bulatao, eds., *Population Growth and Reproduction in Sub-Saharan Africa*. Washington, D.C.: World Bank.

Bongaarts, J., and S. Greenhalgh. 1985. "An Alternative to the One-Child Policy in China." *Population and Development Review* 11(4):585-618.

Boissiere, M., J.B. Knight, and R.H. Sabot. 1985. "Earnings, Schooling, Ability and Cognitive Skills." *American Economic Review* 75:1016-30.

Bond, M. 1983. "Agricultural Responses to Prices in Sub-Saharan African Countries." *IMF Staff Papers* 30.

Bouis, H.E., and L.J. Haddad. 1988. "Comparing Calorie-Income Elasticities Using Calories Derived from Reported Food Purchases and a Twenty-four Hour Recall of Food Intakes: An Application Using Philippine Data." Development Economics Research Centre Discussion Paper 88, University of Warwick, Warwick.

Bourguignon, Francois, William Branson, and Jaime de Melo. Forthcoming. "Adjustment and Income Distribution: A Micro-Macro Model for Simulation Analysis." *Journal of Development Economics*.

Bourguignon, Francois, Jaime de Melo, and Christian Morrisson. 1991. "Poverty and Income Distribution during Adjustment: Issues and Evidence from the OECD Project." *World Development* 19.

Bourguignon, Francois, Jaime de Melo, and Akiko Suwa. 1991. "Distributional Effects of Adjustment Policies: Simulations for Archetype Economies in Africa and Latin America." *World Bank Economic Review* 5(2):339-66.

Boyd, Derek. 1988. "The Impact of Adjustment Policies on Vulnerable Groups: The Case of Jamaica, 1973-1985." In G.A. Cornia, R. Jolly, and F. Stewart, eds., *Adjustment with a Human Face*. Oxford: Clarendon Press.

Bruno, M. 1972. "Domestic Resource Costs and Effective Protection: Clarification and Synthesis." *Journal of Political Economy* 80.

Cain, M. 1983. "Fertility as an Adjustment to Risk." *Population and Development Review* 9:688-702.

Caldwell, J., and P. Caldwell. 1987. "The Cultural Context of High Fertility in Sub-Saharan Africa." *Population and Development Review* 13(3):409-38.

Chadeau, A., and C. Roy. 1986. "Relating Households' Final Consumption to Household Activities: Substitutability or Complementarity between Market and Non-Market Production." *Review of Income and Wealth*, Series 32:387-407.

Chambers, R. 1988. "Sustainable Rural Livelihoods: A Key Strategy for People, Environment and Development." In C. Conroy and M. Litvinoff, eds., *The Greening of Aid: Sustainable Livelihoods in Practice*. London: Earthscan, in association with the International Institute for Environment and Development.

Chambers, R., R. Longhurst, and A. Pacey, eds. 1981. *Seasonal Dimensions to Rural Poverty*. London: Francis Pinter.

Chen, S., G. Datt, and M. Ravallion. 1991. "POVCAL: A Program for Calculating Poverty Measures from Grouped Data." World Bank, Poverty Analysis and Policy Design Division, Washington, D.C.

Chenery, H.B., M.S. Ahluwalia, C.L.G. Bell, J.H. Duloy, and R. Jolly. 1974. *Redistribution with Growth*. Oxford: Oxford University Press.

Chiswick, C.U. 1976. "On Estimating Earnings Functions for LDCs." *Journal of Development Economics* 3:67-78.

———. 1983. "Analysis of Earnings from Household Enterprises: Methodology and Application to Thailand." *Review of Economics and Statistics* 65:658-62.

Chow, G. 1960. "Test of Equality between Sets of Coefficients in Two Linear Regressions." *Econometrica* 28(3).

Cochrane, S. 1979. *Fertility and Education: What Do We Really Know?* World Bank Staff Occasional Paper 26. Washington, D.C.

Cochrane, S., F. Sai, and J. Nassim. 1990. "The Development of Population and Family Planning Policies." In G. Acsadi, G. Johnson-Acsadi, and R. Bulatao, eds., *Population Growth and Reproduction in Sub-Saharan Africa*. Washington, D.C.: World Bank.

Collier, Paul. 1988a. *Macro-economic Policy, Employment and Living Standards in Malawi and Tanzania, 1973-84*. ILO World Employment Programme Research, International Employment Policies, Working Paper 18 (WP2-46/WP.18).

———. 1988b. "Women in Development: Defining the Issues." Policy Research Working Paper 129. World Bank, Washington, D.C.

———. 1989. "Contractual Constraints on Labor Exchange in Rural Kenya." *International Labour Review* 128(6).

———. Forthcoming. "Women and Structural Adjustment." World Bank, Economic Development Institute, Washington, D.C.

Collier, P., and D. Lal. 1986. *Labour and Poverty in Kenya, 1900-1980*. Oxford: Clarendon Press.

Collier, P., S. Radwan, and S. Wangwe. 1986. *Labour and Poverty in Rural Tanzania*. Oxford: Oxford University Press.

Corbo, V., S. Fischer, and S.B. Webb, eds. 1992. *Adjustment Lending Revisited: Policies to Restore Growth*. Washington, D.C.: World Bank.

Cornia, G.A., R. Jolly, and F. Stewart, eds. 1987. *Adjustment with a Human Face*. Vol. 1, *Protecting the Vulnerable and Promoting Growth*. Oxford: Clarendon Press for UNICEF.

Cornia, G.A., and F. Stewart. 1987. "Country Experience with Adjustment." In Cornia, Jolly, and Stewart (1987).

Cornia, G.A., R. van der Hoeven, and T. Mkandawire. 1992. *Africa's Recovery in the 1990s: From Stagnation and Adjustment to Human Development*. A UNICEF Study. New York: St. Martin's Press.

Dankelman, I., and J. Davidson. 1988. *Women and Environment in the Third World: Alliance for the Future*. London: Earthscan.

Dasgupta, P., and D. Ray. 1986. "Inequality as a Determinant of Malnutrition and Unemployment: Theory." *Economic Journal* 96:1011-34.

Deaton, A. 1987a. *The Allocation of Goods within the Household: Adults, Children, and Gender*. Living Standards Measurement Study Working Paper 39. Washington, D.C.: World Bank.

———. 1987b. "Estimation of Own- and Cross-Price Elasticity from Household Survey Data." *Journal of Econometrics* 36.

———. 1988. "Quality, Quantity and Spatial Variation of Prices." *American Economic Review* 78.

Deaton, A., and D. Benjamin. 1988. *The Living Standards Survey and Price Policy Reform: A Study of Cocoa and Coffee Production in Côte d'Ivoire*. Living Standards Measurement Study Working Paper 44. Washington, D.C.: World Bank.

Deaton, A., and A. Case. 1987. *Analysis of Household Expenditures*. Living Standards Measurement Study Working Paper 28. Washington, D.C.: World Bank.

Deaton, A., and J. Muellbauer. 1980. *Economics of Consumer Behaviour*. Cambridge: Cambridge University Press.

———. 1986. "On Measuring Child Costs: With Applications to Poor Countries." *Journal of Political Economy* 94(4):720-44.

Delaine, G., and others. 1992. *The Social Dimensions of Adjustment Integrated Survey: A Survey to Measure Poverty and Understand the Effects of Policy Change on Households*. Social Dimensions of Adjustment in Sub-Saharan Africa Working Paper 14. Washington, D.C.: World Bank.

DeLancey, V. 1990. "Socioeconomic Consequences of High Fertility for the Family." In G. Acsadi,

G. Johnson-Acsadi, and R. Bulatao, eds., *Population Growth and Reproduction in Sub-Saharan Africa*. Washington, D.C.: World Bank.

Demery, David, and Lionel Demery. 1992. *Adjustment and Equity in Malaysia*. Paris: OECD Development Centre.

Demery, Lionel, and Tony Addison. 1987a. *Poverty Alleviation under Structural Adjustment*. Washington, D.C.: World Bank.

———. 1987b. "Stabilization Policy and Income Distribution in Developing Countries." *World Development* 15(12).

———. Forthcoming. "The Impact of Macroeconomic Adjustment on Poverty in the Presence of Wage Rigidities." *Journal of Development Economics*.

Deolalikar, Anil B. 1988. "Nutrition and Labor Productivity in Agriculture: Estimates for Rural South India." *Review of Economics and Statistics* 70.

Dervis, K., J. de Melo, and S. Robinson. 1982. *General Equilibrium Models for Development Policy*. Cambridge: Cambridge University Press.

Devereux, S., and R. Hay. 1987. "Origins of Famine." Food Studies Group, Oxford.

Duncan, A., and J. Howell, eds. 1992. *Structural Adjustment and the African Farmer*. London: ODI/James Currey.

Duraisamy, P., and R. Malathy. 1990. *Impact of Public Programs on Fertility and Gender-Specific Investment in Human Capital of Children in Rural India*. Economic Growth Center Discussion Paper 596. New Haven, Conn.: Yale University.

Edirisinghe, A. 1987. *The Food Stamp Scheme in Sri Lanka: Costs, Benefits and Options for Modification*. Research Report 58. Washington, D.C.: International Food Policy Research Institute.

Edwards, S. 1988. *Exchange Rate Misalignment in Developing Countries*. World Bank Occasional Paper 2/New Series. Baltimore: Johns Hopkins University Press.

———. 1989. *Real Exchange Rates, Devaluation and Adjustment: Exchange Rate Policy in Developing Countries*. Cambridge, Mass.: MIT Press.

FAO (Food and Agriculture Organization). 1986. *Terms of Trade of Pakistan's Agriculture*. Rome.

Ferroni, Marco. 1980. "The Urban Bias of Urban Food Policy: Consequences and Alternatives." Latin American Studies Program Dissertation Series. Cornell University, Ithaca, N.Y.

Ferroni, Marco, and Ravi Kanbur. 1990. *Poverty-Conscious Restructuring of Public Expenditures*. Social Dimensions of Adjustment in Sub-Saharan Africa Working Paper 9. Washington, D.C.: World Bank.

Ferroni, Marco, and A. Valdés. 1991. "Trade and Macroeconomic Linkages and Agricultural Growth in Latin America." *Food Policy* 16(1).

Folbre, Nancy. 1986. "Hearts and Spades: Paradigms of Household Economics." *World Development* 14.

Foster, J.E. 1984. "On Economic Poverty: A Survey of Aggregate Measures." *Advances in Econometrics* 3:215-51.

Foster, J.E., J. Greer, and E. Thorbecke. 1984. "A Class of Decomposable Poverty Measures." *Econometrica* 52:761-66.

Foster, J.E., and A. Shorrocks. 1988. "Poverty Orderings." *Econometrica* 56:173-77.

Frank, O., and G. McNicoll. 1987. "Fertility and Population Policy in Kenya." *Population and Development Review* 13(2):209-43.

Gertler, Paul, and Jacques van der Gaag. 1990. *The Willingness to Pay for Medical Care: Evidence from Two Developing Countries*. Baltimore: Johns Hopkins University Press.

Glewwe, Paul. 1987. *The Distribution of Welfare in Côte d'Ivoire in 1985*. Living Standards Measurement Study Working Paper 29. Washington, D.C.: World Bank.

———. 1991. "Investigating the Determinants of Household Welfare in Côte d'Ivoire." *Journal of Development Economics* 35(2):301-37.

Glewwe, P., and D. de Tray. 1987. "The Poor during Adjustment: A Case Study of Côte d'Ivoire." World Bank, Policy, Planning, and Research, Washington, D.C.

Glewwe, P., and J. van der Gaag. 1987. "Confronting Poverty in Developing Countries: Definitions, Information and Policies." World Bank, Washington, D.C. (December).

Greer, J., and E. Thorbecke. 1986. "Food Poverty Profile Applied to Kenyan Smallholders." *Economic Development and Cultural Change* 35(1):115-41.

Griliches, Z. 1967. "Distributed Lags: A Survey." *Econometrica* 35.

Grootaert, Christiaan. 1983. "The Conceptual Basis of Measures of Household Welfare and Their Implied Survey Data Requirements." *Review of Income and Wealth*, Series 29(1).

———. 1986. *The Role of Employment and Earnings in Analyzing Levels of Living: A General Methodology with Applications to Malaysia and Thailand*. Living Standards Measurement Study Working Paper 27. Washington, D.C.: World Bank.

———. 1990. "Returns to Formal and Informal Vocational Education in Côte d'Ivoire: The Role of the Structure of the Labor Market." *Economics of Education Review* 9(4).

———. 1993. "The Evolution of Welfare and Poverty under Structural Change and Economic Recession in Côte d'Ivoire, 1985-88." Policy Research Working Paper 1078. World Bank, Washington, D.C.

Grootaert, C., and T. Marchant. 1991. *The Social Dimensions of Adjustment Priority Survey: An Instrument for the Rapid Identification and Monitoring of Policy Target Groups.* Social Dimensions of Adjustment in Sub-Saharan Africa Working Paper 12. Washington, D.C.: World Bank.

Habicht, J.-P., and others. 1974. "Height and Weight Standards for Preschool Children: Are There Really Ethnic Differences in Growth Potential?" *Lancet* 2:302.

Hammer, J. 1986. "Population Growth and Savings in LDCs: A Survey Article." *World Development* 14:579-91.

Hansen, S. 1988. "Structural Adjustment Programs and Sustainable Development." Paper prepared for the annual session of CIDIE, August 13-17, Washington, D.C.

Harberger, A. 1986. "Economic Adjustment and the Real Exchange Rate." In S. Edwards and L. Ahamed, eds., *Economic Adjustment and Exchange Rates in Developing Countries.* Chicago: University of Chicago Press.

Harris, J., and M. Todaro. 1970. "Migration, Unemployment and Development: A Two-Sector Analysis." *American Economic Review* 60(1):126-42.

Harvey, C., ed. 1988. *Agricultural Pricing Policy in Africa.* London: Macmillan.

Hausman, J., and W. Taylor. 1981. "Panel Data and Unobservable Effects." *Econometrica* 49.

Hawrylyshyn, O. 1977. "Towards a Definition of Non-Market Activities." *Review of Income and Wealth,* Series 23:79-96.

Healy, M. 1988. *GLIM: An Introduction.* Oxford: Clarendon Press.

Heller, P.S., A.L. Bovenberg, T. Catsambas, K.-Y. Chu, and P. Shome. 1988. *The Implications of Fund-Supported Adjustment Programs for Poverty: Experiences in Selected Countries.* IMF Occasional Paper 58. Washington, D.C.: International Monetary Fund.

Hicks, J.R. 1971. *The Social Framework.* 4th ed. Oxford: Oxford University Press.

Hicks, N., and A. Kubisch. 1984. "Cutting Government Expenditures in LDCs." *Finance and Development* 21(September).

Hill, A. 1990. "Population Conditions in Mainland Sub-Saharan Africa." In G. Acsadi, G. Johnson-Acsadi, and R. Bulatao, eds., *Population Growth and Reproduction in Sub-Saharan Africa.* Washington, D.C.: World Bank.

Hill, T.P. 1977. "On Goods and Services." *Review of Income and Wealth,* Series 23:315-38.

———. 1979. "Do It Yourself and GDP." *Review of Income and Wealth,* Series 25:31-39.

Horton, S. 1988. "Birth Order and Child Nutritional Status: Evidence from the Philippines." *Economic Development and Cultural Change* 36.

Horton, S., R. Kanbur, and D. Mazumdar, eds. 1991. "Labor Markets in an Era of Adjustment: An Overview." Policy Research Working Paper 232. World Bank, Washington, D.C.

Horton, S., and B. Miller. 1987. "The Effect of Gender of Household Head on Expenditure: Evidence from Low-Income Households in Jamaica." University of Toronto.

Hsiao, C. 1986. *Analysis of Panel Data.* New York: Cambridge University Press.

Iliffe, J. 1987. *The African Poor.* Cambridge: Cambridge University Press.

ILO. 1986. *Economically Active Population, Estimates and Projections 1950-2025.* Geneva: International Labour Office.

———. 1989. *African Employment Report 1988.* Addis Ababa: Jobs and Skills Programme for Africa.

Jaeger, W., and C. Humphreys. 1988. "The Effect of Policy Reforms on Agricultural Incentives in Sub-Saharan Africa." *American Journal of Agricultural Economics* 70(5).

Jansen, Doris J. 1991. "Zambia." In Anne O. Krueger, Maurice Schiff, and Alberto Valdés, eds., *The Political Economy of Agricultural Pricing Policy.* Vol. 3, *Africa and the Mediterranean.* Baltimore: Johns Hopkins University Press.

Johnson, M., A.D. McKay, and J.I. Round. 1990. *Income and Expenditure in a System of Household Accounts: Concepts and Estimation.* Social Dimensions of Adjustment in Sub-Saharan Africa Working Paper 10. Washington, D.C.: World Bank.

Johnson, O.E.G. 1986. "Labor Markets, External Developments, and Unemployment in Developing Countries." *IMF Staff Studies for the World Economic Outlook* (July):51-72.

Kakwani, N. 1990a. *Poverty and Economic Growth with Applications to Côte d'Ivoire.* Living Standards Measurement Study Working Paper 63. Washington, D.C.: World Bank.

————. 1990b. *Testing for Significance of Poverty Differences with Application to Côte d'Ivoire.* Living Standards Measurement Study Working Paper 62. Washington, D.C.: World Bank.

Kanbur, S.M.R. 1987. "Measurement and Alleviation of Poverty: With an Application to the Impact of Macroeconomic Adjustment." *IMF Staff Papers.*

————. 1988. "The Implications of Adjustment Programs for Poverty: Conceptual Issues and Analytical Framework." Paper presented to seminar on Implications of Adjustment Programs for Poverty Groups, International Monetary Fund, November, Washington, D.C.

————. 1990. *Poverty and the Social Dimensions of Structural Adjustment in Côte d'Ivoire.* Social Dimensions of Adjustment in Sub-Saharan Africa Working Paper 2. Washington, D.C.: World Bank.

Katseli, L. 1983. "Devaluation: A Critical Approach to the IMF's Policy Presciption." *American Economic Review* 73(2):359-63.

Katz, A.J. 1983. "Valuing the Services of Consumer Durables." *Review of Income and Wealth,* Series 29:405-27.

Katz, A.J., and J. Peskin. 1980. "The Value of Services Provided by the Stock of Consumer Durables, 1947-77: An Opportunity Cost Measure." *Survey of Current Business* 60(7):22-31.

Kelley, A., and J. Williamson. 1984. *What Drives Third World City Growth? A Dynamic General Equilibrium Approach.* Princeton, N.J.: Princeton University Press.

Kennedy, Eileen, and Bruce Cogill. 1987. *Income and Nutritional Effects of the Commercialization of Agriculture in Southwestern Kenya.* Research Report 63. Washington, D.C.: International Food Policy Research Institute.

————. 1989. *The Effects of Sugar Cane Production on Food Security, Health, and Nutrition in Kenya: A Longitudinal Analysis.* Research Report 78. Washington, D.C.: International Food Policy Research Institute.

Killingsworth, M.R. 1983. *Labor Supply.* Cambridge: Cambridge University Press.

Killingsworth, M.R., and J.J. Heckman. 1986. "Female Labor Supply: A Survey." In O.C. Ashenfelter and R. Layard, eds., *Handbook of Labor Economics.* Vol. 1. Amsterdam: North-Holland.

King, E. 1987. "The Effects of Family Size on Family Welfare: What Do We Know?" In D.G. Johnson and R. Lee, eds., *Population Growth and Economic Development: Issues and Evidence.* Madison: University of Wisconsin Press.

Knight, J.B., and R.H. Sabot. 1990. *Education, Productivity and Inequality: The East African Natural Experiment.* New York: Oxford University Press.

Knodel, J., A. Chamratrithirong, and N. Debavalya. 1987. *Thailand's Reproductive Revolution: Rapid Fertility Decline in a Third-World Setting.* Madison: University of Wisconsin Press.

Knodel, J., N. Havanon, and W. Sittitra. 1990. "Family Size and the Education of Children in the Context of Rapid Fertility Decline." *Population and Development Review* 16(1).

Knudsen, O., and P. Scandizzo. 1982. "The Demand for Calories in Developing Countries." *American Journal of Agricultural Economics* 64:80-86.

Kosinski, L., and J. Clarke. 1982. "African Population Redistribution—Trends, Patterns and Policies." In J. Clarke and L. Kosinski, eds., *Redistribution of Population in Africa.* London: Heinemann Press.

Koyck, L. 1954. *Distributed Lags and Investment Analysis.* Amsterdam: North-Holland.

Krueger, Anne O., Maurice Schiff, and Alberto Valdés. 1988. "Agricultural Incentives in Developing Countries: Measuring the Effect of Sectoral and Economy-wide Policies." *World Bank Economic Review* 2(3):255-71.

————. 1991. "Measuring the Effects of Intervention in Agricultural Prices." In Anne O. Krueger, Maurice Schiff, and Alberto Valdés, eds., *The Political Economy of Agricultural Pricing Policy.* Vol. 3, *Africa and the Mediterranean.* Baltimore: Johns Hopkins University Press.

Kumar, Shubh. 1979. *Impact of Subsidized Rice on Food Nutrition in Kerala.* Research Report 5. Washington, D.C.: International Food Policy Research Institute.

Kusnic, M.W., and J. Da Vanzo. 1980. *Income Inequality and Definition of Income: The Case of Malaysia.* Santa Monica, Calif.: Rand Corporation.

Latham, M.C. 1984. "Strategies for the Control of Malnutrition and the Influence of the Nutritional Sciences." *Food and Nutrition* 10(1):5-31.

Lau, L. 1978. "Applications of Profit Functions." In M.A. Fuss and D.L. McFadden, eds., *Production Economics: A Dual Approach to Theory and Applications.* Amsterdam: North-Holland.

Lesthaeghe, R. 1989. "Social Organization, Economic Crises and the Future of Fertility Control in Africa." In R. Lesthaeghe, ed., *Reproduction and Social Organization in Sub-Saharan Africa.* Berkeley, Calif.: University of California Press.

Levy, V. 1985. "Cropping Pattern, Mechanization, Child Labor and Fertility in a Farming Economy: Rural Egypt." *Economic Development and Cultural Change* 33(4):777-91.

Lindauer, D.L., and R.H. Sabot. 1983. "The Public/Private Wage Differential in a Poor Urban Economy." *Journal of Development Economics* 12(February-April):137-52.

Linn, J. 1982. "The Costs of Urbanization in Developing Countries." *Economic Development and Cultural Change* 30(3):625-48.

Lipton, M. 1983. *Poverty, Undernutrition and Hunger.* World Bank Staff Working Paper 597. Washington, D.C.

Lockwood, M., and P. Collier. 1988. "Maternal Education and the Vicious Cycle of High Fertility and Malnutrition: An Analytic Survey." Policy Research Working Paper 130. World Bank, Washington, D.C.

Lucas, R. 1987. "On the Theory of DRC Criteria." *Journal of Development Economics* 14.

Maddala, G.S. 1983. *Limited-Dependent and Qualitative Variables in Econometrics.* Cambridge: Cambridge University Press.

———. 1988. *Introduction to Econometrics.* New York: Macmillan.

Mahieu, F.R. 1990. *Les Fondements de la Crise Economique en Afrique.* Paris: Editions L'Harmattan.

Maine, D., R. McNamara, J. Wray, A. Farah, and M. Wallace. 1990. "Effects of Fertility Change on Maternal and Child Survival." In G. Acsadi, G. Johnson-Acsadi, and R. Bulatao, eds., *Population Growth and Reproduction in Sub-Saharan Africa.* Washington, D.C.: World Bank.

McCarthy, J., and G. Oni. 1987. "Desired Family Size and Its Determinants among Urban Nigerian Women: A Two-Stage Analysis." *Demography* 24(2):279-90.

McDonald, I.M., and R.M. Solow. 1985. "Wages and Employment in a Segmented Labor Market." *Quarterly Journal of Economics* C(4):1115-42.

Meerman, J. 1978. *Public Expenditure in Malaysia: Who Benefits and Why?* New York: Oxford University Press.

Mezzera, J. 1981. "Segmented Labour Markets Without Policy-Induced Labour Market Distortions." *World Development* 9(11/12):1109-14.

Mincer, J. 1976. "Employment and Unemployment Effects of Minimum Wages." *Journal of Political Economy.*

Montgomery, M., and E. Brown. 1990. "Accommodating Urban Growth in Sub-Saharan Africa." In G. Acsadi, G. Johnson-Acsadi, and R. Bulatao, eds., *Population Growth and Reproduction in Sub-Saharan Africa.* Washington, D.C.: World Bank.

Mueller, E. 1976. "The Economic Value of Children in Peasant Agriculture." In R. Ridker, ed., *Population and Development: The Search for Selective Interventions.* Baltimore: Johns Hopkins University Press.

Mundlak, Y., D. Cavallo, and R. Domenech. 1990. "Effects of Macroeconomic Policies on Sectoral Prices." *World Bank Economic Review* 4.

Neary, J., and K. Roberts. 1980. "The Theory of Household Behavior Under Rationing." *European Economic Review* 13(1).

Nerlove, M. 1956. "Estimates of the Elasticities of Supply of Selected Agricultural Commodities." *Journal of Farm Economics* 38.

———. 1958. "Distributed Lags and Estimation of Long-run Supply and Demand Elasticities: Theoretical Considerations." *Journal of Farm Economics* 40.

Ongaro, W.A. 1988. "Adoption of New Farming Technology: A Case Study of Maize Production in Western Kenya." Ph.D. dissertation. University of Gothenburg.

Oni, G., and J. McCarthy. 1988. "Use of Contraception for Birth Spacing in a Nigerian City." *Studies in Family Planning* 17(4).

Payne, P. 1985. "Food System Indicators." In A. Pacey and P. Payne, eds., *Agricultural Development and Nutrition.* London: Hutchison.

Pearce, Richard. 1989. "The Social Dimensions of Adjustment in Angola." Food Studies Group/UNICEF, Oxford.

Pinstrup-Andersen, P. 1985. "An Analytical Framework for Discussing Nutritional Effects of Policies and Programs." In C.K. Mann and B. Huddleston, eds., *Food Policy.* Bloomington: Indiana University Press.

———. 1989. "Government Policy, Food Security and Nutrition in Sub-Saharan Africa." PEW/Cornell Lecture Series on Food and Nutrition Policy, Ithaca, N.Y.

Pitt, Mark M. 1983. "Food Preferences and Nutrition in Rural Bangladesh." *Review of Economics and Statistics* 65:105-14.

Pitt, Mark M., and Mark R. Rosenzweig. 1985. "Health and Nutrient Consumption Across and Within Farm Households." *Review of Economics and Statistics* 67.

———. 1986. "Agricultural Prices, Food Consumption and the Health and Productivity of Farmers." In Inderdjit Singh, L. Squire, and J. Strauss, eds., *Agricultural Household Models: Extensions and Applications*. Baltimore: Johns Hopkins University Press.

———. 1989. "The Selectivity of Fertility and the Determinants of Human Capital Investments: Parametric and Semi-Parametric Estimates." Department of Economics Working Paper 89-30. Brown University, Providence, R.I. (October).

———. Forthcoming. "Estimating the Intrafamily Incidence of Illness: Child Health and Gender Inequality in the Allocation of Time in Indonesia." *International Economic Review*.

Pitt, Mark M., Mark R. Rosenzweig, and M. Nazmul Hassan. 1990. "Productivity, Health and Inequality in the Intrahousehold Distribution of Food in Low-Income Countries." *American Economic Review* 80.

Preston, S., and G. Greene. 1985. "Review of A. Kelley and J. Williamson: What Drives Third World City Growth?" *Population and Development Review* 11(2).

Psacharopoulos, G. 1985. "Returns to Education: A Further International Update and Implications." *Journal of Human Resources* 20:583-97.

———. 1988. "Education and Development: A Review." *World Bank Research Observer* 3(1):99-116.

Pudney, S. 1989. *Modeling Individual Choice*. Oxford: Basil Blackwell.

Pyatt, G. 1990. "Accounting for Time Use." *Review of Income and Wealth*, Series 36:33-52.

Pyatt, G., and E. Thorbecke. 1976. *Planning Techniques for a Better Future*. Geneva: International Labour Office.

Ravallion, Martin. 1988. "Expected Poverty under Risk-Induced Welfare Variability." *Economic Journal* 98(December):1171-82.

———. 1990. "Rural Welfare Effects of Food Price Changes under Induced Wage Responses: Theory and Evidence for Bangladesh." *Oxford Economic Papers* 42.

———. 1992. *Poverty Comparisons: A Guide to Concepts and Methods*. Living Standards Measurement Study Working Paper 88. Washington, D.C.: World Bank.

Ravallion, M., and M. Huppi. 1989. "Poverty and Undernutrition in Indonesia during the 1980s." Agriculture and Rural Development Department Working Paper 286. World Bank, Washington, D.C. (October).

Ravallion, M., and D. van de Walle. 1988. "Poverty Orderings of Food Pricing Reforms." Develop-ment Economics Research Centre Discussion Paper 86. University of Warwick.

Republic of Ghana. 1988. "Ghana Living Standards Survey: Preliminary Results, 1988." Statistical Service, Accra, and World Bank, Africa Region, Social Dimensions of Adjustment Unit, Washington, D.C.

République Rwandaise, Ministère du Plan. 1990. *Consommation et Sources de Revenue des Ménages Ruraux: Enquête Nationale sur le Budget et la Consommation de Ménages*. Kigali.

Reutlinger, S., and A. Selowsky. 1976. *Malnutrition and Poverty: Magnitude and Policy Options*. Baltimore: Johns Hopkins University Press.

Richards, P.J. 1986. "Preserving Jobs under Economic Stabilisation Programmes: Can There Be an Employment Target?" *International Labour Review* 125(4):423-34.

Robinson, S. 1988. "Multisector Models." In H. Chenery and T.N. Srinivasan, eds., *Handbook of Development Economics*. Vol. 1. Amsterdam: North-Holland.

Rogers, A. 1975. *Introduction to Multiregional Mathematical Demography*. New York: John Wiley and Sons.

Rosenhouse, Sandra. 1989. *Identifying the Poor: Is "Headship" a Useful Concept?* Living Standards Measurement Study Working Paper 58. Washington, D.C.: World Bank.

Rosenzweig, Mark R. 1982. "Educational Subsidy, Agricultural Development and Fertility Change." *Quarterly Journal of Economics* 97(1).

———. 1988. "Human Capital, Population Growth and Economic Development: Beyond Correlations." *Journal of Policy Modeling* 10(1).

Rosenzweig, Mark R., and T. Paul Schultz. 1982. "Market Opportunities, Genetic Endowments, and Intrafamily Resource Distribution: Child Survival in Rural India." *American Economic Review* 72:803-15.

———. 1984. "Market Opportunities and Intrafamily Resource Distribution: Reply." *American Economic Review* 74(3):521-23.

———. 1987. "Fertility and Investments in Human Capital: Estimates of the Consequences of Imperfect Fertility Control in Malaysia." *Journal of Econometrics* 36:163-84.

Ruggles, R., and N.D. Ruggles. 1986. "The Integration of Macro and Micro Data for the Household Sector." *Review of Income and Wealth*, Series 32:245-76.

Sahn, D.E. 1988. "The Effect of Price and Income Changes on Food-Energy Intake in Sri-Lanka." *Economic Development and Cultural Change*.

———. 1990. *Malnutrition in Côte d'Ivoire: Prevalence and Determinants.* Social Dimensions of Adjustment in Sub-Saharan Africa Working Paper 4. Washington, D.C.: World Bank.

Sahn, David, and Harold Alderman. 1988. "The Effects of Human Capital on Wages, and the Determinants of Labor Supply in a Developing Country." *Journal of Development Economics* 29.

Sahn, D., and A. Sarris. 1991. "Structural Adjustment and the Welfare of Rural Smallholders: A Comparative Analysis from Sub-Saharan Africa." *World Bank Economic Review* 5(2):259-89.

Saunders, C.T. 1990. "Measures of Total Household Consumption." *Review of Income and Wealth,* Series 26:351-66.

Scandizzo, P., and C. Bruce. 1980. *Methodologies for Measuring Agricultural Price Intervention Effects.* World Bank Staff Working Paper 394. Washington, D.C.

Schultz, T.P. 1982. "Lifetime Migration within Educational Strata in Venezuela: Estimates of a Logistic Model." *Economic Development and Cultural Change* 30(3):559-94.

———. 1987. "School Expenditures and Enrollments, 1960-80: The Effects of Income, Prices and Population Growth." In D.G. Johnson and R. Lee, eds., *Population Growth and Economic Development: Issues and Evidence.* Madison: University of Wisconsin Press.

———. 1988a. "Education Investments and Returns." In Hollis Chenery and T.N. Srinivasan, eds., *Handbook of Development Economics.* Amsterdam: North-Holland.

———. 1988b. "Women and Development: Objectives, Framework, and Policy Interventions." Yale University, New Haven, Conn.

———. 1989. "The Relationship between Local Family Planning Expenditures and Fertility in Thailand, 1976-81." Paper presented at a conference on the Family, Gender Differences and Development, Economic Growth Center, Yale University, New Haven, Conn., September.

Schwartz, A. 1976. "Migration, Age and Education." *Journal of Political Economy* 84(4):701-19.

Scobie, G.M. 1989. "Macroeconomic Adjustment and the Poor: Toward a Research Strategy." Cornell Food and Nutrition Policy Program, Monograph 89-1. Ithaca, N.Y.

Scott, C. 1988. "Testing Survey Methodology in the Context of the SDA Program." World Bank, Africa Region, Social Dimensions of Adjustment Unit, Washington, D.C.

———. 1989. "Estimation of Annual Expenditure from One-Month Cross-Sectional Data in a Household Survey." World Bank, Africa Region, Social Dimensions of Adjustment Unit, Washington, D.C. (June).

Sen, A.K. 1981. *Poverty and Famines: An Essay on Exchange Entitlements.* Oxford: Clarendon Press.

———. 1983. "Poor Relatively Speaking." *Oxford Economic Papers* 35(July):153-69.

———. 1984. *Resources, Values and Development.* Oxford: Basil Blackwell.

———. 1987. *The Standard of Living.* Cambridge: Cambridge University Press.

Sen, A.K., and S. Sengupta. 1983. "Malnutrition of Rural Children and the Sex Bias." *Economic and Political Weekly* 18:855-64.

Singh, I., L. Squire, and J. Strauss, eds. 1986a. *Agricultural Household Models: Extensions, Applications, and Policy.* Baltimore: Johns Hopkins University Press.

———. 1986b. "A Survey of Agricultural Household Models: Recent Findings and Empirical Implications." *World Bank Economic Review* 1(1):149-79.

Sjastaad, L. 1962. "The Costs and Returns of Human Migration." *Journal of Political Economy* 70(5):80-94.

Squire, L. 1981. *Employment Policy in Developing Countries: A Survey of Issues and Evidence.* New York: Oxford University Press.

Stark, O., and R. Lucas. 1988. "Migration, Remittances and the Family." *Economic Development and Cultural Change* 36(3):465-82.

Strassmann, W.P. 1987. "Home-based Enterprises in Cities of Developing Countries." *Economic Development and Cultural Change* 36(1).

Strauss, John. 1984. "Joint Determination of Food Consumption and Production in Rural Sierra Leone: Estimates of a Household Firm Model." *Journal of Development Economics* 14:77-104.

———. 1986. "Does Better Nutrition Raise Farm Productivity?" *Journal of Political Economy* 94.

———. 1988. *The Effects of Household and Community Characteristics on the Nutrition of Preschool Children: Evidence from Rural Côte d'Ivoire.* Living Standards Measurement Study Working Paper 40. Washington, D.C.: World Bank.

———. 1990. "Households, Communities, and the Nutrition of Pre-School Children: Evidence from Rural Côte d'Ivoire." *Economic Development and Cultural Change* 38.

Strauss, John, and Duncan Thomas. 1989. "The Shape of the Expenditure-Calorie Curve." Yale University, New Haven, Conn.

Stryker, J. Dirk. 1991. "Ghana." In Anne O. Krueger, Maurice Schiff, and Alberto Valdés, eds., *The*

Political Economy of Agricultural Pricing Policy. Vol. 3, *Africa and the Mediterranean.* Baltimore: Johns Hopkins University Press.

Svedberg, P. 1988. "Undernutrition in Sub-Saharan Africa: Is There a Sex Bias?" Institute for International Economic Studies Seminar Paper 421. Stockholm.

Taylor, Lance, ed. Forthcoming. *Structuralist Computable General Equilibrium Models: Socially Relevant Policy Analysis for the Developing World.*

Thomas, D., J. Strauss, and M. Hendriques. 1988. "Child Survival, Height for Age and Household Characteristics in Brazil." Development Economics Research Centre Discussion Paper 90. University of Warwick.

Thorbecke, E. 1992. *Adjustment and Equity in Indonesia.* Paris: OECD Development Centre.

Timmer, C.P. 1981. "Is There 'Curvature' in the Slutsky Matrix?" *Review of Economics and Statistics* 62:395-402.

Timmer, C.P., and H. Alderman. 1979. "Estimating Consumption Parameters for Food Policy Analysis." *American Journal of Agricultural Economics* 61(5):982-87.

Timmer, C.P., W.P. Falcon, and S.R. Pearson. 1983. *Food Policy Analysis.* Baltimore: Johns Hopkins University Press.

Todaro, M. 1969. "A Model of Labor Migration and Urban Unemployment in Less Developed Countries." *American Economic Review* 59(1):138-48.

Tsakok, Isabelle. 1990. *Agricultural Price Policy: A Practitioner's Guide to Partial-Equilibrium Analysis.* Ithaca: Cornell University Press.

Tuinenburg, K. 1987. "Experience with Food Strategies in Four African Countries." In J.P. Gittinger, J. Leslie, and C. Holsington, eds., *Food Policy: Integrating Supply, Distribution and Consumption.* Baltimore: Johns Hopkins University Press.

Turvey, R., ed. 1990. *Developments in International Labour Statistics.* London: Pinter Publishers for ILO.

UNDP (United Nations Development Programme). 1991. *Human Development Report 1991.* New York: Oxford University Press.

United Nations. 1981. "Population Distribution Policies in Development Planning." Population Studies 75. New York.

———. 1989. *Household Income and Expenditure Surveys.* National Household Survey Capability Programme. New York.

United Nations Statistical Office. 1968. *A System of National Accounts.* Series F, No. 2, Rev. 3. New York: United Nations.

van der Hoeven, R. 1987. "External Shocks and Stabilisation Policies: Spreading the Load." *International Labour Review* 126(2):133-50.

van de Walle, E., ed. 1987. *The Cultural Roots of African Fertility Regimes.* Proceedings of the Ife Conference, February 25-March 1, 1987, Obafemi Awolowo University and University of Pennsylvania.

van de Walle, E., and A. Foster. 1990. *Fertility Decline in Africa: Assessment and Prospects.* World Bank Technical Paper 125, Africa Technical Department Series. Washington, D.C.

Verma, V., T. Marchant, and C. Scott. 1988. "Evaluation of Crop-Cut Methods and Farmer Reports for Estimating Crop Production: Results of a Methodological Study in Five African Countries." Longacre Agricultural Development Centre Ltd., London.

Vijverberg, W. 1988a. *Nonagricultural Family Enterprises in Côte d'Ivoire: A Descriptive Analysis.* Living Standards Measurement Study Working Paper 46. Washington, D.C.: World Bank.

———. 1988b. *Profits from Self-Employment: A Case Study of Côte d'Ivoire.* Living Standards Measurement Study Working Paper 43. Washington, D.C.: World Bank.

von Braun, J. 1988. "Effects of Technological Change in Agriculture on Food Consumption and Nutrition: Rice in a West Africa Setting." *World Development* 16.

———. 1989. "Commercialization of Smallholder Agriculture: Policy Requirements for Capturing Gains for the Malnourished Poor." International Food Policy Research Institute, Washington, D.C.

von Braun, J., D. Hotchkiss, and Maarten Immink. 1989. *Nontraditional Export Crops in Guatemala: Effects on Production, Income, and Nutrition.* Research Report 73. Washington, D.C.: International Food Policy Research Institute.

von Braun, J., D. Puetz, and P. Webb. 1989. *Irrigation Technology and Commercialization of Rice in the Gambia: Effects of Income and Nutrition.* Research Report 75. Washington, D.C.: International Food Policy Research Institute.

Ward, J., and J. Sanders. 1980. "Nutritional Determinants and Migration in the Brazilian North East." *Economic Development and Cultural Change* 29:141-63.

Westlake, M.J. 1987. "The Measurement of Agricultural Price Distortions in Developing Countries." *Journal of Development Studies* 23.

Westoff, C.F. 1990. "Reproductive Intentions and Fertility Rates." *International Family Planning Perspectives* 16(3):84-89

WHO (World Health Organization). 1983. *Measuring Change in Nutritional Status.* Geneva.

Wolfe, B., and J. Behrman. 1984. "Determinants of Women's Health Status and Health-Care Utilization in a Developing Country: A Latent Variable Approach." *Review of Economics and Statistics* 56:696-703.

————. 1986. "Child Quantity and Quality in a Developing Country: The Importance of Family Background, Endogenous Tastes and Biological Supply Factors." *Economic Development and Cultural Change* 34:703-20.

World Bank. 1980. *Poverty and Human Development.* New York: Oxford University Press.

————. 1981. *Accelerated Development in Sub-Saharan Africa: An Agenda for Action.* Washington, D.C.

————. 1984. *World Development Report 1984.* New York: Oxford University Press.

————. 1986a. *Population Growth and Policies in Sub-Saharan Africa.* Washington, D.C.

————. 1986b. *World Development Report 1986.* New York: Oxford University Press.

————. 1990a. "Federal Republic of Nigera: Health Care Cost, Financing and Utilization." Western Africa Department, Population and Human Resources Operations Division, Washington, D.C. (July 29).

————. 1990b. *World Development Report 1990.* New York: Oxford University Press.

————. 1991a. *Assistance Strategies to Reduce Poverty.* Washington, D.C.

————. 1991b. *Making Adjustment Work for the Poor: A Framework for Policy Reform in Africa.* Washington, D.C.

World Bank and UNDP. 1989. *Africa's Adjustment and Growth in the 1980s.* Washington, D.C.: World Bank.

Yap, L. 1977. "The Attraction of Cities: A Review of the Migration Literature." *Journal of Development Economics* 4(3):239-64.

Zachariah, K., and J. Condé. 1981. *Migration in West Africa: Demographic Aspects.* New York: Oxford University Press.

Zuckerman, E. 1989. *Adjustment Programs and Social Welfare.* World Bank Discussion Paper 44. Washington, D.C.